Theater & Society

ASIA AND THE PACIFIC

series editor: Mark Selden

This new series explores the most dynamic and contested region of the world, including contributions on political, economic, cultural, and social change in modern and contemporary Asia and the Pacific.

Theater & Society

An Anthology of
Contemporary
Chinese
Drama

Haiping Yan, Editor

An East Gate Book

M.E. Sharpe
Armonk, New York
London, England

An East Gate Book

Copyright © 1998 by M. E. Sharpe, Inc.

Library of Congress Cataloging-in-Publication Data

Theater and society : an anthology of contemporary Chinese drama /
Haiping Yan, editor
p. cm. — (Asia and the Pacific)
"An East gate book."
Includes bibliographical references.
ISBN 0-7656-0307-1 (alk. paper). —
ISBN 0-7656-0308-X (pbk. : alk. paper)
1. Chinese drama—20th century—Translations into English.
I. Yen, Hai-p'ing. II. Series.
PL2658.E5T47 1998
895.1′25208—dc21 97-51561
CIP

Printed in the United States of America

Contents

Acknowledgments

Theater and Society: An Anthology of Contemporary Chinese Drama is finally completed for English-speaking readers. Conceived almost eight years ago, this anthology, I hope, contributes to the building of artistic bridges between the different cultures on both sides of the Pacific.

I must thank Mark Selden for his constant support throughout a long working process full of interesting and, at times, unexpected difficulties. Along with his initial invitation to participate in his book series on Asia, I have received generous encouragement, challenges, and help. Harold Shadick, the late Professor Emeritus of Chinese Literature, Edward Gunn, Dominick LaCapra, and Michael Hays at Cornell University have been unfailing sources of support over the years. Martin Coben, Professor Emeritus of Theatre at the University of Colorado at Boulder carefully read part of the translations even though he was battling cancer. Howard Goldblatt, another colleague whom I am fortunate to have in Boulder, provided invaluable help. Wang Zhen the former President of Chinese Drama Publishing House, and Xu Xiaozhong, the current President of Chinese Central Drama Academy, have made specific and continuous efforts to ensure that this project reach its completion.

I would like to thank all the contributors in this anthology and, specifically, to thank Jiang Hong, Timothy Cheek, and Thomas York—three colleagues whose excellent translations of the first two plays discussed in my Introduction are, unfortunately, not included in this book due to space limitations. Their love for Chinese dramatic literature and their commitment to its dissemination and appreciation in an Ensligh-speaking environment have confirmed and sustained my belief in creative cultural translations and productive cross-cultural communications.

Last but certainly not least are my special thanks to Doug Merwin, Patricia Loo, and Angela Piliouras, my editors at M.E. Sharpe. Their tireless efforts and meticulous work have made the process of completing this anthology most pleasant and memorable.

Y.H.

Theater and Society

An Introduction to Contemporary Chinese Drama

Yan Haiping

The five texts presented in this anthology are selected from the hundreds of plays and film scripts written and produced each year in China since 1979. Registering the nation's social, economic, political, and cultural transformations, these works have been published in leading journals and staged in major theaters, provoked powerful responses from Chinese audiences, and caused heated discussions, controversies, and confrontations on a national scale. Representing the most important achievements of contemporary Chinese theater, they also cover its two leading genres, namely, traditional regional music drama and modern spoken drama.[1] The one film script included here, *Old Well,* is nationally and internationally acclaimed. This anthology, the first to present this dramatic and performing literature, offers both vital information about what has come to be called "the dramatic renaissance of the new period" and significant insights into a society that has been undergoing complex structural changes.

"Drama of the new period," like other forms of art and literature of the era, began as a critical response to the Cultural Revolution (1966–1976). Upon emerging from these ten years of civil strife and political fragmentation, many people were frustrated, angry, and deeply shaken. The shared need to express long-stifled emotions found one effective medium in drama, especially modern spoken drama. The first wave of this theatrical movement lasted approximately two years. From 1976 to 1978, two major kinds of plays were produced on stage nationwide. The first comprised new productions of some of the best-known plays created before 1966, such as *Nihongdeng xiade shaobing* (Sentries under the neon light) and *Jiang jie* (Elder sister Jiang). The former is about a group of young soldiers of the People's Liberation Army who come from rural backgrounds but have learned to deal successfully with their new and challenging experiences in Shanghai, the largest and most westernized city in China; the latter is based on the life of a woman revolutionary who maintained her integrity while being imprisoned, tortured, and finally executed by the Guomindang government in the 1940s.[2] As dramatizations embodying the social, cultural, and political values of a "socialist new China," these plays were extremely popular when staged in the 1950s and the early 1960s. During the Cultural Revolution, along with most other literary and artistic works produced since 1949, they were denounced as "poisonous weeds" and consequently banned.[3] The creators of those works were accused of various political crimes and many of them died of persecution.[4] While violent social forces were released in the course of the Cultural Revolution to attack "traditional culture," eight "model plays" in the forms of the Beijing Opera and sinicized Western ballet monopolized the stage of Chinese performing art. Professional theater in general was suppressed; many theater companies were disbanded; modern spoken drama in particular was proclaimed "dead" by Jiang Qing and her followers.[5] The restaging at the national level in the late 1970s of the dramas popular before 1966, therefore, indicated the ending of an era in the nation's cultural and political life and the beginning of what has been called "a dramatic renaissance."

Condemnation of the massive political persecution enforced during the Cultural Revolution was more directly expressed in the second group of plays staged in the late 1970s—plays newly written by both professional and nonprofessional playwrights, including Zong Fuxian's *Yu wusheng chu* (From the depth of silence), Sha Yexin's *Chenyi shizhang* (Mayor Chenyi), Cui Dezhi's *Baochun hua* (Spring flowers), Xing Yixun's *Quan yu fa* (Power versus law), and Su Shuyang's *Danxin pu* (Noble hearts).[6] These plays were constructed with two prominent features: a bitter condemnation of the Gang of Four and an ardent affirmation of senior revolutionary figures who were persecuted during the Cultural Revolution.[7] A nostalgia for the early years of the People's Republic of China (PRC) lent these plays an unspoken sense of tragedy. The tears in the eyes of theatergoers when these dramas premiered marked one of the most intense moments in the nation's contemporary emotional and cultural life.

This nationally shared moment, characterized by its emotional reaction to the repression of the Cultural Revolution and nostalgia for the hopeful and more open early years of the People's Republic, was soon replaced by another wave of more complex theatrical representations. Rather than evoking memories of the past, beginning in the spring of 1979 an increasing number of plays generated debates over the present and its relation to the past and the future. *You zheyang yige xiaoyuan* (There is such a small compound) in Beijing, *Paobing siling de er'zi* (The artillery commander's son) in Shanghai, *Yige wuangu de shengchan duizhang* (A stubborn production team leader) in Anhui, and *Kaolü kaolü* (We shall consider) in Hubei, to name a few, explored sensitive issues such as social inequality and government bureaucracy, touching off debates where they were staged.[8] Finally, a national controversy quickly developed over the one-act play *Jiaru woshi zhende* (If I were real) by Sha Yexin, produced in Shanghai, based on the true story of a young man who manipulated various government officials and gained privileges by impersonating the son of a high-ranking official before being exposed and sentenced to jail.[9] These plays were short and many were crudely crafted, but their appearance indicated that a substantial reexamination of the nation's past, present, and future was under way. After having been forced like most literary and theater journals to cease publication during the Cultural Revolution, the monthly *Jüben* (Drama)—the authoritative forum of the theater world since 1952—resumed its publication and its leadership role in 1979. In the following years the theater world was full of significant controversies. Leading dramatists, critics, theoreticians, and cultural administrators, once allied in their bitter rejection of the repressive policies of the Cultural Revolution, quickly split into different, shifting, and opposing camps over these controversies and the emergence in the early 1980s of a group of assertive playwrights who called their work "the school of critical realism."

One of the most representative controversies generated by these "critical realists" centered on *Xiaojing hutong* (Small Well alley), a five-act drama published in 1981.[10] Its author, Li Longyun, an "educated youth" from Beijing who had worked for many years on an army land reclamation farm, depicted a group of urban residents living in a courtyard named "Small Well" from 1949 to the early 1980s. After surviving various hardships under the Guomindang regime, these hardworking common folk embrace the 1949 revolution with great enthusiasm. Experiencing the remarkable first decade of the People's Republic, they develop a strong sense of national identity and shared social purpose, as well as unconditional belief in the new government and its policies. They throw themselves into the Great Leap Forward of 1958, sacrificing all they have for an imagined national paradise, only to suffer irretrievable individual and collective losses.[11] During the Cultural Revolution, they are in turn confused, frightened, split against one another, and devastated, but they finally reunite in resistance to the political opportunists who seek power while destroying many people's lives in the name of leftist radicalism. The Gang of Four is shown to be sustained by such powerseekers operating at every level of the society including that of the residential neighborhood committee, and their downfall means for the common folk of Small Well a "second liberation." Unlike after their first liberation of 1949, however, in 1979 these common folk take initiatives in asserting their rights to elect their neighborhood committee and democratically organize their community and its leadership. With a cast of nearly thirty characters of different social and individual constitutions and identities, the play presents a nuanced portrayal of the lives of urban working people in Beijing over four decades with a profound sense of history and emotional poignancy.

The Beijing People's Art Theater Company produced the play in 1983. Certain leading figures in dramatic circles and cultural administration in Beijing, however, questioned the decision to bring the play before the public. Although the first act shows that the people of Small Well welcomed the 1949 liberation, they argued, the following acts show only how things went from bad to worse, focusing only on people's "suffering": "It seems as if the Great Leap Forward and the Cultural Revolution were the only two things that we [the Communist Party] have done since liberation—such a representation of PRC history appears rather lopsided."[12] Contending that he was a dramatist, not a historian, the playwright and his supporters argued that a play was not a historical textbook and should not be judged as such. But the play was permitted to run for just three performances with invited guests only. The subsequent bitter controversy involved playwrights, novelists, journalists, critics, theoreticians, and members of the cultural administration at the national level.

The question at the core of the controversy was how to reevaluate and represent some of the most critical and complex experiences of the nation since 1949. Through its portrayal of several moments of socioeconomic and political crisis in the People's Republic, the play captures and explores the problems of the historically conditioned and changing relationship between the socialist state and its citizens, the national body of policymakers and ordinary members of the society. It is imperative, the Small Well story argues, for the Chinese leaders and all citizens to recognize the vital importance of socialist democracy and to develop effective forms of such democracy through which the common folk can employ critical thinking and genuinely participate in the decision-making process of the nation. It was due to unconditional belief in the policies made by the ever narrowing circles of the central leadership and the lack of a community-based participatory socialist democracy that China had suffered such economic fiascoes as the Great Leap Forward and such political disasters as the Cultural Revolution. Underlying such an argument is a conviction that the well-being of the common folk is the ultimate standard for evaluating success and failure in Chinese history. Such a conviction is based upon the author's understanding of his role as a playwright whose vocation is to "speak for the ordinary citizens."

This conviction underlying Li Longyun's emotionally charged play shapes one of the primary principles and organizing features of the school of critical realism. Playwrights such as Zong Fuxian (Shanghai), Zhong Jieying (Beijing), Yao Yuan (Jiangsu Province), and Li Jie (Jilin Province) who loosely gathered under the banners of this school, despite their many differences shared the basic view that working people's daily experiences and ethical sentiments were the sources of their creative activity, and that enacting social and cultural critiques in dramatically effective ways was the essential function of theater. Their pointed critiques of contemporary Chinese society were therefore woven together with their pronounced emotional attachment to the well-being of the ordinary majority, a commitment that had been one of the essential components in the legitimacy of the PRC government and its proclaimed programs. Li Longyun once summarized his thoughts on playwriting in the following lines.

> I grew up in the southern part of the old city of Beijing, the little alley where we lived had a rather civilized name, "the small well." The small well alley looked old and tumbledown, but in my heart and in my memories it is lively and filled with tenderness. Like a gracious mother, it offered me a gentle breast to rest upon, provided me a space to begin my toddling. I believe that every writer has a piece of land that his heart calls home, and every homeland has its own smell, color, ethos, and culture. It is upon this homeland a writer's life is dependent and by which a writer's death is defined. My homeland has formed the most essential feelings in the depth of my heart, it has shaped a particular sense of self-respect in me, it tells me about kindness and beauty, about integrity and firmness, and what is the dignity of common folk living at the bottom of a society.[13]

The sentiments expressed by Li Longyun in these lines were shared by many playwrights of critical realism active in the first half of the 1980s. It is the working people's lives and their profound sense of human dignity and equality that render *Small Well Alley* and its likes critical of aspects of the PRC's history and affirmative of the values of a socialist morality deeply resonating with Chinese folk egalitarian ethics.

Responding to these ethical sentiments from another angle but sharing similar views on socialist democracy and socially engaged theater, another group of playwrights in the early 1980s sought to employ premodern historical materials to create dramas that were allegorically relevant to the contemporary social situation. They employed the form of modern historical drama that was invented by Guo Moruo in the 1920s and has been developed by spoken dramatists ever since, and they drew upon Chinese history for dramatic motives. Among the modern historical plays produced in the early 1980s, *Li Shimin, Prince of Qin* was one of the most influential.[14] Written by Yan Haiping (the author of this introduction), then a student at Fudan University in Shanghai, *Li Shimin, Prince of Qin* dramatizes the early years in the political life of Li Shimin, later the grand emperor of the Tang dynasty—a dynasty that represents the pinnacle of China's imperial history (A.D. 627–650). Exploring the turbulent events that led to the founding of the Tang dynasty, the play's thematic vision is based on the classical concept of *minben* (民本), a prominent concept in Chinese political philosophy and history which asserts that the foundation of any dynasty lies in the common people and their minds and hearts, reminding its audience that "the commoners are the currents of the river, and the kings and the nobles are the boats riding it; the river carries the boats but also buries the boats."[15] With its epic-style dramatization of the conflict between Li Shimin, who was pressured to recognize the demands of the peasants and their essentiality to the lasting stability of the Tang dynasty, and his father, Li Yuan, and elder brother, Li Jiancheng, who adhered to the desires of the nobility and the supremacy of imperial authority, the play reenacts a historical story with critical significations relevant to post–Cultural Revolution society.

The production of the play by the Shanghai Youth Theater Company in 1981 created a stir nationwide. While the enthusiastic audience crowded in for ninety performances in the heat of Shanghai's summer and some critics embraced it with even greater enthusiasm, other critics, newspaper editors, and cultural administrators denounced it for deviating from Marxist historical materialism. Li Shimin and his father, Li Yuan, and brother, Li Jiancheng, they argued, were all members of the imperial ruling class; their conflict was a pure power struggle among the members of the ruling elite and did not concern any significant policy difference. That the author chose an emperor as her protagonist showed how far she had wandered from Marxist class theory and how "dangerously she had gone astray."[16] The author responded that the core of Marxism was its historical dialectic, and that vulgar materialism would only lead to nihilistic attitudes toward the nation's rich and complex history.[17] Focusing on the tensions between the commoners' needs and the ways in which the members of the governing body come to terms with such needs, the author summarized her reading of Li Shimin's story:

> Witnessing how the peasants rebelled against the Sui dynasty, Li Shimin was awestruck; searching into the rise and the fall of past dynasties, Li Shimin further recognized the formidable forces of the commoners and their importance to the long-term stability and prosperity of his dynasty. "The Son of Heaven," he wrote, "if he follows *Dao* [Heaven], people will support him, and if he violates *Dao,* people will discard him," because "*Dao* sees as the people see, *Dao* hears as the people hear." This is the lesson that Li Shimin learned from his experiences as one of the founding generals of the Tang dynasty as well as from his understanding of history, this is the core of his thoughts on policymaking and governing. Those who respond to the needs of the

people will govern, and those who ignore the needs of the people will perish. In the past, in the present, as in the future, even the greatest leaders of our nation have to be tested and judged by this basic law of historical process.[18]

Such a rereading of history has an interesting doubleness. Clearly criticizing the PRC leadership—especially Mao Zedong—for the destructive consequences of such social turmoils as the Cultural Revolution, it at the same time registers deep influences of Mao's teaching on human history and the relationship between "the commoners" and "the kings and the ministers." By remembering the past in such a way, it reevaluates the present and leaves no room for any leaderships—past or present—to be exempt from the "historical judgment" of the commoners. Although a symposium on the play organized by the Shanghai branch of the Association of Chinese Dramatists was riven with high political tension and deep divisions among participants of considerable sociocultural status and influence, subsequent discussions became increasingly enthusiastic, involving all the major theater journals and critics in the country.[19] The play was soon made into a television series shown nationwide and was adapted into regional music forms and performed in small cities and towns.[20] While other modern historical plays of the same period have different thematic concentrations and theatrical effects, their dramatic constitutions are woven with similar convictions of the historical inescapability and ethical legitimation of the judgment on any governing body from "the commoners." Chen Baichen's *Dafengge* (Song of the wind), Lu Jianzhi and Fang Jiaji's *kunqü*-style *Tangtaizong* (The Grand emperor of Tang), and Zhen Huaixi's *puxian*-style music drama *Xintinglei* (Tears shed at the Xin Pavilion) are among the most significant examples.[21]

Rereading the nation's past on the one hand and examining the current conditions of working people and their needs on the other, many of the critical realists of the early 1980s sought to rediscover history and to confront the severe problems and crises in Chinese society in order to revitalize what they saw as the spirit of socialist modernization. Such efforts were questioned by other dramatic activities with more individualist impulses. There emerged another group of playwrights who attempted to break away from what they saw as the alienating, antiartistic, and ultimately illusory role of social and moral leadership with which Chinese intellectuals—including the critical realists—seemed obsessed. Looking to the West for inspiration, these playwrights discovered Western modernism in their eager, albeit tentative, pursuit of "the modern."[22] As early as 1980, some influence of the theater of the absurd appeared in works by such playwrights as Jia Hongyuan and Ma Zhongjun in Shanghai, and very quickly such influences appeared with more thematic substance in theater circles in Beijing.[23] A formally experimental play titled *Absolute Signals,* by Gao Xingjian, a scholar in modern French literature, was produced in 1982 in Beijing; its dramatization of the sensitive social issues of youth unemployment and juvenile delinquency attracted positive responses, though its highly innovative visual image of socially detached individuals went largely uncommented.[24] The following year, *Bus Stop,* by the same author, was staged by the People's Art Theater Company, and with it Western-style experimental modernism came of age in China. Still interacting with the social concerns of realist playwrights, the play shows certain structural and ideological departures—much more significantly than most works of critical realism at the time—from traditions of the theater in particular and Chinese culture in general since the 1950s. It is the first text in this anthology.

A seemingly Beckettian play, *Bus Stop* dramatizes a group of people who have been waiting for ten years at a bus station somewhere between country and city for a bus that is to take them to the city. One bus after another passes but none stops at their station. While waiting and agonizing over their individual dreams and desires, they hardly notice that one silent, middle-aged man leaves the bus station after several buses have passed: "He strides away without turning his head even once. Music rises, the melody evoking a painful and persistent search."[25] By the end of the play, people begin to realize that perhaps this bus stop has been suspended and the bus route changed; they finally decide to stop waiting and get ready to walk on their own feet to the city. Realistic in characterization and symbolistic in overall structure, the play provoked immediate controversy in Beijing cultural circles, followed by heated discussion in major cultural centers throughout the nation. Some critics stressed the play's creativity and hailed its message that people should actively take charge of their lives rather than waste their lives in passive waiting. Other critics contended that the play contained a basic questioning if not a fundamental negation of the organization of contemporary Chinese society, a condescending attitude toward the deluded "pitiable multitude," and an elitist and individualistic impulse embodied in the "silent man" walking alone to the city.[26]

The controversy occurred in 1983, a time when a serious debate at the highest levels of the state and cultural spheres was intensifying, and a socioideological metamorphosis in the world of literature and art was quickly unfolding. At the center of the debate were efforts to read the economic and political disasters and implied theoretical problematics of PRC history as symptoms of a systematic "alienation" inherent in socialist theory and practice. Led by senior theorists such as Wang Ruoshui, then the deputy editor of *People's Daily,* and supported by such figures as Zhou

Yang, then the minister of culture, the theory of "socialist alienation" was proposed while a rediscovery of humanist discourse in the early writings of Karl Marx was conducted.[27] Wang, Zhou, and their supporters were arguing that the Chinese socialist project had over the decades turned into the opposite of the ideal of socialism—had become alienated from itself—and that the Marxist theory of class struggle in the hands of the "ultraleftists" had been used to fabricate class struggles in a socialist society; such fabrications served not only to legitimize their violation of many people's personal freedom and their denial of the human dignity of the citizens but to "justify sheer cruelty in their pursuit of power."[28]

Responding to this theory of socialist alienation and the proposed humanistic remedy, former Politburo member Hu Qiaomu and other theorists insisted upon two major points. First, the problems that occurred in Chinese socialist practice could be rectified while the socialist system as a whole still had its great vitality and could further mature. That such disasters as the Great Leap Forward and the Cultural Revolution were stopped, criticized, and indeed denounced provided the evidence that the socialist system had in itself an effective rectifying mechanism. The problems that Wang, Zhou, and their supporters pointed to, therefore, could not be defined as predetermined results of the systematic alienation of socialism itself, and to define them as such could lead to the dangerous conclusion that socialism was intrinsically alienating if not fundamentally flawed. Second, humanism and its variants, including the version in the young Marx, was historically inseparable from and in fact a vital part of the ideology of the bourgeoisie. This was why Marx himself in his mature writings turned away from this creed and developed his dialectic and historical materialism. Adopting this Western and bourgeois ideology to solve the problems in Chinese socialist practice was therefore historically utopian and theoretically misleading.[29] The appearance of *Bus Stop* added to this debate a particular dimension by providing Hu Qiaomu and his supporters, including He Jingzhi and Feng Mu, a dramatic illustration of bourgeois humanist individualism with an overall negation of the socialist practice and history of contemporary China.

The significant critical attention the play received can be seen in the discussion organized by the editorial committee of *Xijübao* (On theater), the equivalent of *People's Daily* in the theater world, and participated in by Tang Yin, Du Gao, and Zhen Bonong, three important cultural critics. In their response to the play, these critics also articulated their views on the forces operative in the formation of the school of "Western modernism," on the debate about socialist alienation theory and humanism, and on the general climate in the cultural world at the time. They saw in all these "theories of socialist alienation" and "schools of Western modernism" a fundamental rejection of socialism and Marxism and, by implication, a crisis of the socialist consciousness that could undermine the "foundation of our country":

> Some of our theorists tend to view and judge our historical experiences of socialist practice and its problems with pessimism and formulate the misleading theory claiming that the socialist system constantly generates its own "alienation." ... This theory can easily be accepted by some of our young writers who have become fundamentally doubtful about socialism. When we are criticizing ultraleftism and its effects on art and literature, creative experiments in the theater are the refreshing fruits with which we have every reason to be pleased. Yet our critiques of ultraleftism seem to have caused serious confusion in the minds of some young authors as well. They take the critique of ultraleftism as a fundamental abandonment of Marxist views on art and culture and total denunciation of the achievements of socialist literature and art and its revolutionary tradition. And their "innovations" turn out to be mere echoes of Western modernists. Taking the capitalist art of the West as the ultimate "world art" and canceling the fundamental distinctions between socialist art and capitalist art, their dramatic "innovations," as a result, become imitations of "the theater of the absurd," products of the declining Western culture.[30]

The response from these critics was consequential. *Bus Stop* was stopped after ten performances in July 1983, and the play was judged "seriously flawed." At about the same time, the debates on "alienation theory" and "the young Marx's humanism" vs. "the old Marx's class struggle" concluded with Zhou Yang's self-criticism for having misunderstood Marx and Wang Ruoshui's removal from office. Such administrative conclusions, however, did not resolve the complex questions raised in these debates and certainly did not prevent enthusiasm for Western culture and ideology from further growing in the Chinese cultural world.

More books on Western modernist theater were quickly and often inadequately translated into Chinese and disseminated in literary, dramatic, and theoretical circles. Plays by emerging Chinese playwrights of various schools ranging from "absurdism" to "surrealism" continued to be staged in rapidly increasing quantity from 1983, and the first peak of experimental modernism was reached in the mid-1980s. *Jieshang liuxing hongqunzi* (Red skirts are the fashion) by Jia Hongyuan and Ma Zhongjun and *Yige shengzhe dui sizhe de fangwen* (A visit from a dead man) by Liu Shugang were among the most acclaimed and controversial plays.[31] In *Red Skirts,* a "model socialist worker" alienates her co-workers because of her ideological pretension—however reluctant—of being a virtuous role model and her socially induced dishonesty. In *A Visit,* a fashion designer fights the "social prejudices" against private ownership and courageously sets up and runs her own business, while her lover, who is marginalized by his temporary working status in a state-run theater company, emerges as the true moral hero by saving a passenger assaulted by a murderous criminal on a public bus at the expense of his own life. Despite the measures taken by some cultural administrators to criticize or ban some of those plays, their rising popularity testified that theater circles in particular and the cultural world in general were living in a profoundly different climate—one in which not only Marxist notions of class and class struggle were questioned in their relation to Chinese society but a whole range of social ethics and moral values established since 1949 were, implicitly or explicitly, deconstructed as forms of "hypocrisy of ultraleftism." As an "era of pluralism" in the cultural arena was heralded by some quickly rising new writers,[32] it appeared clear that the value system of humanistic individualism was reshaping the orientation and organizing features of Chinese art and literature. It was represented in literary, artistic, critical, and theoretical works in rapidly increasing quantity, although such individualism was harshly and constantly criticized and indeed denounced from on high.

The quest for "modern subjectivity," proclaimed by leading modernists and indicated by the bulk of modernist plays produced since the mid-1980s, is at the heart of Western-inspired and Western-oriented experimental modernism. Among the features of "modern subjectivity," the claim of individuality and individual creativity is most prominent. The theory of "socialist and revolutionary realism," which stressed the sociopolitical nature and function of art and literature and had been the dominant theory in China since the 1950s, was rejected by the modernists, who asserted that such theory over the decades had become a political cliché that had frozen the natural blossoming of modern Chinese culture. To liberate Chinese literature and art from stifling orthodoxy, many experimental modernists declared that art in its essence was independent of politics, not representing any socioeconomic group or class. Rather, artistic works were expressions of individual creativity and universal humanity. In searching for such expressions of transcendental individual-universal humanity, they embraced and absorbed Western modernism with great enthusiasm while undergoing a process of multilayered psychocultural transference. The thematic motives of modernism, such as epistemological uncertainty, existential agony and despair, and ontological nothingness, articulated in the West by the post–World War II generation, in short, were captured, appropriated, transplanted, and reproduced in a radically different sociohistorical context, namely, post–Mao China. Such a practice was of course not, as modernists themselves claimed, apolitical or cleansed of sociopolitical implications.

They were both socially and politically charged expressions rooted in the desire to break away from particular sociopolitical constraints. But contrary to the assertions of Du Gao and others, they were not mere imitations of European modernist theater either. The historically specific dynamics in this complex process of discovery, appropriation, and reproduction can be seen in all the works of experimental modernism mentioned above and others. In his essay on modernism and contemporary Chinese literature, written in 1987, Gao Xingjian articulates the features of such Chinese modernist organizing principles quite clearly:

> The movement of contemporary Chinese literature toward modernity shares some features with Western modernism, but it cannot possibly repeat the process of development of modern Western literature. The school of modernism that has emerged in China, in general terms, is rather different from that of Western modernism . . . Unlike Western modernism, which is underlined by a negation of the self, Chinese modernism is founded on an affirmation of the self; it exposes the absurdities in the realities of Chinese society but does not—as Western modernism does—take absurdity as constitutive of the existential conditions of humanity. . . . A critical skepticism about the old humanism is the point of departure for Western modernism; but for Chinese modernists, the rediscovery of humanism that was lost under the social conditions of modern and contemporary Chinese society is their core. Such rediscovered humanism is imbued, in effect, with the spirit of romanticism.[33]

Such a "rediscovered humanism" filled with the spirit of "romanticism," while not overtly rejecting collectivism, focuses on the individuality of the citizens that had been radically deemphasized if not erased in contemporary Chinese public discourses. Gao's *Bus Stop,* the earliest modernist play, is certainly one of the representative works of this dramatic school. Samuel Beckett's *Waiting for Godot* provided a situational structure and dramatic impulse for Gao's play, but *Bus Stop* has an unmistakably Chinese quality in its individual characterizations and structural implications, which are both underlined by the social and historical conditions of Chinese society in the post–Mao era. Beckett's play, more specifically, explores the loss of the meaning of humanity in the postwar West, and Gao's play centers on what he sees as the blindness of the multitude who have been trapped by illusory group-bound conventions and promises throughout their lives. As an embodiment of epistemological negation of Western modernity, *Godot* offers nothing, indeed cancels almost any possibility, for change. As an embodiment of disillusionment about Chinese socialist practices, *Bus Stop* offers the "silent man," who is clearly a trope for humanistic enlightenment and an individual search for direction in a moment of social transformation and political uncertainty.

Situated in and responding to this moment of transformation and uncertainty, dramatists writing in the vein of critical realism and experimental modernism in the first half of the 1980s adopted distinctively different organizing principles in their playwriting and theatrical production. Their differences, however, were largely submerged by their shared support of Wang Ruoshui and Zhou Yang, first for their advocacy of "humanism in early Marx," and later through a variety of confrontations with what both called "ultraleftism," namely, the complex and by no means homogeneous cultural and political forces persisting in the society that were critical of their dramatic and theatrical practices. The battle waged over the banning of the play *WM* (We) in 1985 shows how the major members of both schools functioned as allies in a national controversy. The play *WM* is hence chosen as the second text in this anthology.

Written by Wang Peigong and produced by the Theater Troupe of the Air Force in Beijing, *WM* offers a tender and nearly melancholic portrayal of "educated youth" in their struggle to cope with their drastically changing living conditions and to find meaning in their lives. The play begins with a scene of a "collective household" in the countryside during the Cultural Revolution and ends with a reunion at a fancy city restaurant in the mid-1980s. The seven characters in the play are from different social and family backgrounds: the status and identities of their parents range from those of a senior army officer, a cadre who gained power during the Cultural Revolution, and a hardworking industrial worker to those of intellectuals, a "rightist," and a "capitalist roader."[34] Their lives, registering important aspects of Chinese society over a decade and capturing significant historical moments of these years, are characterized by emotional ruptures and political disillusionments. Despite all they have suffered, however, they remain deeply bound by their shared youth spent in the "collective" and their memories of a sunny childhood in the 1950s, crystallized in the team song of the "Young Socialist Pioneers." The play ends with them humming the melody of the song and poignantly echoing—with explicit mockery and implicit nostalgia—a group of children, another generation of Young Pioneers, singing in the distance.

Structurally, the play is divided into four parts, with a series of intertwined individual stories using two drummers to set the rhythm of the unfolding events and accentuate each character's often unspoken feelings or subconscious. Drawing on such modernist elements as streams of consciousness in the forms of overlapping or parallel monologues, *WM* is substantiated by a realistic characterization. The significance of such structural innovation certainly goes beyond the realm of pure theatrical techniques. Registering such sentiments of experimental modernism as an ever growing sense of alienation among once genuinely connected characters, the play is at the same time suffused with a longing for social justice, equality, and the ideals that informed most plays of critical realism in the early 1980s. The reform era in *WM* is no longer an imagined future invested with hope for socialist democracy (as in *Small Well*), belief in the "laws of history" in accordance with which the will of the commoners prevails (as in *Li Shimin*), or desires of romantic individualism (as in *Bus Stop*). The reform era in the play has turned into a trying reality in which some old problems persist and new problems emerge while drastic social changes dislocate everyone and redefine everything. Compared with the three texts discussed above, *WM* offers a much more fluid narrative that aims to capture these complex social conditions and the individuals feeling caught in them without any conclusive evaluations. As the author said in an interview, "We don't want to define those characters in ready-made categories of good or bad, . . . we just want to accurately represent their experiences, their emotional crises, to show the barely discernible changes in human relations under changing social realities."[35] In fact, *WM* is one of the few plays of the mid-1980s that touches upon the subtle disintegration of the moral fabric of human relations under the gradually developing commodification of society.

Some leading members of the Air Force Cultural Bureau were displeased with the play. The young people, they argued, all appeared self-serving and petty, they lacked a belief in socialism and a sense of purpose for their lives. The only person among the seven characters who had kept his ideals and integrity appeared most abstract, and he was literally losing his eyesight. One sees in the play how these young people had lost their socialist dreams but no indication of how they could regain their ideals. The production, judged too "gloomy, low-spirited, and decadent," was permitted two dress rehearsals with a small group of invited guests to solicit comments and suggestions for its revision.[36] Wang Gui, the director of *WM* and also the head of the troupe, rejected these criticisms as ultraleft orthodoxy. Arguing that the play realistically reflected the life experiences of the generation of "educated youth," he refused to make any revisions and turned the first "dress rehearsal with invited guests only" into a full-fledged evening performance witnessed by a large group of critics, reporters, writers, and theorists. Although praise quickly appeared in major newspapers and journals, the Air Force Cultural Bureau canceled all rehearsals and further possibilities for public performance.

The controversy immediately reached the national level, and the decision to ban the play provoked anger and protest. Numerous dramatists from the schools of critical realism and experimental modernism protested the decision, calling it "brutal and confused administrative interference."[37] The Society of Dramatic Literature, a newly established subgroup of the

Association of Chinese Dramatists, soon decided to sponsor a production of the play by collecting donations from such sympathetic groups as the Chinese Society of the Disabled, led by Deng Xiaoping's elder son, Deng Pufang.[38] They then invited artists from different theater companies to perform it. The Shanghai People's Theater Company, meanwhile, also decided to stage the play. While the rehearsals were proceeding in both cities, numerous newspapers and journals reported on the play and its surrounding controversy, and when the two productions were brought to the public in October the reviews were full of unanimous praise.

The overwhelming praise for *WM*, like the resolute ban it provoked, indicate as much about the complexity of the moment in which it appeared as about the meaning of the production itself. With the decollectivization being enforced in the rural areas, by 1985 the urban economy had entered preliminary stages of denationalization. The cultural climate, the most sensitive barometer of Chinese socioeconomic and political life, was likewise transforming. In late 1984 the Fourth Congress of Literature took place in Beijing, and Hu Qili, then a standing member of the Politburo, gave a keynote speech promoting efforts to create "a vast sky of artistic freedom" and denouncing "inappropriate administrative interference" in literature and art.[39] In the early spring of 1985, the Fourth Congress of Theater also took place in Beijing, at which Xi Zhongxun, then secretary of the Central Disciplinary Committee of the Communist Party, made a speech similarly denouncing "ultraleft interference." The institutional implications of these speeches were demonstrated in the striking reconfigurations of the standing committees of the Writers Association and the Dramatists Association that were accomplished at both congresses: a significant number of those who had supported the controversial "new works of the new period" since the early 1980s were elected to replace some of the increasingly unpopular previous members of both committees;[40] and the once controversial writer Wang Meng was soon to assume the office of minister of culture. The production of *WM* was hailed as "a new chapter of modern Chinese spoken drama," and *Small Well Alley* was finally restaged for the public in the spring of 1985 after its five painful years of being kept at bay.[41]

The *WM* production, therefore, occurred at a significant transitional moment in the world of art and literature. The transition, however, was far more complex than what the performance of the play and its emotionally charged controversy had contained. The appearance of *Small Well Alley* looked tragically belated on the changing Chinese sociocultural scene. "Chinese reform" as a synonym for "Chinese modernization" was by now identified not only with decollectivization of the rural economy but with the partial denationalization, commodification, and internationalization of the urban economy, and voices echoing such socialist ethics as the collective well-being of the working people were likely to be judged old, outdated, and somewhat "ultraleft." Welcomed by its Beijing audience, *Small Well* was received as a gesture about a dispute in the past rather than as an artistic work auguring the future, and the moral values of the honest, hardworking common folk with their preference for the collective well-being affirmed in the play appeared out of step with the culture of the day. That none of the plays Li Longyun wrote after *Small Well* was nearly as influential indicates the changed sociopolitical conditions following in the wake of the reform process. Leading critical realists, after their hard-won battles over the "ultraleftists" who often attempted to ban their works in the first half of the 1980s, were confronted with growing new problems after the mid-1980s.

The cultural world of these years embraced Western-style modernism that was accompanied by escalating importation of European and American cultural products; books on Western literature, philosophy, political science, art, and theories were hastily translated and published. The theater world from 1985 onward was increasingly dominated by "modernist" dramas. These dramas, like some of the earlier modernist experiments, absorbed certain Western modernist sentiments on alienation from the state and a rebellious spirit toward sociocultural orthodoxy. More important, and unlike some of the earlier modernist dramas, they further inherited great amounts of sociocultural nihilism built within the organizing principles of Western modernist theater, in the light of which the ideology of Marxist socialism and its moral traditions were rejected. The spirit of individual rebellion against society embodied in Western modernism was transplanted into the Chinese context to deconstruct established cultural and moral systems, even as the conventional values of Western modernity were penetrating China to fill the ideological void created by such modernist deconstruction and the furthering of economic denationalization and internationalization. As such literary terms as "absurdism," "surrealism," "expressionism," or simply "modernism" were dancing through theater or literary journals and cultural circles, waves of Western consumer goods were sweeping across Chinese society. There appeared in cultural circles an equation of the modern West with the modern world, modernization with westernization, and Western-style modernity with universal humanity. While this Western-oriented modernism was reaching its second apex in the latter half of the 1980s, "the West is best" sentiments began to dominate the theater world as well as the society at large.[42]

Responding to the challenges that modernist theater with a nihilistic turn posed, but insisting on the "Chineseness" of their theatrical practices, some of the critical realists consciously appropriated the modernist techniques. Among the innovations in playwriting evident since the mid-1980s were structural changes: well-made plots often gave way to series of episodes; the orderly unfolding of stories began to split into multiple lines of development in which time and space or past and present were manipulated with greater flexibility; complex, ambiguous, and at times allegorical images increasingly replaced well-defined and linearly developed characters. When realists employed these putatively Western modernist techniques they began to appear more familiar to Chinese eyes and even turned out to be something very close to many aesthetic formulations of Chinese traditional music drama. The rich trove of traditional music drama then was emphatically rediscovered by critical realists. Such features of Western modernist theater as the fluidity of time and space, symbolism of imagery, and performative theatricality, some critical realists asserted, were in fact originally borrowed by Western dramatists from dramatic cultures of the East. Bertolt Brecht's interest in Beijing Opera, which inspired him to crystallize his theories of alienation effect and the epic theater, was the most cited and discussed example. Creative combinations of European modernist semiotics and the aesthetic codes of traditional Chinese drama, some of the leading dramatists of critical realism argued, marked the most promising direction for modern Chinese theater. The effort to carry out such combinations resulted in one of the most influential and provocative dramas of the 1980s: the *chuanjü*-style play *Pan Jinlian: The History of a Fallen Woman* of 1986, a realist redramatization of an ancient Chinese story in the form of regional music drama that rather consciously and effectively incorporated Western modernist elements.[43] *Pan Jinlian* is the third text and the only regional music drama in this anthology.

Written by well-known playwright Wei Minglun in the form of traditional *chuanjü* with one prelude and four parts, *Pan Jinlian* reappropriates the traditional story of "lascivious" Pan Jinlian by recontextualizing her life in juxtaposition with various fictional and historical characters from different times and places. Jia Baoyü, the hero of the Qing-period novel *The Dream of the Red Chamber,* Wu Zetian, the female emperor of the Tang dynasty, Anna Karenina, the heroine of Leo Tolstoy's classic novel, *Feifei,* a divorcée of modern China, and her friend, a contemporary woman judge, are but a few of those presented in this representation of Pan Jinlian's tragic story. The play, the author announced, is a protest against the "oppression of the female gender" rooted in Chinese traditional culture and persisting in different forms in modern Chinese society.[44] Moreover, the place where the story takes place is "across countries and continents, unconstrained by specific locations," implying that this protest is relevant to cultures and societies everywhere.[45] The "fallen" woman, Pan Jinlian, viewed as one among all the women in the world who have suffered male oppression, is reevaluated from cross-national, transhistorical, and multicultural perspectives as the victim of patriarchal power structures. Compared with such plays as *WM* that also incorporate traditional Chinese and Western modernist techniques, *Pan Jinlian,* with a regional music form and folk-style language familiar to Chinese audiences in both urban and rural areas, appears more coherent and complete in its aesthetic stylization and more dynamic and effective in its dramatization. The play creates virtually an entirely new form of Chinese regional music drama that cannot be fully defined by reference to categories of realism or modernism, traditional or modern. The author himself styled it *"chuanjü of the absurd."*

Stimulating many theatergoers of both traditional music drama and modern spoken drama with its refreshing thematic treatment and formal innovations, and disturbing some others with its radically different reinterpretation of the traditional story, *Pan Jinlian* touched off another heated nationwide debate. Some acclaimed the play as a milestone in contemporary cultural history and a powerful protest against Chinese "feudal morality" and its contemporary variation, "ultraleft orthodox morality," which imposed feudalistic restrictions on relations between male and female citizens. Wei Minglun's redramatization of Pan Jinlian, they argued, revealed the necessity of "sexual liberation" not only for Chinese women but for the nation's search for sociocultural modernity.[46] The concept of "sexual liberation," directly translated from English, was thus formally introduced and quickly disseminated in contemporary Chinese literary criticism. Others, however, denounced the play as a grave sociocultural misrepresentation in which a hedonistic, self-indulgent, and thoroughly traditional woman is glorified as an icon for women's liberation. "This play is written and produced with explicit pragmatic social purpose," a senior critic wrote; "it is certainly not just about a traditional story and a woman who was victimized by China's feudal tradition. The play's immediate implications for Chinese society in the 1980s are more than visible, as the author himself also declared. In our society today, while rapidly increasing numbers of middle-aged and younger men are carrying on extramarital and premarital affairs, and the percentage of teenagers' love affairs has also been quickly rising, Wei's Pan Jinlian, who is driven by her impulsive individual sexual desires to 'justifiably' murder her husband, can indeed help those men to achieve and justify their 'sexual liberation.' The sex is liberated, but this has nothing to do with women's liberation."[47] As in some of the previous controversies, the oppositions had little interest in the complexity of the play as a many-layered artistic work and less patience to explore the issues broached by it:

problems of gender in the gender-blind discourse of state socialism, the issue of sex in a society in which only four decades earlier Confucian patriarchy was still the official ideology and concubinage was legal, and the changing configurations of gender, sex, and class in a women-friendly and at the same time paternalistic state that is presently dismantling some of its established social mechanisms while generating a market economy, with all its usual women-hostile consequences, such as the return of the oldest form of sexual exploitation—prostitution. All these issues and more that are contained in this play and its receptions, unfortunately, have not been explicated in this debate.

Unlike the debates over *Small Well* or *WM,* however, the controversy about *Pan Jinlian* was quickly concluded with a general affirmation of the play as a great artistic work offering a powerful critique of both "feudalist moral codes" and "ultraleft orthodoxy" about human sexuality. It is significant that although leading cultural luminaries of the reform era such as Wang Meng and Liu Zaifu celebrated the flourishing of an "era of cultural pluralism,"[48] in the theater world *Pan Jinlian* hardly engendered genuine critical exchanges and substantial controversy at all. Instead, Chinese dramas written and produced in the late 1980s were regularly acclaimed by critics as protests against "feudal ultraleftism" or as arguments for "reform and open-door policy," "modernity," and "individuality." Until, that is, the social and political explosion of 1989 and the imposed silence that followed June 4.

The national success of *Pan Jinlian,* and the brief but highly visible controversy it aroused, temporarily masked the disturbing fact that from the mid-1980s the theater world as a whole was drastically declining. Film, television, and various popular entertainments flourishing in urban areas since the mid-1980s surpassed theater as the medium attracting national attention. As early as 1983, more than one hundred new films were released annually, and 87 percent of the households in Beijing and Shanghai already had television sets.[49] "Every evening," a noted dramatist wrote in 1983, "several TV channels offer interesting programs, more than ten cinemas show various Chinese and foreign films, each theater stages musical dramas, dancing dramas, and other popular performances—people now have many choices for a leisured evening. If we want to attract the audience to come and see our spoken dramas, we have to offer something special."[50] Theater, in short, had been increasingly challenged by the rapidly changing social conditions and larger patterns of the nation's cultural life.

Emblematic of those changes, the Chinese film and television industries had been visibly rising since the mid-1980s. As the percentage of urban households that had television sets increased with unprecedented speed and programs and channels with commercial advertisements multiplied, so did the time that people spent in front of the television. Although the sociocultural impact of the television industry on the general public was increasing in the mid-1980s, the film industry, which reached its most productive period in its quantity and technical quality, captured most of the public attention.[51] The rise of the once humble Xian Film Studio best exemplified such changes. Led by Wu Tianming, appointed manager of Xian Film in 1983, the studio produced a series of national hits and, in 1985, sold more copies of its films than any other studio in the country. In 1987, its films won seven of the eleven national Golden Rooster Awards and several prestigious international prizes.[52] Provoking strong responses at a variety of international film festivals while stirring excitement and controversy within China, these films registered the dynamics of modern Chinese history as much as the changes in the history of Chinese film.

Wu Tianming was recognized as one of the most forceful figures in film by the mid-1980s and an outstanding director in national and international film circles. Among eleven awards he received as a film director, five were international; among the five films he had directed, *Old Well,* released in 1986, was awarded two national and three international prizes.[53] With a narrative style strikingly distinguished from those of realist films made by such leading senior directors as Xie Jin and Wu Yigong, *Old Well* fascinated audiences with its innovative use of heavy color and strong light, creative appropriation of folk and rural imageries, highly assertive and theatrical cinematic representation, and enormous emotional energy. The film focuses on villagers who live and labor under the harshest physical conditions. Generation after generation of these villagers searched for water, the most precious source of life and hope, in a severely barren mountainous area. Their heroic-tragic persistence and the allegorical significance of their struggles are powerfully revealed through the cinematic narration, which is at once brutally realistic and intensely symbolic. Rewriting the realist tradition of Chinese film with its allegorical narrativity, *Old Well* paved the way for and heralded most creative features of the "fifth generation" of Chinese film directors. Embraced by Chinese viewers and acclaimed by Western critics, it significantly altered the landscape of Chinese cinematic culture. It is the only film script in this anthology.

The national and international recognition of Wu Tianming's *Old Well* caused complex but positive reactions as well as nationwide controversy in China. Some cultural critics and administrators asserted that the film gained attention in the West by representing Chinese society and people's lives in a most degrading way, exaggerating and even fabricating China's dehumanizing rural poverty and backwardness to please Western critics and audiences who held culturally and racially prejudiced stereotypes about the inferior "yellow race." Others contended that the film embodied the most precious spirit of the Chinese people and its culture, namely, the indomitable tenacity and determination to live and to develop under the most severe natural and social conditions. The international recognition the film won, they further argued, should be celebrated as a victory of Chinese culture asserting itself in the world and not taken as negative evidence against the film itself. As the Chinese economy, according to the general orientation set up by the reform policies of the nation, must find ways to enter the international economy, Chinese cultural production must make every effort to enter the global cultural market. *Old Well* was exemplary in taking the lead in "going into the world."[54]

The debate over *Old Well* concluded with unequivocal praise of the work by most members of the Chinese cultural world, but the complex questions regarding export-oriented cultural products in the international economic and cultural market were far from being resolved. Although 1985 to 1987 became known as the "golden years of Chinese film" for the unprecedented influence that film exerted throughout the nation compared with other performing arts, particularly spoken drama, financial support from the government for the film industry soon declined. This reduction of government financial support generated an urgent need for alternative resources. From 1987 onward, driven by the need to find more adequate financial support, attracted by the glamour and wealth that international recognition implied, and further pushed by the policies designed by the Chinese reform leadership to promote production for export, the Chinese film industry resorted to foreign investment and to making films for international markets. Competition for overseas financing among film directors intensified, and some turned completely to the Western film market starting in the late 1980s. Zhang Yimou's *Raise the Red Lantern* (1991) and *Shanghai Triad (1995) and Chen Kaige's Farewell My Concubine* (1993) and *Temptress Moon* (1997) were among the latest sensations so created. That the majority of the Chinese audience showed less and less interest in these films, even deeply disliking Zhang's *Red Lantern* in particular, contrasted sharply with the nationwide enthusiasm that Wu Tianming's *Old Well* once evoked.[55]

The problematic implications of the increasing fame of certain Chinese films since the late 1980s in the world film market can be partly seen in the marketing and distribution of Zhang Yimou's *Red Lantern*. Financed from Hong Kong and Japan and catering to the Eurocentric mindset that has dominated the international cultural market in general and film market in particular, *Red Lantern* offered a brilliant cinematic fabrication and a conscious exoticization of the Chinese concubine system in the 1920s and its erotic politics. The high-profile coverage and sensational praise the film received in the Western media contrasted with the ambiguous comments in Chinese newspapers, revealing an emerging process of "orientalizing" Chinese culture and people, a process consciously joined by some Chinese artists who won international fame bestowed by Western patronage with monetary rewards.[56] This process has begun to induce serious critical examinations.

Meanwhile, the television industry had been undergoing intensifying commercialization since the late 1980s. Media products from Hong Kong, Taiwan, Japan, and the West were imported in increasing quantities, and by 1988 nearly 60 percent of television programs in Shanghai and Beijing were imported from the West or Japan or patterned after Hong Kong and Taiwan commercial styles.[57] As many Western scholars of contemporary China have emphasized, the rise of the television industry in the 1980s was one of the most significant developments in modern Chinese cultural history. Unlike its counterpart in the West, however, its rapid development since the mid-1980s was generated not only by the growing forces of the domestic economy and technology but also by the aggressive expansion of Western consumer culture and its variations in the "Kong/Tai" (Hong Kong and Taiwan) style into China.[58]

These changes in film production and the rise of the television industry, emblematic of the formation of a performing arts market in China and the changes in the nation's cultural life, were inseparable from, and to a certain degree illustrative of, an overall economic and social transformation. The increasing commodification of society and the further opening of the nation to Western multinational capital and ideology, particularly since the late 1980s, have been structurally redefining the modes of production and the fundamental ways of life of the Chinese. When pursuit of material wealth began to dominate society's imagination and dictate the lives of individual citizens, cultural activity that was not yet commercialized appeared increasingly superfluous and anachronistic. While the government was cutting funds on one hand and the declining audience was cutting the box office on the other, the theater world as a whole was rapidly sinking into total crisis. By 1988, in the words of Yin Ruocheng, then vice minister of culture, "a large percentage of spoken drama companies nationwide are nearly dead." His solution: "We must disband more theater companies at all levels, adopt a contract system, and promote tourist performances."[59]

Confronted with this crisis, dramatists of critical realist and experimental modernist persuasions responded in very different ways. Many of the realists were disturbed by commercialization and what they called "Hongkongization" and "Taiwanization" of Chinese culture. As early as 1985, after Hu

Qili's speech on artistic freedom, leading dramatists of critical realism gathered in Beijing to discuss "freedom of artistic creation and artists' historical missions." Wang Peigong, the author of *WM,* evoked the threat of cultural commodification to spoken drama in the following comments:

> All the programs produced by the central television network for the Spring Festival this year, including that Hong Kong–style "New Year's Eve Show" and that traditional music drama preluded by a comic actor embracing a big shoe-shaped piece of gold, were utterly disappointing to the mass audience. "So *this* is called 'freedom of art?!' " many asked. Some answered: "Why make such a fuss? This is merely the beginning!" If such a "beginning" continues, more of the audience will be driven out of theater and cinema. How then can we talk about literary and artistic prosperity? Such a "beginning," I don't need to repeat, will make some men of letters "freely" run into fatal pitfalls![60]

Echoing Wang's comments, Zhong Jieying, another noted playwright of the Beijing People's Art Theater Company, warned: "Please cherish what we have finally won, namely, the right to write what we truly feel and think about our lives. If we let our art be dominated by those fashionable performances that imitate Hong Kong and Taiwan tastes and let money-dictated publications including pornography dominate our society, freedom will lose its true value and become just another form of falsehood."[61] Most dramatists of the critical realism school shared these views, as many essays printed in journals and speeches made at meetings indicate; yet how to further understand or deal with those "pitfalls" and "falsehoods," few of them seemed to know.

Similarly uncertain about the fate of modern Chinese drama, and indeed the future direction of the country as a whole, dramatists of experimental modernism responded to the changing situation with diverse views. Some followed the impulses offered by European modernist "negative theology" and went further and further into an isolated agony and despair over the "ultimate meaninglessness of being"; others turned into unconditional admirers and proponents of Western modernity and its ideology, identifying the idealized images created by eighteenth-century European rhetoric of "liberty," "equality," and "fraternity" with historical realities. They shared, however, the rhetorical assertion that the socially engaged and committed tradition of modern and contemporary Chinese literature and art was the culprit responsible for the multiple crises of Chinese culture in general and Chinese drama in particular.[62] Literature and art, some of them insisted, were expressions of individual subjectivity endowed with universal humanity, and anything that involved social issues was doomed as pseudoart repugnant to "our modern audience." Such pseudo art and literature, it was further argued, were deeply rooted in the tradition of classical Chinese aesthetics, which emphasized the social and ethical function of literary activity and was simply a feudal legacy that should be eradicated from "modern" ways of artistic thinking.[63] Critical realism, with its announced engagement with the social, political, cultural, and emotional conditions of the nation, was thereby viewed as another variant of "ideological orthodoxy," a descendant of "feudalism" and its modern reincarnation, "ultraleftism," outdated, petrified, and bound to be discarded by "new waves of world history."[64] Increasing numbers of playwrights of critical realism, including Zong Fuxian, Xin Yixun, Li Jie, and Li Longyun were implicitly criticized and at times explicitly ridiculed.[65]

It is here that the problematic tensions between the school of critical realism and that of experimental modernism became explicit. As early as 1985, in an interview with an American journalist, Li Longyun made the following comments:

> What's most attractive about a writer is his or her own character, and what is most appealing about a nation is its own cultural spirit and form of living . . . A play is significant internationally if it is characterized by its own unique artistic style and resonates with its own profound cultural traditions. I believe that our productions of plays like *Rhinoceros* and *Bald Soprano* cannot surpass the productions by Western theater companies, but I dare say that there is no theater in the entire world that can produce a better production of *Teahouse* than the Beijing's People's Art Theater Company.[66]

More polemical phrases like "superficial imitators," "self-styled westernizers," and "trick players and claptrappers" were coined by some critics to characterize some of the modernists, indicating the degree to which this conflict was emotionalized.[67] While modernist plays staged in cities like Shanghai accounted 74 percent of all the productions mounted in the years from 1985 to 1989, a large proportion of these dramas, with intentionally obscure language and westernized images, were less and less appealing to the general public.[68] Despite the effusive praise they received from some theater critics, the theater of experimental modernism in the late 1980s was losing the genuine cultural energies and critical thrusts operating in the pioneering modernist works of the earlier years and, more important, was losing the remaining part of the general audience for spoken drama.

The deep tension between the two drama schools voiced by some critics and dramatists, such as Wang Peigong and Li Longyun, interestingly enough, has never been adequately explored in the theater world. As China's structural economic changes encouraged further commodification of society and were closing the social spaces once occupied by such non-commercial forms of culture as spoken drama, a sizable proportion of the nation's leading playwrights and drama theoreticians either remained silent on topics of urgent social relevance or stretched themselves to comply with whatever currents that were carrying the day. Those who insisted upon the organizing principles of socially engaged critical realism and "Chinese cultural styles" in their literary practice and theories often appeared defensive and reactive rather than creative or initiative; Zong Fuxian and Xi Yixun, among others, managed to criticize their own playwriting with explicit anxiety and hidden ambivalence.[69] While further socioeconomic changes forced even the most ontological or transcendental modernists to confront the empty theater houses in the late 1980s, most of them seemed desperately frustrated and deeply lost rather than capable of asserting alternatives as they once appeared so confident in doing. The ambivalent responses of some—and the significantly absent responses of others—to the crises of Chinese spoken drama since the mid-1980s indicate the historical profundity and complexity of the crisis in relation to a changing society.

As the decade of the 1980s was ending, financial support for theater from the government was further reduced to subsistence or a lower than subsistence level. The Ministry of Culture in 1987–1988 began to enforce an "employee contract system" in theater companies for their new hiring, and such basic principles as job security, free medical care, and other benefits were done away with. For those dramatists who joined the companies before this contract system was enforced and hence still retained some benefits, particularly free medical care, the State Council adopted a new policy that "strongly encouraged" them to stop being dependent on the company for their income and to take the initiative to organize individual performances to make a living for themselves. Meanwhile, more theater companies were disbanded. In 1987 alone, for instance, five spoken drama troupes in Liaoning Province were closed.[70] The degree of change in government policy in the late 1980s was demonstrated emphatically when *Jüben* (Drama), the national drama journal that was founded in 1952 and contained essentially the entire history of contemporary Chinese drama ever since—except during the Cultural Revolution years—lost its annual funding from the cultural administration in 1988.[71] The editors and staff members of the journal refused to let it be closed. They made a historically unprecedented and emotionally charged national appeal for donations, and managed to continue its publication. The national theater journal *Xijübao* (On theater), on the other hand, did not lose its funding entirely. But with its funding drastically reduced it was compelled to change its title to *Zhongguo xijü* (Chinese theater), and it started issuing "popular editions" containing photos of sexualized women and violent, sensational stories to increase revenues.[72] Moneymaking had become the real priority for theater companies and drama publishing houses at all levels, and more theater companies were turned into nightclubs.[73] A large number of playwrights gave up playwriting and started working for the television industry or joined other lucrative commercial activities; a larger number of actors left the stage of spoken drama and contracted for various commercial performances to make a living; driven by the profit-making pressures at home and lured by the spells of Hollywood films and American-style mass culture industries abroad, many artists left the country altogether and joined the largest "brain drain" from China in the twentieth century.[74]

Still, some of the finest playwrights, directors, and dramatic artists of the nation remained with their chosen vocation and continued their creative efforts. The dramatic works of fine artistic quality written and produced in the last two years of the 1980s, therefore, cannot be fully appreciated without understanding the turbulent social, economic, and cultural situation in which Chinese dramatists struggled. Faced with a wide array of night entertainment, neon-light advertisements for Western consumer goods such as MTV, legal or illegal imported videotapes, magazines, and pornography, Hong Kong, Taiwan and American television programs and Rambo films, discos and Japanese-style karaoke singing, theater productions appearing in the last years of the 1980s were not only outstanding artistic works but heroic triumphs for the much undermined, confused, and distressed world of Chinese spoken drama. *Sangshuping jishi* (Sangshuping chronicles) was such a play, and it is therefore chosen as the last dramatic text in this anthology.[75]

Staged by the Central Drama Academy in Beijing in 1988, *Sangshuping* is set in a northern Chinese village during the late years of the Cultural Revolution. It dramatizes how the "high rhetoric" of militant radicalism during the Cultural Revolution had no real connection at all with the villagers' lives and was used only by traditional patriarchal forces in the socioeconomically backward countryside. The patriarchal tradition perpetuated by rural poverty and the victimization of women by such cultural traditions and economic conditions are both emphatically dramatized. The love stories of the young and their tragic endings are movingly represented. As a condemnation of the die-hard patriarchal and traditional forces operating through "ultraleftism" during the Cultural Revolution, the play did not go beyond the accomplishment of plays of critical realism like *Small Well Alley*. The crucial difference between the plays produced in previous years and *Sangshuping Chronicles,* however, lies in the fact that the former's critiques of social, political, and cultural illnesses were intertwined with their authors' call for a genuine practice of socialist ethics and democracy in accordance with the common folk's needs and desires, while the latter holds the patriarchal mentality of "the common folk" in rural China perpetuated by their extreme economic poverty as one more major source of the social illnesses persisting in society. The causes of the tragedies of Sangshuping, the play suggests, are not only the abuse of power by officials and their institutional mechanisms, but the extreme rural poverty and the cruel ignorance of the peasantry rooted in their poverty and associated traditional values.

Such a difference is particularly striking when one compares this play with the film *Old Well,* which deals with a similar type of rural lives. While Old Well's villagers share many of Sangshuping's problems, their human spirit to not only persist but struggle to change their lives is recognized and represented with intimate understanding and deep emotional resonance. In Sangshuping, no such spirit survives. Whereas the two leading women characters in *Old Well* assert their strong individualities and their ability to define their own forms and values of living, in *Sangshuping* the two leading women characters become simply victims—one goes insane and the other commits suicide. *Old Well* unfolds with the life of Wangquan, a young man with a modern education who returns to his home village to live, suffer, work, and fight; *Sangshuping* is seen through the observant eye of Zhu Xiaoping, in whom the authorial voice speaks. Unlike Wangquan, Zhu is the only character in the play who is not from the village but from another world—China's large urban centers. Although his sociopolitically privileged family background is presented with critical reflection in the play when Zhu is shown using it to help the villagers, his constant gaze is clearly enacted as a perspective of "the modern" that organizes this dramatic narrative of "the traditional." Indeed, one may well argue that *Old Well* is a story told as the villagers live through it, while the Sangshuping story is told as a self-conscious modernist sees it. Many of the critical insights into the Chinese peasantry in the play are certainly invaluable in heightening the sense of urgency to "enforce fundamental social reform" and "eliminate feudalistic ignorance," as the director of the play puts it.[76] But the structuring of the play is also underlined by a narrative distance that allows a fair amount of objectification of the villagers. By turning them into carriers and victims of "feudalistic" ignorance and cruelty without any intrinsic resources for effective change, the play implies a prescription for saving the Chinese peasantry from itself—a "modernization" that seems a negation of the "backward lives" of the Sangshuping village rather than a consolidation of the desires and strengths for change coming from its inhabitants.

The much emphasized focus of the production is on aesthetic experimentation. Incorporating elements of traditional Chinese music drama and techniques of Western modernist theater in an innovative, unique, and coherent performing style, the play is full of images of poetic richness and allegorical suggestiveness, fluid spatial constructions and temporal transmutations, and expressive representations of individual characters' feelings and their shared living situation. As the performance was going on in the Academy's little theater, all noted theater critics and cultural administrators in Beijing, including Yin Ruocheng, then the minister of culture, hailed it as "the crystallization of the finest achievements of contemporary Chinese dramatic art."[77] While such celebration is grounded in the remarkable aesthetic experimentation of this production, it cannot substitute for substantial explication of the complex signification of the play and its prescriptive "call for fundamental social reform." As if being somewhat displaced by the promotion of its aesthetic innovation in itself, discussions of any substance about the play—its form in relation to its content, for instance—were visibly absent in the entire celebration of this "theatrical triumph." The show "closed after fewer than twenty performances at the Academy's little theater."[78]

Such triumphs on stage, moreover, were fewer and fewer, as the prescriptions for the nation's modernization with a "global vision" were intensifying in the public discourse, indicating the degree to which tensions between the public program for "national progress" and the lives of China's ordinary citizens were growing. After the tragic events of 1989, no one can say that the theater world remained unchanged, but the essential tensions and crises discussed above persisted and developed. While market-led reform was in temporary retrenchment from late 1989 to late 1991, there appeared a momentary resurgence of spoken dramas reasserting "socialist spirit and morality."[79] After Deng Xiaoping's trip to southern China in the spring of 1992 and the Fourteenth Party Congress in the fall calling for speeding up the implementation of reform policies gearing the society toward a "socialist market economy," however, this momentary resurgence was eclipsed and commodification further dictated sociocultural trends.[80] Although a "middle-class theater" was advocated by some critics and dramatists in the late 1980s and then again in the early 1990s, most Chinese artists who remained in their profession seemed to have realized that they were living in a painful period during which the most they could do might be to keep their dramatic activity alive on a small scale and continue to prepare for a resurgence in the future—whatever that might be.[81] In his essay "Our Hope for Spoken Drama Lies in the New Century," Zhao Yaoming, a noted playwright in Nanjing, predicted that it would take thirty or so years for China to succeed with its market reforms and to turn itself into "a prosperous, democratic, socially integrated, and culturally developed country" with a fully established middle class. Until then, it seemed to Zhao, modern spoken drama, conditioned by the necessities of Chinese social history, had no alternative but to continue its struggle to survive in its diminished and diminishing social spaces.[82]

While hope for the revitalization of modern Chinese drama seemed to be placed by some critics and dramatists in the twenty-first century, with an ideal audience of an imagined Chinese middle class, some American- and Western-run commercial theaters began to gain social and institutional ground in cities like Shanghai.[83] Meanwhile, the last group of playwrights and dramatists were leaving the realm of spoken drama; 95 percent of the students in the 1992 class at the Shanghai Drama Academy chose to write television scripts to fulfill the requirements for their degrees.[84] A news item in *South Evenings* on July 21, 1993, reported that playwrights in Beijing had all stopped writing plays; some retired, some started working for commercial television, and some "jumped into" the "sea of business." The situation in such provincial centers of spoken drama as Hubei and Liaoning was even worse than in Beijing. In the south, Shanghai, Nanjing, and Guangzhou are faring slightly better; there have been occasional productions of spoken dramas, but they are by and large not well attended.[85] Among the few plays to win some national media coverage in the beginning of the 1990s, one was an adaptation of Harold Pinter's *The Lover* in Shanghai in August 1992, containing a lovemaking scene; another was a new play called *Taiyang wan* (Harbor of the sun) by Chu Yue in Beijing in May 1993, which had a female nude scene.[86] While female nudity was certainly not the sole attraction of these two plays, they did not seem to offer much for sustained artistic or social discussion. As a Chinese scholar noted in 1994: "Since a certain kind of capitalism is developing in China now, theater companies can no longer operate as they have since the inception of the People's Republic in 1949."[87]

Modern Chinese drama continues to exist, however, no matter how small its scale of production and how limited its social influence may be for the moment. Contemporary dramatists are still searching for ways to keep their art alive, no matter how much they have to turn to commercial activities for their living.[88] In the early 1990s in Nanjing a series of innovative performances in small and at times temporary theaters were produced by artists who put their limited individual financial resources together, and "the Nanjing little theater movement" became nationally known.[89] In Beijing, there also appeared various sponsoring programs, and all the shows produced in the 1990s have had substantial public or private donations. *Niao ren* (Bird men), a three-act spoken drama, was mounted by the People's Art Theater in April–May 1993 with such subsidies and was extremely well received by the audience.[90] In Shanghai, artists organized stage readings of noncommercial scripts, and some of them led to formal and successful public productions. *Loushang de marjin* (The Karaoke upstairs), staged by the Shanghai People's Theater in June 1994, was one such success. In all these productions supported by various financial sources, the organizing principles of experimental modernism developed since the early 1980s clearly leave their marks on dramatic texts and performances, particularly in their structural constitutions and technical effects; but a return of critical realism in their dramatic narratives is also undeniable and potent.

The return of critical realism in the first half of the 1990s is in fact beginning to show increasing prominence in the struggling theater world. *The Karaoke Upstairs* is a case in point. Written by Zhang Xian, formerly a student of Shanghai Drama Academy and currently the most active playwright in Shanghai, the play dramatizes the life of a young female receptionist at a luxury hotel who prostitutes her body to help her struggling working-class family, and the life of a female stockbroker who has done away with any family ties while devoting her body and soul to the speculations at the newly opened and fluid "futures market." The former has an elder brother whose salary as a factory worker cannot keep the family going but who condemns his once "sweetest baby sister" for being "brazenly immoral," and the latter has a temporary lover from Taiwan who seems to be plunged into a desperate search for "human feelings" in Shanghai by his transnational property and wealth. As the brother is reduced to seeking help from his sister after he admits that he actually wants "the immoral money," the love-hungry man from Taiwan sinks into a hysterical rant on the inhumanity of the world after he realizes that his longing for "feelings" is returned with the financial calculation of his Shanghai female partner for "blue chips." The play ends with the stockbroker sitting at the window of her hotel room gazing into the silent starry sky of a busy Shanghai night, as the "sweetest baby sister"-turned-prostitute at the hotel reception desk hums the "Team Song of the Young Pioneers" that every Chinese child since 1949 knows by heart, remembering her elementary-school days when she was the youngest and most beloved of her class: "Father," she says with a choking voice, "I have received an A again for my Chinese literature test." The production had five evening performances, and each had a full house in attendance.[91]

Sharing the dramatic dynamics of critical realism but with more allegorical significance, *Bird Men* is also among the noteworthy plays of the 1990s. Centering on a group of Beijing residents who love Beijing Opera and the traditional culture of bird breeding, the play dramatizes how their encounters with Westerners and overseas Chinese generate tensions. As the story unfolds, a sociocultural gathering place for those who breed their birds and practice the art of Beijing Opera is one day taken over by an overseas Chinese and turned into a psychoanalysis clinic, holding all those bird breeders and Opera lovers as patients. The place is visited by a representative of an international organization for bird protection; through an English translator, this representative accuses the bird breeders of various cruelties against birds, including violating bird rights by putting them into beautiful cages. Meanwhile, he awards a medal to a Chinese Dr. Chen, who specializes in "birdcology" and makes vivid specimens out of living rare birds, asserting that "specimen making of rarity is a great contribution to preserving and collecting rare birds and animals of the world."[92] As the overseas Chinese uses Freud to analyze the "Chinese neuroses" and the Western representative actively forces "international regulations" into the culture of Chinese bird breeding, the leading character of the play—a longtime Beijing Opera performer—turns both of them into objects of investigation. By showing how the overseas Chinese knows precious little about China and Freud is fundamentally incoherent, he unmasks this expert on "Chinese neuroses" as a cultural charlatan. By showing how Dr. Chen is a bird killer with obsessive compulsions for sinister acquisition, he tells the representative of "bird protectors international" to never again "come and issue these sorts of medals!" When the representative protests his right to come and issue medals since "now we live in a single globalized world," the Beijing Opera performer replies: "You are protected by the consular jurisdiction; otherwise you need to worry about your doggy-life! Now guys, get him out!"[93] Although the play never spares the Beijing Opera master his sense of profound crisis, it offers an allegorical story that clearly registers not only a probing self-reflection but a certain nationalist impulse that is critical of both the Chinese Dr. Chen and the Western representatives. With its mixture of Chinese and Western humor, modern and traditional as well as official and colloquial language styles, the play seized the imagination of the audience in Beijing and topped the list of most popular shows in 1994.

Despite the often overwhelming difficulties in mounting them on the public stage, the return of critical realist dramas with an allegorical turn persists. Such a return can also be seen in the continuing efforts to stage modern historical dramas of realist-allegorical significance in the mid-1990s. *Xinhai chao* (The tidal currents in the year Xinhai), a powerful dramatization of the mass movement in Sichuan Province in 1911 to protect the Chinese railway construction against the encroachment of Western imperialist forces with which the Manchu court was collaborating, was produced in 1991. *Shangyang*, a play about a famous minister in the Warring States (17–11 B.C.) who resolutely sought to reform the court, promote economic growth, and consolidate the state by establishing the legal system and carrying out its enforcement, was staged in 1996. Shangyang was put to death by the nobility after the old emperor died, but the systems and mechanisms established by his reform remained as the core of the great success of the state of Qin.[94] The implications of both plays for the continuing Chinese reform and its shifting, contested, and contradictory orientations in the late twentieth century are striking and certainly complex. Dramatists of the 1990s return to history and the lives of ordinary citizens for their artistic inspiration under extremely difficult conditions and with enormous tenacity. The scope of their activity and the influence of their works is nowhere near those of the critical realists in the early 1980s, certainly. The spirit with which they probe the problems and crises in a structurally changed and changing China through dramatic creations, however, will register as a unique chapter with yet-to-be-recognized significance in the history of modern Chinese drama.

The future of modern Chinese drama and dramatists, as a leading scholar of Chinese theater in the modern West once remarked, depends on the future of China's modernization and its repositioning in a "global village" that seems increasingly dominated by multinational and transnational capital.[95] Caught in the historical confluence that has transformed a reform that inspired hopes for socialist democracy into a reform led by the market economy, the playwrights who emerged in the early 1980s and their younger colleagues have to structurally reconstitute themselves and their art while keeping their creative spirit and social commitment alive, confronting the drastically altered conditions of their lives and their country in ever more complex relations to the world at large. A rethinking of their professional mission and a redefinition of their identities are essential to the survival of modern Chinese dramatists and the development of Chinese dramatic culture. It is indeed time to anthologize contemporary Chinese drama, including film scripts, that have been produced since the beginning of the reform era. This anthology, I hope, offers those who love Chinese theater and Chinese culture in particular, and love human creativity and human creations in general, an opportunity to reflect upon what has happened in the turbulent past two decades and to ponder what might be created in the future—in China as in the world.

Notes

1. There is another category of Chinese dramatic literature, namely, "modern historical drama." Regional music drama (which has had a long history beginning in the twelfth century) and modern spoken drama (which made its appearance in 1907 and has

been developing since) are often viewed as the two major genres of modern Chinese theater. Modern historical drama, created by Guo Moruo in 1923 and practiced by many distinguished Chinese dramatists ever since, may well be ranked as another major genre in modern Chinese theater. For more information on the aesthetic features and significance of this genre, see Yan Haiping, "Modern Chinese Drama and Its Western Models: A Critical Reconstruction of Chinese Subjectivity," *Modern Drama,* March 1992, pp. 54–64; Yan Haiping, "Male Ideology and Female Identity: Images of Women in Four Modern Chinese Historical Plays," *Journal of Dramatic Theory and Criticism,* fall 1993, pp. 61–81.

2. The government under the Nationalist Party (Guomindang), headed by Chiang Kai-shek, ruled China from 1928 to 1949 before the Chinese Communist Party, led by Mao Zedong, came to power and founded the People's Republic of China.

3. Colin Mackerras, *Chinese Drama: A Historical Survey* (Beijing: New World Press 1990), p. 167.

4. Lao She and Tian Han were among the most prominent spoken dramatists who died during the Cultural Revolution. Between the years 1966 and 1976, the membership of the Writers Association dropped from 1,059 to 865. Most of the decrease was due to deaths, and most of these deaths occurred between 1966 and 1969, the height of the Cultural Revolution. See Bonnie S. McDougall, "Writers and Performers, Their Works, and Their Audiences in the First Three Decades," in *Popular Chinese Literature and Performing Arts in the People's Republic of China, 1949–1979,* ed. Bonnie S. McDougall (Berkeley and Los Angeles: University of California Press, 1984), p. 304, n. 69.

5. See "Xinchangzheng yü xinshiming: fukan zhi duzhe" (New long march and new mission: to the readers on the day when *Drama* resumes its publication), *Jüben* (Drama), January 1979, p. 2. Mao Zedong's wife, Jiang Qing, was one of the members of the Cultural Revolution Committee in 1966 and leader of its radical "Gang of Four." The very few spoken dramas that were allowed to be staged professionally during the decade, carrying political messages promoted by the Gang of Four, indicated the minimal possibility of survival for spoken drama on the professional stage as a whole. It should be noted, however, that amateur performances of dramatic stories created by amateur writers in factories, schools, and other working units in urban areas were widespread. Those performers also brought their shows to rural areas. In the rural areas where the land was fertile and farming was comparatively advanced, many production teams used their resources to organize young people to create their own amateur performances as well.

6. Zong Fuxian, *Yü wusheng chu* (From the depth of silence), *Renmin xiju* (People's theater), December 1978, pp. 49–76; Sha Yexin, *Chenyi shizhang* (Mayor Chenyi), *Jüben* (Drama), May 1997, pp. 2–40; Cui Dezhi, *Baochun hua* (Spring flower), *Jüben* (Drama), April 1979, pp. 2–47; Xing Yixun, *Quan yü fa* (Power versus law), *Jüben* (Drama), October 1979, pp. 2–34; Su Shuyang, *Danxin pu* (Noble hearts), *Renmin xiju* (People's theatre), May 1978, pp. 16–80.

7. Zhang Chunqiao, Yao Wenyuan, Jiang Qing, and Wang Hongwen represented the radical forces during the Cultural Revolution. The term "the Gang of Four" was used by Mao Zedong in referring to them critically at a Politburo meeting in the late 1960s and has been used extensively since 1979, when the four were arrested by Ye Jianying, one of the ten marshals of China, with the support of the army and Hua Guofeng, then the first vice chairman of the Chinese Communist Party and the prime minister of the PRC. Many of those plays are fictional, of course, but some were dramatizations of the lives of senior revolutionaries. For example, *Shuguang* (Dawn), by Zhao Huan (1977), is about the life of He Long; *Chen Yi chushan* (Chen Yi coming out of the mountains), by Ding Yishan (1979), is about the life of Chen Yi. Both He and Chen were among the ten marshals of the PRC.

8. Li Longyun, *You zheyang yige xiaoyuan* (There is such a small compound), staged by the Children's Repertoires Theater of China in Beijing, April 1979; Zhou Weipo et al., *Paobing siling de er'zi* (The artillery commander's son), *Wenhui bao* (Wenhui daily), Shanghai, June 10, 1979; Li Min, *Yige wuangu de shengchan duizhang* (The stubborn production team leader), *Anhui xiju* (Anhui drama), March 1979; Xue Zheng, *Kaolü kaolü* (We shall consider), *Jüben* (Drama), August 1979.

9. Sha Yexin, *Jiaru woshi zhende* (If I were real), *Qishi niandai* (The seventies), Hong Kong, January 1980.

10. Li Longyun, *Xiaojing hutong* (Small Well alley), *Jüben*, May 1981, pp. 36–76. A complete English translation of the play by Jiang Hong and Timothy Cheek of Colorado College is available upon request. Much to the editor's regret, it cannot be included in this anthology due to the limits of space.

11. The Great Leap Forward was launched by Mao Zedong and the PRC leadership in 1958 to speed up growth of the national economy. The movement failed, resulting in a widespread famine from 1959 to 1963. See Maurice Meisner, *Mao's China and After* (New York: Free Press, 1986), pp. 204–251.

12. Archivists of *Jüben*, "Guanyü jige huaju de zhengyi" (Regarding the debates on several spoken dramas), *Jüben* (Drama), February 1985, p. 94.

13. Li Longyun, "Yü meiguo jizhe de tanhua" (A conversation with an American journalist), *Yingju yuekan* (Film and drama monthly), July 1985, p. 7.

14. Yan Haiping, *Qinwang Li Shimin* (Li Shimin, prince of Qin), *Jüben* (Drama), October 1981, pp. 10–47.

15. See Yan Haiping, "Xizuo *Qinwang Lishimin* de yixie xiangfa" (Reflections on writing *Li Shimin, prince of Qin*), *Jüben* (Drama), September 1982, pp. 87–90.

16. Wang Guorong, "Ping *Qinwang Lishimin*" (On *Lin Shimin, prince of Qin*), *Jiefang ribao* (Liberation daily), July 1, 1982.

17. Yan Haiping, *Qinwang Li Shimin: jüben yü pinglun* (Li Shimin, prince of Qin: Text and Criticism) (Beijing: Chinese Drama Publishing House, 1985), pp. 144–168.

18. Yan Haiping, "Jinjin shi kaishi: Woxie *Qinwang Li Shimin* ("This is just the beginning: I write *Li Shimin, Prince of Qin*"), in *Li Shimin, Prince of Qin: Text and Criticism*, p. 150.

19. Li Zehou's review of the play is one of the fine examples. See *Li Zehou shinianji: 1979–1989* (Collections of Li Zehou's writings from 1979–1989) (Anhui: Anhui's Publishing House for Art and Literature, 1994), pp. 49–51.

20. The television series, *Qinwang Li Shimin* (Li Shimin, prince of Qin), was written by Yan Haiping, directed by Zhang Ge, and produced by Shanghai Television Station, December 1982. In 1982, the play was awarded the national prize for excellence in drama by the Association of Chinese Dramatists and the Chinese Ministry of Culture.

21. Chen Baichen, *Dafengge* (Song of the wind), *Jüben* (Drama), January 1979; Lu Jianzhi and Fang Jiaji, *Tangtaizong* (Grand emperor of Tang), *Jüben* (Drama), April 1982; Zhen Huaixi, *Xintinglei* (Tears shed at the Xin Pavilion), *Jüben* (Drama), August 1982.

22. See "Daoyan de hua" (Words from the director), in the program for the production of Samuel Beckett's *Waiting for Godot* by the Shanghai Drama Academy, 1987.

23. Ma Zhongjun, Jia Hongyuan, and Jü Xinhua, *Wuwai you reliu* (There are warm currents outside of this house), *Jüben* (Drama), June 1980, pp. 55–65.

24. Gao Xingjian and Liu Huiyuan, *Juedui xinghao* (Absolute signals), *Shiyue* (October), a literary quarterly, no. 5, 1982.

25. Gao Xingjian, *Chezhan* (Bus stop), *Shiyue* (October), no. 3, 1983, pp. 119–138.

26. See "Bianzhe an" (Notes from the editor) to "*Chezhan* sanren tan" (A dialogue among three critics on *Bus Stop*), *Xijubao* (On theater), March 1984, pp. 3–7.

27. Wang Ruoshui, "Wei rendaozhuyi bianhu" (An apology for humanism), *Wenhui bao* (Wenhui daily), Shanghai, January 17, 1983.

28. Wang Ruoshui, "Lun yihua" (On alienation), *Xinwen jie* (News front), no. 2, 1980; Zhou Yang, "Makesizhuyi de jige wenti" (On several theoretical issues in Marxism), *Renmin ribao* (People's daily), March 9, 1983.

29. Hu Qiaomu, "Guanyu rendaozhuyi he yihua wenti" (On humanism and the question of alienation), *Xinhua wenzhai* (New China digest), March 1998, pp. 1–17.

30. "Chezhan sanren tan" (A dialogue among three critics on *Bus Stop*), Xijübao (On Theuter), March 1984, pp. 3–7.

31. Jia Hongyuan and Ma Zhongjun, *Jieshang liuxing hongqunzi* (Red skirts are the fashion), staged by the Youth Theater Company of China, June 1984; Liu Shugang, *Yige shengzhe dui sizhe de fangwen* (A visit from a dead man), *Jüben* (Drama), May 1985.

32. See Liu Xinwu and Li Li, "Liu Xinwu tan xingshiqi de bianhua" (Liu Xinwu on the literary changes in the new era), *Wenhui yuekan* (Wenhui monthly), no. 5, 1988.

33. Gao Xingjian, "*Chidao de xiandaizhuyi yü dangjin zhongguo wenxue*" (The slow arrival of modernism and contemporary Chinese literature), a speech at the Conference on Contemporary Chinese Literature and Modernism held in Hong Kong, October 11, 1987, in Gao Xingjian, *Meiyou zhuyi* (No -isms) (Hong Kong: Tiandi Publishing House, 1996), p. 102.

34. Wang Peigong and Wang Gui, "*WM*" (We), *Jüben* (Drama), September 1985, pp. 6–23. "Rightist" is a political category formally coined and used in the political campaign of 1957 in which half a million people (most of them intellectuals) were labeled as "antisocialist rightists" and punished accordingly. The category continued to exist in Chinese political life until the end of the Cultural Revolution. "Capitalist roader" was a political label coined and used during the Cultural Revolution (1966–1976), referring to those political leaders who allegedly wanted "to restore capitalism in China instead of developing socialism." See Meisner, *Mao's China and After*, pp. 167–397.

35. Staff reporter of *Jüben*, "Fang Women de zuozhe" (An interview with the author of *WM*), *Jüben* (Drama), August 1985, p. 51.

36. See Yi Min, "*Women* fengbo de shizhong" (The beginning and the end of the controversy on *WM*), *Jüben* (Drama), November 1990, pp. 18–26.

37. Ibid., pp. 18–26.

38. The Society of Dramatic Literature was established in 1985, included many active playwrights of the Dramatists Association, and was chaired by Wang Zhen, the former director of the Chinese Drama Publishing House. See *Jüben* (Drama), November 1985, p. 91.

39. "Xuexi Hu Qili tongzhi zai zhongguo zuojia di sici daibiao dahui shang de zhuci" (Discussions on Hu Qili's speech at the Fourth Chinese Writers' Congress), *Jüben* (Drama), March 1985, pp. 27–30.

40. "Cong minzhu dao tuanjie de dahui" (A democratic and unifying conference—on the Fourth Congress of Theater), *Yingjü yuekan* (Film and drama monthly), June 1985, pp. 3–5. For the names of the members in the newly elected secretariat of the Association of Chinese Dramatists, see *Xijübao* (On theater), June 1985, p. 3.

41. Wang Buping, "Huajü yishu de xinpianzhang" (A new chapter of modern Chinese spoken drama), *Jüben* (Drama), September 1985, pp. 25–27; Wang Yüsheng, "Wei xiaojing hutong gongyan erzuo" (For the eventual public production of *Small Well Alley*), *Xijübao* (On theater), March 1985, pp. 12–13.

42. Wan Shuyuan, "Xijü chongbai yü guannian cuojue" (On the phenomenon of worshiping Western theater and its implied conceptual illusions), *Yingjü yuekan* (Film and drama monthly), July 1987, pp. 17–19; Bai Ren, "Waiguo ren shuo . . ." (The

foreigners say . . .), *Xijübao* (On theater), July 1986, p. 50; Ye Tingfang, "Women de shenmei yishi yao jinru xiandai lingyü" (Our aesthetic consciousness should be modernized), *Xijübao* (On theater), October 1985, pp. 18–21.

43. Wei Minglun, *Pan Jinlian: yige nüren de chenlunshi* (Pan Jinlian: The history of a fallen woman), *Xinhua wenzhai* (New China digest), February 1986, pp. 87–99. *Chuanjü* is one of the major Chinese regional music theater forms, originated in Sichuan province; "chuan" means Sichuan, and "jü" means drama.

44. Wei Minglun, "Wo zuozhe feichang huandan de men—Pan Jinlian xiaxiang" (I am having a very absurd dream—some fanciful thoughts on Pan Jinlian), *Xinhua wenzhai* (New China digest), February 1986, p. 101.

45. Wei Minglun, *Pan Jinlian, Xinhua wenzhai* (New China digest), February 1986, p. 87.

46. Liu Binyan, "Cixiang fengjian youling de lijian—ping chuanjü *Pan Jinlian*" (A sharp sword against feudalism—on *Pan Jinlian*), *Xinhua wenzhai*, (New China digest), September 1986, pp. 102–104.

47. Zhang Yihe, "Chuanjü *Pan Jinlian* de wenti yü qüshi" (The pitfalls and trendy impulses in chuanjü *Pan Jinlian*), *Xijübao* (On theater), October 1986, pp. 40–45.

48. See *Renmin wenxue* (People's literature), January–February 1987. Gao Xingjian, *Meiyou zhuyi* (No -isms), p. 105.

49. Huang Weijun, "Wodui huajü qiantu zhi duanxiang" (My thoughts on spoken drama's future), *Xijübao,* July 1983, p. 34.

50. Wang Zhen, "Huajü de miren, caiyou huajümi" (Spoken drama has to be fascinating to have its fans), *Xijübao* (On theater), May 1983, p. 14.

51. *Zhong guo wenhua nianjian* (Yearbook of Chinese culture) (Beijing: People's Publishing House, 1986–1987).

52. Lan Mu, "Wu Tianming yü xiying de qiji" (Wu Tianming and the miracle of Xian Film Studio), in *Laojing: zhongguo mingzuoxuan—dianying* (*Old Well:* Chinese masterpieces—film), volume 1, edited by Jiao Xiongping (Taipei: Wanxiang Publishing, 1990), p. 127.

53. Ibid.

54. Chen Kun, "Yangwang Chang'an—zheli you ge Wu Tianming" (Look up toward Chang'an—there is a Wu Tianming), *Dazhong dianying* (Popular films), September 1987.

55. See, for instance, Dang Yang, *Haiwai feihong* (Letters from overseas) (Beijing: Chinese Federation of Arts and Literature Publishing House, 1996), pp. 93–103; Zhu Ling, "A Brave New World? On the Construction of 'Masculinity' and 'Femininity' in *The Red Sorghum Family*," in *Gender and Sexuality in Twentieth-Century Chinese Literature and Society*, ed. Lu Tonglin (Albany: State University of New York Press, 1993).

56. I use the concept of "orientalizing" in the way that Edward Said articulates it in his *Orientalism* (New York: Vintage Books, 1978). Orientalism, simply put, is a way of defining, creating, controlling, manipulating, and maintaining the cognitive dichotomy between the Western Self and its Other—the Orient and the Oriental—with the former occupying certain "positional superiority" to the latter politically, intellectually, culturally, and morally.

57. This percentage is based on unpublished letters from television producers and critics in both cities from 1987 to 1988.

58. Herbert I. Schiller's essay, "Transnational Media: Creating Consumer Worldwide," *Journal of International Affairs* 47 (summer 1993), contains important information regarding this aspect of Chinese media.

59. Ling Sheng, "Huajü jiang zouchudigu: ji Yin Ruocheng buzhang yü xijüjie renshi de tanhua" (Spoken drama will overcome its crisis: the conversations between

Minister Yin Ruocheng and representatives of the theater circles from northeastern provinces), *Xijübao* (On theater), January 1988, pp. 4–8.

60. "Chuangzuo ziyou yü lishi shiming" (Artistic freedom and historical mission—a group discussion), *Jüben* (Drama), April 1985, pp. 33.

61. Ibid., p. 34.

62. Xia Yan, "Guanyü wenxue yü yishu" (On literature and the arts), an interview with Xia Yan by Li Ziyun, *Renmin wenxue* (People's literature), May 1988.

63. Ibid.

64. Deng Hindun, "Zhongguo xiandai xijü meixue yantao de lishi huigu" (Historical reflections on the studies of modern Chinese dramatic aesthetics), *Shanghai xijü* (Shanghai theater), April 1987, p. 8; Qian Jianping, "Huajü wutai de zaodong—jianlun yizhong xijü pinge" (The restless forces in spoken drama—considerations on a new dramatic style), *Shanghai xijü* (Shanghai theater), February 1988, pp. 33–34.

65. See, for instance, Yü Jun, "Xiandai yishi yü xijü fazhan" (Modern consciousness and the development of drama), *Jüben* (Drama), June 1988, p. 77; many articles of a similar kind can be found in Shanghai's *Shanghai xijü,* 1986–1989; Beijing's *Xijübao,* 1986–1989; and Nanjing's *Yingjü yuekan,* 1986–1989.

66. Li Longyun, "Yü meiguo jizhe de tanhua" (A conversation with an American journalist), *Yingjü yuekan* (Film and drama monthly), July 1985, p. 8.

67. Dong Jian, "Lishi de zhuanzhe yü huajü de mingyun" (The transformation of history and the fate of drama), in *Wenxue yü lishi* (Literature and history) (Nanjing: Jiangsu People's Publishing House, 1992).

68. Yü Shuqing, "Xianshi, youzai zhaohuan xianshi zhuyi—jian tan xinshiqi Shanghai de huajü wutai" (Reality is again calling for realism—spoken drama in Shanghai during the reform era), *Shanghai xijü* (Shanghai theater), February 1990, p. 7.

69. Zong Fuxian, "Wode kunhuo yü zhuiqiu" (My confusions and my searches), *Jüben* (Drama), August 1988.

70. From the archives of the Liaoning Province Branch of the Association of Chinese Dramatists.

71. The editors, "Zhi duzhe" (To the readers), *Jüben* (Drama), December 1988, p. 27.

72. See *Zhongguo xijü* (Chinese theater), January–March 1989.

73. Feng Zi, "Jüzuojia de shiming" (Playwrights' vocation), *Jüben* (Drama), July 1988, p. 27.

74. The real number of artists who left China in and since the early 1980s is not adequately documented, although it is well known that the losses of artistic talent across the nation are considerable. The Shanghai Philharmonic Orchestra, for instance, had lost one-third of its musicians by 1986 to Western Europe, the United States, and Canada, among others. After losing 111 members over the past two decades, it currently has 155 musicians and staff members, among whom 20 or so hold passports and reportedly wish to go abroad, according to the orchestra's personnel archives for 1986–1990.

75. Chen Zidu, Yang Jian, and Zhu Xianping, *"Sangshuping jishi"* (Sangshuping chronicles), *Jüben* (Drama), April 1988, pp. 4–28.

76. Xu Xiaozhong, "Sangshuping jishi shiyan baogao" (A report on the stories of Mulberry village experiment), trans. Faye C. Fei, *TDR,* summer 1994, pp. 106–109.

77. Ibid.; also *Xijübao* (On theater), June–August, 1988.

78. Faye C. Fei and William H. Sun, "Stories of Mulberry Village and the End of Modern Chinese Theatre," *TDR,* summer 1994, p. 132.

79. See *Jüben* (Drama), 1990–1992. *Rishi* (Eclipse, 1990), by Tong Dinmiao, Fang Zi, and Gu Tiangao (from Beijing), *Tianbian you yizu shenghuo* (Sacred fires burning on the horizon, 1990), by Zhen Zhenghuan (from Shandong), *Qingjie* (The complex, 1991),

by Xü Yan (from Guangzhou), *Fuqin de chezhan* (Father's station, 1991), by Su Lei (from Beijing), and *Daqiao* (The grand bridge, 1991), by He Guofu (from Shanghai), were among the most notable.

80. In 1992, Deng Xiaoping visited the special economic zones in the coastal areas of southern China. The speeches he made during the visit virtually ended the debates on "the nature of the Chinese reform" that had been escalating after the tragedy of June 4, 1989, centering on the differences between socialist reform and capitalist reform. The core of his speech was as follows: "Socialism's real nature is to liberate the productive forces, and the ultimate goal of socialism is to achieve common prosperity." See Maurice Meisner, *The Deng Xiaoping Era* (New York: Hill and Wang, 1996), p. 516. Deng's proposals for achieving a more rapid pace of development through the adoption of capitalist methods were canonized at the Fourteenth Congress of the Communist Party of China, which met in Beijing from October 12 to October 18, 1992. See Meisner, *Deng Xiaoping Era,* p. 480.

81. See, for instance, Shao Hongda, "Guanyü huajü fazhan de da shihua" (Some honest remarks on the development of spoken drama), *Jüben* (Drama), February 1988, p. 58.

82. Zhao Yaoming, "Women ji xiwang yü xinshiji de huajü" (Our hope lies in spoken drama of the new century), *Yingjü yuekan* (Film and drama monthly), February 1992.

83. The theater built in the American International Center–Shanghai Center located on the Nanjing Road is a prominent example.

84. *Shanghai xijü* (Shanghai theater), September 1992.

85. "Jüzuojia zai zuoshenme?" (What have the playwrights been doing lately?), *Nanfang wanbao* (South evening news), July 21, 1993.

86. See *Qiaobao* (The China press), August 31, 1992; *Zhongguo ribao* (China daily), May 2, 1993.

87. David Jiang, "Shanghai Revisited," *TDR,* summer 1994, p. 79.

88. Ibid., pp. 75–80.

89. The "little theater movement" was described in a letter by Dong Jian, the leading theater scholar and critic in Nanjing, dated June 5, 1994.

90. Gou Shixing, *Niao ren* (Bird men), *Xin jüben* (New drama), March 1993, pp. 3–21.

91. The play has not been published yet. For a brief report on the production, see the Shanghai *Xinmin wanbao* (Xinmin evening news), June 16, 1994, when it was staged in June 1994 in the small theater of the Shanghai People's Theater. The audience, a mixture of university students and urban residents, was very responsive to the emotional turbulence enacted among the four characters in the play.

92. Guo Shixing, *Niao ren* (Bird men), *Xin jüben* (New drama), March 1993, p. 17.

93. Ibid., p. 21.

94. He Feng, *Xinhai chao* (The tidal currents in the year Xinhai), *Jüben* (Drama), May 1991, pp. 23–46; Yao Yuan, *Shangyang* (Shangyang), see Li Rong's report, "Lishijü nenfou zaidu huihuang?" (Can modern historical dramas regain their glory?), *Jiefang ribao* (Liberation daily), September 12, 1996.

95. Mackerras, *Chinese Drama,* p. 223.

Theater & Society

Bus Stop

A lyrical comedy on life in one act

By Gao Xingjian*

Translated by Kimberly Besio

Cast of Characters

THE SILENT MAN, middle aged
GRAMPS, sixty-some years of age
YOUNG WOMAN, unmarried, twenty-eight years old
HOTHEADED YOUTH, nineteen years old
SPECTACLES, thirty years old
MOTHER, forty years old
MASTER WORKER, forty-five years old
DIRECTOR MA, fifty years old

Ages of the characters are all when they first come onstage.

Place: A public bus stop on the outskirts of town

In the middle of the stage stands a sign for a public bus stop. Due to many years of wind and rain, the words on the sign have weathered away to illegibility. On one side of the bus-stop sign there is an iron railing; those waiting for the bus line up within the railing. The railing forms the shape of a cross; the length of each direction is uneven. There is a certain symbolic implication to this—perhaps it stands for an intersection in a road, perhaps

*Gao Xingjian is currently living in Paris and is the recipient of the Chevalier de l'Ordre des Arts et des Lettres from the French Ministry of Culture. Before he left China in 1988, he was trained as a scholar of French literature. He has been actively publishing plays, novels, novellas, short stories, and literary theoretical writings since the early 1980s. *Bus Stop* was one of his earliest plays and won him a national reputation. Published in the literary quarterly *Shiyue* (October), March 1983 (pp.119–138), the play was staged by the Beijing People's Art Theater Company.

A partial translation of this play by Geremie Barmé is included in the collection *Trees on the Mountain,* ed. Stephen C. Soong and John Minford (Hong Kong, The Chinese University Press, 1984), pp. 379–386.

a crossroads in life, perhaps just a stop along the way in each character's individual journey through life. Characters can enter from any direction.

(SILENT MAN *enters, carrying a bag over his shoulder, stops, and waits for the bus.* GRAMPS *enters empty-handed.*)

GRAMPS: Did the bus just go by?

(SILENT MAN *nods his head.*)

GRAMPS: Are you going into town?

(SILENT MAN *nods.*)

GRAMPS: If you want to take the bus into town on a Saturday, you need to set out early. If you wait until people get off work you won't be able to squeeze your way on.

(SILENT MAN *smiles faintly.*)

GRAMPS: (*Looks back*) Still not a trace. This is Saturday afternoon, when everybody wants to go to town, and yet there are even fewer buses than usual. If you're a step too late, and hit rush hour, oh my! When everybody gets off work, at that point you see some excitement all right! Everybody crowds together—it's like squeezing pus out of a boil, but you have to have the strength. There's no way someone as old as me can manage! Anyway, I've made it here ahead of everyone. Even those who get off early haven't gotten a move on yet. I didn't even dare take my afternoon nap. (*Sighs, yawns*) If it wasn't that I have something to do in town tonight and absolutely *must* go, nothing could tempt me to chance rush hour. (*Pulls out cigarettes*) You smoke? (SILENT MAN *shakes his head.*) It's best not to. You can't even buy any good ones anymore, not to mention spending all that money, and then there's the chance of getting bronchitis. As soon as you hear that some Great Front Doors[1] have arrived, OK, then you have a line forming out the door and onto the street, even doubling back on itself once or twice. Each person has a two carton limit. And just when it looks like you're at the front of the line the clerk turns around and leaves. You can ask and ask, but they don't pay a bit of attention to you. Is this any way to "serve the customer"? It's all for show. Actually, those Great Front

---

[1]"Great Front Door" is the name of a popular brand of cigarette in China.

Doors have all gone out the "Great Back Door"![2] It's just like taking a bus. You'll be standing in line, just as you ought to, when someone will sneak in front of the line and wave his arms at the driver. He's "got connections," humph, that's what it's *called* anyway. By the time you've hurried over, kathunk, the door has shut again. This is what they call "serving the passenger," and there's nothing you can do but stand helplessly and watch. Everybody has seen it, but nothing can be done about it! (*Looks toward the wings*) Enough, someone's coming. You stand first, I'll stand behind you. As soon as the bus comes it'll be chaos, whoever is stronger will push ahead to get a seat. That's the way it is these days!

(SILENT MAN *smiles faintly.*)

(YOUNG WOMAN *enters, holding a pocketbook, and stands a short distance away from them.*)

(HOTHEADED YOUTH *enters. He seats himself on the railing with a little jump, pulls out a filter cigarette from his shirt pocket, and uses a butane lighter to light up.*)

GRAMPS: (*To the* SILENT MAN) See, as I said, that's the way it is these days!

(SILENT MAN *taps on the railings with his fingers to express agreement.*)

YOUTH: How long you been waitin'?

(GRAMPS *pretends he hasn't heard.*)

YOUTH: How long d'you have to wait between buses?

GRAMPS: (*Impatiently*) Go ask the bus company.

YOUTH: Very funny! I'm asking you.

(SILENT MAN *takes a book from his bag and begins to read it.*)

GRAMPS: Me? I'm not a dispatcher!

---

[2]"The back door" is a euphemism for goods or services, ostensibly meant for the public, being sold or exchanged through unofficial channels for individual favors.

YOUTH: I asked you how long you'd been waiting.

GRAMPS: Kids! Is that any way to ask?

YOUTH: (*Seeing his mistake*) Old Grandfather.

GRAMPS: I'm not your grandfather.

YOUTH: (*Mockingly*) Then sir . . .

GRAMPS: No use.

(YOUTH, *thus rebuffed, begins to whistle, stares at* GRAMPS *out of the corners of his eyes, swings his legs.*)

GRAMPS: This is to rest your arms on while waiting in line. It's not a seat.

YOUTH: What's the harm in sitting on it? It isn't hemp stalk.

GRAMPS: Didn't you notice that the railing is bent?

YOUTH: Was it my sitting on it that did that?

GRAMPS: If everybody sat on it and swung their legs, how could it not be bent?

YOUTH: Is it yours?

GRAMPS: I'm concerned because it's public property.

YOUTH: What are you gassing about? Why don't you just go home and share your babblings with your old lady? (*His swings become more pronounced.*)

GRAMPS: (*Controls his temper, just barely manages to keep himself from exploding, turns toward the* SILENT MAN) You see . . .

(SILENT MAN *has been reading, paying no attention to their conversation.* SPECTACLES *runs on.*)

GRAMPS: (*To the* YOUNG WOMAN) Stand in line, it'll be chaos in a bit. (YOUTH *jumps down from the railing, pushes ahead to stand in front of the* YOUNG WOMAN.)

(MOTHER *hurries on stage, straining to carry a large suitcase.*)

GRAMPS: It should be first come first served.

YOUNG WOMAN: (*To* GRAMPS, *in a voice so small it can barely be heard*) It doesn't matter, I'll just stand here.

(*The sound of a bus coming is heard. The* MASTER WORKER *strides on, carrying a bag of tools, and lines up at the end. The bus sound comes nearer; everybody faces the direction the sound is coming from. The* SILENT MAN *puts away his book. Everybody moves forward.*)

YOUNG WOMAN: (*Looking back at* SPECTACLES) Don't push!

GRAMPS: Line up! Everybody line up.

(*The sound of the bus passing in front of everybody.* YOUTH *suddenly moves around* GRAMPS *and the* SILENT MAN *and runs to the front.*)

ALL: (*Facing the* YOUTH) Oh! . . . Oh!

(*The bus doesn't stop.*)

ALL: Stop! Why doesn't it stop? Hey!

(YOUTH *chases after it a few steps, as the sound of the bus fades into the distance.*)

YOUTH: Bastard!

GRAMPS: (*Indignantly*) If you behave like that there's no way the bus will stop for us.

MOTHER: Hey! You in front, stand in line.

SPECTACLES: (*To the* YOUTH) Stand in line. Stand in line, did you hear?

YOUTH: What's it to you? I'm in front of you at any rate.

MOTHER: There are so few of us, wouldn't it be nice if we could all stand in line and take our turn?

SPECTACLES: (*To the* YOUTH) You line up in back of the others.

GRAMPS: (*To the* SILENT MAN) No upbringing.

YOUTH: And you have upbringing?

MOTHER: You won't stand in line and yet think that's reasonable?

GRAMPS: (*Slowly and deliberately*) What I said was you don't stand in line while waiting for the bus—no upbringing at all!

YOUTH: If your foot itches[3] get your old lady to take your shoes off for you—what are you messing with me for?

MOTHER: It's too bad that you young people have learned to behave like such ruffians.

SPECTACLES: Everybody's asking you to stand in line; how can you be so rude?

YOUTH: Who didn't stand in line? The bus didn't stop—what are you yelling at me for?

SPECTACLES: Stand in back of the others!

YOUTH: In front of you anyway!

GRAMPS: (*So angry that he is shaking*) Go stand in line!

YOUTH: Who do you think you're bluffin'? You think I'm afraid of you?

GRAMPS: You'd like to hit somebody, huh?

(*The* SILENT MAN *goes over and stands in front of the two of them.* YOUTH *sees that he is strong and well built, and can't help being a little scared, draws back a step, covers his weakness by leaning against the railing.*)

YOUTH: *You* make the bus stop if you're so capable. (*Leans against the railing and sways*)

---

[3]"Foot itches" is homophonous in Chinese with "upbringing."

GRAMPS: Young fellow, your education was wasted.

YOUTH: So what if my education was wasted? If you've so much book learnin' how come you're not taking a limo into town?

GRAMPS: Standing in line while waiting for the bus is nothing to be ashamed of. It's common social morality. Didn't your teachers in school teach you that?

YOUTH: Didn't have that lesson.

GRAMPS: Didn't your Mum and Dad teach you?

YOUTH: If your Ma taught you so much, how is it you didn't make it onto that bus?

(GRAMPS *chokes back his words for a moment, looks toward the* SILENT MAN, *but the* SILENT MAN *has started reading again.*)

YOUTH: (*Pleased with himself*) Since you didn't push your way onto the bus, didn't you live all these years for nothing?

SPECTACLES: Everybody is waiting for the bus, let's be a bit more self-disciplined.

YOUTH: Aren't I in line? Ahead of you!

SPECTACLES: You came after some others. (*Points to the* YOUNG WOMAN)

YOUTH: Then let her get on first. But when the bus comes she has to push her way on.

YOUNG WOMAN: (*Turns away and ignores him*) Obnoxious!

YOUTH: (*To* GRAMPS) If you can push your way on, then push. If you can't, then don't blame me. You'll never be able to push your way on, so don't block the way for those behind you. Old Grandfather, if you're so cultured and wise how come you don't understand the principles of pushing your way onto the bus? I haven't had much formal education, but at least I know how to do that.

(*The sound of a bus*)

MOTHER: Here comes the bus. Stand in line everybody.

YOUTH: (*Still leaning against the railing, to the* YOUNG WOMAN) I'm right behind you. When you can't push your way on, don't blame me for running over you.

YOUNG WOMAN: (*Frowns*) You go in front.

(*The sound of the bus gets nearer. The* SILENT MAN *puts away his book. The* MASTER WORKER, *who has been squatting on the ground throughout, stands up, and everybody presses forward against the railing.*)

SPECTACLES: (*To the* YOUNG WOMAN) Try to get close to the side, then grab on to the door handle.

(*The* YOUNG WOMAN *glances at him but doesn't respond. Everybody moves forward toward the direction the bus is coming from. The* YOUTH *is outside the railing, following after the* YOUNG WOMAN.)

GRAMPS: Stop! Stop!

SPECTACLES: Hey! . . . Stop!

MOTHER: We've all waited so long!

YOUNG WOMAN: The last run didn't stop.

YOUTH: Son of a bitch . . .

MASTER WORKER: Hey!

(*Everybody chases the bus to one corner of the stage.* YOUTH *suddenly surges in front.* SPECTACLES *makes a grab for him.* YOUTH *shakes him off,* SPECTACLES *catches hold of his sleeve, and* YOUTH *turns around and punches him. The sound of the bus goes off in the distance.*)

SPECTACLES: You dare hit me?

YOUTH: What're you going to make of it?

(*The two go after each other.*)

GRAMPS: They're fighting! They're fighting!

MOTHER: The young these days!

YOUNG WOMAN: (*To* SPECTACLES) Stay out of his way!

SPECTACLES: You delinquent!

YOUTH: (*Rushing at him*) I'll get you!

(*The* SILENT MAN *and the* MASTER WORKER *come forward and separate the two of them.*)

MASTER WORKER: Everybody hold your punches! Hold your punches! Haven't you anything better to do?

SPECTACLES: Stinking delinquent!

YOUTH: You bastard!

MOTHER: Such ugly language! Don't you have any shame?

YOUTH: Where does he get off grabbing at my clothing!

SPECTACLES: All I did was pull him back. Why won't you wait in line?

YOUTH: Quit your showing off for that skirt; if you have the guts let's go off and duke it out.

SPECTACLES: You think I'm afraid of you? Stinking delinquent.

(YOUTH *rushes forward again, is caught by the wrists by the* MASTER WORKER, *and can't move.*)

MASTER WORKER: Quit making trouble—stand in back.

YOUTH: What's it to you?

MASTER WORKER: Get back there! (*Twists the* YOUTH's *wrists and drags him to the back of the line*)

GRAMPS: Right, don't let him make a ruckus so that nobody can get on the bus. (*To the* SILENT MAN) He'll respond to that.

(*The* SILENT MAN *hasn't heard; he has started reading again.*)

YOUTH: I was in front! Are only you all allowed to go into town, and I'm not?

MOTHER: Nobody has said you can't go into town.

GRAMPS: (*To the* MOTHER) We all have business in town—he just wants to make a ruckus. There are those types who specialize in making a ruckus when getting on the bus, you know, they're called "three hands"; you have to be careful of them.

(*They all feel for their wallets, with the exception of the* SILENT MAN *and the* MASTER WORKER.)

YOUTH: What makes you such an expert? Old hick.

(*The* YOUNG WOMAN *and the* MOTHER *exchange glances and smile.* GRAMPS *glares at them discontentedly.*)

MOTHER: (*Hurriedly changing the subject, to* SPECTACLES) It's not worth your while fighting him. If you start a fight you'll be on the losing end.

SPECTACLES: (*In a heroic manner*) If we had a couple more troublemakers like that then nobody would be able to get on the bus. Are you going into town too?

MOTHER: My husband and child are both in town. Squeezing onto the bus on a Saturday is really a headache. Boarding is just like fighting a battle.

SPECTACLES: Why don't you get a work assignment in town?

MOTHER: Who doesn't want a work assignment in town, but you have to have a way to get it.[4] (*Sighs*)

---

[4]In the early 1980s when this play was written, virtually all jobs were assigned by the government. Life in town was easier, and the schools in town were superior to those in the country. Thus, a work assignment in town was much desired and difficult to obtain. Often, as in the Mother's case, only one spouse would be able to get a work assignment in town and the couple would choose to live apart, either for the sake of the children's education or in the hope that eventually the other half of the pair would be able to transfer to town as well.

YOUNG WOMAN: Two buses in a row have passed by—neither has stopped.

SPECTACLES: They only dispatch a bus from the starting point when the seats are full. Do you have business in town?

(YOUNG WOMAN *nods*.)

SPECTACLES: Actually, it might be better for you to board the bus at the starting point; where do you live?

(YOUNG WOMAN *glances at him guardedly, doesn't respond. Snubbed,* SPECTACLES *pushes up his glasses.*)

(*The* SILENT MAN *shuts his book, looks back toward the direction the buses have come, seems a bit impatient, and again buries his head in his book.*)

GRAMPS: How annoying; I need to get to the Cultural Palace in town by 7:00 sharp.

MOTHER: You're really ready to have a good time. Are you going to see a play?

GRAMPS: No such luck. No, let the town folks watch plays; I'm catching a round of chess.

MOTHER: What?

GRAMPS: Catching a round of chess—chariots, horses, gunners, don't you understand? Checkmate!

YOUNG WOMAN: Oh, Chinese Chess—Gramps you're really an addict.

GRAMPS: Young woman, I've played chess all my life.

SPECTACLES: Everybody has his own passion; if you're not mad about something life isn't worth living.

GRAMPS: You're right about that! I've researched every book on chess ever published, from "Heavenly Master Zhang's Complete Compendium of

Secret Chess Stratagems" to the recently published "One Hundred Solutions to Checkmate in Chinese Chess." I can lay them out for you without a step out of order. Do you play?

SPECTACLES: Once in a while, just for fun.

GRAMPS: That's no good! Chess is an art, a specialized field of knowledge!

SPECTACLES: That's true, it isn't easy to play well.

GRAMPS: Have you ever heard of Li Mosheng?

MOTHER: (*Sees that the* MASTER WORKER*'s bag of tools is touching her suitcase, and pulls her bag toward herself*) Are you a carpenter?

MASTER WORKER: Yeah.

SPECTACLES: Which Li Mosheng?

MOTHER: Are you working even on a Saturday?

MASTER WORKER: (*Disinclined to respond*) Mmh.

GRAMPS: You play chess, but have never even heard of Li Mosheng?

SPECTACLES: (*Apologetically*) Doesn't ring a bell.

MOTHER: Do you repair chair legs? At our house—

MASTER WORKER: (*Contradicting her*) I do cabinetry.

GRAMPS: Don't you read the evening paper?

SPECTACLES: Lately I've been busy reviewing my lessons, preparing for the college entrance exams.

GRAMPS: (*Flatly*) Oh, you don't really know the basics yet.

MOTHER: (*Turning and addressing the* YOUNG WOMAN) Is your family in town too?

YOUNG WOMAN: No, I have something to do.

MOTHER: (*Looks her up and down*) Meeting a friend?

(YOUNG WOMAN *gives an embarrassed nod.*)

MOTHER: Is he a nice young man? What does he do for a living?

(YOUNG WOMAN *lowers her head and draws in the dirt with her toe.*)

MOTHER: Will you be setting the date soon?

YOUNG WOMAN: You do go on! (*Takes a handkerchief from her purse and fans herself with it*) Why doesn't that bus come?

SPECTACLES: The dispatcher must have gotten talking to someone and forgotten the time.

MOTHER: Is this any way to "serve the passenger"?

GRAMPS: On the contrary, the passengers have to serve them! If there's no one waiting at the bus stop how can they show off how vital they are? Just be patient and wait.

MOTHER: I could have finished washing a big load of laundry by now.

YOUNG WOMAN: You have to hurry home on a Saturday to do laundry?

MOTHER: That's married life for you. My better half can hold a book, but can't do much else. A handkerchief is small, right? Well, he can't even wash *that* clean. If you're looking for a mate, don't go for a bookworm like him. If he knew how to manage at all he would have found a way for us all to live together in town long ago.

GRAMPS: Isn't that trouble of your own making? Can't you just have him transfer to the suburbs? Every week you have to wait for the bus like this, then squeeze onto it—how can you stand it?

MOTHER: I have a child. I have to consider my Peipei. You know what the level of education is like in the schools on the outskirts of town. Hardly anybody from there can pass the college entrance exams! (*Shooting her lips out toward the* YOUTH) I don't want to let my Peipei end up like that, and ruin his future.

(*The sound of the bus*)

YOUNG WOMAN: The bus is coming!

SPECTACLES: It's really coming, and it's empty!

MOTHER: (*Picks up her bag*) Don't crowd—we'll all be able to board, and everybody will have a seat.

YOUTH: (*To* GRAMPS) You had best watch your feet a bit more closely. Don't trip and drop your wallet. You wouldn't be able to get to your money to buy a ticket. Then you'd *really* look a fool.

GRAMPS: Young fella, don't think you're such a marvel, sooner or later you're gonna be sorry. (*To everybody*) There's no hurry. Everybody get in line to board the bus.

(*Energized, they form a neat line. The sound of the bus gets closer.* DIREC-TOR MA *rushes on with his overcoat unbuttoned. Swinging both hands, he goes straight toward the front of the bus stop.*)

ALL: Hey! What are you doing? Don't you know the rules? Get to the back of the line!

DIRECTOR MA: (*Unconcerned*) I'm just taking a look. You all just keep standing in line.

SPECTACLES: Haven't you ever seen a bus before?

DIRECTOR MA: I've never seen anybody like you. (*Glares at him*) I'm looking for somebody.

(*The sound of the bus passes by in front of everybody, and again it doesn't stop.* DIRECTOR MA *gallops to the front of the bus stop.*)

DIRECTOR MA: (*Waving his arms*) Hey! Hey! Old Wang! Master Wang! It's me, Old Ma from the state-run store.

(*Everybody scatters as they chase after the bus together.*)

SPECTACLES: Why doesn't the bus stop?

YOUNG WOMAN: Several in a row, and none have stopped. Oh, I wish it would stop!

MOTHER: There are only a couple of people on that bus. Why doesn't it stop!

DIRECTOR MA: (*Pointing in front, pursues the bus, yelling*) Pick up one. Open the front door a second. I'm Old Ma from the state-run store. Just me . . .

GRAMPS: (*Pointing at the bus, scolds*) Have you ever seen such a driver? Do you pay any attention at all to your passengers?

MASTER WORKER: Damn!

YOUTH: (*Picks up a rock and smashes it against the side of the bus*) I'll smash you.

(*The sound of the bus goes off into the distance. The* SILENT MAN *stares after it fixedly.*)

DIRECTOR MA: All right! You bus company folks had better not expect anything from *me* ever again.

GRAMPS: You're Director Ma from the state-run store?

DIRECTOR MA: (*Swaggering a bit*) What can I do for you?

GRAMPS: Do you know the driver?

DIRECTOR MA: They've changed people; it's that damned pragmatism.

GRAMPS: I guess they just don't appreciate your past favors, Director Ma.

DIRECTOR MA: Oh, don't bring up that kind of exchange of favors. Next time someone from the bus station comes by, it will be strictly public business handled publicly. (*Pulls out cigarettes*) You smoke?

GRAMPS: (*Stares at the cigarette brand*) No, thanks, I came out without my glasses.

DIRECTOR MA: They're Great Front Door.

GRAMPS: Those are hard to get.

DIRECTOR MA: You can say that again! The other day when someone from the bus station came looking for them I sold them twenty cartons wholesale. I never expected that they would treat me like this. It's really no joke.

GRAMPS: Could you sell *me* a carton wholesale?

DIRECTOR MA: Well, it's not easy to manage with an item in such short supply.

GRAMPS: Those Great Front Doors all went out the back door. No wonder the buses never stop where and when they're supposed to.

DIRECTOR MA: What do you mean by that?

GRAMPS: Nothing.

DIRECTOR MA: What do you mean, "nothing"?

GRAMPS: Oh, nothing in particular.

DIRECTOR MA: What do you mean, "nothing in particular"?

GRAMPS: Nothing in particular just means nothing in particular.

DIRECTOR MA: You mean something by that "nothing in particular just means nothing in particular."

GRAMPS: Well then, you tell me what it means.

DIRECTOR MA: The meaning behind your "nothing in particular just means nothing in particular" is obvious. You're saying that as the director I set a bad example by "opening the back door" right?

GRAMPS: You said it, I didn't.

(*The* SILENT MAN *strides back and forth agitatedly.*)

SPECTACLES: (*Reading his English flash cards*) Book, pig, desk, dog, pig, dog, desk, book . . . [5]

MASTER WORKER: What country's English is that you're studying?

SPECTACLES: English is English. There's no such thing as what country's English. Oh . . . this is American English. The Americans and the English all speak English, but the pronunciation is different. It's kind of like the word "I." You say "aah," they say "oi." Nowadays, if you want to get into college you have to pass a foreign language test. I hadn't studied one before. I had to begin from scratch. Can't just sit here waiting and waiting for the bus. I would waste a lot of precious time just waiting for the bus.

MASTER WORKER: You go ahead and study. Go ahead.

MOTHER: *and* YOUNG WOMAN: (*Simultaneously facing the audience and talking to themselves*)
My Peipei is waiting for me to return and make sweet dumplings.
WE AGREED TO MEET AT 7:15 AT THE GATE TO THE PARK, ACROSS FROM THE
He won't eat white-sugar-filled, nor sweet-bean-filled, nor almond-
ROAD, UNDER THE THIRD LAMPPOST. I'LL BE HOLDING A PURPLE PURSE; HE'LL
filled, he'll only eat sesame-filled . . .
BE LEANING ON A FLYING PIGEON BICYCLE . . .

(*The* SILENT MAN *walks in front of them, looks at them sadly. They stop speaking.*)

DIRECTOR MA: (*To* GRAMPS) I ask you what is "an item in short supply."

GRAMPS: You can't buy it.

DIRECTOR MA: As far as the customer is concerned it means you can't buy it, but to those of us in the commercial department it's called insufficient flow of goods. An insufficient flow of goods creates a contradiction in supply and demand. How would you resolve this contradiction?

GRAMPS: I'm not a director.

---

[5]Expressions in italics were originally in English.

DIRECTOR MA: But you're a customer! Would you be able to stop smoking?

GRAMPS: I've tried quite a few times.

DIRECTOR MA: Don't you know that smoking is hazardous to your health?

GRAMPS: I know.

DIRECTOR MA: You know, and yet you still smoke? You see? Despite all that propaganda! Isn't family planning advocated every year? But have pregnancies gotten any less? The population keeps rising! Adults can't give it up, and youngsters still wet behind the ears keep getting hooked one after the other. The numbers of those who smoke grow faster than the tobacco leaves. You tell me. Can a supply and demand contradiction like this be resolved?

(*The* SILENT MAN *slings his bag over his shoulder, prepares to leave, then hesitates.*)

SPECTACLES: (*Recites in a loud voice*) *Open your books! Open your pigs* . . . wrong. *Open your dogs* . . . no, that's not right!

GRAMPS: Can't they just produce more?

DIRECTOR MA: Now that's a good question! But that would be up to the production unit. Can those of us in the commercial unit solve the problem? You blame us for opening the back door, but if we can only take care of a few people with connections by way of the back door, how can we sell things openly by way of the front door? Don't you see, there will always be people who will be able to get hold of things and those who won't. If everybody could get hold of things there wouldn't be any contradictions.

YOUNG WOMAN: Blah, blah, blah! This is driving me crazy!

MOTHER: You don't really know the meaning of the phrase. Wait until you're a mother. Then you'll really know what it's like to be driven crazy.

(*The* SILENT MAN *turns. The* YOUNG WOMAN *meets his glance, and immediately looks down. The* SILENT MAN *doesn't notice, and strides off. He doesn't look back. Soft music begins; the music expresses a kind of pain and a stubborn searching and longing. The sound of the music gradually diminishes. The* YOUNG WOMAN *gazes in the direction he has gone, as if she has lost something.*)

MASTER WORKER: If I may interrupt . . . (DIRECTOR MA *and* GRAMPS *turn their heads.*) I wasn't talking to you two—you two go on with your comic routine.

DIRECTOR MA: You think our discussion is a comic routine? I'm educating a customer! (*Continues trying to convince* GRAMPS) You don't understand the situation we in the commercial unit are in. Don't you admit that you're just sulking? Do you think it's easy being a director? Just try it!

GRAMPS: I couldn't.

DIRECTOR MA: You just try it and see!

GRAMPS: I'm convinced, I'm convinced!

DIRECTOR MA: (*To the* MASTER WORKER) Do you see? You see?

MASTER WORKER: See what? Are you talking about that gentleman wearing spectacles?

SPECTACLES: (*Making sentences*) *Do you speak English? I speak a litter . . .*

YOUTH: (*Mimicking him, in an unnatural voice*) Ai . . . si . . . pi . . . ke . . . ai . . . li . . . tu . . . er

SPECTACLES: (*Angrily*) *Are you pig?*

YOUTH: *You're* the bullshitter![6]

YOUNG WOMAN: Don't quarrel, all right? I can't stand it!

MASTER WORKER: Sir, what time does your watch have?

SPECTACLES: (*Looks at his watch. Gives a start*) What? How can this be . . . ?

---

[6]The Youth has heard the English phrase above as the Chinese *fangpi,* which means "bullshit."

MASTER WORKER: It's not running?

SPECTACLES: It would be better if it weren't . . . somehow a whole year has passed!

YOUNG WOMAN: You're fooling us!

SPECTACLES: (*Looks at his watch again*) Truly. We've been waiting at this bus stop for one full year!

(*The* YOUTH *puts his fingers in his mouth and whistles with all his strength.*)

GRAMPS: (*Glares at them*) Rubbish!

SPECTACLES: It's not rubbish. If you don't believe me, look.

MASTER WORKER: Quit bluffing. That's impossible!

MOTHER: Why does my watch say it's only 2:40?

YOUTH: (*Moves over to her*) It's stopped!

MASTER WORKER: What are you yelling about? (*To* GRAMPS) Look at yours.

GRAMPS: (*Trembling, barely manages to pull out his pocket watch*) Why is it wrong?

YOUTH: You have it upside down.

GRAMPS: One . . . ten. It's stopped.

YOUTH: (*Gloating*) It can't even keep up with the others. Your watch is just like you—it's worn out too!

DIRECTOR MA: (*Shaking his wrist, listening*) Why has my watch stopped also?

MOTHER: Look at the date. Doesn't yours have a calendar?

DIRECTOR MA: The thirteenth month, forty-eighth—strange! This is an imported Omega!

YOUTH: Maybe its innards are plastic?

DIRECTOR MA: Move aside!

SPECTACLES: My watch is electric. It can't be wrong. Look, it's still running. I bought it last year. It's never once stopped. It's an electric watch with six functions. It tells the year, month, date, hour, minute, second . . . Look, hasn't one full year passed!

MASTER WORKER: You're giving me a heart attack with your bluffing. So what if it's an electric watch? Electric watches have been known to be wrong.

GRAMPS: Listen to you. We have to believe in science. Electricity is science; science can't bluff. We're in the electronic age now! Something must have gone wrong.

MOTHER: Are you saying we have been at this bus stop waiting for one year?

SPECTACLES: Yes. It truly has been one year. A year three minutes and one second, two seconds, three seconds, four seconds, five seconds, six seconds . . . look, it's still running.

YOUTH: Hey, it's the truth, folks, it really has been one fuckin' year.

(*The* YOUNG WOMAN *runs away and covers her face with both hands. Everybody is solemn.*)

MOTHER: (*Talking to herself*) They will have run out of clean clothes long ago. He can't do anything. He wouldn't know how to patch pants. Peipei must have cried himself nearly to death calling for his mama. My poor Peipei . . .

(*The* YOUNG WOMAN *squats down. The others slowly form a circle around her.*)

SPECTACLES: (*Softly*) What's wrong?

MASTER WORKER: Are you hungry? I have an extra fried cake in my bag.

GRAMPS: Does your stomach hurt?

DIRECTOR MA: (*To the audience in a loud voice*) Is there a doctor in the house? Can somebody who knows something about medicine take a look at her?

MOTHER: (*Controls herself; walks over and bends over the* YOUNG WOMAN) Where does it hurt? Tell me. (*Strokes her hair*)

(YOUNG WOMAN *buries her head in the* MOTHER's *breast and begins to sob bitterly, choked with tears.*)

MOTHER: This is a woman's matter. You all move away.

(*The group drifts off.*)

MOTHER: Now, tell me, what's wrong?

YOUNG WOMAN: Big sister, I'm so unhappy . . .

MOTHER: (*Caressing her*) Lean against me. (*She sits down on the ground, has the young woman lean against her, whispers into her ear.*)

GRAMPS: (*Visibly aged, sighs*) I guess I missed that chess match . . .

DIRECTOR MA: You were going into town just to play a game of chess?

GRAMPS: I've waited and waited. I've waited a whole lifetime just for that one match.

YOUNG WOMAN: No! No! He won't wait any longer . . .

MOTHER: Silly girl. He'll wait.

YOUNG WOMAN: No, he won't. You don't understand.

MOTHER: How long have you known each other?

YOUNG WOMAN: It will only be our first meeting. At 7:15, by the entrance to the park. Across the road, under the third lamppost . . .

MOTHER: You've never seen each other before?

YOUNG WOMAN: A classmate of mine who found work in town introduced us.

MOTHER: Don't be sad. You can find another. There are lots of young men in the world.

YOUNG WOMAN: No. Never again. No one will ever wait for me again!

DIRECTOR MA: (*Faces the audience, talking to himself*) I should leave. All I was going to do was go to the Tongqing building to have a meal and a couple of drinks. Someone had invited me, someone with connections. I don't have to wait a whole year just to go into town to have a drink. Don't I have liquor at home? Even some world-famous Maotai in a white porcelain bottle tied with red string . . . I'm not bragging, I would only need to say a few words, wouldn't have to bother to raise a finger, and there would be someone delivering it to my door. I don't have to. (*In a loud voice*) I don't have to!

GRAMPS: (*Agitated*) I *must* play that match!

DIRECTOR MA: (*To the audience*) This is what you call a chess fanatic. There are all sorts of strange people in this world, to wait a whole year just to play a game of chess. (*To GRAMPS, with good intentions, pitying him*) It's not as if I don't play a little chess. But I'm not as crazy about it as you are. You're a chess addict. Come to my house and we'll have a cup or two. I'll keep you company in your addiction, and we'll have a good time. We'll drink a little, play a little. Gramps, you're so old, why waste your time waiting for the next bus? Come with me.

GRAMPS: (*Disdainfully*) With you?

DIRECTOR MA: Gramps, just among the hundred or so in our store, there are no less than ten section chiefs, and division chiefs. And yet none are my equal. If you don't believe me, go ask them.

SPECTACLES: (*Reading*) *Pig, book, desk, dog,* . . . *k* . . . *g* . . . *k* . . .

GRAMPS: (*So agitated that he is shaking*) . . . Do you read the evening paper?

DIRECTOR MA: Never miss a day! I only subscribe to the evening paper. The town's evening paper is delivered to the suburban post offices by noon; by afternoon one is distributed to our store. I always keep it to read after I've eaten dinner. There's nothing I don't know about news in town, a day after the fact.

GRAMPS: Then do you know of Li Mosheng?

DIRECTOR MA: Eh, that opera singer who has recently made a name for himself singing female roles? Superb!

GRAMPS: And you play chess. I'm talking about the current national grand master in chess.

DIRECTOR MA: Oh, you mean the champion of the chess tournament, something Li. He has the same surname as my mother-in-law.

GRAMPS: So what if he's the champion? His chess isn't that special.

DIRECTOR MA: Old fellow, are you saying you could be the champion?

GRAMPS: The evening paper published the strategy he took the championship with. It . . . it wasn't anything I hadn't studied before. Wasn't it just because he lives in town? If I lived in town . . .

DIRECTOR MA: (*Laughing*) That championship would have been yours.

GRAMPS: Well, I wouldn't go that far. Anyway, I wrote him a letter and set up a match with him at the Cultural Palace in town. It was for this evening, eh, a year ago this evening! When playing chess you shouldn't take back a false move, and as a person you shouldn't break a promise.

DIRECTOR MA: You have a point.

SPECTACLES: (*Memorizing furiously, painfully*)   *Bik, pook, desgdokpikboog* . . . How unnatural!

YOUTH: You still farting around with that foreign bullshit?

SPECTACLES: (*Irritably*) I'm different from you. You can loaf around and do nothing, but I need to take the college entrance exams! I only have this one last chance. If the bus doesn't come soon I'll be too old to register for the exams. I've waited and waited. It's such agony to have wasted one's youth like this. You don't understand! Leave me alone.

YOUTH: I'm not stopping you, am I?

SPECTACLES: (*Pleading*) Please, leave me alone. Just let me have a little peace and quiet, OK? Can't you mess around somewhere else?

YOUTH: Not in town at any rate! (*Moves away, thoroughly bored; suddenly bursts out*) Are only townies allowed to walk on the streets in town? Aren't I human? Why can't I go into town and take a stroll? I'm going, no matter what!

MASTER WORKER: (*Annoyed*) What're you squawking about? Can't you just sit down and relax! (*Squats down; tears off a piece of old newspaper from out of his bag and brings out some tobacco leaves, shreds them up and rolls a cigarette*)

(*Silence. The stage lights dim. There seems to be the sound of a bus off in the distance, then barely perceptible music sounds. The music of the SILENT MAN is reintroduced faintly. Everyone listens with tense concentration. It seems like the sound of the wind, then it fades away again.*)

DIRECTOR MA: (*To the audience*) They're all possessed. (*To the group*) Aren't you all ready to give up; why don't we get going?

YOUTH: Go where?

DIRECTOR MA: Go back home.

YOUTH: I thought you wanted to go to town.

DIRECTOR MA: D'you think I'm out of my mind? It's so far away, why go into town just to drink some rotten wine? I'm not that stuck on it.

YOUTH: (*Sadly*) I just wanted to go to town to have some yogurt.

DIRECTOR MA: I'm talking with someone. What are you wrangling with me about, kid? (*To* GRAMPS) I'm going, even if you aren't.

(*Everybody looks at each other, their interest aroused a bit.*)

GRAMPS: Oh . . . (*Gazes at* DIRECTOR MA; *stares blankly, doesn't know what to do*)

MOTHER: (*Gazes at* GRAMPS) Sir . . .

YOUNG WOMAN: (*Gazes at the* MOTHER) Big sister . . .

SPECTACLES: (*Hesitantly, gazing at the* YOUNG WOMAN) You . . .

MASTER WORKER: (*Seeing* SPECTACLES'S *movement*) Hey!

(DIRECTOR MA *walks in front of the* MASTER WORKER, *cocks his head, hinting that he should follow him.* MASTER WORKER *is still looking toward* SPECTACLES. DIRECTOR MA *lowers his head and gazes at the* MASTER WORKER's *tool bag, prods it with his foot. This breaks the circle formed by their gazes.*)

YOUTH: Hey, what about that guy? Did he bug out?

GRAMPS: Who left?

YOUTH: You really *are* out of it. That guy who was in line in front of you, he ditched us. He didn't say a word, just bugged on out of here.

GROUP: (*Except for the* YOUNG WOMAN, *they begin to get excited*) Who? Who? Who are you talking about? Who left?

GRAMPS: (*Slaps his thigh, suddenly realizing what has happened*) Right. At the beginning I said a few words to him. He didn't make a peep—just left.

MOTHER: Who? Who are you saying has left?

SPECTACLES: (*Remembers*) He had a bag slung over his shoulders. He was right at the front of the line, always reading . . .

MOTHER: Oh! When you two started fighting he pulled you apart!

MASTER WORKER: Right. How come we didn't see when he took off?

SPECTACLES: He couldn't have gotten on the bus, could he?

DIRECTOR MA: Do you think they opened the front door for him?

YOUNG WOMAN: (*Dazedly*) The bus didn't stop at all. He went off toward town by himself.

DIRECTOR MA: Did he go this way, or that way? (*Points toward opposite directions*)

YOUNG WOMAN: He took off along the road toward town.

DIRECTOR MA: Did you see him?

YOUNG WOMAN: (*Sorrowfully*) He even looked over toward me. Then he went on ahead without looking back.

SPECTACLES: I bet he made it to town long ago.

YOUTH: Had to have!

GRAMPS: Why didn't you say something earlier?

YOUNG WOMAN: (*Frightened and uneasy*) Isn't everybody waiting for the bus . . .

GRAMPS: He was really clever . . .

YOUNG WOMAN: When he looked at you his eyes had such an unblinking expression. It was like he was looking right through you . . .

DIRECTOR MA: (*A little nervous*) He couldn't have been a cadre sent from town to investigate, could he? He didn't pay any attention when we were speaking. When I was educating the old man here?

YOUNG WOMAN: No, not then. He was walking back and forth, as if preoccupied with something . . .

DIRECTOR MA: He didn't gather any evidence . . . for instance the situation with distributing cigarettes? Opening the back door to sell Great Front Doors?

YOUNG WOMAN: I didn't hear him say a word.

DIRECTOR MA: Why didn't you give him some feedback about the bus company? The masses certainly have opinions about that!

GRAMPS: These days when you go out, it's tough getting from one place to another. (*Strokes the iron railing with his hand, turns within the railing, pondering*) Where is this transportation? Could we be waiting in the wrong place?

MASTER WORKER: (*Uneasily*) Old man, what are you saying? Isn't this the stop into town?

GRAMPS: Is it possible that we should be boarding from over there?

SPECTACLES: (*Looks across*) That's the stop in the opposite direction.

MASTER WORKER: (*Relieved*) Oh, you startled me sir. (*Squats down*)

GRAMPS: (*To the audience in a quavering voice*) Are you all waiting for the bus too? (*Speaking to himself*) Can't hear. (*In a slightly louder voice*) Are you all waiting for the bus to go back to the countryside? (*Speaking to himself*) Still can't hear. (*To* SPECTACLES) Young'un, I'm a little hard of hearing. Ask them if they are all going back to the countryside. If they're all going back, maybe we shouldn't put ourselves through all this just to get to town.

DIRECTOR MA: (*Shaking his head and sighing*) After all, town isn't paradise. We might as well go back. My son must be just about to get married. (*To the* MASTER WORKER) Do you do carpentry, mister?

MASTER WORKER: Yeah.

DIRECTOR MA: Why don't you make my son a set of furniture? Wasting time like this won't do your business any good. I'd treat you fairly.

MASTER WORKER: Nope.

DIRECTOR MA: Besides your pay, I'll take care of your meals. I'll even throw in two packs of foil-wrapped Great Front Doors. (*To himself*) Don't be always going on about those Great Front Doors. If someone from Management Section of the Commerce Department overhears you'll be in trouble. Huh, I don't even know what your workmanship is like.

MASTER WORKER: I do cabinetry. I work with hardwood. I make carved mahogany chairs, and ebony screens. Can you afford to have something like that made? It's a skill handed down from my ancestors!

DIRECTOR MA: You act like you're such hot stuff! Let me tell you, in town the fashion is for sofas. Who wants your carved chairs—they're too hard on the rear end.

MASTER WORKER: The things I make are for people to look at, not for people to sit on.

DIRECTOR MA: Now I've heard everything. You think you can just make things for show?

MASTER WORKER: At present you can bang gongs and still not find people with my skill. An export company in town has hired me to start a class to teach apprentices.

DIRECTOR MA: Well then wait, just wait. But I want to go back. Is there anybody who wants to come with me?

(*Silence. The light gets even dimmer. In the distance there is the sound of the bus. The* SILENT MAN *theme music plays again, light but clear. That searching beat gets more and more distinct.*)

SPECTACLES: Listen. Listen! Did you hear? That . . .

(*The sound of the music fades away.*)

SPECTACLES: How come you didn't hear? That man must have gotten to town long ago. We can't wait any longer. Useless waiting, fruitless suffering . . .

GRAMPS: He's right. I've waited a lifetime, waiting like this, and waiting. I've gotten old waiting!

MOTHER: (*Simultaneously*) If I had known this trip would be so difficult I wouldn't have brought such a big bag; it would be a shame to throw away the dates and the sesame now.

YOUNG WOMAN: (*Simultaneously*) I'm exhausted. I probably look a wreck. I can't think of anything else. If only I could sleep.

YOUTH: Quit your yammering! I could have crawled into town by now!

MASTER WORKER: Then why don't you just crawl off?

YOUTH: You crawl. I'll be right behind you!

MASTER WORKER: These two hands of mine do the work of a craftsman. A man isn't a maggot in a vat of manure!

SPECTACLES: (*Facing the audience*) Hey, hey! Are you still waiting for the bus? There isn't any sound. (*Loudly*) Is there anybody still waiting for the bus across the way?

YOUNG WOMAN: It's pitch black. I can't see a thing. It's late. There won't be another bus coming along.

MASTER WORKER: Then I'll wait until dawn! There's a bus sign erected here—they can't be fooling us, can they?

DIRECTOR MA: What if the bus doesn't come? Are you going to stupidly wait here a whole lifetime?

MASTER WORKER: I have a craft. In town they want my craft. What does anybody want from you?

DIRECTOR MA: (*His pride wounded*) Someone invited me to eat. I just don't feel like eating!

MASTER WORKER: Then why don't you go back home?

DIRECTOR MA: I've been thinking about it for quite a while now. (*Worried*) We're out in the boondocks here. There's nothing in either direction. If I should set off a dog out there in the dark . . . Hey, does anybody want to go back home with me?

GRAMPS: I was thinking of going back. But the road home is black as ink. It would be even harder to travel. (*Sighs*)

YOUTH: (*Pulls himself up; slaps his rear end*) Shall we go?

DIRECTOR MA: All right. The two of us will keep each other company.

YOUTH: Who's going with you? I'm going into town to have yogurt.

MASTER WORKER: They take perfectly good milk, and then put it aside to drink when it's sour. What kind of taste is that? And then there's that town beer, it's just like horse piss! Just because it's from town doesn't make it better, you good-for-nothing!

YOUTH: I just want some. I'm going for that yogurt—I'll empty five containers in a single breath. (*To* SPECTACLES) Don't waste your time with them, the two of us should just go!

SPECTACLES: What if the bus comes right after we go? (*Facing the audience, speaking to himself*) But what if the bus comes, and doesn't stop again? When I reason it out I feel I should go, but maybe . . . what if? I don't worry about anything but that "what if." I must make a decision! *Desk, dog, pig, book,* to go or to wait? To wait or to go? This is one of life's really difficult decisions. Perhaps it has been destined by fate that I must wait for a lifetime. Till I'm old, till I die. But then, can't one take charge of one's future? Why accept the dictates of fate? On the other hand, what is fate? (*Asks the* YOUNG WOMAN) Do you believe in fate?

YOUNG WOMAN: (*Softly*) Yes.

SPECTACLES: Fate is just like a coin. (*Brings a coin out from his pocket*) Do you believe in this? (*Throws it down and then picks it up*) Is it heads, or is it tails? *Pig, book, desk, dog,* then it's decided. *Are you teachers? No. Are you pig?* No, I'm not anything. *I am I.* I am I! You don't believe in yourself, and yet you believe in this? (*Mocking himself, he flips the coin in the air and then catches it.*)

YOUNG WOMAN: Well then, what should we do? I don't even have the strength to make a decision.

SPECTACLES: Let's play with our fate then. Heads, we keep on waiting. Tails, we go. Here we go! (*He throws the coin up in the air. It falls to the ground. He retrieves it, and covers it with the palm of his hand.*) Shall we go, or shall we wait? Shall we wait, or shall we go? Let's take a look at our fate!

YOUNG WOMAN: (*Quickly pressing the back of* SPECTACLES'S *hand with her palm*) I'm afraid! (*She realizes that she is touching his hand and hurriedly draws back her own.*)

SPECTACLES: You're afraid of your own fate?

YOUNG WOMAN: I don't know. I don't know anything.

YOUTH: Huh, these two are really something. Hey, are you going or not?

MASTER WORKER: Are we ever going to have an end to this? Those who want to go, go! There's a bus-stop sign erected here, and people waiting. How come a bus doesn't come? How can the bus driver draw a salary if he doesn't come collect the passengers' ticket money?

(*Silence. The sound of the bus and the* SILENT MAN *music simultaneously float across the stage. It gets more and more distinct, and the beat becomes even more pronounced.*)

DIRECTOR MA: (*Waving his arms, seeming to want to drive away the distraction that is troubling them all*) Hey, is anyone going?

(*The sound of the music fades away.* GRAMPS, *who has been leaning against the bus-stop sign and dozing off, lets out a snore.*)

GRAMPS: (*Without opening his eyes*) Has the bus come?

(*The others don't answer.*)

YOUTH: We're all being worn away right along with that wooden sign; I'm really down. (*Does a headstand, then dejectedly slumps to the ground*)

(*Everybody squats or sits on the ground. The sound of the bus is heard, but nobody moves. They just listen attentively. The sound of the bus gets louder, and the light gets brighter as well.*)

YOUTH: (*Still prone on the ground*) Hey, it's coming!

MOTHER: It's coming at last. Old man, wake up. It's dawn already, and the bus is about to come!

GRAMPS: It's coming? (*Hurriedly stands up*) It's coming!

YOUNG WOMAN: Could it be that it won't stop again?

SPECTACLES: If it doesn't stop again, we'll block it!

YOUNG WOMAN: It won't stop.

GRAMPS: If they don't stop again it will be dereliction of duty!

MOTHER: But what if they just don't stop?

YOUTH: (*Suddenly jumps up*) Mister, do you have a big nail in your bag?

MASTER WORKER: What for?

YOUTH: If they don't stop again, I'll make 'em blow a tire. Then nobody will get into town!

YOUNG WOMAN: You can't be serious. Tampering with transportation is a crime.

SPECTACLES: We had better block the bus. Let's all get in the middle of the road and form a line.

MASTER WORKER: That'll do it!

YOUTH: (*Picks up a club*) Quick, the bus is coming!

(*The sound of the bus gets closer; everybody stands up.*)

YOUNG WOMAN: (*Yelling*) Stop—bus!

MOTHER: We have already waited a year!

GRAMPS: Hey, hey! Stop!

DIRECTOR MA: Hey—

(*Everybody throngs to the front edge of the stage, blocking the road. The bus horn sounds.*)

SPECTACLES: (*Directing everybody*) One, two!

EVERYBODY: Stop! Stop! Stop!

SPECTACLES: We've waited a whole year for nothing!

THE GROUP: (*One after another, waving their arms and yelling*) We can't wait any longer! Stop! Stop! Stop, bus! Stop!

(*The bus sounds its horn unceasingly.*)

GRAMPS: Get out of the way! Quick, get out of the way!

(*Everybody hurriedly dodges out of the way, then hurriedly chases after the bus, crying out.*)

YOUTH: (*Rushes forward brandishing his stick*) I'll pound you!

SPECTACLES: (*Holding him back*) You'll get run over!

YOUNG WOMAN: (*Closing her eyes in terror*) Aaah—

MASTER WORKER: (*Charges forward, hauls him back with one hand*) D'ya want to get killed?

YOUTH: (*Struggles free, chases behind the bus; throws the stick in his hand away*) I hope you fucking fall into the river and feed the turtles.

(*The sound of the bus goes off into the distance. The set quiets.*)

MASTER WORKER: (*Blankly*) They were all foreigners.

MOTHER: It was a tour bus with foreigners in it.

SPECTACLES: What's so special about that? He's just driving for foreigners.

GRAMPS: (*Mumbling*) It wasn't even full.

MASTER WORKER: (*Brokenhearted*) Couldn't we have just stood in the back? It isn't as if we wouldn't have bought tickets!

DIRECTOR MA: Do you have any foreign-exchange currency?[7] They'll only accept foreign money.

---

[7]At this time China had a two-currency system. "Foreign-exchange currency" (*waihuijuan*) was used by foreign visitors and to buy imported goods. "People's currency" (*renminbi*) was used within China by Chinese citizens for domestically produced goods and services. According to law, foreigners were allowed to use only foreign-exchange currency and the average Chinese citizen was allowed to use only *renminbi*. This two-currency system ended in 1994.

GRAMPS: (*Stamping his foot*) But this isn't a foreign country!

YOUNG WOMAN: I said it wouldn't stop. It just didn't stop.

(*At this point one car after another drives by in front of them. Cars come and go, in all colors, accompanied by all sorts of sounds.*)

DIRECTOR MA: This is too ... too infuriating! Making monkeys of the passengers like this! If you're not going to stop, don't erect a sign! If the bus company isn't rectified, there's no way transportation will ever improve. You all should write a letter from the masses. And I'll personally deliver it to the upper echelons of the Transportation Department. (*Pointing at* SPECTACLES) You write it!

SPECTACLES: What should I write?

DIRECTOR MA: What should you write? Just write this and that—hey, you're an intellectual. Can't you even write a letter from the masses?

SPECTACLES: What would be the use of writing a letter? Won't we still be here waiting as before?

DIRECTOR MA: Well then, just keep waiting if you've a mind to. What am I getting anxious about? I've long ago given up on that meal in town. I'm only racking my brains for your sakes. Go ahead and wait then. It'll serve you right to wait!

(*Silence. The* SILENT MAN *theme music begins lightly, but as a quick and light three-beat variation; it carries a taunting feel to it.*)

SPECTACLES: (*Looks at his watch, startled*) My gosh!

(*The* YOUNG WOMAN *moves over close to look at his watch. The beat of the music accompanies what is read below, bounding along.*)

SPECTACLES: (*Repeatedly—following the indicator button*) May, June, July, August, September, October, November, December—

YOUNG WOMAN: January, February, March, April—

SPECTACLES: May, June, July, August—

YOUNG WOMAN: All together one year and eight months.

SPECTACLES: And we had just passed one year only a little while ago.

YOUNG WOMAN: Now it's two years and eight months.

SPECTACLES: Two years and eight months—no, that's wrong. It's already been three years and eight months. No! Wrong. Five years and six . . . no, seven, eight, nine, ten months . . .

(*Everybody is stunned. They look at each other in blank dismay.*)

YOUTH: Really fucking crazy!

SPECTACLES: I'm quite sane!

YOUTH: I wasn't talking about you—I'm saying that mechanism has mental problems.

SPECTACLES: A mechanism doesn't have a mind. Further, a watch is a mechanism that measures time. And time can't be influenced by whether someone is sane or not.

YOUNG WOMAN: Don't say any more, all right? I'm begging you!

SPECTACLES: Don't stop me. No, the problem isn't with me. I don't have any way to stop the flow of time. You all look. Come and look at my watch.

(*Everybody circles around and looks at his watch.*)

SPECTACLES: Six years—seven years—eight years—nine years, ten full years even as we're speaking!

MASTER WORKER: Could it be? (*Catches hold of* SPECTACLES's *wrist; shakes it; listens; looks at it.*)

YOUTH: (*Also comes forward, pulls the setting button on the watch*) Aha, there are no numbers now are there? Huh, the truth comes out. (*Grabs hold of* SPECTACLES's *arm and lifts it up high*) As soon as I pull it, it doesn't move! (*Pleased with himself*) That doohickey really had me going there.

SPECTACLES: (*Solemnly*) What do you know? Time is still passing whether we can see it or not. Time is an objective entity. There are formulas by which it can be deduced and calculated. T is equivalent to the radical sign; alpha plus beta multiplied by sigma is the square of something or other. It's all right there in Einstein's Theory of Relativity!

YOUNG WOMAN: (*Hysterically*) I can't stand it, I really can't stand it!

GRAMPS: Preposterous! (*Coughs*) To make, make passengers wait at the bus stop until their hair turns white with age . . . (*Is immediately transformed to doddering old age*) Absurd . . . too absurd . . .

MASTER WORKER: (*Brokenheartedly*) The bus company must have purposely plotted against us, huh? But what did we ever do to the bus company?

MOTHER: (*Transformed to a state of utter exhaustion*) Peipei, my poor Peipei and his father, their clothes must have been reduced to tatters long ago. Not to mention having nothing clean to wear . . . He doesn't even know how to thread a needle . . .

(*The* YOUTH *walks over to one side and kicks a stone around, kicks it left, then right. Then he sits dejectedly, prone on the ground. He spreads his legs apart and gazes vacantly into space.*)

YOUNG WOMAN: (*Woodenly*) I really feel like crying.

MOTHER: Just let yourself cry then. There's nothing to be ashamed of.

YOUNG WOMAN: Big sister, the tears won't come.

MOTHER: That's the way it is for us women. A woman's fate is to wait, endlessly wait. First, we wait for a young fellow to come find us. Then, when we finally do get married, we wait for children to be born. Then we have to wait for them to grow into adulthood. And by then we've gotten old . . .

YOUNG WOMAN: I've already gotten old, I've already waited until old age . . . (*Lies against the* MOTHER's *shoulder.*)

MOTHER: If you want to cry, then go ahead and cry it out. You'll feel better once the tears have come. I'd really like to throw myself on his chest, and cry my heart out . . . not for any particular reason . . . at least, not for any reason I can say . . .

DIRECTOR MA: (*Sorrowfully, to* GRAMPS) Old man, will it be worth it to you? What's wrong with staying at home and enjoying your old age in comfort? Amusements like music, chess, calligraphy, and painting are meant for whiling away your time, for personal enjoyment. But you insist on going into town to vie for eminence. You're throwing away your life on the road, and all for the sake of those couple of lumps of carved wood. Is it worth it?

GRAMPS: What do you know? You're just a businessman after all. Playing chess is about gusto. It's about spirit. To live on this earth you have to have some spirit!

(*The* YOUTH, *extremely bored, walks behind SPECTACLES and claps him on the shoulder forcefully, breaking into his meditation.*)

SPECTACLES: (*Furiously*) You don't understand what it is to suffer, so you're apathetic. Life has left us behind. The world has forgotten us. Your life is trickling away before your eyes. Do you understand? You don't understand! You might be able to muddle along like this, but I can't . . .

MASTER WORKER: (*Sadly*) I can't go back. I'm a cabinetmaker, a hardwood furniture maker! I wasn't going into town just to make a few bucks. I have a craft. Sure, I can make a living in the countryside. It's a cinch to make bed frames, tables, cupboards, and my family wouldn't starve. But how can I squander the skills passed on from my ancestors just on things like this? You might be a director, but you can't understand this.

SPECTACLES: (*Pushing aside the* YOUTH) Go away, let me alone for a while. (*Suddenly bursts out*) I need quiet! Do you understand? Quiet! Quiet!

(YOUTH *moves away obediently, acts as if he is about to give a loud whistle, but pulls his fingers back just as he has stuck them in his mouth.*)

YOUNG WOMAN: (*Facing the audience, talking to herself*) I used to have quite a few dreams—some of them were rather beautiful . . .

MOTHER: (*Facing the audience, talking to herself*) Sometimes I too would really like to dream . . .

(*The women's speeches below are interwoven and linked together; each speaks to the audience, neither one interacts with the other.*)

YOUNG WOMAN: I dreamed that the moon could laugh out loud . . .

MOTHER: But I always fall onto the bed and sleep. I'm always extremely exhausted and extremely sleepy. I never get enough sleep . . .

YOUNG WOMAN: I dreamed that he was holding my hand, and whispering softly into my ear. I really wanted to cuddle up close to him . . .

MOTHER: As soon as I open my eyes, there are Peipei's socks with a hole in them, his toe sticking out . . .

YOUNG WOMAN: Now I don't have any dreams at all . . .

MOTHER: His father has another snag in his sweater cuff . . .

YOUNG WOMAN: But there are also no black bears charging toward me . . .

MOTHER: Peipei wants a little electric car . . .

YOUNG WOMAN: Also nobody chasing after me fiercely . . .

MOTHER: Tomatoes are twenty cents a half-kilo . . .

YOUNG WOMAN: I'll never dream again . . .

MOTHER: These are a mother's concerns. (*Turns her head toward the* YOUNG WOMAN) When I was your age I wasn't like you.

(*Below is a dialogue between the two.*)

YOUNG WOMAN: You don't know. I've changed too. I've gotten so petty. I can't stand seeing the other girls wearing pretty clothes. I know this is awful, but when I see the girls in town wearing high heels, it makes me feel bad inside. I feel they're walking all over me, parading around in front of me just to upset me. Big sister, I know this is awful . . .

MOTHER: I understand, I don't blame you . . .

YOUNG WOMAN: You don't know. I'm jealous, sickeningly jealous . . .

MOTHER: Don't be silly. It's not your fault . . .

YOUNG WOMAN: I keep wishing I could wear a more colorful outfit—one of those one-piece dresses, the kind with a zipper. But I don't even dare to make a dress like that. It would be so wonderful to be in town. The streets are full of people wearing such dresses. But could I wear something like that in public around here? Big sister, you tell me!

MOTHER: (*Stroking her hair*) Wear whatever you like. Don't wait until you're my age. You're still young. A young fellow will fall for you some day. You will kiss, and make love to each other. You will bear him a child, and his affection for you will deepen . . .

YOUNG WOMAN: Go on . . . dear sister, keep talking . . . do I have any white hair?

MOTHER: (*Parting her hair*) No. Really!

YOUNG WOMAN: Don't try to fool me!

MOTHER: Well, only one or two strands.

YOUNG WOMAN: Pull them out for me.

MOTHER: You can't see them. You shouldn't pull them out. The more you pull out, the more there will be.

YOUNG WOMAN: Please, dear sister!

(MOTHER *pulls out a white hair for her, then suddenly hugs her and begins to cry.*)

YOUNG WOMAN: Big sister, what's wrong?

MOTHER: I have a lot of gray hairs. Am I completely gray?

YOUNG WOMAN: No, no . . . (*Hugs her, they start crying together*)

YOUTH: (*Sitting on the ground; slaps a dollar bill on the ground; fumbles for three playing cards in his pocket and flings them to the ground*) Who'll take me on? Five dollars a pop! I'll play it all on this one round.

(GRAMPS *feels his own pocket.*)

YOUTH: No need to feel for your money. These are my own earnings from doing odd jobs. Whoever's lucky can just pick it up. I'm not going to waste my time here.

(GRAMPS *and* DIRECTOR MA *crowd around him.*)

YOUTH: Which of you will ante up? Three dollars in my left hand. Two dollars in my right. I'm the banker—here's five dollars. That's my bus fare into town and back, and my yogurt money.

DIRECTOR MA: A young fellow like you, why can't you behave yourself?

YOUTH: Enough of that. Go on home and teach your son. Old man, won't you try your luck? If you win both won't that be five dollars? If you get it right, you're lucky. If you lose, you're unlucky. At your age, what's so special about a couple of bucks? You can have a drink on me.

(MASTER WORKER *walks over.*)

YOUTH: Heavenly Gate, Earthly Gate, Green Dragon, White Tiger— where will you place your bet?

(MASTER WORKER *aims a swat at him.*)

YOUTH: I won't go into town, OK? I won't eat yogurt. Will that make you happy? (*Bursts into tears*) Let the fucking town folks stroll around on the town streets!

GRAMPS: Pick 'em up, young feller, pick 'em up.

(*The* YOUTH *wipes away tears with a dirty hand. He blows his nose, picks up the bills and the playing cards, hangs his head and sobs. Silence. The sound of a bus in the distance intertwines with intermittent playing of the* SILENT MAN *theme music. The beat is fast, transformed into a happy tune.*)

SPECTACLES: The bus won't come. (*Makes a decision*) Let's go. Like that man. While I stupidly waited at this bus stop, others have made it to town and have accomplished something long ago. There's nothing to wait for!

GRAMPS: He's right. Young woman, stop crying. If you had gone with that man your baby would have learned to walk by now, to say nothing of you having gotten married and had a child. I've waited and waited. I've gotten all hunchbacked with waiting. (*With difficulty*) Let's go—(*Staggers a bit*)

(SPECTACLES *hurriedly supports him.*)

GRAMPS: I'm just afraid that I won't make it ... Are you going too, ma'am?

YOUNG WOMAN: Big sister, are you still going into town?

MOTHER: (*Combing the* YOUNG WOMAN's *hair*) It's really too bad. Such a nice young woman and nobody wants you? I'll introduce you to someone! (*Lifts her bag*) I really shouldn't have brought such a heavy bag.

YOUNG WOMAN: I'll carry it for you.

DIRECTOR MA: Do you make purchases for an organization, ma'am?

GRAMPS: Are you going or not?

DIRECTOR MA: (*Lost in thought*) If we're talking about quality of life, a small village in the countryside is more peaceful. Just take crossing the street in town. Old man, with those red and green lights, who's to say you won't be hit by a car in a blink of an eye?

MASTER WORKER: I'm going!

YOUTH: (*His spirit revived*) Shall I grab a carrying pole and carry you?

DIRECTOR MA: What are you jeering about? I have high blood pressure. My arteries have hardened. (*Indignantly*) I'm not going to make myself miserable! (*Exits, turns his head back once more*) I forgot to take my tranquilizing and restorative powder made out of a compound of wolfberry and formalin and soaked in sorghum spirits.

(*Everybody watches* DIRECTOR MA *as he exits.*)

GRAMPS: Did he go home?

MOTHER: (*Mumbling*) He went home.

YOUNG WOMAN: (*Listlessly*) Don't go home!

YOUTH: Let him go his way, and we'll go ours.

MASTER WORKER: (*To* SPECTACLES) Why aren't you leaving?

SPECTACLES: Let me look one last time. I want to see if there are any buses still coming. (*Wipes off his glasses, puts them on again*)

(*The group scatters in all directions, as they hesitantly mill around. Some act as if they are leaving. Others stand still again. Still others bump into each other.*)

GRAMPS: Get out of my way!

YOUTH: Mind your own business!

MOTHER: This is really a mess.

SPECTACLES: Ah, life, ah, life . . .

YOUNG WOMAN: What kind of life is this?

SPECTACLES: It's life all right. We're still living, aren't we?

YOUNG WOMAN: We'd be better off dead.

SPECTACLES: Then why not die?

YOUNG WOMAN: To come into this world for such a little while and then to die, what a waste!

SPECTACLES: Life ought to be meaningful.

YOUNG WOMAN: But not to die, to keep living like this, how senseless!

(*The group stays in the same spot marking time, turning in circles. It is as if they are mesmerized.*)

MASTER WORKER: Let's go!

YOUNG WOMAN: No—

SPECTACLES: Not going?

YOUTH: Go!

MOTHER: Let's just go.

GRAMPS: Go—

(*Silence; the sound of rain*)

GRAMPS: Has it started sprinkling?

YOUTH: Grandpops, if we hang around any longer it'll start hailing.

MASTER WORKER: (*Looking at the sky*) This damn weather! It's fine one minute, lousy the next.

MOTHER: It's really coming down.

(*The sound of rain falling hard and heavily*)

MOTHER: What shall we do?

GRAMPS: (*Muttering to himself*) Need to find a place to get out of the rain . . .

YOUNG WOMAN: (*Tugs the* MOTHER's *hand*) Let's go, if we get drenched we'll get drenched.

YOUTH: (*Stripping to the waist*) If we don't go, we'll get poured on for nothing. Heavens! Why doesn't it just let down knives?

SPECTACLES: (*To the* YOUNG WOMAN) This won't do. If you get soaked through you'll catch a cold.

MASTER WORKER: It's just a shower, no big deal. It'll clear up as soon as these clouds pass. (*Brings a piece of tarpaulin out from his bag and tents it over the heads of* GRAMPS *and the* MOTHER)

MOTHER: You're well prepared.

MASTER WORKER: I have been working out away from home for quite a few years. You can't help but run into wind and rain. I'm used to it. (*To everybody*) Everybody come and get out of the rain for a while.

(*The rain comes down in sheets.* SPECTACLES *and the* YOUNG WOMAN *quietly come to stand under the tarpaulin.*)

MASTER WORKER: (*To the* YOUTH) You actin' dumb again?

(*The* YOUTH *gets under the tarpaulin. The light dims.*)

GRAMPS: When you're young this type of cold autumn wind and rain doesn't seem a big deal. But when you're old, and have rheumatism, it's another matter.

SPECTACLES: (*To the* YOUNG WOMAN) Are you cold?

YOUNG WOMAN: (*Shivering*) A tiny bit.

SPECTACLES: Your clothes aren't warm enough—put my jacket over your shoulders.

YOUNG WOMAN: What about you?

SPECTACLES: I'm fine. (*He is so cold his teeth are chattering.*)

YOUTH: (*Pointing at* SPECTACLES*'s watch*) Is that gadget still running? What year is it *now*?

YOUNG WOMAN: Don't look at your watch!

MOTHER: But we don't know what month of what year it is now.

YOUNG WOMAN: It's best not to know.

(*Sounds of wind and rain. The dialogue below is conducted amid the fluctuating sound of wind and rain. The voices overlap.*)

YOUTH: Ah, the ditches are overflowing . . . sure could get a few fish now . . . Grandpops, I'll make a bet with you . . .

YOUNG WOMAN: (*Simultaneously*) . . . Just sitting like this . . . rain, rain, the wind is chilly . . . but my heart feels quite warm . . . sitting together like this touching his shoulder . . .

SPECTACLES: (*Simultaneously*) . . . It's better this way . . . misty, the fields, that little hill across the way, the road to our future lives, all hazy . . . she's really gentle . . . really kindhearted . . . really good . . .

GRAMPS: Young feller, you're not getting any younger. If you keep stupidly messing around like this how will you ever make something of yourself!

YOUNG WOMAN: (*Simultaneously*) . . . Your glasses are all steamed up.

SPECTACLES: (*Simultaneously*) . . . She's so lovely . . . why am I just noticing . . . Ah, steam, don't wipe it off. This way everything is misty . . .

(*The speeches below are divided into three groups, basically conducted simultaneously, but intersecting each other occasionally. The various dialogues and monologues being conducted are sometimes dominant, sometimes weak; sometimes one group will stand out, sometimes another.*)

Group One

GRAMPS: (*Dominantly*) You ought to apply yourself to a craft. Otherwise no young lady will ever want to be with you.

YOUTH: (*Dominantly*) There's no one to take me on. What's the use . . .

GRAMPS: (*Dominantly, winks*) Isn't there a master worker right in front of you?

YOUTH: (*Dominantly, gathering his courage*) Sir, would you consider taking on an apprentice?

MASTER WORKER: (*Less dominantly*) Depends on what kind.

YOUTH: (*Less dominantly*) What kind would you take on?

MASTER WORKER: (*Less dominantly*) Learning a craft isn't like academics. You just want somebody who is good with their hands, and diligent.

YOUTH: (*Dominantly*) Do you think I would do?

MASTER WORKER: (*Dominantly*) Just a tad oily, but you'll do.

Group Two

SPECTACLES: (*Less dominantly*) I've already gone past the cutoff age for taking the college entrance exams. What's the use of going on? My youth has passed me by without my realizing it . . .

YOUNG WOMAN: (*Less dominantly, nudging him with her shoulder*) You can still take the entrance exam for night school. And then there's always correspondence school! You'll get in, you'll definitely get in.

SPECTACLES: (*Dominantly*) Do you think so?

YOUNG WOMAN: (*Dominantly*) I do. (*As* SPECTACLES *furtively takes her hand*) This isn't right. Don't be like this. (*Hurriedly draws her hand back, turns away and puts her arm around the* MOTHER's *shoulders;* SPECTACLES *hugs his knees and listens to them talk*)

Group Three

MOTHER: (*Weakly*) There was a time, I was walking at night. It was rainy then too, raining hard and without letup. I felt like there was somebody following me. I turned my head and looked back stealthily. It was raining hard; I couldn't see clearly. I could just tell there was somebody also holding an umbrella. Not close, but not far. If you speeded up a few steps he would follow. If you slowed down, so would he. My skin was all over goosepimples, my heart was pounding . . .

YOUNG WOMAN: (*Less dominantly*) And then?

MOTHER: (*Less dominantly*) I barely made it to my doorway . . .

(*Below the group begins to chat together, everybody talking at once.*)

MOTHER: I stood still. That person passed under the streetlight. I took a look; it was a woman also. She was frightened too. Afraid, both because she had no one to keep her company, and because she might run into someone bad.

MASTER WORKER: There really aren't that many bad people in this world. But you can't let down your guard. I don't plot against others. But what if they plot against me?

GRAMPS: That's the problem—that plotting. I crowd you. You step on me. If we all looked after each other a bit more, life would be a whole lot easier.

MOTHER: Wouldn't it be nice if everybody could be this intimate, such kindred spirits?

(*The set quiets. The cold wind murmurs.*)

MASTER WORKER: Move in.

GRAMPS: Squeeze a little closer together.

SPECTACLES: Everybody put your backs together.

MOTHER: This way it's warmer.

YOUNG WOMAN: I'm ticklish.

YOUTH: Hey, no one would want to tickle anyone here!

(*Everybody presses together more closely. Amid the sound of the cold wind's roar comes the voice of . . .*)

DIRECTOR MA: Wait, wait—don't leave!

MASTER WORKER: (*To the* YOUTH) What's that yelling about? Go take a look.

YOUTH: (*Pokes his head out from under the tarpaulin*) It's Director Ma from the state store.

(DIRECTOR MA *runs on, shivering, and hurriedly burrows under the tarpaulin.*)

MOTHER: You'll catch your death in those wet clothes. Quick, take them off.

DIRECTOR MA: I hadn't gotten very far when . . . when . . . when . . . a-choo! (*Sneezes again and again*)

GRAMPS: You insisted on going back by yourself. If you had stayed with the rest of us you wouldn't look like a drowned rat now.

DIRECTOR MA: Old man, you're still alive and kicking I see.

GRAMPS: Can't drop dead in the middle of the road, can I? Are you still planning on going into the city to have a meal with your "connections"?

DIRECTOR MA: Are you still going for that game of chess that was probably called long ago?

GRAMPS: Can't I go meet some chess buddies?

MOTHER: Don't bicker.

DIRECTOR MA: It's that annoying, rotten mouth of his.

GRAMPS: Look at your behavior.

MOTHER: We're all under one piece of tarpaulin to escape the rain—

DIRECTOR MA: It was he who first hurt—ah—(*sneeze doesn't come out*)

MOTHER: You'll be better once the sun comes out.

DIRECTOR MA: Huh, this rain!

GRAMPS: This's rain? It's snow!

(*From beneath the tarpaulin everybody sticks out hands or feet to feel.*)

YOUNG WOMAN: It's rain.

SPECTACLES: (*Sticks out his foot and stamps it*) That's snow.

YOUTH: (*Runs out, jumps up and down*) Ha, it really is friggin' hailing.

MASTER WORKER: You gettin' wild again, young'un? Hold it steady!

(YOUTH *obediently goes back to holding up the tarpaulin. The wind and the rain are now accompanied by various other sounds—it sounds like a car starting, and then as if a car were braking. The* SILENT MAN *theme music begins to play indistinctly. This time the sound is stentorian.*)

MOTHER: We can't go after all. (*Gathers up her bag*) We'll have to keep waiting until I don't know when . . . this rain, snow, it keeps coming down without an end in sight . . .

SPECTACLES: (*Lowers his head and memorizes his English flash cards*) *This is rain, that is snow.*

GRAMPS: (*Scratching out chess moves on the ground*) Gunner seven across to eight, horse nine across to five.

(*The* YOUNG WOMAN *is lost in thought. She walks out of her character from under the canvas. She clearly changes step by step. By the time she arrives in front of the audience's seats she has completely detached herself from the character in the play. The light on stage gradually dims completely.*)

YOUNG WOMAN: Who cares whether it's rain or snow. Whether it is three years, five years, or a decade. How many decades do you have in a life?

(*Below the three voices speak at once.*)

YOUNG WOMAN: Your whole life wasted like this.
SPECTACLES: (*Simultaneously, subordinate*) *It rain, it rained.*
GRAMPS: (*Simultaneously, even more subordinate*) Horse nine forward to eight, gunner four retreat to three.

YOUNG WOMAN: To waste time like this, will we keep on wasting it forever?
SPECTACLES: *It is raining, it will rain?*
GRAMPS: Pawn six across to five, chariot five forward to one.

YOUNG WOMAN: And will you grumble like this, and suffer like this?
SPECTACLES: *It snow, it snowed.*
GRAMPS: Assistant five retreats to six, gunner four across to seven.

YOUNG WOMAN: Will you keep on suffering forever, as you wait forever?

SPECTACLES: *It is snowing and it will snow.*
GRAMPS: Chariot three forward to five—assistant five retreat to six!

YOUNG WOMAN: The old are already old. Those to be born will come into the world.
SPECTACLES: *Rain is rain, snow is snow.*
GRAMPS: Chariot three forward two, gunner four retreat to one.

YOUNG WOMAN: When today is past, there will still be a today. The future will always be the future.
SPECTACLES: *Rain is not snow, snow is not rain.*
GRAMPS: Elephant five retreat to three, gunner four across to seven.

YOUNG WOMAN: Are you going to keep on waiting like this, grumbling your whole life?
SPECTACLES: *Rain isn't snow and snow isn't rain!*
GRAMPS: Elephant seven retreat to five, chariot three forward to seven, checkmate!

(*The stage turns bright; the* YOUNG WOMAN *has already returned to the stage and back to her character. The sound of wind and rain has stopped.*)

MASTER WORKER: (*Looking at the sky*) Didn't I say the rain wouldn't last long? Isn't that the sun showing its face? (*To the* YOUTH) Put away the tarp.

YOUTH: Aye! (*Hurriedly folds up the tarp*)

MOTHER: Shall we get going?

YOUNG WOMAN: (*Looking at* SPECTACLES) Are we still going?

GRAMPS: Where are you heading?

YOUTH: Into town, mister?

MASTER WORKER: You'll follow me at any rate.

GRAMPS: Are you still going into town? Can I make it at my age?

SPECTACLES: Won't you still have to walk if you head home?

GRAMPS: You have a point there.

MOTHER: But my bag is really heavy.

SPECTACLES: I'll carry this bag for you, ma'am. (*Picks up the big suitcase*)

MOTHER: Thanks so much. Granddad, watch where you put your feet. Don't step in a puddle.

YOUNG WOMAN: Be careful! (*Supports* GRAMPS)

GRAMPS: You all go on ahead. Don't let this old geezer hold you back. As for me, could I trouble you to dig me a grave wherever I fall? Don't forget to stick a marker on it. Just say here lies a chess fanatic who died without regret. No particular talent, just played a lifetime of chess. Always kept thinking about finding a chance to go into the Cultural Palace in town to show his stuff. I waited and waited. I've withered away, and I'll be planted on the road into town.

YOUNG WOMAN: Don't talk like that!

GRAMPS: What a good young woman! (*Takes a look at* SPECTACLES; SPECTACLES, *a little self-conscious, pushes up his glasses.*) Director Ma, are you going or not?

DIRECTOR MA: I'm going! I have to go into town to lodge a complaint against the bus company! I'm going to find their manager and ask him who, after all, they think they're driving buses for, their own convenience or in service to the passengers? They have to take responsibility for making the passengers suffer like this. I'm going to court and sue. I want them to make reparations for their passengers' damages—health and all those years of life!

YOUNG WOMAN: Stop fooling—whoever heard of a lawsuit like that?

DIRECTOR MA: (*To* SPECTACLES) Look at the bus-stop sign. What stop is this? What time does your electric watch have now? Record it all. We'll go find the bus company and settle their hash!

SPECTACLES: (*Looking at the sign*) What the . . . , there's no station name?

GRAMPS: Strange.

DIRECTOR MA: Why put up a sign if there's no station name? Look again more carefully.

YOUNG WOMAN: He's right, there isn't.

YOUTH: Mister, we've been waiting for nothing. We've been cheated by the bus company!

GRAMPS: Take another look. There's a sign—how can there not be a station name?

YOUTH: (*Runs to the other side of the sign, to* SPECTACLES) Come look. It seems like there was a piece of paper pasted here. There's just a few marks left.

SPECTACLES: (*Examining it closely*) Probably it was an announcement.

DIRECTOR MA: Where did that announcement go? Look for it and see.

YOUNG WOMAN: (*Looking in all directions on the ground*) It's been windy and rainy. It more than likely disappeared long ago.

YOUTH: (*Stands on the iron railing, looks at the bus-stop sign*) Even the traces of glue are awfully gray. It was ages and ages ago.

MOTHER: What? This stop has been abolished? But just last Saturday I . . .

YOUNG WOMAN: Which last Saturday was that?

MOTHER: Wasn't it just the week before, before, before, before, before . . .

SPECTACLES: Tell us, the Saturday of what month and what year? (SPECTACLES *practically pastes himself to his wristwatch and stares.*)

YOUTH: You don't need to stare at it. That's a big waste. You ought to have changed the battery long ago.

MASTER WORKER: No wonder none of the buses stopped.

GRAMPS: We waited at this stop for nothing?

SPECTACLES: You bet we waited for nothing.

GRAMPS: (*Heartbroken*) Then why is this sign still erected here? Isn't that just teasing people?

YOUNG WOMAN: Let's go! Let's go!

DIRECTOR MA: That won't do. We must go bring an action against them!

SPECTACLES: Bring an action against whom?

DIRECTOR MA: The bus company! Is it acceptable to deceive the passengers like this? I'm ready to risk my director's position!

SPECTACLES: You might as well bring an action against yourself. Who told us not to look clearly? Who told us to wait aimlessly like this? Let's go; there's nothing to keep waiting for.

MASTER WORKER: Let's go!

EVERYBODY: (*Mumbling*) Let's go, let's go, let's go, let's go, let's go . . .

GRAMPS: Can we still make it?

MOTHER: Could it be that the road to town was flooded, so that the bridge was washed away and the road is impassable?

SPECTACLES: (*Impatiently*) How could it be impassable? Haven't quite a few cars already passed?

(*From a distance there is again the sound of cars. Everybody silently gazes toward it. At this point the sound of cars comes from all directions. Everybody is at a loss and panic-stricken. The heavy rumbling of cars keeps drawing near. The theme music of the* SILENT MAN *floats elegantly above the rumble of the multitudinous cars like a cosmic sound. All fix their gaze ahead of themselves. Some walk out toward the audience; some remain on stage. All transform out of their characters. Along with this the lights also fluctuate, shining on the actors with different degrees of brightness. The light on stage is essentially extinguished.*)

(*The lines below are spoken by the seven at the same time. The speeches of*

A, F, and G are woven together to make one group and form complete sentences.)

ACTOR A *playing the* YOUNG WOMAN: Why don't they go? Hasn't everything that should be said already been said . . . Then why don't they go? Time has all flowed away to no purpose! . . . I really don't understand, really don't understand . . . Aren't they all going? . . . If you really want to go, then go . . . then just tell them to go quickly! Why are they still not going? . . . Everybody quickly go . . .

ACTOR B *playing* DIRECTOR MA: . . . There are times in your life when you really have to wait. Have you ever stood in line to buy ribbon fish? Oh, you don't cook! Then you must have lined up to wait for the bus? Lining up is waiting. If you have stood in line a long time and it turns out that what is being sold isn't ribbon fish at all, but a washboard for washing clothes—now the washboards in town work really well; they don't harm your clothes. But you have a washing machine. Didn't you stand in line all that time for nothing? You can't help but be boiling mad. Therefore, I say, it doesn't matter if you wait. What matters is that you first be clear what you're waiting for. If you line up and line up, and wait in vain for half your lifetime, or perhaps your whole lifetime, aren't you just playing a big joke on yourself?

ACTOR C *playing* MASTER WORKER: . . . waiting, really doesn't matter. People wait because there's always some good prospects ahead. If they don't even have any good prospects, that's tragic . . . it's called despair to use the language of that young fella Spectacles. Despair is just like drinking DDVP. DDVP is for poisoning flies or mosquitoes. Why would somebody try to make themselves suffer by drinking DDVP? If they don't die, they'll be taken to the hospital to have their stomach pumped. That's even more distasteful . . . Oh yeah, have you ever walked at night? You're out there in the middle of nowhere, and what's more it's overcast. There's nothing but darkness in front of you. Won't you just get further and further from where you want to be? *Then* you have to wait for dawn. But if it's bright daylight, and you still put off leaving, aren't you just being stupid?

ACTOR D *playing* MOTHER: The mother says to her son: walk, darling, walk! But the child can never learn. You might as well let him crawl on his own. Of course, sometimes you can support him. Later on, let him go from one corner to another groping the wall. And then he'll walk to the doorway . . . You also have to allow him to fall. Just help him back up. A child can't learn to walk without tripping. To be a mother you have to be patient about this. Otherwise, you're not qualified. No, you don't know how to be a mother. Therefore, I say it's really hard to be a mother. But isn't it also difficult to be human?

ACTOR E *playing* GRAMPS: Everybody says it's harder to act in a comedy than a tragedy. In a tragedy even if the acting doesn't make the audience cry, the actors can cry. But a comedy? That's not the case. If the audience doesn't laugh you can't be up on the stage enjoying yourself. What's more, if the audience isn't happy you can't tickle them—no one would be willing to be an audience then. Therefore, I say it's harder to act in a comedy than in a tragedy. It's clearly a comedy, but you still have to assume a really sorrowful manner and one by one lay out all the laughable aspects of human life for the audience to see. Therefore, I say it's much harder to be a comic actor than to be a tragic actor.

ACTOR F *playing* YOUTH: . . . don't understand . . . it seems that . . . they're waiting . . . of course it's not a bus stop . . . it's not a terminus stop . . . they would like to go . . . then they ought to just go . . . finished saying . . . we're waiting for them . . . ah, go . . .

ACTOR G *playing* SPECTACLES: . . . really don't understand . . . perhaps . . . they're waiting . . . time isn't a bus stop . . . life isn't a bus stop either . . . actually, they don't really want to go . . . then just go . . . finished saying what ought to be said . . . we're waiting for them . . . go!

(*From all directions the sounds of speeding cars get ever closer, interspersed with the sound of horns from all types of cars. The light on stage brightens. The actors have all returned to their characters. The* SILENT MAN *theme music becomes a great and yet humorous march.*)

SPECTACLES: (*Gazing at* YOUNG WOMAN, *tenderly*) Let's go.

YOUNG WOMAN: (*Nodding her head*) Ummhmm.

MOTHER: Oh, my bag?

YOUTH: (*Gaily*) I have it right here.

MOTHER: (*To* GRAMPS) Take care where you step. (*Goes to support* GRAMPS *by the arm*)

GRAMPS: Thank you.

(*Everybody is taking care of each other, and holding each other up. They are just about to start off.*)

DIRECTOR MA: Hey, hey—wait a minute, wait a minute, I'm tying my shoelace!

The End[8]

---

[8]The published version of this play was followed by the author's "Several Suggestions Concerning the Performance of This Play." See Geremie Barmé's translation, p. 386.

WM

By Wang Peigong
Playscript revised for performance by Wang Gui*
Translated by Thomas Moran

Cast of Characters

YUE YANG (General), the son of a retired serviceman, and later a soldier himself

LI JIANGSHAN (Hatoyama[1]), the son of a "capitalist roader," and later the writer and director of made-for-television movies

YÜ DAHAI SA(Chief[2]), the son of a member of the standing committee of a municipal revolutionary committee, and later the manager of a private enterprise

---

*Wang Peigong is a senior professional playwright at the Theater Troupe of the Political Department of the Air Force in Beijing. Wang Gui is a senior director of the same troupe and was the head of the troupe before he was removed from his office in 1985 due to the national controversy caused by *WM,* which he directed. Among their numerous works, *WM* was one of the most influential in China.

For the text used for this translation, see *Jüben* (Drama), September 1985, pp. 6–23. The original title in Chinese uses the letters "WM," which is the author's abbreviation of the *pinyin* romanization of the Chinese word *women,* meaning "we" or "us" (in the Chinese title, "WM" is followed by *women* written in characters). Taken as ideographs, rather than English letters, "W" and "M" represent people who have fallen and people who are standing, which is a reference to the ups and downs in the lives of the play's seven characters. To those in the audience with a bit of English, the letters in the title also suggest "women" and "men." For another translation of most of the first act, see Wang Peigong, "Urbling Winter," translated by Geremie Barmé and John Minford, in *Seeds of Fire: Chinese Voices of Conscience,* ed. Geremie Barmé and John Minford (Hong Kong: Far Eastern Economic Review, 1986), pp. 105–117.

[1]Hatoyama (Jiu shan) is the name of the head of the Japanese military police in the revolutionary Beijing Opera *The Red Lantern* (Hong deng ji). (See also notes 45 and 51.)

[2]Yü Dahai's nickname is "da tou," but the literal meaning, "big head," is less important than the figurative meaning, "head," "leader," or "chief," which is a gesture toward the power and status of Yü's father.

JIANG YI (Wheelbarrow[3]), the son of a worker, and later an assistant director in the propaganda department of a government bureau

BAI XUE (Princess[4]), the daughter of an intellectual, and later fine arts editor at a publishing house

PANG YUN (Sister[5]), the daughter of an office worker, and later a graduate student

ZHENG YINGYING (Sad Sack[6]), the daughter of a "rightist," and granddaughter of a capitalist

A female DRUMMER and a male KEYBOARDIST

Introduction

(*The* DRUMMER *and the* KEYBOARDIST *bound onto the stage and strike up the cheerful tune "The Gold and Silver Shuttles." The players enter and dance together in modern fashion.* YUE YANG *crosses through this happy dance; he appears to appreciate the music, but he also seems to be searching for something.*)

DRUMMER: (*With enthusiasm*) Hello, comrade! Welcome to the party!

(YUE YANG *seems not to hear; he brushes by.*)

DRUMMER: (*Loudly*) Hey! Comrade soldier!

(YUE YANG *stops.*)

DRUMMER: (*With concern*) What's the matter? Are you hard of hearing?

YUE YANG: It's my eyesight that isn't so good; there's nothing wrong with my hearing. I can hear that you're pretty good on those drums. Sounds like machine gun fire.

---

[3]In Chinese, Jiang Yi's nickname is "banche," which is a wooden handcart or wheelbarrow. The name calls attention to Jiang Yi's working-class background.

[4]Combing Bai Xue's given name with her nickname in Chinese, "gongzhu," yields "Baixue gongzhu," or "Snow White."

[5]Pang Yun's nickname is "xiunü," which means "nun" or "sister in a religious order."

[6]"Sad Sack" is a rough equivalent for the rather affectionate Chinese "xiao kelianr," which means "little pitiful one."

DRUMMER: (*Smiles*) You're too kind. I heard that several heroes had returned from the front.[7] Might you be . . . ?

YUE YANG: (*Flatly*) No. I'm no hero. (*Crosses to one side, sits*)

DRUMMER: Fascinating. (*To the* KEYBOARDIST) Hey, what do you think of this guy?

KEYBOARDIST: Oh, it's General!

DRUMMER: (*With surprise*) General? He's a general?

KEYBOARDIST: (*Laughs*) It's his nickname. He's a grunt who would like to be a general.

DRUMMER: Oh, so we can say that he is a disciple of Napoleon.

YUE YANG: You cannot! I do not worship Napoleon!

KEYBOARDIST: The General is a disciple of Marx.

DRUMMER: (*To* YUE YANG) What were you thinking about just now?

YUE YANG: Me? I was thinking about my friends.

KEYBOARDIST: (*Walks to the front, pulls* YUE YANG *to his feet*) All of your friends are right here! (*Spins* YUE YANG *around so that he faces the group*)

YUE YANG: (*Excitedly*) My friends! Hello!

(*The others stop dancing; they call out happily and run toward* YUE YANG, *whom they embrace joyfully.*)

YUE YANG: (*Introducing the others*) This is my group of friends from the collective. Hatoyama, Chief, Wheelbarrow, Princess, Sister, and . . . Sad Sack.

---

[7]During the summer and fall of 1985, when *WM* was first performed, the Chinese media ran many stories about soldiers returning from the fighting on the Vietnamese border.

(*As* YUE YANG *introduces each member of the group, he or she strikes a pose and then proceeds to put on drab, bulky winter clothing.*)

YUE YANG: (*Putting on his winter garb*) The "collective"! . . . That's a term that is fast fading from memory. Someday people will have to go to the dictionary to find out what it means. But we won't forget what it means. Not in a lifetime can we forget! The collective. What does that mean to us? . . . (*Sighs a sigh of deep and conflicting emotions, shivers and joins the others*)

Act One
Winter 1976[8]

(*The players imitate the sound of a whistling wind. They move mechanically in dull, arduous labor.*)

LI JIANGSHAN: (*Unable to hold out any longer*) Man! I can't take it anymore!

JIANG YI: As leader of this collective, I solemnly order that we wrap it up! Let's go home!

(*The group struggles against a cold wind as they walk back to their barracks.*)

YUE YANG: Hey! When shit freezes it sure is hard![9]

YÜ DAHAI: Hard and stinking!

LI JIANGSHAN: "Hard and stinking."[10] Isn't that just like us?

---

[8]Although the authors do not specify the setting for any of the acts in the play, Act One obviously takes place somewhere in China's far northeast and the other three acts in Beijing or another major eastern city. When the play begins, Yue Yang and the others have been in the countryside for between two and five years after having been sent there from their urban homes during the middle period of the Cultural Revolution, when as many as twelve million teenagers were dispatched to rural areas. This rustication campaign removed potentially disruptive former Red Guards from city streets and eased problems caused by high urban unemployment (the government, of course, claimed a more revolutionary purpose for the campaign).

[9]In the original, it is unclear why Yue Yang makes this remark. In their translation, Geremie Barmé and John Minford make a safe assumption and add the information that Yue Yang speaks after kicking a frozen "turd." Wang Peigong, "Urbling Winter," p. 105.

[10]"Hard and stinking" is the second part of a well-known *xiehouyü* (two-part saying), of which usually only the first part, "a stone in a latrine" (*maokeng lide shitou*), is said, leaving the second part, which the speaker intends as a criticism of someone, unsaid and

JIANG YI: Hatoyama!

LI JIANGSHAN: Really, that's what the brigade leader said. Didn't you hear him?

BAI XUE: If intellectuals are the "Stinking Ninth Category,"[11] then we sent-down youths are the stinking number what?

LI JIANGSHAN: The stinking tenth category!

YÜ DAHAI: Stinking shit category![12]

ZHENG YINGYING: (*Shrilly*) Stinking shitballs!

(*A burst of laughter from the group*)

YUE YANG: (*Sternly*) Haven't you taken enough abuse from other people? Do you have to insult yourselves? (*Angrily*) Let's go!

(*Silence. They push open a door, enter a room, and one by one collapse from fatigue.*)

LI JIANGSHAN: (*Lying down*) When we first got here, I thought this place was a real dump. It doesn't seem so bad now.

JIANG YI: Well, there's no place like home.

YÜ DAHAI: This goddamn place is home? (*Sings*) "Out on the frontier, a thousand miles from home . . ."

YUE YANG: Will you knock off the goddamn singing?

(*Suddenly, there is a clap of thunder and a loud gust of wind.*)

---

merely implied. See John S. Rohsenow, *A Chinese-English Dictionary of Enigmatic Folk Similes* (Tucson: University of Arizona Press, 1991), s.v. "maokeng lide shitou."

[11]During the Cultural Revolution, intellectuals were ranked next to eight other categories of undesirables, which were, in order, as follows: landlords; rich peasants; counterrevolutionaries; bad elements; rightists; renegades; enemy agents; and capitalist roaders. Warren Kuo, ed., *A Comprehensive Glossary of Chinese Communist Terminology* (Taipei: Institute of International Relations, 1978), s.v. "chou lao jiu."

[12]The pun here is on "ten" and "shit," which are homophonous except for tone in Chinese.

ZHENG YINGYING: (*Crying out in alarm*) The door! . . . The door's been blown off its hinges!

(*None of the men stir.*)

YÜ DAHAI: If it has blown off its hinges, then it has blown off its hinges. That saves us opening and closing it.

BAI XUE: Hey, get up, fix it!

LI JIANGSHAN: Oh, Uncle Lei Feng,[13] save us, save the pitiful sent-down youths!

JIANG YI: (*To* YUE YANG) We'd better fix it, otherwise we'll be cold tonight.

LI JIANGSHAN: Wheelbarrow, this is a lot better than your dad had it back in the evil old society, huh?

YUE YANG: Wind! Snow! Tribulation! Come on, give us all you've got!

LI JIANGSHAN: (*Sings*) "Learn from the pine . . ."

YÜ DAHAI and YUE YANG: (*At the top of their voices*) " . . . growing on Mt. Tai . . ."[14]

BAI XUE: The snow is blowing in! What a bunch of lazy bastards!

YUE YANG: Princess, stop yelling! If you keep yelling, then tonight when a big, black bear comes into your room, I'm not going to save you.

(*The men laugh.*)

ZHENG YINGYING: Oh, heavens!

---

[13]After his death, PLA enlisted man Lei Feng (1940–1962) became the centerpiece of a "learn from Lei Feng" campaign that eulogized "Chairman Mao's good soldier" in print, film, and song. Lei Feng was praised for his loyalty, selflessness, and courage in service to Mao, the party, and the people, as detailed in the diary he left behind.

[14]From the libretto of the revolutionary Beijing Opera *Spark amid the Reeds* (Lu dang huo zhong). Wen Mu, *Lu dang huo zhong,* ed. Wang Cengqi et al. (Beijing: Zhongguo xijü chubanshe, 1964), p. 51. In 1967, the opera was revised and its name changed to *Shajiabang.*

PANG YUN: (*To the other women*) If they really don't fix it, what are we going to do?

BAI XUE: If they don't fix the door, then we don't fix dinner.

PANG YUN: Right!

ZHENG YINGYING: Right! We won't cook!

YÜ DAHAI: If you don't cook, then we'll drink the northwest wind—we'll starve. Which is perfect for "recalling past suffering and praising present happiness."[15] (*Sings*) "The sky is full of stars . . ."

THE MEN: (*Lying down, singing*) ". . . the crescent moon shines on. There's a meeting at the production brigade . . ."

BAI XUE: (*With annoyance*) Bastards! A bunch of bastards!

YUE YANG: Who are you swearing at?

BAI XUE: You guys, who else? Girls have been raped in their barracks, because they didn't keep their doors shut and locked. Or haven't you heard?

(*The men fall silent. YUE YANG is the first to leap up; the others get up slowly after him; they fix the door. BAI XUE smiles. The women begin to cook. The fire's glow lights up their faces. The door is closed and locked.*)

BAI XUE: Okay, let's eat. Boiled water and two pieces of cornbread each.

(ZHENG YINGYING *passes out the cornbread.* LI JIANGSHAN *crosses to one side.*)

ZHENG YINGYING: Where are you going? Come eat!

LI JIANGSHAN: I'm going to wash my hands.

JIANG YI: Aren't we the little gentleman, so fastidious!

---

[15]Beginning in the early 1960s, the party conducted a campaign to encourage the people to "recall the sufferings of the old society and praise the sweetness of the new society." Lau Yee-fui, Ho Wang-yee and Yeung Sai-cheung, *Glossary of Chinese Political Phrases,* ed. Nancy Ma et al. (Kowloon, Hong Kong: Union Research Institute, 1977), s.v. "Yi ku si tian."

(*Ignoring* JIANG YI, LI JIANGSHAN *washes and dries his hands.*)

LI JIANGSHAN: Hey, where are my dirty clothes?

ZHENG YINGYING: Don't shout! Come eat! (*Gives* LI JIANGSHAN *his cornbread*)

LI JIANGSHAN: (*Softly*) Listen, I don't want you to wash them. In that bunch there's . . . a pair of underpants.

ZHENG YINGYING: (*Unconcerned*) So what? You're so prissy!

(*They eat in silence.* BAI XUE *flicks a little something into* YUE YANG's *bowl with her chopsticks.*)

LI JIANGSHAN: (*Trying a mouthful of food*) Okay, Princess, don't be partial!

(*Laughing,* BAI XUE *gives a little to* LI JIANGSHAN *as well.*)

YÜ DAHAI: And you've forgotten me!

BAI XUE: What's so special about a little hot sauce? (*Gives* YÜ DAHAI *a bit*) There was only a little left. That's it.

JIANG YI: Give me what's left. I'll add some boiled water to it and drink it.

BAI XUE: Wheelbarrow, pour me a bowl of water!

JIANG YI: Right.

LI JIANGSHAN: Wheelbarrow, pour me a bowl of water!

JIANG YI: It's right in front you. Pour it yourself.

LI JIANGSHAN: Huh?

(ZHENG YINGYING *pours a bowl of water for* LI JIANGSHAN. LI JIANGSHAN *takes it, smiles.* ZHENG *and* LI *share it.*)

YÜ DAHAI: (*Not without jealousy*) Hatoyama, you're always lucking out. Wipe that shit-eating grin off your face. Sad Sack, don't play favorites, or next time I won't help you with your work.

JIANG YI: Workpoint recordbooks! (*Gives each his or her recordbook*) Here's yours, and yours, and yours . . .

YÜ DAHAI: (*Reads, then*) Goddamn it. Five workpoints again!

JIANG YI: What's wrong with five workpoints? If a teacher gave you a five, you'd flip.[16]

YÜ DAHAI: (*Figuring*) One workpoint is equal to one point four cents. Five times point four is two, plus five . . . A day's work is just seven cents! Seven cents, guys!

LI JIANGSHAN: How much do you think you're worth? Who told you to come down to the countryside with us for "reeducation"?

JIANG YI: Really, Chief. I heard your father has been named to the standing committee of the city revolutionary committee.

YÜ DAHAI: (*Spits out a mouthful of food*) Bah! Dirt in the food.

YUE YANG: Wheelbarrow, why does ten workpoints worth of work get only five workpoints? That's not right!

JIANG YI: I complained, but the brigade says sent-down youths get half workpoints. It's the regulation.

LI JIANGSHAN: Hear that? What assholes!

YUE YANG: (*Angrily*) Go to sleep! Go to sleep!

(*The men and women retreat to their respective sides of the barracks and lie down to sleep.*)

YÜ DAHAI: Didn't we just eat? Why is it that as soon as I lie down, I'm hungry?

YUE YANG: Cut the bullshit!

LI JIANGSHAN: Chief, are you really hungry?

---

[16]A "five" is equivalent to an "A."

YÜ DAHAI: If I say anything, it'll be bullshit.

JIANG YI: I don't think anybody was this hungry even during the famine years.[17]

YÜ DAHAI: If everybody doesn't take turns starving, how are we going to "keep class struggle constantly in mind"?

LI JIANGSHAN: Very perceptive!

YUE YANG: That's ridiculous!

LI JIANGSHAN: (*To* JIANG YI) Hey, I'll teach you a trick. You have to keep your mind off your hunger. Did you read *The Battle of Sangkumryung?*[18] If there's no water, you deliberately think about plums. If you're hungry, you say to yourself, "I've eaten so much! I'm full to bursting. . . . First, it was stuffed buns, then it was dumplings . . ."

JIANG YI: No good. The more I think about food, the hungrier I get.

(YÜ DAHAI *chuckles to himself.*)

LI JIANGSHAN: Chief, that's the trick your father uses when he writes up reports, right?

YÜ DAHAI: (*With venom*) Fuck off!

YUE YANG: (*Angrily*) I'm going to punch the next guy who says anything.

(*The men are quiet. Silence. Sobbing is heard from the women's side.* PANG YUN, *who is reading a book by flashlight, nudges* BAI XUE.)

BAI XUE: (*Moving closer to* ZHENG YINGYING) What's the matter? What is it?

---

[17]Literally, the "three difficult years" (*san nian kunnan shiqi,* 1959–1961), a time when perhaps twenty million starved to death as a result of the ruinous agricultural policies of the Great Leap Forward.
[18]The battle of Sangkumryung was fought in Korea in the autumn of 1952 between Chinese and U.S. forces. For the novel to which Li Jiangshan refers, see Lu Zhuguo, *Shangganling* (Beijing: Renmin wenxue chubanshe, 1965).

ZHENG YINGYING: (*Holding her stomach*) I . . . my belly hurts.

BAI XUE: Hungry?

ZHENG YINGYING: No, that's not it. It's . . . that time of the month.

BAI XUE: Everything okay?

ZHENG YINGYING: No. I don't have any toilet paper or anything.

PANG YUN: Here's a newspaper that just came today.

ZHENG YINGYING: (*Cries out sharply, throws the paper to one side*) Are you nuts? There are . . . editorials and photographs in that paper!

BAI XUE: Which proves that the editorials are extremely timely! (*Quietly*) I'm telling you, whenever there's no paper, this is what I use! Go on!

(ZHENG YINGYING *takes care of her problem.*)

PANG YUN: (*With concern*) Still uncomfortable?

ZHENG YINGYING: Much better, thanks.

PANG YUN: (*Sadly*) I really envy you all. I'm already three months late. I've got anemia, edema . . . I'm not going to be much of a woman after this.

ZHENG YINGYING: Listen girls, just now I dreamt of my grandmother . . . She was dead. But she was watching me.

BAI XUE: That just shows how much you miss your grandmother.

ZHENG YINGYING: You have no idea. My mother was pregnant with me when my father was labeled a rightist. That's when he died. I lost my mother later. They hung a sign that said "reactionary capitalist" around my grandfather's neck, and they beat him to death in the street. They smashed the piano he bought me too. . . . That left my grandmother and me. If anything should really happen to her . . . (*She is on the verge of tears.*)

BAI XUE: Don't you know? Dreams are the opposite of what's real. Sleep.

(*Leaning against* BAI XUE, ZHENG YINGYING *sleeps.* PANG YUN *reads.*)

BAI XUE: You're still reading?

PANG YUN: I'm cold, I'm hungry, and I can't sleep.

BAI XUE: Are you still dreaming about going to college? There is no way they'll let us take the exam. You have to be "recommended," understand? Sleep with them and they'll recommend you! (*Chuckles*) Feel like giving it a try?

PANG YUN: Why don't you try it?

BAI XUE: Me? Ha! (*Sighs*) Going to college isn't worth dog shit. And I'm not even talking about the idiots they call "university students" today. My dad was graduated from a famous school, studied overseas, knows four languages, and all the same he's raising ducks at cadre school! . . . Go to sleep! As they say, "happiness is a good sleep."

(*The women are quiet.* YÜ DAHAI *tosses and turns; he can't sleep; he farts.*)

BAI XUE: (*Loudly*) Hey, you over there! Cut it out!

YÜ DAHAI: (*Feigning alarm*) Who was it? Who has disturbed Princess's sweet dreams? That's a crime worth ten thousand deaths! (*Laughs softly*) Don't be offended; except for a little cornbread, all I have in my stomach is dried sweet potato. . . . My farts can't stink.

(*Someone's stomach growls.*)

LI JIANGSHAN: Shh! Listen . . . what's that stirring? Demons and monsters, class enemies of all kinds are howling.

(*Someone laughs.*)

YUE YANG: (*Jumping up*) What do you say I go and "pluck" a chicken?

LI JIANGSHAN: Long live the General!

YÜ DAHAI: I'll go with you.

YUE YANG: No need. A surprise attack is a job for a lone soldier!

YÜ DAHAI: (*Pokes* JIANG YI *meaningfully*) Wheelbarrow, you go with him, stand lookout.

JIANG YI: Nobody goes! Brigade Captain Bai has been keeping an eye on us. He told me that a sent-down youth in another village stole a chicken, and the villagers caught him and poked his eyes out!

LI JIANGSHAN: (*Shivers*) God, they'd do it, too.

YÜ DAHAI: (*Clenching his teeth*) Fuck Brigade Captain Bai.

YUE YANG: (*Coldly*) What Bai was implying was . . .

JIANG YI: It's the same old thing. They can get away with murder.

YUE YANG: Did Bai the Wolf tell you that himself? Well, today he gets his. Chief, the dagger!

YÜ DAHAI: (*Hands* YUE YANG *a knife*) Be careful!

JIANG YI: (*Imploringly*) Really, General, if you steal from anybody, don't steal from him.

LI JIANGSHAN: General, whatever you do, don't steal from old aunt and uncle Wang. They've been pretty good to us; they sent over some sweet potatoes!

YUE YANG: I know the score! I steal only ill-gotten goods! (*Grabs the knife and rushes out*)

(BAI XUE *gets up; she stops* YUE YANG *outside the door.*)

BAI XUE: Honorable General, you're a chicken thief?

YUE YANG: Humph! Sometimes even a good man from Liang Mountain will steal chickens.[19]

---

[19]The good men of Liang Mountain are the 108 bandits assembled under the leadership of the Robin Hood–like Song Jiang in the seventeenth-century Chinese novel *Shui hu zhuan* (Outlaws of the marsh. It is also called *The Water Margin*), by Shi Naian. The

BAI XUE: Some good man you are. You don't plan on keeping your eyes?

YUE YANG: If they knock them both out, I'm out of luck. If they leave me one, then I'll still be a general. (*Shuts one eye*) See, like Potemkin![20] (*He is about to go.*)

BAI XUE: (*Quickly*) Don't go.

YUE YANG: What's with you?

BAI XUE: Don't go. If they want chicken, let them go.

YUE YANG: (*Laughs sadly*) You're really a fool! You think this is what, gluttony?

BAI XUE: Whatever, don't go. I . . . I don't want you to go!

YUE YANG: (*Gazes at* BAI XUE; *slowly*) It's just the way I am. If I resolve to do something, nothing can change my mind, not even . . . you. (*He pulls* BAI XUE *to him tightly and kisses her roughly.*)

BAI XUE: (*She is struck dumb; suddenly, she slaps* YUE YANG.) You bastard! Bastard!

YUE YANG: Right. But this "bastard" really has his spirits up now! (*Pushes* BAI XUE *away and runs off.*)

(BAI XUE *touches her cheek and watches* YUE YANG *as he moves away.* YUE YANG, *with adroit, practiced moves, steals a chicken.* BAI XUE *waits.* YUE YANG, *holding a chicken and in high spirits, runs toward center stage.*)

YUE YANG: (*Shaking the chicken in* BAI XUE's *face.*) Look!

(BAI XUE *does not say a word; she turns and goes into the barracks.*)

---

novel was a favorite of Mao Zedong's in his youth, but during the Cultural Revolution Mao positioned the book and its protagonist as the targets of a propaganda campaign. (See also note 23.)

[20]Grigory Alexandrovich Potemkin (1729–1791), Russian general and statesman and lover of Empress Catherine II, lost his left eye while in his early twenties. George Soloveytchik, *Potemkin* (London: Thorton Butterworth, 1938), pp. 49–50.

THE GROUP: (*Crying out*) Welcome General, returning home in triumph!

YUE YANG: (*Does a lively impersonation of Lin Biao*[21]) "Young generals of the Red Guards! The hard facts have proven once again . . . there is much to be gained by sending urban youth to the countryside!" (*Throws the chicken down.*) There you go!

(*Cheering, all dash forward; in a rush, they kill and pluck the chicken.*)

YÜ DAHAI: Kill the chicken!

THE GROUP: Kill! Kill! Kill!

LI JIANGSHAN: Pluck its feathers!

THE GROUP: Pluck! Pluck! Pluck!

YUE YANG: Wash it clean!

THE GROUP: Scrub! Scrub! Scrub!

(*The players lie down to blow on the flames to raise the fire over which they will roast the chicken.*)

YUE YANG: Who can contribute a little kindling?

YÜ DAHAI: Burn this! (*Passes over some paperback books*) My dad sent me a complete set of the "Criticize Lin Biao and Confucius" material.[22]

---

[21]As national defense minister and vice chairman of the party's Central Committee, Lin Biao (1907–1971) oversaw the growth of the PLA in power and influence during the Cultural Revolution; in 1966, he became Mao's designated successor. Donald W. Klien and Anne B. Clark, eds., *Biographic Dictionary of Chinese Communism* (Cambridge: Harvard University Press, 1977), vol. 1, pp. 559–567. A split grew between Mao and Lin "over the political role of the army and other policy issues," and in July 1972 it was reported that the previous fall Lin had been killed in a plane crash while trying to escape to the Soviet Union after his plan to assassinate Mao and take power was uncovered. Philip Bridgam, "The Fall of Lin Piao [Biao]," *China Quarterly,* July–September 1973, pp. 427–428 (See also note 22.)

[22]In August 1972, the party journal *Hong qi* (Red flag) launched a campaign against Lin Biao. "Zhangwo shehui zhuyi shiqi jieji douzheng de guilü" (Grasp the laws of class struggle in the socialist era), *Hong qi,* August 1972, pp. 40–42; cited in "Quarterly Chronicle and Documentation," *China Quarterly,* October–December 1972, p. 762. The campaign against Lin was subsequently joined to a movement to criticize Confucian ideas, a movement used by the Gang of Four to curtail the power of the Prime Minister Zhou Enlai. (See also note 21.)

ZHENG YINGYING: How about criticism of Song Jiang, do you want that?[23]

YUE YANG: Toss it here! Burning it down to ash is a pretty thoroughgoing criticism.

JIANG YI: (*Grabs the book* PANG YUN *has been reading*) Hey, burn this too.

PANG YUN: That's Hatoyama's.

YUE YANG: (*Takes the book, reads*) Ai Siqi, *Philosophy for the Masses*.[24] This we have to keep. Wheelbarrow, what about those newspapers of yours?

(*They all cheer; someone makes a move to grab the papers.*)

JIANG YI: Nothing doing! Those have articles by Liang Xiao on the revolution in education that we're supposed to study and discuss.[25]

LI JIANGSHAN: "Stop your windy nonsense!"

JIANG YI: What did you say, asshole?

LI JIANGSHAN: Me? ... I was reciting a line from a poem of the Chairman's, okay?[26] Hey, the chicken's ready!

---

[23]From the perspective of the party, the ideological problem with the novel *Outlaws of the Marsh* was the return of its bandit-hero, Song Jiang, to the service of the emperor: "[Song Jiang] pushes capitulationism [sic], practices revisionism, changes [the name of the bandits' meeting hall] from [Unite in Revolt] Hall to [Be Loyal to the Emperor] Hall, and accepts the offer of amnesty and enlistment." *Peking Review*, September 12, 1975, p. 7. (See also note 19.)

[24]Ai Siqi (1910–1966) was an important writer on Chinese communism and Marxist-Leninist philosophy. From 1953 until his death, Ai was with the party's Marx-Lenin Institute in Beijing. Klien and Clark, eds., *Biographic Dictionary of Chinese Communism, 1921–1965*, vol. 1, pp. 1–3.

[25]Liang Xiao, homophonous with "two schools," was a pseudonym of the "mass criticism group of Beijing and Qinghua universities," which was active as a mouthpiece for radical elements between 1974 and 1976.

[26]On December 31, 1975, two of Mao Zedong's poems, "The Jinggang Mountains Revisited" and "Two Birds: A Dialogue," were broadcast to a national radio audience. The latter poem contains the line "no farting" (*bu xü fangpi*), rendered in an official translation as "stop your windy nonsense," which is spoken by the roc, a mythical bird

(*They each grab a piece of chicken and start to eat.*)

YÜ DAHAI: Yeah, I heard that this time the campaign is aimed at . . . (*Gestures to indicate someone of short stature*)

YUE YANG: (*Startled*) But didn't he say that "men of ability are hard to find"?[27]

BAI XUE: Yes! And things had just started to get a bit better . . .

ZHENG YINGYING: And on New Year's Eve he said, "everywhere the orioles sing and the swallows dart."[28]

LI JIANGSHAN: But that poem also had the line, "stop your windy nonsense," right?

(THE GROUP *is puzzled. All are silent.*)

YÜ DAHAI: (*Heaves a long sigh*) It's the same shit over and over. In another seven or eight years it'll be time for another . . .[29]

---

that in the poem represents Marxist revolutionaries, as a rebuke to the sparrow, which stands in for revisionists. Mao Zedong, "Ci er shou," *Renmin ribao* (People's daily), January 1, 1976, p. 1; and Mao Zedong, "Two Poems," *Peking Review,* January 2, 1976, pp. 5–6. (See also note 28.)

[27]Yu Dahai has indicated Deng Xiaoping, who was the implied target of a February 1976 article in the *People's Daily* that criticized "capitalist roaders still taking the same road." "Wuchan jieji wenhua da geming de jixü he shenru" (The continuation and deepening of the Great Proletarian Cultural Revolution), *Renmin ribao,* February 6, 1976, p. 1; cited in "Quarterly Chronicle and Documentation," *China Quarterly,* June 1976, p. 427. On April 7, 1976, Deng was dismissed from all posts by resolution of the Central Committee. "Resolution of the Central Committee of the Communist Party of China on dismissing Teng Hsiaoping [Deng Xiaoping] from all posts both inside and outside the party," Xinhua (New China news agency), in *Foreign Broadcast Information Service,* April 7, 1976. Yue Yang is apparently quoting a comment Mao made about Deng around the time of Deng's rehabilitation in 1973, which ended Deng's long absence from the scene after he was first purged in 1967.

[28]This is from the first of the two poems mentioned in note 26. An editorial in the *People's Daily* claimed that this line referred to the "excellent situation at home and abroad"; of particular interest to Zheng Yingying and the others would have been a comment in the same editorial that "more than ten million school graduates have gone to the vast countryside where they are persevering in the revolution and growing steadily." "Shishang wu nanshi zhiyao ken dengpan" (Nothing is hard in this world if you dare to scale the heights), *Renmin ribao,* January 1, 1976, p. 2; cited in *Peking Review,* January 2, 1976, pp. 8–10.

[29]In a talk delivered at the Tenth National Congress of the Communist Party of China in August 1973, Gang of Four member Wang Hongwen said, "In 1966, when the Great Proletarian Cultural Revolution was just rising, Chairman Mao already pointed out: 'Great disorder across the land leads to great order. And so once again every seven or

LI JIANGSHAN: (*Lies down*) Another seven or eight years . . .

YUE YANG: (*With annoyance*) Don't talk about that! Princess, get out the guitar, play something!

BAI XUE: (*Softly*) I can't. A rat bit through one of the strings.

YUE YANG: Shit! Tomorrow I've got to get us a cat!

LI JIANGSHAN: (*Deliberately*) A black cat or a white cat?

YÜ DAHAI: Ha! Any cat that catches rats is a good cat.[30]

JIANG YI: (*Nervously*) You all watch what you say over there, okay? Are you looking for trouble?

YÜ DAHAI: Oh, we didn't mention any names. What's wrong with you?

LI JIANGSHAN: Enough! How about the revolutionary masses settle down a bit!

(YUE YANG *watches the fire. Suddenly, he begins to sing a melancholy but forceful tune, a song well known to* THE GROUP *from its younger days: "The Anthem of the Young Pioneers."*)

YUE YANG: (*Sings*) Are you prepared?
We are always prepared!
We are the Young Pioneers . . .

---

eight years. Monsters and demons will jump out themselves. Determined by their own class nature, they are bound to jump out.' " Wang Hongwen, "Report on the Revision of the Party Constitution," *Peking Review,* September 7, 1973, pp. 30–31.

[30]In the early 1960's, Deng Xiaoping remarked famously that "so long as it raises output, private farming is permissible. White or black, so long as a cat can catch mice, it's a good cat." This version of what Deng is supposed to have said was quoted by his enemies as evidence of Deng's capitalist tendencies in a 1967 article in the *People's Daily.* See "Zhongguo nongcun liang tiao daolu de douzheng" (Struggle in China's countryside between two roads), *Renmin ribao,* November 23, 1967, p. 1; cited and translated in Paris H. Chang, "Struggle between the Two Roads in China's Countryside," *Current Scene* 6 (February 15, 1968), p. 8. According to Kenneth Lieberthal, Deng's aphorism dates to a 1962 meeting of the party Secretariat that Deng convened to review the data on individual farming. Kenneth Lieberthal, "The Great Leap Forward and the Split in the Yan'an Leadership: 1958–1965," in *The Politics of China: 1949–1989,* ed. Roderick MacFarquhar (Cambridge: Cambridge University Press, 1993), p. 123.

(*At first, the others listen quietly, then all join in*)

THE GROUP: (*Sings*) The masters of the future
We are sure to be.
Da da da dee da,
Dee dee da dee da!

(*As they Sing, they forget themselves, and the sound of their singing rings clearer and clearer.*)

THE GROUP: (*Sings*) Little brothers,
Little sisters,
Our future is unlimited.
The masters of the future
We are sure to be.

Da da da dee da,
Dee dee da dee da!

(PANG YUN *begins to cry.* ZHENG YINGYING *starts to cry as well. The young men's eyes also begin to tear.*)

BAI XUE: (*Choking back tears*) We're crying?! For what! No matter how beautiful a dream is, it's still just a dream. No matter how grim reality is, it's still real.

YUE YANG: (*Laughs bitterly*) I want to be a general? How many generals have been purged?

PANG YUN: I haven't got a chance.

ZHENG YINGYING: The piano . . . smashed to pieces! The last sound it made was so beautiful.

LI JIANGSHAN: What does life mean, anyway?

JIANG YI: My dad always says that life is just three meals a day, plus two shots of booze and sleep. Well, he's right, if you think about it.

YÜ DAHAI: He's right my ass! So what are we on this planet for?

LI JIANGSHAN: Human beings . . . human beings are just specks of dust.

ZHENG YINGYING: Wretched little pieces of stone.

YUE YANG: I'll tell you what we are, we're bricks. If you want to build the Great Wall with us, no problem. If you want to stack us up into a chicken coop, that's fine too. It all depends on how you use us.

YÜ DAHAI: (*Grimly*) What they've done is take you and throw you aside. Ah! (*Hits a bowl rhythmically*) Each one of us is a brick!

THE GROUP: (*In unison*) North, south, east, west, we go where we are moved!

YUE YANG: You say your life is tough?!

THE GROUP: (*Listlessly*) Think about the six thousand miles of the Long March!

LI JIANGSHAN: You say your work is hard?

THE GROUP: (*Worn out beyond endurance*) Think about the evil old society . . .

(*Following the last line above, the players, with the exception of* BAI XUE, *tumble left and right and fall asleep.*)

BAI XUE: (*Plucks at the guitar with the missing string, summons up a little energy and softly sings "The Song of the Sent-Down Youth"*) "An oil lamp's glow shines on the wall. The night is dark and lonely. Look back at the past so far in the distance, where is the road home?" (*She slips off to sleep.*)

(*The* DRUMMER *and* KEYBOARDIST *come quietly toward center stage.*)

DRUMMER: Are they frozen? They all have such odd, agonized smiles on their faces!

KEYBOARDIST: People who freeze to death all have that smile.

DRUMMER: Wake up! Wake up! There is disaster on the way!

KEYBOARDIST: Look! Those flashes of light!

DRUMMER: Listen! The earth is roaring in anger! (*Plays a roll*)

THE GROUP: (*Awoken by the commotion, they yell out*) Earthquake! It's an earthquake![31]

(*There is a loud rumbling. The walls of the barracks collapse. All tumble away, then run, as they fight to survive the earthquake. Finally, the noise fades. The players huddle together; they peer out a window.*)

YUE YANG: Look! Everything's gone black! What's happened to the village? The people?

YÜ DAHAI: Gone. Everything's wiped out!

LI JIANGSHAN: The sun? How can the sun have been destroyed too?[32]

ZHENG YINGYING: Look at all that snow! Where can we hide?

YUE YANG: Come! Huddle together.

PANG YUN: (*Terrified*) The earth has cracked open, hasn't it? Is it going to swallow us up?

JIANG YI: (*Despairingly*) Finished! (*Wildly*) We are finished!

YÜ DAHAI: Stop yelling! We're still alive! Let me think!

THE GROUP: Let us think!

YUE YANG: Closer together! Huddle up tightly! Don't fall asleep again! Stick together! Don't split up again!

(*The group huddles together and is as still as if sculpted from stone.*)

---

[31]Even though the dates do not match, the authors are alluding to a disastrous earthquake in Tangshan, Hebei Province, on July 28, 1976, which killed more than 200,000. An earthquake was a traditional portent of dynastic change, and Chinese audiences would take this scene as a reference to the deaths of Zhou Enlai on January 8, 1976, and Mao Zedong on September 9, 1976.

[32]The sun, of course, stands for Mao Zedong.

DRUMMER: "As long as the flint remains, the spark cannot die."[33] "If Winter comes, can Spring be far behind?"[34] Didn't any of you notice? By the time the last murderous gust of the west wind had faded away, spring had returned. The ice has broken up; the snow has melted; tender buds of hope are bursting on the branches of the trees! This is the spring for which you have longed for so many years! Quick! Run into the fields, run down the roads! Breathe, run, sing!

(*One by one, the group comes around. Dazed but happy, they peel off their winter clothing and throw it to the ground. Each walks off as he or she pleases. Breathing deeply, running and leaping, they head into spring.*)

Act Two
Spring 1978

(*The members of the collective are together once again. They are busy reviewing notes and memorizing theorems and formulas.*)

YUE YANG: (*Happily*) Does everyone have an admission card for the exam?[35]

PANG YUN: It's like a dream!

LI JIANGSHAN: General, what area tests are you taking?

YUE YANG: Aerospace engineering, marine engineering . . . anything that's got a connection with the military!

---

[33]This is the penultimate sentence of an essay Lu Xun published in 1936 in praise of Chinese student activists and those citizens who supported them. Lu Xun identifies his inspiration as the following comment by Zhang Dai (1597–1679), a scholar of the late Ming: "Loyal officials and righteous men appear most often when the country is in crisis; they are like sparks struck from a flint—a flash which quickly fades; if the rulers of the people do not preserve these sparks quickly, the fire will be extinguished." Lu Xun, " 'Ti wei ding' cao" ("As yet untitled," a draft), *Lu Xun quan ji* (The complete works of Lu Xun) (Beijing: Renmin wenxue chubanshe, 1981), vol. 6, p. 435; Lu Xun, *Selected Works* (Beijing: Foreign Languages Press, 1961), vol. 4, p. 249.

[34]The last line of Shelley's "Ode to the West Wind," in which the poet invites the wind to "by the incantation of this verse, / scatter, as from an unextinguished hearth / Ashes and sparks, my words among mankind!" *The Complete Poetical Works of Shelley,* ed. Thomas Hutchinson (Oxford: Clarendon Press, 1904), p. 640.

[35]Yue Yang and the others are preparing for a college entrance examination.

YÜ DAHAI: I'm doing economics. What China needs is management expertise.

PANG YUN: It doesn't matter what area test you take, just as long as you pass.

JIANG YI: But our residency cards are still for out in the countryside.[36]

YUE YANG: I've burned all that stuff!! I've really burned my bridges behind me!

LI JIANGSHAN: "In one year win the battle, in three years win the war." By the year 2000 we'll achieve the Four Modernizations! We can do it! We can do it by then!

ZHENG YINGYING: But for now we've got to get ready for this test. Every morning my grandmother has been sending me off with one fritter, two hard-boiled eggs, and a prayer that I'll score one hundred percent. But I still feel so unsure.

LI JIANGSHAN: (*Consolingly*) We all feel the same way. We wasted all that time.

BAI XUE: And what did we learn? Only how to criticize and condemn, how to turn in blank exam papers, how to break windows, how to beat up our teachers . . .

(*They all laugh loudly.*)

JIANG YI: Let's go! When they're through grilling us, we'll be burnt-out.[37]

YÜ DAHAI: To get done, we've got to be grilled! No one lose heart!

YUE YANG: Right! Let's go for it! Ah, goddamn!

---

[36]Under residency rules that were not relaxed until the mid-1980s, each citizen had a registered permanent residence and could not move to a new location to live or to work without permission.

[37]This begins a running pun on two pairs of homophones; the words for "to take an exam" and "to grill" or "to roast" are both pronounced "kao," and both "bewildered" and "burnt" are pronounced "hu."

(With mixed emotions, the group enters the examination hall in single file. One by one they exit. They are absolutely exhausted, their faces pale, as if they have been stricken ill.)

YÜ DAHAI: *(To* YUE YANG*)* How did you do?

YUE YANG: Absolutely . . . not so great!

LI JIANGSHAN: Oh, my god! I screwed up again!

ZHENG YINGYING: *(On the verge of tears)* 1843! It was 1843! What an idiot! 1843 . . .[38]

JIANG YI: Hey, it's over. Don't keep worrying about it.

BAI XUE: Quick, over here! Sister . . .

(They all surround PANG YUN, *who has fainted and collapsed.)*

YUE YANG: Water! Get some water!

YÜ DAHAI: Is it low blood sugar? She should rest.

PANG YUN: *(Coming to)* No . . . I . . . I have to take the test.

BAI XUE: Are you crazy?

ZHENG YINGYING: How can you take a test in the shape you're in?

PANG YUN: I . . . I can do it! *(Struggles to rise but faints again)*

LI JIANGSHAN: She'd better go home.

YUE YANG: I'll go talk to them.

---

[38]A question that would elicit this answer is "In what year was the Treaty of Humen signed?" The Treaty of Humen, which is also known as the Treaty of the Bogue, attached provisions to the Treaty of Nanjing that contained imperialist clauses and had opened five Chinese ports to foreign trade in 1842. The Treaty of Humen further granted most-favored-nation status to the United Kingdom and stipulated that British citizens could settle permanently in specified areas. *Cihai (The Encyclopedia of Words)* (Shanghai: Shanghai cishu chubanshe, 1989), s.v. "Humen tiaoyue."

PANG YUN: No! (*She reaches out and grabs* YUE YANG *by the leg, stopping him.*) . . . I have to take this test! (*She is close to tears.*) I . . . I can pass! . . . I have to pass this test! (*She is overcome with sobbing.*)

(*The others are frightened and discouraged.*)

DRUMMER: (*Uncomprehendingly*) How did things come to this?

YUE YANG: Yes, how can it have come to this? . . . Is it because these days there is only this one "golden road,"[39] or is it because we've been held up for so long and have almost lost all hope, and so we're grabbing with everything we've got at this last chance to realize our dreams?

KEYBOARDIST: (*Runs on, holding several sheets of paper*) The scores are in!

(*Each takes his or her report card; many different emotions register on their faces.*)

PANG YUN: (*As if she cannot believe her eyes*) I passed? I passed! I . . . really passed! (*Wild with joy*) . . . Look you guys! I made it over the cutoff! Ha ha ha ha ha! I passed! I passed! . . . (*Suddenly, she sobers, looks at her friends and is shaken and embarrassed; softly*) I'm . . . I'm sorry . . . I . . . How stupid of me. How could I? I wasn't deliberately trying to . . . I really didn't mean anything! (*She looks at the others imploringly.*)

(*The others look at* PANG YUN; *some turn their heads away, others make an effort to smile.*)

YUE YANG: (*Crosses toward* PANG YUN; *with sincerity*) Congratulations!

JIANG YI: Yeah! You've brought honor to the collective.

LI JIANGSHAN: That's right! If one of us has passed, then that isn't bad at all!

(*Abruptly,* PANG YUN *covers her face and cries; sobbing, she bows toward the others, turns and walks off alone.* YUE YANG *motions to* BAI XUE. BAI XUE *and* ZHENG YINGYING *follow* PANG YUN.)

---

[39] A reference to the phrase "the golden road of socialism."

(*By a riverbank. The men exchange sad looks. Suddenly, they break out in laughter that they can no longer contain. They laugh until they have to sit down, quite out of breath.*)

LI JIANGSHAN: My . . . my god! Damn if Wheelbarrow didn't say so . . . When . . . when they're through grilling us, we'll be burnt-out!

YUE YANG: Completely fucking burnt-up! Ha ha ha ha!

YÜ DAHAI: (*Pokes* JIANG YI) Hey, how do you hawk burnt meatballs again?

JIANG YI: (*Mimics a hawker's cry*) Burnt— . . . oh, fuck it! Who's going to buy burnt meatballs?

YUE YANG: Chief, let me see your scores. (*Takes* YÜ DAHAI*'s score report; reads*) You jerk, you passed!

YÜ DAHAI: (*Laughs bitterly*) I passed, but there is no way I'm going to get into college. I know my place. (*He slowly tears the score report to pieces.*)

LI JIANGSHAN: Why?

YÜ DAHAI: My father's being disciplined.[40] You didn't know? (*Throws the shreds of paper into the river; walks off.*)

(*The men watch* YÜ DAHAI *as he goes*)

LI JIANGSHAN: (*Softly*) No way. They can't still be "implicating nine generations of the family in the crimes of one," can they?[41]

---

[40]Yu Dahai's father is being punished for his transgressions during the Cultural Revolution.

[41]The set phrase that Li employs, "zhu lian jiu zu," refers to the wide distribution of responsibility and punishment for certain crimes under traditional penal codes. During the Qing dynasty, for example, the penalty for treason was the execution of not only the offender but also all those over fifteen years of age among the offender's father, grandfather, sons, grandsons, brothers, brothers' sons, maternal grandfather, father-in-law, and brothers-in-law. Richard J. Smith, *China's Cultural Heritage: The Ch'ing [Qing] Dynasty, 1644–1912* (Boulder, Colorado: Westview Press, 1983), p. 240; and Derk Bodde and Clarence Morris, *Law in Imperial China: Exemplified by 190 Ch'ing Dynasty Cases (Translated from the "Hsing-an hui-lan") With Historical, Social, and Juridical Commentaries* (Philadelphia: University of Pennsylvania Press, 1967), p. 286.

JIANG YI: China never changes in this respect. Take you, for example, Hatoyama. I'll tell you what's going to happen. You will definitely be the first called back to the city, and you'll have no problem finding a job. You have unlimited prospects. General has it made, too. But the rest of us, if our dads don't retire early, then we're out of luck.[42] We have to take goddamn tests! (*Slaps his rear*) Tests! They shouldn't rehabilitate only the old guys; they should lend a hand to us youngsters! (*He sadly wipes his eyes and walks away.*)

(LI JIANGSHAN *looks at* YUE YANG. YUE YANG *watches the river.*)

LI JIANGSHAN: (*Puts his arm around* YUE YANG's *shoulder; softly*) What do you plan to do?

YUE YANG: I'm still thinking about it. (YUE YANG *slowly stands up, lightly removes* LI JIANGSHAN's *arm from around his shoulder, hangs his head and exits.*)

(*A shaken* LI JIANGSHAN *watches the river roll on.*)

(*On the street,* YUE YANG *bumps into* JIANG YI.)

YUE YANG: Where are you heading? What's with all this stuff you're carrying?

JIANG YI: I'm . . . going to see some relatives.

YUE YANG: (*Teasing* JIANG YI) You jerk, you're not telling the truth! (*Indicating the cartons of cigarettes and bottles of wine that* JIANG YI *is carrying*) You've got "firecrackers," "hand grenades" . . . What "mountain" are you planning to blow up?

JIANG YI: Hey, what can I do? I have to get a doctor to write me a medical excuse so that I can stay in the city. I'll see what happens after I get settled.

YUE YANG: (*Surprised*) You're not going to take the exam again next year?

JIANG YI: Next year? Next year the cutoff will be even higher! The test will be even harder! I don't have the brains to compete in that game.

---

[42]In the Maoist economy certain types of employment could be inherited by a child upon the retirement of the parent.

YUE YANG: What do you think you're doing? There is always a chance if you try.

JIANG YI: And if farts could start fires then matches wouldn't be worth a dime. I'm telling you, you should get moving now. What if by some chance the policy changes again? Cry, because it will be too late for you. (*Exits in a rush*)

(YUE YANG *is lost in thought; he turns and walks away.* YUE YANG *arrives at* YÜ DAHAI's *apartment;* YÜ DAHAI *is reading.*)

YUE YANG: What's up, Chief?

YÜ DAHAI: Not a damn thing. Reading, thinking. You?

YUE YANG: Just out for a stroll. I'm not studying; I've got nothing to do. If I try to study, I can't anyway.

YÜ DAHAI: Here, take a look at these: *Exploration; Starlight; The Big Earth.* . . . They're what they call "unofficial magazines."[43]

YUE YANG: God, what lousy paper. It's not even good enough for toilet paper.

YÜ DAHAI: Never mind the quality of the paper, some of the articles are fucking excellent! They've got reprints of campaign speeches from some universities in Beijing too.[44]

YUE YANG: What, I don't see you for a few days and in the meantime you turn into a philosopher? Reading this stuff isn't worth shit! Hey, weren't you planning to . . .

---

[43]These are examples of unofficial publications associated with the Democracy Wall activity that flourished between December 1978 and March 1979. These magazines often began as wall posters and evolved into inexpensively printed periodicals of limited press runs.

[44]Yü Dahai is referring to elections held in the late 1970s and early 1980s to choose deputies to people's congresses in Beijing's districts and counties. These contests were significant in that they were the first elections in more than a quarter century in which the number of candidates exceeded the number of posts to be filled. For an account of the election activity at Beijing University by a student of that institution, see "The Wind Rises from the Duckweed," in *Wild Lilies, Poisonous Weeds,* ed. Gregor Benton (London: Pluto Press, 1982), pp. 88–97.

YÜ DAHAI: (*Kicks a stack of books*) Look here. I just bought these through a friend: a complete set of college economics and management texts. But I've figured things out. If China doesn't solve fundamental, systemic problems, then this stuff (*he kicks a book*) is no better than toilet paper. A lot of people pay lip service to "building socialism," but I wonder if they really understand what socialism is? Come on, take a look at some of these magazines. It doesn't matter if everything they say is right or not. I guarantee you won't be the same after you read them. The writers are all young people. Take a look at what they're thinking, at what they're doing. (*With some self-importance*) In my opinion, China's future rests on the shoulders of young people like ourselves. (*Slaps* YUE YANG *on the back; quoting from a poem by Li Bai*) "Heaven has blessed us with talent for a reason!" Give it a shot, brother!

(YUE YANG *is taken aback. He looks at* YÜ DAHAI *as if he were a stranger.*)

(JIANG YI *and* LI JIANGSHAN *enter.*)

JIANG YI: Hey! News flash! Hatoyama's connections have had him transferred back to the city! What did I tell you? (*Everybody looks at* LI JIANGSHAN)

LI JIANGSHAN: (*Uneasily*) I really don't know anything about it. It was all arranged by my old man's secretary. . . . Don't look at me that way.

(*The others look at* LI JIANGSHAN *and laugh.*)

LI JIANGSHAN: (*Alarmed*) . . . Don't look at me that way, brothers!

(*All but* LI JIANGSHAN *depart without a word.* LI JIANGSHAN *sighs repeatedly.*)

(LI JIANGSHAN *comes to call on* ZHENG YINGYING.)

ZHENG YINGYING: (*Feigning indifference*) I hear you've been transferred home.

LI JIANGSHAN: Does that make you happy?

ZHENG YINGYING: Happy? Of course it makes me happy.

LI JIANGSHAN: Then why aren't you smiling? Tell me! Why aren't you smiling?

(LI JIANGSHAN *begins to take* ZHENG YINGYING *in his arms.*)

ZHENG YINGYING: (*Gently moves to free herself*) Don't . . .

LI JIANGSHAN: (*Distressed*) You're all like this! Even you are acting like this! . . . It's like I'm not Hatoyama anymore. It's like I'm Wang Lianju![45]

ZHENG YINGYING: No one has said a word against you.

LI JIANGSHAN: Am I a fool? Can't I tell? Look me in the eye and tell me that you're not deliberately putting distance between us.

ZHENG YINGYING: (*Sighs softly*) The distance between us has been there from the start!

LI JIANGSHAN: (*Laughs bitterly*) Distance! . . . I've known about this "distance" since I was a kid. In kindergarten the teacher always gave me the biggest apple. Adults spoiled me no matter how much trouble I made. Every Saturday my friends' parents came to get them on bicycles. I was the only one who rode in a exhaust-farting car. . . . But then one night, people started spitting on me, throwing stones at me. Suddenly, I was the "bastard son of a capitalist roader," and nobody wanted anything to do with me! . . . I gritted my teeth and went to the countryside. In the collective it was as if I'd become human again. (*His voice breaks.*) Am I not anymore? Huh? Why can't it always be like it was in the collective? Huh? What's wrong with that?

ZHENG YINGYING: (*She doesn't know what to say.*) I . . . (*Sighs, takes* LI JIANGSHAN's *hand in hers*) I'm so sorry for you.

(LI JIANGSHAN *angrily tightens his grip on* ZHENG YINGYING's *hand.*)

ZHENG YINGYING: (*Cries out from the pain*) Let go!

LI JIANGSHAN: (*Drops* ZHENG YINGYING's *hand contemptuously, moves away, then turns back toward* ZHENG) You pity me? Go ahead and

---

[45]Wang Lianju is a former underground communist who turns traitor to act as police inspector for the puppet government under the Japanese occupation in *The Red Lantern.* (See also notes 1 and 51).

pity me! Just remember, I have power! I am going to find a way to get you all called back! And I also want . . . to marry you!

(ZHENG YINGYING *is startled; she pauses, then laughs.*)

LI JIANGSHAN: What are you laughing at? I'm completely serious!

ZHENG YINGYING: That's what's funny! (*Turns her back*) Go.

LI JIANGSHAN: (*Crosses to* ZHENG YINGYING, *turns her around*) I am going to tell them we have already . . .

ZHENG YINGYING: You take what we had too seriously! Do you think that what we did back there matters anymore, now that we're here? Do you think your parents are going to agree that what happened between us is so important? Do you think they are going to allow you to marry the daughter of a rightist, the granddaughter of a capitalist? Just because I helped you wash a few clothes? Because we shared a little . . . affection? What a joke!

LI JIANGSHAN: Don't give me that stuff about having to be well matched socially and economically. I despise that sort of feudal thinking. I'll say it again, I want to marry you!

ZHENG YINGYING: Impossible.

LI JIANGSHAN: (*Crestfallen*) You don't believe me?

ZHENG YINGYING: (*Brokenheartedly*) I don't believe myself! I don't believe the society I live in! . . . Enough! There's . . . nothing we can do about this. . . . (*Her eyes fill with tears; she sobs.*) Who . . . who put this distance between us?

LI JIANGSHAN: (*Angrily*) I don't want to hear that word! I don't want to hear it!

ZHENG YINGYING: (*Calming down*) But from my mother's womb I've understood the meaning of that word. (*Sadly*) Go.

(*They stare at each other silently.* LI JIANGSHAN *seems to be about to reach out for* ZHENG YINGYING, *but the distance between them grows larger and larger.*)

(BAI XUE *and* YUE YANG *enter a small grove of trees. BAI XUE is carrying a portfolio, brushes, and paint. She is in a good mood.*)

BAI XUE: Hey! Come here! Stand still! Lean against that tree.

YUE YANG: I'm telling you, I'm not joking.

BAI XUE: I'm serious too. My uncle wants me to take the entrance exam for the art institute, says he knows the director, but I still have to submit some work. I'm going to take you and this beautiful spring day and put you in a painting together.

YUE YANG: (*Somewhat dispirited*) You're thinking of taking me with you, right, to be your full-time model?

BAI XUE: You would be very suited for that, except your expression is too melancholy. But for this painting it's perfect. I've even thought of a title. I'm going to call this one "Spring."

YUE YANG: Why won't you agree to my leaving?

BAI XUE: Lean your head to the side a bit. Keep that pose.

YUE YANG: There are only three days left in the recruitment period. I've got to get back to the countryside to sign up! Do you understand?

BAI XUE: Darn, I've messed it up. (*Sighs*) Okay, what are you saying? Damn your dream of being a soldier.

YUE YANG: It's not a dream. It is an achievable goal! I found out that after one year in the service, I can take the exam for a military academy.

BAI XUE: And after two more years, you get out, get assigned as a platoon leader, twenty-third grade, salary 52.50 a month—and you've got to pay for your own food. I've made my own inquiries.

YUE YANG: And if I work hard for ten years? Twenty years? Get some combat experience? Why can't I make division commander or brigade captain?

BAI XUE: And if midway you're demobilized? The rule is you always go back to where you came from: "We're sorry, please stay in the countryside for the rest of your life." Don't do this to me! What if they don't let you test for the academy? What if you fail? What if you never make it to combat? What if you do and get killed? My god, that's horrifying!

YUE YANG: I know, I know. But at least I would have tried.

BAI XUE: And me?

YUE YANG: (*Puzzled*) You? What problems do you have?

BAI XUE: You've made up your mind to work for something twenty years down the line. So I'm supposed to wait twenty years for you, is that it? Alone, by myself, just so I can call myself the wife of a general? . . . No, I'm not interested. It doesn't matter if you have a job or not; it doesn't matter how much money you make; I don't care about any of that! I just want to be able to see you, touch you.

YUE YANG: (*Comes forward impulsively, gently takes* BAI XUE *in his arms*) Bai Xue!

BAI XUE: (*Presses close to* YUE YANG) Don't go. Don't go. . . . I don't have to go to art school, if that's going to keep us apart for two or three years. . . . (*Strokes* YUE YANG's *face and neck; gently*) We've already wasted a lot of our springtime; there isn't much of it left. . . . We can't. . . . We can't cause more pain for ourselves. I like your decisiveness, and I hate it! . . . Don't, don't leave me. Just hold me like this. . . . You'll always be my prince, General.

YUE YANG: (*Passion gone, calmly*) And if I insist on going?

BAI XUE: (*Pushes* YUE YANG *away; also calmly*) Then I will find someone else right away!

YUE YANG: You? Find someone else? (*Laughs loudly*)

BAI XUE: (*Enraged*) What? You don't believe me?

YUE YANG: (*Laughing*) I believe you! I believe you! I believe you! My beloved Princess! (*He moves to hug* BAI XUE.)

(BAI XUE *ducks away from* YUE YANG. YUE YANG *chases;* BAI XUE *dodges; they continue around the tree. Vexed, BAI XUE grabs a paint brush and points it at YUE YANG.*)

BAI XUE: You just dare come closer! I'll give you a face full of paint!

YUE YANG: Okay. I surrender! (*Laughing, he leans against the tree.*)

(BAI XUE *makes a "humph" sound, turns to the easel and begins to paint.*)

YUE YANG: Hey, really. I'm leaving tomorrow. (*Sighs*) Those seedlings we planted back then have already grown into trees! We can't keep wasting time.

BAI XUE: Leave! As soon as you're gone, I'm going to find someone else.

YUE YANG: Hey, don't kid around.

BAI XUE: You just try it and see. (*Folds up the portfolio; is about to go.*)

YUE YANG: (*Grabs* BAI XUE) What about our feelings? Hm? My love for you? You don't take any of that into account?

BAI XUE: (*Disdainfully*) Haven't you failed to take those things into account? You're a selfish bastard! (*Yanks herself free of* YUE YANG, *exits in a rage.*)

YUE YANG: (*Angrily*) Me? I'm selfish? (*Angry and frustrated, he tears a branch from a willow tree and with it he whips the ground with all his strength.*[46] *Suddenly, he stops.*)

(*The melody of "The Anthem of the Young Pioneers," mixed with the past laughter of the group, is heard.* YUE YANG *listens. His friends crowd around.*)

ZHENG YINGYING: Are you really going?

YÜ DAHAI: Don't go. We'll go into business together.

JIANG YI: If you leave like this, Princess is going to be heartbroken!

---

[46]The willow is traditionally associated with the sorry of parting.

LI JIANGSHAN: Wait a while longer. Director Hu Yaobang of the Central Organization Department just made an important speech about the problem of sent-down youths.

PANG YUN: Think it over again, okay?

YUE YANG: I've thought it over, and I've decided. I don't intend to wait any longer. I'm going to use my own two legs to walk my own road.

JIANG YI: Why isn't Princess here?

YUE YANG: Go check on her for me. Give her some encouragement; look after her. Consider it your duty as a member of the collective. Tell her I've gone. (*Looks at the willow branch he is holding*) I'll take this with me; I'll stick it on the sentry box I'm heading for. (*Holding up the branch, he exits slowly without looking back; his friends wave good-bye.*)

ZHENG YINGYING: (*Sighs; unhappily*) He's gone. What about us?

(*In silence, the group splits up and all disappear into the trees, which sway in the spring wind. BAI XUE enters carrying the portfolio; she walks alone back and forth amid the trees. JIANG YI crosses toward BAI XUE.*)

JIANG YI: You should go see him off.

BAI XUE: He shouldn't go!

JIANG YI: He asked me to look after you.

BAI XUE: (*Rashly*) I told him, as soon as he left, I'd take up with someone else!

JIANG YI: (*Immediately*) I . . . I'll be your model, okay?

BAI XUE: (*Taken aback at first, she laughs.*) Fine! Stand still. Lean against that tree. (*She arranges her brushes and paints.*)

(JIANG YI *doesn't know what to do; finally, he strikes a stiff, unnatural pose. BAI XUE lifts her head and looks; she throws down her brush angrily, turns and walks away. JIANG YI hesitates for a second, then hurries after BAI XUE. In uniform, a dignified YUE YANG crosses between BAI XUE and JIANG YI.*)

Act Three
Summer 1981

(*The group enters, mimicking in chorus the drone of cicadas: "dog days—, dog days—."*)

YUE YANG: From the great southwest, transferred out to the great northwest. What have I accomplished over the past few years? (*Furrows his brow as he thinks it over*) What does a soldier do? Go to war, go home to the barracks, serve as duty officer, stand sentry duty, perform public service. . . . It seems like there's never any free time, but then it seems like I never do anything.

DRUMMER: Has your dream of becoming a general come true?

YUE YANG: That's just a dream. It will always be a dream. I'm a soldier who loves to dream.

(YUE YANG *and* PANG YUN *walk by each other.*)

PANG YUN: (*Stops suddenly*) General? . . . General!

YUE YANG: (*Turns his head, stumped for a moment*) . . . Sister? (*They shake hands*) Hey, how can I still call you that? I should say, comrade student! (*Pauses*) How are things going?

PANG YUN: No big news.

YUE YANG: Don't say that! Going to college isn't big news? You're on your way to . . .

PANG YUN: I've got an appointment.

YUE YANG: You have a boyfriend then?

PANG YUN: Not really. (*Changing the subject*) How are you? Are you in the academy?

YUE YANG: (*Pained, but with indifference*) I'm afraid I haven't been that lucky. I spent my first year in combat. Then I thought I'd take the exam for the academy, but the doctors said my memory wasn't good enough. I wasn't allowed to take the test. They don't let me take the test, I don't take it, that's that. Anyway, I'll finish my commitment and then come back to civilian life.

PANG YUN: (*Something dawns on her.*) Didn't Princess come to meet you?

YUE YANG: (*Calmly*) What do you mean? (*Angrily*) Are you making fun of me?

PANG YUN: You . . . What are you talking about?

YUE YANG: Don't you know? You really don't know?

PANG YUN: I haven't been in touch with any of them for more than two years.

YUE YANG: Oh. (*Pauses*) We broke up.

PANG YUN: (*Amazed*) What? . . . Why?

YUE YANG: Why? There is no why. . . . She's with someone else. That's the way it is.

PANG YUN: (*Wants to ask more questions, but it is too awkward to do so*) . . . Oh.

YUE YANG: (*Despite himself, he goes on.*) Do you know who she is with? . . . Wheelbarrow!

PANG YUN: Huh?!

YUE YANG: Pretty goddamn amusing. Wheelbarrow!

PANG YUN: I really never imagined. . . . What can I say, General? Are you doing okay?

YUE YANG: (*Laughs*) I got over it a long time ago. You get going. Your boyfriend is waiting for you! (*Gently pushes PANG YUN on her way*) Say hello for me.

(PANG YUN *waves, exits.* YUE YANG *follows her for a few steps, smiles faintly, and waves. The sound of a siren rises. The sound of the siren blends into the whistling of bombs and the concussion of explosions.* YUE YANG *freezes, looks all around blankly.*)

(YUE YANG *and* LI JIANGSHAN *walk together talking. They run into* YÜ DAHAI.)

YUE YANG: (*Going forward in greeting*) Chief!

YÜ DAHAI: (*Happily surprised*) General!

(YÜ DAHAI *and* YUE YANG *shake hands.* LI JIANGSHAN *extends his hand to* YÜ DAHAI; YÜ DAHAI *looks at* LI JIANGSHAN *but does not take his hand.*)

YUE YANG: Chief, are you still manning the stoves in that mess hall?

YÜ DAHAI: Yeah.

YUE YANG: Still taking college courses?

YÜ DAHAI: I'm still studying. Self-study. (*With concern*) Are you still in the service?

(YUE YANG *smiles and nods his head.*)

LI JIANGSHAN: General, come back. If you need a job, I can take care of it.

YUE YANG: Think of a way to help Chief!

LI JIANGSHAN: He works for a state factory. His case wouldn't be so easy to manage. And he doesn't get along with his superiors. Besides, two years ago he got mixed up in that business over "existentialism."[47]

YÜ DAHAI: "Ism," "ism," "ism." You're boring me!

YUE YANG: (*Changing the subject*) It's so muggy.

LI JIANGSHAN: I'll take you to a dance tonight. They're going to have

---

[47]This refers to Yü Dahai's earlier flirtation with the unofficial press and, by extension, Democracy Wall.

videotapes, blue movies. Think you can handle it? The old men have closed their eyes! Chief, do you want to come with us?

YÜ DAHAI: Are you going to take my shift?

LI JIANGSHAN: (*Can restrain himself no longer*) What is it with you? Did I do something to make you angry?

YÜ DAHAI: Tell me, how many times have you switched jobs in the past couple of years?

LI JIANGSHAN: I can't say for sure.

YÜ DAHAI: (*Still half-jokingly*) As often as you change your goddamn clothes, right? You go wherever things are good.

LI JIANGSHAN: And I'm going to switch again. I'm looking into a job with a television station. I'm going to do a little directing.

YÜ DAHAI: (*To* YUE YANG) Did you hear that? Directing. What a crock of shit!

LI JIANGSHAN: (*Angrily to* YÜ DAHAI) It's not a sure thing, but there's a good chance. You don't believe me?

YÜ DAHAI: I believe you. How could I not believe you? You're a member of the Chinese aristocracy, right?

YUE YANG: Just drop it.

YÜ DAHAI: (*Ignoring* YUE YANG; *lashing out at* LI JIANGSHAN) Why is it so hard for somebody like me to get anywhere? Why is it so easy for you? I'm telling you, any "freedom" and "democracy" that there is in China goes to serve young "gentlemen" like yourself. There's none left for the regular folk.

YUE YANG: (*Furiously*) Are you guys coming or not? I'm leaving!

LI JIANGSHAN: (*Casually rocks back and forth on the balls of his feet; to* YÜ DAHAI) Please, tell me, what solution to this problem do you have?

YÜ DAHAI: (*Very angrily*) I don't have any solution. But don't be so self-satisfied, you jerk. You have your motorcycle, you go dancing, you drink, you have your women . . . you just play around. Is that all there is to life? I'm poor but I have my integrity! What do you have? You're just a hollow shell. You're a shit!

(YUE YANG's *head begins to ache as he watches the other two fight.*)

LI JIANGSHAN: Right, I'm a shit. (*Laughs*) But what about the way you're chasing after Sad Sack? What do you call that? What do you want with her?

YÜ DAHAI: You fucking dump her and now you tell me I can't look after her or help her out?

LI JIANGSHAN: Oh, things are just great now! Everything's fine! With this new policy in effect, she has tens of thousands of *yuan* coming into her hands. So hurry up and marry her! Glory to the Old Ninth. You're moving up in the world!

YÜ DAHAI: (*Indignantly*) You! . . . (*Makes a fist*)

LI JIANGSHAN: I'm selfish, you're noble. You're most admirable, very upright! Completely without fault! Your intentions are pure! You're something else, you managed to latch on to a little "surplus value" without having to dirty your hands.[48]

(YÜ DAHAI *gives* LI JIANGSHAN *a slap in the face, knocking* LI *to the ground.*)

YUE YANG: (*Rushes to break it up*) Chief! Don't!

LI JIANGSHAN: (*Gets up; calmly*) General, stand aside. (*To* YÜ DAHAI) Hit me again! Vent a little anger for Sad Sack.

YÜ DAHAI: (*Softly*) I'm just saying that a person has to make his life count for something! (*Pushes* LI JIANGSHAN *away with all his strength, exits*)

---

[48]In Marxist theory, surplus value is the difference between the real value of the work done or the commodities produced by a worker and the wages paid to that worker by the employer. Tom Bottomore, ed., *A Dictionary of Marxist Thought* (Cambridge: Harvard University Press, 1983), s.v. "surplus value and profit."

YUE YANG: (*Dejectedly*) Chief's gone. . . .

LI JIANGSHAN: (*Upset*) Gone. . . . (*Pained*) I'm so stupid! Why did I say those things?

YUE YANG: (*Not looking at* LI JIANGSHAN) Is that true, what he said?

LI JIANGSHAN: What?

YUE YANG: About you and Sad Sack.

LI JIANGSHAN: (*Sighs*) It's true.

(YUE YANG *looks at* LI JIANGSHAN, *then walks away silently.* LI JIANGSHAN *sits dejectedly.*)

LI JIANGSHAN: Chief, forgive me! I didn't mean anything. I really wish you nothing but the best, with all my heart!

(*Thinking over his troubles,* YÜ DAHAI *stands by a river.*)

YÜ DAHAI: Good-bye happiness.

(*Elsewhere,* ZHENG YINGYING *waits impatiently for* YÜ DAHAI.)

ZHENG YINGYING: Why haven't you shown up? I've had so many annoying letters and phone calls from people either asking for money or from men proposing marriage! I don't dare leave the house, and you're nowhere to be found. I'm scared to death!

YÜ DAHAI: Don't wait for me anymore. Let's just . . . end it here!

YUE YANG: (*Sitting alone by the river*) My head really hurts! How did things turn out like this?

LI JIANGSHAN: If, because of those stupid things I said . . . (*He is startled by this thought.*)

ZHENG YINGYING: Did he . . . hear some rumor?

YÜ DAHAI: No. . . .

YUE YANG: How did things turn out like this? Have we forgotten friendship? Have we forgotten that we were together in the collective? . . . (*Covers his head with his hands*)

YÜ DAHAI: (*Wretchedly*) I knew it was over when she changed from an ugly duckling into a swan.

ZHENG YINGYING: (*Thinking back*) He was happy for me, but . . . he had to force a smile. I showed him those letters of proposal as a joke, but . . . he didn't laugh! (*She is frightened.*)

YUE YANG: (*Frustrated and baffled*) Do money and status mean more than love and friendship?

YÜ DAHAI: Don't forget public opinion, . . . rumor and slander!

LI JIANGSHAN: Don't take what I said seriously! I admit, it was just jealousy! After all, I loved her. I still love her!

YUE YANG: How can things be so messed up?!

YÜ DAHAI: (*With a forced smile*) Now you two are all set. It doesn't matter anymore that she's the daughter of a "rightist" and the granddaughter of a capitalist.

LI JIANGSHAN: Can something that has been lost be found again?

YÜ DAHAI: What have I got left? I've lost the last thing that was precious to me. All I have are failure and defeat. Doesn't that make me an empty shell too? (*Despairingly*) I need a drink! Give me something to drink! (*Drinks as if crazed*)

LI JIANGSHAN: (*Stands*) I've lost myself. I can't lose my friends as well.

ZHENG YINGYING: (*Stands when* LI JIANGSHAN *stands*) I've already lost Hatoyama. I can't lose Chief too.

YUE YANG: (*Stands when* LI *and* ZHENG *stand*) Chief, where are you?

KEYBOARDIST: (*Solemnly*) He got drunk and got in a fight. He's been thrown in jail!

YUE YANG, ZHENG YINGYING, and LI JIANGSHAN: What?! (*Startled, they watch as* YÜ DAHAI *is thrown into a jail cell. He struggles. Large, powerful but unseen hands push him, and he falls to the floor.*)

YUE YANG: (*Despairingly*) Chief! Chief!

ZHENG YINGYING: Chief!

LI JIANGSHAN: (*Brokenheartedly*) Chief.

(YÜ DAHAI *comes to; he sits up in a daze.*)

YÜ DAHAI: It's dark out? Damn! I'm late for work. (*He gets up and runs, but hits a wall.*) Where's the door? Where's the door? (*Gropes*) This is crazy! Am I dreaming? (*Bites his hand and finds that it hurts*) Where am I? . . . What is this place? (*Realizing where he is, he is terror stricken.*) How did I get here? Let me out! I've got to get to work. Master Liu is waiting for me to come on shift so he can go eat. He's got somebody sick at home too. . . . (*Losing hope*) Okay, I'll just stick it out for a week. . . . No! How can I stay here? What will people think? At the factory, General, Sad Sack . . . (*Pounds the door with his fists*) Open up! Open the door! Let me out! . . . How can it be so stuffy in here? There's no air! It's so hot! . . . I'll never do it again! If I promise not to do it again, can you let me out? Okay? Let me out! Ah . . . (*Crying, he leans against the door.*)

(ZHENG YINGYING *cries hopelessly.*)

YUE YANG *and* LI JIANGSHAN *are in the middle of a discussion.*)

LI JIANGSHAN: This problem of his won't be easy to clear up. There's this new crackdown on crime, you know. What can I do?

YUE YANG: I don't care what trouble there is between the two of you, you've got to think of something. We can't let Chief be ruined by this.

LI JIANGSHAN: (*Slowly*) Well, then we have to find Wheelbarrow.

YUE YANG: Wheelbarrow?

LI JIANGSHAN: There is no other way. The son of a bitch is doing okay for himself. He's a cadre. He does political work in some government bureau. And, as it happens, his office oversees Chief's factory. So, if Wheelbarrow were to give the word . . .

YUE YANG: Okay . . . you go see him. (*Quietly moves to one side*)

LI JIANGSHAN: (*Understandingly*) You're not coming with me? That's okay. I hear he's been assigned housing. He's getting married.

YUE YANG: (*Thinks it over; decisively*) Let's go.

(*Quietly, they move off.*)

(JIANG YI *is fixing up his new apartment.* YUE YANG *and* LI JIANGSHAN *enter.*)

LI JIANGSHAN: Wheelbarrow!

(*It seems* JIANG YI *has already grown unaccustomed to this name; he does not answer.*)

LI JIANGSHAN: (*Slaps* JIANG YI *once on the back*) Hey! Wheelbarrow!

JIANG YI: Hey, hey! Hatoyama, brother! . . . (*Sees* YUE YANG *and is struck dumb*)

LI JIANGSHAN: Hey, the new place looks good!

JIANG YI: (*Hastily*) It's a mess. Come on in, sit down. (*Turns on a fan*) It's really hot. . . . (*Fawningly to* YUE YANG) General, when did you get back? You didn't write. I could have gone to meet you at the station.

LI JIANGSHAN: We came to talk about Chief.

JIANG YI: Yes, I just heard. Tell me, how could he do such a thing?

LI JIANGSHAN: (*Interrupting*) We don't want to talk about any of that. You have to help him.

JIANG YI: . . . Okay! All it takes is one word from General and yourself. You want a soda?

YUE YANG: (*Stands*) Let's go. (*Motions to* LI JIANGSHAN)

(LI JIANGSHAN *places a plaster figure of the Venus de Milo on the table.*)

JIANG YI: It's . . . Venus? Very nice! Very pretty!

LI JIANGSHAN: It's for you.

JIANG YI: Thank you. Thank you very much. (*Looks it over appreciatively*) This must have cost a good bit. And they're hard to find these days.

LI JIANGSHAN: Princess might like it.

YUE YANG: She's . . . she's doing well?

JIANG YI: (*Casually*) She's okay. I'm not real sure. We haven't seen each other in two months.

LI JIANGSHAN: (*Not understanding*) Aren't you getting married?

JIANG YI: Yes. We took care of the marriage registration two days ago.

LI JIANGSHAN: Which goddamn sentence is the truth?

(JIANG YI *laughs, hands them a photograph.*)

YUE YANG: (*His face turns pale*) Who is this woman?

JIANG YI: My fiancée.

LI JIANGSHAN: What?! You son of a bitch . . .

YUE YANG: What about Princess? You just . . .

JIANG YI: Guys . . . listen to me. Princess and me . . . I thought about it and thought about it, and we just weren't compatible. Imagine it, that family of hers and my family . . . My parents and . . .

YUE YANG: So why did you . . . lead her on?

JIANG YI: There . . . there wasn't any "leading her on." There was mutual consent. And furthermore, . . . she said it herself, she said that when you left, she would take up with someone else right away. I'm . . . I'm really . . . I'm sorry.

LI JIANGSHAN: You fucking moved right in, didn't you? How can you face your friends? While General's at the front fighting, you . . .

YUE YANG: Don't mention that!

JIANG YI: I . . . I have to ask you to forgive me. You know, I've always . . . I have my pride like everybody else . . . but deep down I still . . . I knew that I couldn't marry her. I'm not good enough for her. She . . . she doesn't even love me anyway. General, the feelings between the two of you are still strong. If you wanted to start things up again with her, I could arrange . . .

YUE YANG: That's enough! (*Looks at* JIANG YI *with disgust; to* LI JIANGSHAN) Let's go!

LI JIANGSHAN: Hey, Wheelbarrow, you really couldn't stoop any lower.

JIANG YI: Won't you stay for a while?

LI JIANGSHAN: Hey, wait a minute. (*Comes back, picks up the photograph*) I've seen this woman!

JIANG YI: (*Flustered*) How . . . how could that be?

LI JIANGSHAN: I have seen her. She's Bureau Director Wang's daughter. She's your boss's daughter, right? Ha ha! You jerk, what do you have to say now? Ha ha ha ha!

YUE YANG: (*Catching on*) Ha ha ha ha!

JIANG YI: (*Stares at the other two in rage; suddenly, laughs heartily, more loudly than* YUE YANG *and* LI JIANGSHAN) Ha ha ha ha!

(JIANG YI's *laughter sobers* YUE YANG *and* LI JIANGSHAN.)

JIANG YI: (*With venom*) Laugh! Why aren't you laughing? Laugh at me! I'm scrambling up the social ladder! I'm riding a woman's petticoats! I'm using people to pull myself up in the world. Why don't you guys laugh? How am I any worse than you? By what right do you become officials just because your fathers are officials? How come I'm fucking doomed to live in a tenement? You want to laugh at me for going after the daughter of a bureau director? Fine! Say I don't love her. I'm still going to marry her. Sooner or later you're going to have to treat me with respect.

YUE YANG: (*Struck dumb by* JIANG YI's *confession*) So this is how you treat Princess?

JIANG YI: (*Laughs coldly*) How did she treat you? Yeah, she's pretty, but "pretty" isn't necessarily a good thing. I would come off the night shift and I would have to go out with her to window-shop. I would have to throw down my homework and go with her to listen to some horseshit symphonic orchestra. I admit it myself, I was just some dog she played with . . . Pretty Princess! Now I understand what kind of Princess she is.

YUE YANG: What do you mean?

JIANG YI: She's "painted skin."[49]

YUE YANG: Shut up! Stand up!

YUE YANG *faces* JIANG YI. *In his imagination,* YUE YANG *picks up a whip and flogs* JIANG YI. JIANG YI *faces* YUE YANG.)

JIANG YI: Do you want to give me a whipping?

YUE YANG: Yeah, very much.

JIANG YI: Whip to your heart's content. Why don't you go to it?

YUE YANG: (*Bitterly*) Because I'm a soldier!

(LI JIANGSHAN *pulls* YUE YANG.)

JIANG YI: Humph! (*Sings as if nothing is the matter*) "The masters of the future, we are sure to be . . ." (*Suddenly, dances a few steps, then sadly wipes tears from his eyes*)

(LI JIANGSHAN *pulls* YUE YANG *to the riverbank, where they sit.*)

---

[49]In the seventeenth-century tale "The Painted Skin," a murderous demon deceives her victims by wearing a painted human skin that makes her appear to be a beautiful woman. For a translation, see Pu Songling, *Strange Stories from a Chinese Studio,* translated by Herbert A. Giles (Shanghai, Hong Kong, Singapore: Kelley and Walsh, 1936), pp. 47–57.

YUE YANG: Just now I must have looked pretty horrible, huh?

LI JIANGSHAN: You looked very dignified. Have you taken a good look at me? (*Takes out a flashlight, turns it on, shines it up onto to his face*) Much uglier than Wheelbarrow, right?

YUE YANG: What are you talking about?

LI JIANGSHAN: There's no hope for me. (*With bitterness*) I'm rotten inside.

YUE YANG: (*Angrily*) How could you be hard-hearted enough to let Sad Sack go?

LI JIANGSHAN: It wasn't like that. . . . It wasn't like that! . . . I promised her. I told her I would take charge of my own life. But I had no choice. My parents put pressure on me. They want to make me into somebody I'm not. The woman I love, they won't let me love. Women I don't love are lined up for me to choose from. The same old lady who slammed her door in my face when I was down, sweet-talked me and got me drunk, then she got her daughter all made up and sent her to my bed. . . . It's also my own fault. Most of us act like beasts when we're drunk. . . . (*The seduction of an inebriated* LI JIANGSHAN *is illuminated by the flashlight.*)

LI JIANGSHAN: I can't see her again. I'm too filthy! (*Feels nauseous*) It's like I've fallen into a sewer, I'm covered in filth! . . . I keep moving from place to place, but everywhere I go, people suck up to power, beat other people down, lie, cheat. You could say I have a lot of friends, but not one of them is a real friend. They all just want to use me. (*Smiles a smile full of irony*) They use me, I use them! But you few, real friends of mine, not one of you has come to me! Chief curses me, but don't think I hate him. No! Actually, I'm glad he does. Really! (*Stands*) We're so pitiable. I've put my hopes in Art now. Do you think I'll finally find myself in Art? (*Hangs his head, exits*)

(YUE YANG *is deep in sober, troubled thought.*)

(YÜ DAHAI *and* ZHENG YINGYING *argue stubbornly.*)

YÜ DAHAI: Go away!

ZHENG YINGYING: No!

YÜ DAHAI: Go away!

ZHENG YINGYING: I won't!

YÜ DAHAI: I'm begging you, go away!

ZHENG YINGYING: I will not!

YÜ DAHAI: I won't open the door.

ZHENG YINGYING: I'll wait.

YÜ DAHAI: I'll never open the door!

ZHENG YINGYING: I'll wait forever.

YÜ DAHAI: (*Growing frustrated*) How can you be so shameless? I've already thrown you over!

ZHENG YINGYING: (*Fighting back tears*) Go ahead, criticize me. I'm listening.

YÜ DAHAI: I've been convicted of assault. I've been fired. Do you realize this? No one will ever want me again!

ZHENG YINGYING: I want you! . . . I want you!

YÜ DAHAI: I don't want you. Leave! Go away!

ZHENG YINGYING: You need money, right? I have a certificate of deposit here for twenty thousand *yuan*. There's more too. . . . If it's money that has opened this rift between us, take it! It's yours.

YÜ DAHAI: No! It's yours.

ZHENG YINGYING: I don't want it. All I want is you!

YÜ DAHAI: (*Sighs*) I have no job and nothing to live for. Do I still exist? Twenty thousand *yuan*. The monthly interest is probably several times my old salary. (*Grievedly*) I'm supposed to take your money and spend it on food and drink and just party my life away? Not do anything with my life? What would that make me? Some kind of zombie? Some kind of bum? . . . Why do you love a bum like me? What do you want from me?

ZHENG YINGYING: I think you're still a good man!

YÜ DAHAI: Okay. (*Opens the door*) Give me that certificate! (*Takes the certificate*) This is a loan, a loan, do you understand? There is only one thing I can do. I'll start a business, open a private company and turn my ideals into reality. If I go broke and we become paupers, then I'll marry you and work like an ox to pay you back! If I make money, I'll pay you back, and we'll be even. Then I can hold my head up when I ask you to marry me! Okay?

ZHENG YINGYING: (*Laughs*) Okay. It's all in your hands! I just want to hear you say one thing: we're the same, you and me, we're both worth something!

YÜ DAHAI: (*Crying*) Sad Sack! Dear Sad Sack, I love you! (*Hugs ZHENG YINGYING tightly*)

(YÜ DAHAI *and* ZHENG YINGYING *kiss affectionately. The group mimics in chorus the drone of cicadas: "dog days—, dog days—."*)

(BAI XUE, *lying on a sofa, is lost in wistful thought.*)

BAI XUE: Paint? Paint what?! The brushes are dry. The paint's dry. There's no more turpentine. What a bastard he is! I wasted so much time on that bastard! Bastard. What a bastard!

(BAI XUE *cries, then laughs; over the sound of her laughter is heard snatches of her earlier conversations with* YUE YANG.)

BAI XUE: *Don't go. I . . . I don't want you to go!*

YUE YANG: *It's just the way I am. If I resolve to do something, nothing can change my mind, not even . . . you! (The sound of a kiss)*

BAI XUE: *You bastard! Bastard!*

(*A pause*)

BAI XUE: *You just dare come closer! I'll give you a face full of paint!*

YUE YANG: *Okay. I surrender! . . . I'm leaving tomorrow. . . . Those seed-*

lings we planted back then have already grown into trees! We can't keep wasting time.

BAI XUE: *Leave! As soon as you're gone, I'm going to find someone else.*

(*The sound of* YUE YANG's *laughter is heard.*)

BAI XUE: (*Mutters*) Bastard, bastard! (*Leans against her easel, cries silently, then dances; she trips over a kitten*) Oh! Whose kitten? (*Stands still*) You're so cute. Why are you all alone? (*Picks up the kitten*) Here, baby, come to me. I want you. What should I call you? Sad Sack? No, I can't call you that. That's the name of an old schoolmate of mine. I'll call you . . . I'll call you Bai Xue. How's that? Little Bai Xue! Little Mimi. Where are all your friends? Oh, they've abandoned you? No matter! We'll be friends! I'll give you milk to drink. I'll sing you songs. (*Sings*) "Little darlings, little darlings, give us a hint and let us guess." (*Can't go on singing*) You don't like that one? Okay, we'll switch to a nicer one. (*Sings a melancholy tune*) "An oil lamp's glow shines on the wall. The night is dark and lonely . . ."

(YUE YANG *enters, looks at* BAI XUE.)

BAI XUE: (*Singing to the kitten*) "Look back at the past, so far in the distance. Where is the road home?"

(YUE YANG *silently watches* BAI XUE. BAI XUE *lifts her head, discovers* YUE YANG *standing there. There is an awkward silence.*)

YUE YANG: (*Breaking the silence*) I'm very happy that you still remember the old songs.

BAI XUE: (*Willfully affecting a relaxed air*) Oh, I just thought of it by chance to sing for this kitten. Right, Mimi? (*To* YUE YANG) You've come to settle the score with me? I'm sorry, I don't remember anything. When I read a book, I forget each page as I turn it. And I never read a book twice.

YUE YANG: If you tear up and toss aside all your yesterdays, page by page, then your book isn't complete. Your life will become scattered and lost.

BAI XUE: Did you come here to deliver this bit of philosophy to me?

YUE YANG: I came to see someone who was once a friend of mine. She and I share some sweet memories, and we went through some hard times together. . . . Actually, I came to ask how she is going to live from now on.

BAI XUE: (*Laughs*) How will I live? The way I'm living now, of course!

YUE YANG: How long can you go on living like this?

BAI XUE: Is that any business of yours? Listen, my life is fine! What is so great about Wheelbarrow? I can find a dozen guys like him anytime.

YUE YANG: Wheelbarrow may have done some hateful things, but he's still making an effort. But what about you? (*Walks toward the easel*) You still haven't finished your painting of spring, and all around you it's already summer. Very soon it's going to be fall! How are you going to feel when everyone else is reaping the results of their efforts? What will you think then?

BAI XUE: Me? I won't think anything. I'll have lived, that's enough!

YUE YANG: Fine. This was a wasted trip! You just lie there on the couch, play with your cat, . . . waste your talent, waste your life, . . . right up until you're a chattering old woman! (*Turns and walks out*)

BAI XUE: (*Jumps up*) Hateful! Really hateful! (*She walks back and forth wringing her hands; suddenly, she stops and stares blankly at her unfinished painting, "Spring."*)

YUE YANG: (*Angrily*) I think I really have turned into a stupid grunt. I can't understand anything! (*Pauses*) I'll go back to my unit. It may be a little lonely—what do they say? "In the day, G.I. watches G.I.; in the night, G.I. watches starlight"—and there's a lot of noise and squabbling, but compared to this place it sure is uncomplicated. (*Hears something*) What's that? What are the cicadas doing singing at night? No, who's that laughing?

(*The sound of* BAI XUE'*s laughter rises; her shadow appears and disappears amid the trees.*)

YUE YANG: No, who's that crying?

(*The soft sound of sobbing is heard.*)

YUE YANG: Is that really someone crying? . . . (*Steps to one side*)

(*A young woman chokes back tears and walks listlessly toward the river.*)

YUE YANG: (*Steps back to center stage*) Who's there? What are you doing? (*The woman is about to leap into the river; startled,* YUE YANG *dashes forward and pulls her back.*) . . . Huh?! Sister?!

(PANG YUN *recognizes* YUE YANG; *she begins to weep bitterly.*)

YUE YANG: What's the reason for this?

PANG YUN: He tricked me.

YUE YANG: Because some guy took advantage of you, you want to kill yourself? What do you think I should do, then?

PANG YUN: (*Moaning*) You're a man . . .

YUE YANG: And you're no average woman. You're a college student.

PANG YUN: So what? I've had enough!

YUE YANG: What are you doing this for, really? Love?

PANG YUN: (*Growing angry*) Love? Where is there any love? It's just lies! It's all lies. My father lied to my mother, and then he left her! My mother collected scrap paper and sold popsicles to make enough money to send me to school. I . . . I told her I would finish school before I got a job. I told her I would definitely wait to have a boyfriend. But I lied! (*Laughs sorrowfully*) It's retribution! All that has happened to me is retribution for what I've done. He was married all along . . . and his wife is a real bitch. She came into my house and smashed my things up. She called me a tramp in front of everybody! I have my pride! I'm somebody too! . . . You . . . you still won't let me die?

YUE YANG: That's right! I won't let you kill yourself.

PANG YUN: Why can't I? My life belongs to me! I'm not asking for anything, and I have nothing to give. I'm sick of living! General, please help me put an end to this stupid, empty life!

YUE YANG: I won't.

PANG YUN: Don't soldiers kill people?

YUE YANG: (*Angrily*) That's on the battlefield, killing the enemy!

PANG YUN: (*She shivers*) It's cold. I'm freezing!

(YUE YANG *hurriedly takes off his shirt and drapes it over* PANG YUN's *shoulders. There is a terrible scar on* YUE YANG*'s bare chest.* PANG YUN *is speechless; not knowing what to say or do, she turns away.*)

YUE YANG: (*Smiles bitterly*) It's ugly, right? But this is nothing. Our company commander was hit in the eye and blinded. Our deputy company commander, who was just one year out of the academy, died in my arms. Just before he died, he said something odd. He said, "My wife's nickname is 'Tuantuan,' and our little girl's called 'Yuanyuan': 'Tuantuan Yuanyuan.'" Half a year went by before I understood what he meant. Together, those names mean "surround and protect." He meant that we soldiers surround and protect life! ... And you say that your life belongs only to you! How do you think that makes us feel? What do I say to my buddies when I go back to the unit? Huh?

(PANG YUN *stops crying. She lifts her head and stares at the scar on* YUE YANG's *chest. She stands slowly, then gives the shirt back to* YUE YANG. YUE YANG *puts on the shirt.*)

YUE YANG: I'll walk you home.

(PANG YUN *hesitates briefly, then walks forward.* YUE YANG *moves to follow her but almost walks into the river.* PANG YUN *quickly pulls* YUE YANG *back. Astonished,* PANG YUN *looks into* YUE YANG's *eyes.* YUE YANG *walks off with* PANG YUN.)

(YUE YANG *enters.*)

DRUMMER: General, it's been an exciting summer, huh?

YUE YANG: (*Shakes his head*) Like watching a foreign film.

DRUMMER: Are you going to keep watching?

YUE YANG: No time. I'm going back to my outfit.

DRUMMER: Well, when you're back at your post, what are you going to tell your buddies?

YUE YANG: I'll tell them that they shouldn't think of civilian life as so happy, or so wonderful, or so peaceful! There is loneliness here too, and depression. Here people also struggle and sacrifice. . . . Am I right?

DRUMMER: You would seem to be. When will we see each other again?

YUE YANG: Wait until fall. Don't they say "settle accounts in the autumn"? (*Smiles slightly, puts on his uniform jacket and cap, salutes crisply*) I'll see you in the fall! (*Exits*)

(THE GROUP *loudly mimics the singing of cicadas: "dog days—, dog days—."*)

Act Four
Autumn 1984

(*The members of the group all wear attractive, well-pressed fall clothing.*)

DRUMMER: The osmanthus has bloomed. Autumn has arrived. The sky is clear and bright. The world is awash in color. It is the season for reaping and the season for reflection.

(*The group comes together. Smiling, they greet one another, shake hands and embrace politely. They sit down together at a table.*)

DRUMMER: Ah! This is a rare event. You are all together again. But isn't someone missing?

YÜ DAHAI: That's odd. He invited us and there's no sign of him.

LI JIANGSHAN: General will show up only when the bit players are assembled.

BAI XUE: Judging by the postmark on his letter, he should have gotten back a week ago.

ZHENG YINGYING: The handwriting in the letter is a mess. I have a feeling that it's not his writing.

PANG YUN: It's his.

YÜ DAHAI: (*To* JIANG YI) So, Team Leader, I hear you've been promoted to office director.

JIANG YI: Assistant.

YÜ DAHAI: Oh. What have you been doing? Publicizing the "Five Points of Attention and the Four Beautifications"?[50] Ha ha ha ha!

JIANG YI: (*Laughs*) Oh, just busy running around in circles. Busy running around in circles.

LI JIANGSHAN: Don't give us this "oh, nothing" stuff. You're doing all right. You should take us out to dinner! (*To* YÜ DAHAI) And then there's you, the big-shot manager!

YÜ DAHAI: Sure, sure. So, we'll go Dutch treat, right? Where should we go?

PANG YUN: (*To* ZHENG YINGYING) So, how much money have you made?

ZHENG YINGYING: (*Shrugs her shoulders*) The devil knows. Ask him.

YÜ DAHAI: (*Laughs*) I can't say for sure, either. Ah, money! Worldly possessions, worldly possessions. You can't take them with you.

DRUMMER: (*Sighing*) Ah.

PANG YUN: (*To* BAI XUE) Princess, I hear that your painting "Spring" won an award. I hear it's worth twenty-two thousand American dollars on the foreign market.

BAI XUE: I'm not selling. When are you going to America?

PANG YUN: What?

BAI XUE: Aren't they sending you over to do graduate study?

PANG YUN: Yes. But I . . . Can you give "Spring" to me? Make me a copy?

---

[50] A reference to the mid-1980s campaign that called on citizens to attend to politeness, cultural refinement, order, hygiene, and morality, and to beautify outlook, language, behavior, and the environment.

BAI XUE: I don't really feel like painting at the moment. I'll give you a different one, okay?

PANG YUN: I've always thought that in "Spring" I could see my . . .

DRUMMER: Hm?

BAI XUE: Oh . . .

ZHENG YINGYING: (*Involved in a conversation with* LI JIANGSHAN) I understand. I understand.

YÜ DAHAI: (*Crossing over*) What are you talking about? His television play? (*Puts his arm around* ZHENG YINGYING's *shoulder; to* ZHENG YINGYING) Have you told him? (*To* LI JIANGSHAN) We voted for you.

LI JIANGSHAN: Thank you. Thank you.

YÜ DAHAI: But you know why your movie won't win an award? It was in the tabloids, those "romances" of yours . . .

ZHENG YINGYING: (*Interrupting*) What does that have to do with his moviemaking?

LI JIANGSHAN: (*To* YÜ DAHAI) You don't know what it's like in the arts. We're in business just like you. But with you everything is out in the open. With us everything is done under the table. Every trick in the book is used. Drop it. Let's not talk about this. It's boring!

YÜ DAHAI: What do you say to working with me, Mr. Director? (*To* ZHENG YINGYING) Huh, it's a good idea, right?

ZHENG YINGYING: You want him to work with a hustler like you? (*To* LI JIANGSHAN) Don't listen to him. You stick to writing and directing.

LI JIANGSHAN: I'm not planning to switch, anyway. Things are the same, no matter where you go. (*Lights a cigarette and moves to one side*)

YÜ DAHAI: (*To* ZHENG YINGYING) Where did you go yesterday? I made a point of finding time to come home to see you, and I brought you some good, new Japanese clothing that I managed to get my hands on. But I waited all afternoon for you for nothing!

ZHENG YINGYING: Thanks for thinking of me. (*Laughs*) Sweetheart, you've finally learned what it's like to have to wait. (*Pauses*) I went to watch Hatoyama do a shoot, okay? Afterward, I invited him out to dinner, and then we talked for a while about old times. It got late. Should I ask for your forgiveness?

YÜ DAHAI: What's the big deal? Next time, just say something. (*He is about to walk away from* ZHENG YINGYING.)

ZHENG YINGYING: (*Blocking his way*) When you came home yesterday, was it to tell me that you agree to go to court for a divorce?

YÜ DAHAI: (*Laughs*) Okay. When I have time, I'll divorce you.

ZHENG YINGYING: (*Flaring*) What are you laughing about?

YÜ DAHAI: Hey, remember where you are. (*Kisses* ZHENG YING-YING's *hand, moves away*)

DRUMMER: (*Exclaims in English*) How modern!

KEYBOARDIST: (*Laughs*) They sure are modern enough!

LI JIANGSHAN: (*Crosses to* YÜ DAHAI) What's up with you two?

YÜ DAHAI: (*Shrugs*) She hasn't hit menopause yet, has she?

LI JIANGSHAN: She's lonely. Be a little more considerate of her.

YÜ DAHAI: (*Smiles wryly*) I'm so busy I don't even have time for myself.

LI JIANGSHAN: Everyone needs a little love to make things bearable. (*To* JIANG YI) Right, Wheelbarrow?

JIANG YI: (*Nods his head*) It's no good having only money. (*Sighs*) But, then again, it's no good having only the other and no money.

YÜ DAHAI: What did you mean by that? I've been blinded by money, is that it? Well, excuse me. I buy government bonds at three thousand, five thousand a pop. I gave ten thousand to repair the Great Wall! Please, if you don't mind my asking, Mr. Office Director . . .

JIANG YI: Assistant!

YÜ DAHAI: Mr. Assistant Office Director, how much did you contribute?

JIANG YI: Don't compare yourself with me. I'm trying to live up to your example.

YÜ DAHAI: Oh, my hat's off to you! If you hadn't turned your back on me, I never would have gotten to where I am today, right?

LI JIANGSHAN: Listen, "let's talk just of friendship and not of other things."[51] Okay?

ZHENG YINGYING: I agree! (*To* YÜ DAHAI) What are you trying to start?

JIANG YI: (*Sighs; to* YÜ DAHAI) You're better off than me now. You don't have to come home from a day on the job and sit down to study for your diploma.

LI JIANGSHAN: No one has it easy. What does a human life amount to, anyway?

ZHENG YINGYING: A wretched little piece of stone!

PANG YUN: (*In English*) Small potatoes!

YÜ DAHAI: What?

LI JIANGSHAN: (*In Chinese*) Potatoes. Small potatoes . . .

(*Everyone falls silent. There is a long pause.*)

JIANG YI: What's keeping General?

ZHENG YINGYING: Really!

YÜ DAHAI: An accident?

LI JIANGSHAN: There's still fighting at the front. Maybe he's gone back to the front.

PANG YÜN: (*Leaping to her feet*) He . . . ?!

---

[51]In Act Six of *The Red Lantern*, this is Hatoyama's opening gambit in an unsuccessful attempt to bribe Li Yühe into revealing a code used by the communists. *Hong deng ji* (The red lantern) (Beijing: Renmin chubanshe, 1970), p. 36. (See also notes 1 and 45.)

BAI XUE: What is it, you chicken thief?!

(YUE YANG *is seen laughing and carrying a chicken, which he throws to the others. The group looks at* YUE YANG. *Laughter and shouting from years before is heard as the group kills and plucks the chicken.* YUE YANG *puts on his uniform cap, salutes, then exits.*)

YÜ DAHAI: He can't really have become a general and forgotten us?

PANG YUN: (*Upset*) He'll never become a general now.

BAI XUE: How do you know?

(*Silence.* YUE YANG *appears; he is in low spirits.*)

THE GROUP: General?

LI JIANGSHAN: Where have you been? We've been waiting forever!

(YUE YANG *does not speak. His countenance is downcast as he looks at the group.*)

YUE YANG: Excuse me, but which one of you is my "fiancée"? Speak up! Who is it? Who wrote this despicable, anonymous letter to the top brass? (*Holds out the letter*)

(JIANG YI *takes the letter. The others crowd around.*)

JIANG YI: (*Reading*) "Head wound . . . possibility of loss of sight . . . should retire from duty as soon as possible . . ." This . . .

YUE YANG: (*Deeply hurt*) This came just at the right time. It swept away my last shred of hope for a promotion! (*Shouts angrily*) Who wrote it?!

THE GROUP: Who was it? (*They stare at one another, then speak at once.*) That's really lousy! Really unthinking! Immoral! Who did it?

BAI XUE: (*Unperturbed*) Quit scolding. It was me.

THE GROUP: You?

YUE YANG: You . . . Do you understand the consequences of this practical joke?

BAI XUE: Of course I understand! I just wanted you to come back and finish "Autumn" with me.

YUE YANG: (*Extremely upset*) You! You . . . you! (*He is speechless.*) Fuck!

BAI XUE: Go ahead, swear! I deserve it. I'll go to your superiors and explain everything, okay?!

LI JIANGSHAN: Princess, how could you be so selfish?!

YÜ DAHAI: Haven't you ruined things for him?

JIANG YI: You went too far!

ZHENG YINGYING: Why do you still want to toy with him?

PANG YUN: (*Yelling out suddenly*) It wasn't her! . . . I wrote the letter!

YUE YANG: (*Startled*) You . . . ?

PANG YUN: That summer when you saved my life, that's when I found out. I went to talk to your doctors. . . . I had a reason to write that letter. . . . Tell us, what were the results of the checkup?

KEYBOARDIST: Examination results: Yue Yang, male. Nineteen seventy-nine: received a head injury in battle, cerebral concussion, optic nerve severely damaged; vision in the right eye reduced to twenty percent of normal, complete blindness in the right eye in the future.

YUE YANG: (*Dejected, he sits; baffled, he laughs.*) Satisfied? (*All are silent.*)

THE GROUP: (*Softly*) General . . .

YUE YANG: General! General! (*Laughs*) That's a dream! A bright, shining, glorious dream. But a dream is just a dream. (*Laughs sorrowfully*) Why am I blaming you? I'm really stupid! . . . (*To his friends*) Dreams are the opposite of what's real, right? (*Softly and with disappointment*) I am going to go blind.

PANG YUN: (*Deeply apologetic*) General!

YÜ DAHAI: General, come home! I'll use everything I own to get you cured, even if we have to send you overseas. We'll get your sight back.

ZHENG YINGYING: And there's me too! I'll contribute my part.

YUE YANG: I want to be a soldier.

LI JIANGSHAN: Come home, General! You've given enough already. I want to film the story of your life. I'll make a film called *The General of Tomorrow*. I want you for the leading role. I'm going to make that movie. I'll make it. I'm definitely going to make it!

YUE YANG: I want to be a soldier!

PANG YUN: Come home! I want to be with you for the rest of our lives! I can live with nothing. I . . . I've loved you for a long time. I need a place where I can put my love. (*Under her breath*) That scar . . . that scar . . . that scar of yours . . .

YUE YANG: I want to be a soldier.

(*The others lose their patience.*)

YÜ DAHAI: With one eye, what kind of a soldier do you think you'll be?!

ZHENG YINGYING: Are you crazy?!

JIANG YI: Face facts!

LI JIANGSHAN: What's wrong with you?!

BAI XUE: Why do you just have to be a solider?!

YUE YANG: (*Excitedly*) I'm addicted to soldiering, all right? . . . You haven't seen your friends die on the battlefield! You can't understand! . . . No, I have no chance of making general now, but how many military men really do have any chance to make general? But as long as I'm not completely blind, I can still follow my dreams! No matter what you all think of me, I'm happy with myself. To live, a man's got to have spirit; he's got to give a little something back; he's got to make something of his life. Otherwise, the day will come when he can't go on. Don't try to talk me out of this! Nobody forces anybody else to do what they don't want to do, all right? Hey, come on, let's sing a song. (*Sings*) "Are you prepared?"

THE GROUP: (*Joining in*) "Always prepared, we are the Young Pioneers."

(*The players look at one another. Suddenly, they feel self-conscious. There is embarrassed laughter. They stop singing. From the wings comes the resonant, happy sound of children singing "The Anthem of the Young Pioneers." The group listens, enthralled.*)

YUE YANG: It's children singing.

DRUMMER: That's right. They're going out onto the streets and into the alleys to pick up trash. Shall we join them?

YUE YANG: (*Moved by the innocence of childhood*) Let's join them!

THE GROUP: Should we? . . . Let's go. . . . Let's go! . . . Come on!

(*In high spirits, singing, shouting slogans such as "no littering," and waving brooms and mops, the group joins the ranks of the Young Pioneers.*)

The End

Pan Jinlian

The History of a Fallen Woman

by Wei Minglun*

Translated by David Williams,
with the assistance of Xiaoxia Williams

Does Heaven know why things happen when they do?
The protagonist of every tragedy belongs not only to history,
but to poetry as well, even though such a person has a
historical identity.
A tragedy's heroine is guilty, but at the same time innocent!
— Belinsky, *On Hamlet*

Cast of Characters

From the original story of *Pan Jinlian:*
PAN JINLIAN
WU SONG
WU DALANG
XIMEN QING
ZHANG DAHU
MATCHMAKER WANG
FIRST RASCAL, SECOND RASCAL, THIRD RASCAL

---

*Wei Minglun is presently the best-known playwright of *chuanjü,* one of the major regional music drama forms in China. Since 1950, when he was only nine years old, he has been a professional actor, then director, and finally playwright of the *chuanjü* troupe of Zigong City in Sichuan Province. He started his playwriting in 1955 and began to win national recognition in the early 1980s when two of his plays were awarded the prize of excellence in drama for 1981–1982 by the Association of Chinese Dramatists and the Ministry of Culture. Among his numerous works, *Pan Jinlian* was one of the most controversial and influential. This translation is based on the play as reprinted in *Xinhua wenzhai* (New China digest), February 1986, pp. 87–99. It was originally published in *The Dramatists' Friend* magazine, vol. 2, 1986.

Other interpolated characters:

LÜ SHASHA

SHI NAI'AN

WU ZETIAN

JIA BAOYÜ

ANNA KARENINA

A SMALL-TOWN MAYOR

HEAD JUDGE OF THE PEOPLE'S TRIBUNAL (female)

RED MAID

A MODERN PUNK

SHANGUAN WAN'ER

There are also a number of men and women doubling in supporting roles. These, from within and outside the original *Pan Jinlian,* include four soldiers, neighbors, hunters, a fierce tiger, a family servant, four women, an honor guard, and other characters.

Time: Across dynasties and generations

Place: Across continents and nations, in no specific location

Scene: A complex stage set is not required, but you will need special lighting effects. The backdrop should have a large old-style Chinese character for "play," (戏). With each scene change, this character should appear in a different calligraphic style. On either side of the stage is a two-level platform; on the one to the audience's left appears the word (荒) (absurd), and on the one to their right, the word (诞) (ridiculous).

SHE?

Offstage CHORUS: (*Sings*)

> A man of learning fictionalized Jinlian,
> And gave Wu Song his place in theater lore.
> An altar was defiled with shining knives,
> And mourning clothes were soaked with bloody gore.

(*The curtain slowly rises. The lights gradually come up on a group of carved statues depicting the scene "Wu Song Kills His Sister-in-Law." There are white candles and white drapes.* WU SONG *glares harshly at* PAN JINLIAN. *Two soldiers accompany* MATCHMAKER WANG. *One neighbor is recording her confession as three other neighbors stand watching fearfully at the side. As soon as the* CHORUS *stops, the crowd of soldiers comes to life.*)

WU SONG: (*A harsh cry*) Kill!

(MATCHMAKER WANG *gives a strange yell and seizes the door, wishing to escape. However, the soldiers catch her, lift her up, and carry her offstage horizontally. The neighbors scatter like startled birds or animals, and exit one after the other.*
   In the style of traditional Chinese drama, WU SONG *kills his sister-in-law. He performs handsprings and does acrobatic feats involving a chair. Using the short knife he has been holding in his mouth, he begins to tear at the neck of* PAN JINLIAN's *mourning clothes. He cuts to the level of her chest in a single stroke.* PAN JINLIAN *cries out tragically and clasps her chest. Her body sinks down slowly, like a leaf.*
   Blackout. Darkness everywhere, except one light on JINLIAN *lying on her stomach in a pool of blood as her eyes slowly close. This light gradually fades to blackness.*
   The wooden clapper sounds. On the steps on one side of the stage appears an ANCIENT LITERARY SCHOLAR *with a traditional thread-bound Chinese book.*)

ANCIENT SCHOLAR: Snake fangs hide in green bamboo;
                     A bee can sting with deadly dart.
                     Both these lack the poison which
                     Lies hidden in a woman's heart.

Ladies and gentlemen; as my book says in Chapter 26, Wu Song is going directly to Lion Mansion after he has killed a wanton woman. If you want to know what follows in the book, now listen to my tale as it unfolds in the succeeding chapters.

(*On the steps on the other side of the stage appears a* MODERN YOUNG WOMAN *holding a pair of binoculars in her hand.*)

MODERN WOMAN: Who is telling that story?

ANCIENT SCHOLAR: Who is asking that question?

MODERN WOMAN: Who? It's so cloudy!

ANCIENT SCHOLAR: Do you wish to see a thousand miles?[1]

MODERN WOMAN: With the help of my binoculars.

(*Together:*) Look!

(*They pass through the clouds, searching, and meet at the center of the stage.*)

MODERN WOMAN: You!

ANCIENT SCHOLAR: You!

MODERN WOMAN: Who are you?

ANCIENT SCHOLAR: Listen, and I'll tell you. (*Sings in the* kunqü *style*[2])

> I've written of millions of brave soldiers.
> My massive work will live a thousand years.
> For heroes, I have words of praise;
> Corrupt officials I oppose.
> Loyalty and righteousness I foster.
> My writing is like holy scripture.
> I myself am the humble scholar Shi Nai'an
> I myself am the humble scholar Shi Nai'an.

MODERN WOMAN: Ah, truly you are the author of *The Water Margin*.[3] For a long time, I've heard of your name, and I've always wanted to consult with you. (*Reaches out to shake his hand*) Hello!

SHI NAI'AN: (*Cupping one hand in the other before his chest, in the traditional Chinese greeting*) Men and women ought not to touch each other. What sort of a person are you? How shocking!

---

[1] In Chinese, the phrase *yü qiong qian li mu* is a line from the Tang poet Wang Zhihuan's poem "Ascending the Crane Pagoda," meaning "If you want to see a thousand miles farther. . . ." In current usage, it is often followed by the next phrase, ". . . you should ascend another flight of stairs."

[2] *Kunqü* is a renowned Chinese traditional music drama form characterized by refined melodies performed on wind instruments.

[3] One of the greatest classics of Chinese literature, *The Water Margin* by Shi Naian (also called *Outlaws of the Marsh*) is based on historical events. It tells the interwoven stories of 108 men and women who rebel against the Song government, form a brotherhood in the wilderness, and eventually receive an imperial pardon. The nearest analogue in English literature is the tales of Robin Hood and his fellow outlaws. Separate episodes are the sources for many Beijing Opera plays.

MODERN WOMAN: Are you asking me? (*Sings a modern pop song*)

> My origin lies in a beautiful state,
> A society full of bright sunlight,
> Where women are joyful and sweet,
> With youth, energy, and beauty.
> Our thoughts are acute,
> Our ambition is high.
> I'm a 1980s woman, I say with pride;
> I'm a 1980s woman, I say with pride.

(*Attempts to pull* SHI NAI'AN *into a ballroom-style dance*)

SHI NAI'AN: This is preposterous! A manifest absurdity! (*Gazes at the* MODERN WOMAN, *sizing her up*) What is your name?

MODERN WOMAN: Lü Shasha.

SHI NAI'AN: Where does your family reside?

LÜ SHASHA: Number 5 Garden Street.[4]

SHI NAI'AN: Garden Street. (*Strokes his beard*) Your abode is not far from Purple Stone Street, is it?

LÜ SHASHA: (*Laughs*) Quite far. I let my thoughts fly with the wings of my imagination across the boundaries of time and space, to arrive before you and express my respect. At the same time, however, I do feel just a touch of regret.

SHI NAI'AN: What cause do you have for regret? I will listen with respectful attention.

LÜ SHASHA: As the author of *The Water Margin,* you praise the heroic peasants who gathered on Mount Liang[5] and revolted against their imperial lords. Your sympathy for the peasant rebellion shows that your heart is in the right place. Regrettably, however, in the middle of your book you condemn women much too harshly. And you kill so many of them!

---

[4]Lü Shasha is a fictional character in a contemporary Chinese novel titled *Huayuanjie wuhao* (Number 5 Garden Street).

[5]An actual mountain in present-day Shandong Province, used as the base camp by the 108 heroic outlaws.

SHI NAI'AN: Silence! They were a bunch of wantons and prostitutes, whom I have denounced in both writing and speech. Once I condemned them, their reputations were determined for all time. If you do not believe me, then observe . . .

(SHI NAI'AN *ascends a platform, and points with his sword to the side of the stage. Four young women appear in a whirling dance.*)

LÜ SHASHA: Who are you?

FIRST WOMAN: Yan Xijiao![6]

SECOND WOMAN: Pan Qiaoyun![7]

THIRD WOMAN: Mrs. Jia![8]

FOURTH WOMAN: Bai Xiuying![9]

LÜ SHASHA: Goodness gracious, they were all made from the same bad model! All women who have fallen, sinful women; who is the worst among them?

SHI NAI'AN: Pan Jinlian . . .

(PAN JINLIAN *appears in the traditional clothing and demeanor of a courtesan and walks forward in a seductive manner. From her hand trails a silk handkerchief. The four women accompany her as they dance, aping her at every step.*
   The four women withdraw. PAN JINLIAN's *silk fan covers half her face. She turns her head and strikes a pose, with a come-hither look in her eye.*)

---

[6]In Chapter 20 of *The Water Margin*, a woman who betrayed her husband, Song Jiang, the eventual leader of the outlaw band.

[7]In Chapter 45 of *The Water Margin*, a woman who carried on an adulterous relationship with a monk in her husband's absence. Her husband discovered the affair and killed them both.

[8]A name shared by several characters who marry into the Jia family in *Dream of the Red Chamber*, any of whom can be taken to signify moral impurity.

[9]In Chapter 51 of *The Water Margin*, an itinerant actress whose "temperamental" character caused a great disturbance in a city where she was performing, leading to her own death.

SHI NAI'AN: You sources of disaster! You causes of calamity! Women and small-minded people are more trouble than they're worth.[10]

LÜ SHASHA: Old sir, that is only acording to your "subjective lenses."

SHI NAI'AN: What do you mean, my "subjective lenses"?

LÜ SHASHA: Traditional prejudice!

SHI NAI'AN: Orthodox wisdom!

LÜ SHASHA: I admit that your "orthodox wisdom" still has some influence today. But we modern people can't always be completely led around by the nose by you ancient ones.

SHI NAI'AN: Can it possibly be that you are considering reversing history's verdict on Pan Jinlian?

LÜ SHASHA: No, the words "reversing history's verdict" are too simplistic. (*She ascends her platform.*) I'm looking at things from a 1980s point of view. I am reevaluating Pan Jinlian, and I think about how this innocent and frail woman sank step by step into depravity . . .

(*Loud noises come from the gongs and drums, and four men enter, with long sleeves covering their faces.* LÜ SHASHA *and* SHI NAI'AN *exit. These four men—*ZHANG DAHU, WU DALANG, XIMEN QING, *and* WU SONG—*all fold up their sleeves and strike a pose. They then circle* PAN JINLIAN *while dancing.*

PAN JINLIAN *moves her fan to reveal her face. Her expression is not the same as before; it has changed to the gaze of a "Qing Yi" character.[11] In the following line, she uses the vocal tone appropriate to this type of woman.*)

PAN JINLIAN: (*Plaintively*) The suffering—ah!

---

[10]A paraphrase of a widespread saying originally found in the teachings of Confucius.

[11]In Beijing Opera, a type of character noted for her repressed and reserved emotions, observation of wholesome morality, and elegant manners.

RESISTANCE

Offstage CHORUS: (*Sings*)

> A cruel defloration never sees the light of day,
> But the chapel overflows with Buddhist sutras on display.
> The shadows of the knife or of the slaughter are invisible.
> The peaceful "tock" alone of the temple block is audible.

(*A group of worshipers gathers in the small private Buddhist hall of a family long known for its exemplary morality and goodness. The patriarch, ZHANG DAHU, has his back to the audience. He recites Buddhist scriptures inaudibly. The stage is calm, with only the monotonous sound of the wooden temple block.*)

SERVANT: (*Upstage*) Wu Dalang, come along with me!

(*The SERVANT leads WU DALANG onstage. WU DALANG looks around; he appears to be cautious and anxious.*)

WU DALANG: (*Thinking out loud*) The master has summoned me. My two feet tremble with fear. (*Follows the SERVANT into the courtyard*) I, your humble servant Wu Zhi,[12] kowtow before my master, Zhang Dahu. (*He does so.*)

ZHANG DAHU: Don't be so formal. Please, sit on the stool.

WU DALANG: Thank you for your kindness, sir. (*He sits on the stool, in a somewhat calmer mood.*)

ZHANG DAHU: Elder Wu, how has your business been lately?

WU DALANG: Thanks to your kindness, although my business is small, I'm doing well. Also, I'm a bachelor and my needs are few, so I'm not in bad shape.

ZHANG DAHU: Since your financial circumstances are adequate, why don't you get married?

WU DALANG: Uh ... not to hide the truth from you, sir, when a man reaches the age of forty-five, his clothes become ragged with no one to

---

[12]Wu Zhi is Wu Dalang's given name. "Da" means "the elder," and "lang" means "son."

mend them. Of course, I would like to get married, but my appearance is working against me. I'm weak and mediocre; who could possibly have a good opinion of me?

ZHANG DAHU: Don't give up on yourself. You're honest and tolerant, sincere and law abiding. All these characteristics mean that you measure up to the ideal of a virtuous, obedient subject. I congratulate you. (*Bows with clasped hands, and sings*)

> The star of blessing shines upon your life.
> Your old age sees you furnished with a wife.
> A decade ago, I hired a girl, a peasant
> In this time, her beauty's grown quite pleasant.
> She's quick and skillful at embroidering birds,
> At music, singing, and reciting poets' words.
> All here is calm, and yet she's often gloomy.
> The seer I questioned told the reason to me:
> Last life, she failed to make a marriage with you.
> This life, she'll surely pay her debt that's due.
> All in the world is under fate's decree;
> Fate, unseen, drives everything we see.
> You, a baker, will possess this flower—
> Heaven wills it with its mighty power!

WU DALANG: Can this be true? (*Sings*)

> I've been a bachelor for years and years;
> Sent by Heaven, a lovely wife appears.
> I'm happy and suspicious, both;
> Delighted and perplexed, both.
> Shorty Wu has a conscience; I wonder
> If this wedding may not be a blunder.
> A young woman married to ugliness—
> Sire,
> To me, this match means happiness,
> To her, it brings fatal distress.

ZHANG DAHU: Heaven has arranged this match, so you should not decline it. Now, I will call her out so you can see her, and then we will talk further. (*Calls out*) Servant!

SERVANT: (*Enters*) Yes, Master?

ZHANG DAHU: Summon Jinlian to make some tea to serve to the guest.

SERVANT: Yes, sir. (*Calls out*) Listen, Jinlian, make some tea and serve it to the guest.

PAN JINLIAN: (*Answering from within*) Coming!

(*The* SERVANT *leaves.* ZHANG DAHU *begins to recite Buddhist scriptures inaudibly.* WU DALANG *does not dare to pursue the conversation further, so he sits off to one side, and dozes off.* PAN JINLIAN *strolls onstage.*)

PAN JINLIAN: (*Sings*)

Last night, autumnal moonglow made the gardens bright.
I leaned upon the rail and saw a twin star's light.
My parents died when I was still a baby,
When young, I ached for warmth and friendship daily.
I weary of depending on this wealthy family.
I love to hear the flower vendors' calls; my soul
Follows the tiny butterfly over the wall.
Like a sleepwalker, through the crowd I float,
Searching for someone to share my heart.

ZHANG DAHU: Why hasn't she come yet? (*Pounds the table*)

(*The gongs and drums beat quickly.*[13] PAN JINLIAN *responds and comes forward holding a teacup with both hands.*)

PAN JINLIAN: Master, please have some tea.

ZHANG DAHU: Our honored guest is over there; now hurry and serve the tea to him.

PAN JINLIAN: Right away, Master. (*Bows her head while offering the tea*) Honored guest, please have some tea.

(WU DALANG *accepts the tea. He raises his head and looks up. It seems as if he is meeting a legendary goddess, and he is struck dumbfounded.* PAN JINLIAN *looks down at the dwarf, who is staring blankly while holding the teacup. She stifles a laugh, but she cannot help smiling.*)

CHORUS: (*From behind the curtain*) Ah, the sharp contrast—

WU DALANG: (*Aside, sings*)

From Heaven has fallen a beauty most attractive!

---

[13]The rhythm used here is called *yun li bai* (white cloud).

PAN JINLIAN: (*Aside, sings*)

> The earth has cast up a midget most repulsive!

ZHANG DAHU: (*Aside, sings*)

> That ugly old dwarf is only three inches tall.
> This young pretty maid has a hundred-charm smile.

PAN JINLIAN: (*Aside, sings*)

> I laugh because I don't know why you're so uneasy.

WU DALANG: (*Aside, sings*)

> I wish to find a place to hide, because my heart's
> so queasy.

ZHANG DAHU: (*Aside, sings*)

> This girl is like a thorny wild rose bush.
> That dwarf obeys the law, but with a spirit made
> of mush.

WU DALANG: (*Sings*)

> I am entering the land of dreams!

PAN JINLIAN: (*Sings*)

> Are things as suspicious as they seem?

WU DALANG: (*Sings*)

> I wish I knew what to do . . .

PAN JINLIAN: (*Sings*)

> I must ask a question, too . . .

ZHANG DAHU: (*Sings*)

> I will lead, but I won't state my views.
> I will listen to whatever reply ensues.

WU DALANG: (*Wishing to decline the marriage*) But, Master . . .

ZHANG DAHU: Go home and think things over very carefully. Come back tomorrow and we'll settle matters once and for all.

WU DALANG: I will obey your command. Farewell!

PAN JINLIAN: Excuse me, honored guest, your teacup!

(WU DALANG *only then suddenly realizes that he is still holding his teacup. He returns it to her with a gesture of thanks. He wants to say something, but instead he holds back. With a sad and troubled expression on his face, he leaves the hall.*)

ZHANG DAHU: Jinlian, what do you think of this person?

PAN JINLIAN: An ugly person does many strange things. It's quite amusing. (*Smiles with tightly pressed lips*)

ZHANG DAHU: You may smile all you want, but your old Master will insist upon bestowing you, in writing, upon Wu Dalang. Accompany him "smiling" for the rest of your life!

PAN JINLIAN: (*Alarmed*) Ah! (*She doesn't believe him, and innocently asks*) Old Master, with all due respect, were you speaking in jest just now?

ZHANG DAHU: In jest? Hmph! I thought you kept on saying that you were weary of a rich, noble household, and that you'd rather marry into a poor, mean one. I can help you achieve your aim by marrying you off to the dwarf baker. The work of baking will certainly reduce the pride in your bones!

PAN JINLIAN: (*Dropping the tea tray, and giving out a long cry*) My heavens! (*Sings*)

> Vile play! This deliberate mismatch occurs at
>   your behest;
> You pose as Buddha, but your heart is cruel.
> The book of marriage becomes the book of Hell.
> This servant girl is forced to do as you request.
> A slave is like a mute who eats bitter thatch.
> The sharpness pricks her mouth like fire;
> She cannot swallow without pain,
> She cannot give voice to her rage.
> She suffers from her smothered ire.
> Two rows of teardrops etch her face.

ZHANG DAHU: Oh, crying is useless. If you are open to talks and discussions, this marriage might be changed or modified.

PAN JINLIAN: Please, explain *how* it might be changed. How could it *possibly* be modified?

ZHANG DAHU: (*Changing to a low, menacing tone of voice*) You do not wish to wed Wu Dalang. Very well; it is either do that, or you will become the concubine of your old Master. It must be the one or the other. Jinlian, listen to me now . . .
(*Sings*)

> One-half of this city is mine.
> As my wife, your status will be great.
> A servant being served—how rich a fate!
> You'll have slave girls as my concubine.
> Reflected in my glory, you will shine.
> I'll play the cowherd, you the pretty weaver.
> We will be inseparable forever.[14]

PAN JINLIAN: (*Sings*)

> You are a beast in human form,
> You are a beast in human form.
> With sneering face, you ask me to wed *whom*?
> Bitterness lies everywhere, I learn.
> No matter whom I wed, distress and doom!
> Is there some third way that I can turn?
> Yes—to sink into the lotus pond and end my gloom.

(PAN JINLIAN *quickly starts to flee the Buddhist hall. A gust of night wind blows through the open door. She pauses.*)

ZHANG DAHU: The wind is blowing so wildly that the trees are shaking. Don't do anything rash.

CHORUS: (*From behind the curtain*)
The treetops toss and the branches sway!
The wind says, "Don't go!" the moon, "Please stay!"

PAN JINLIAN: (*With great emotion induced by the turbulent scene, sings*)

---

[14]A famous couple from Chinese mythology. The woman, Zhi Nü, originally a star, fell in love with the cowherd Niu Lang. She descended to the earth as a human being, married him, and bore him two children. Both Zhi Nü and Niu Lang became constellations, but her mother kept them separate by means of a river, the Milky Way. On the seventh day of the seventh lunar month of every year, however, sympathetic magpies build a bridge across this river so they can meet. The image is thus highly ironic here.

Grass and trees have sympathies, the moon and
wind are smiling.
My young womanhood is blossoming.
Truly I should stay alive a few more years,
Though forced to swallow bitter wine with tears.

ZHANG DAHU: Whom will you marry?

PAN JINLIAN: (*Sings with conviction*)

I would greatly prefer to wed the dwarf
Than be the consort of a jackal or a wolf.

ZHANG DAHU: (*At his wit's end, sings*)

This rose has jabbed my hand with her prickly thorn.
The mermaid simply will not take my bait.
Verbal art cannot compare with force.
In this Buddhist hall, why not just take her as my mate?

(*The gongs and drums play loudly. PAN JINLIAN sees the dangerous situation. She seizes the door, wishing to escape, but ZHANG DAHU grabs and restrains her. He turns her body and shuts the door. With a leering smile, he draws her close to him, intent on assaulting her. PAN JINLIAN resists fiercely, and bites DAHU hard on the wrist.*)

ZHANG DAHU: (*In pain*) Aaaaah!

(*JINLIAN grabs a candlestick and raises it in self-defense.*)

ZHANG DAHU: Just keep this up, missy, and I will see to it that you *do* marry the dwarf! Your life will be a sea of bitterness with no shore!

(*Blackout. The drums and gongs play, and then the pipa[15] plays a solo. On one platform there appears a resplendently dressed YOUNG MAN wearing a magnificent golden headdress.*)

YOUTH: (*Sings in the Shaoxing-opera style[16]*)

---

[15]*Pipa*, a plucked string instrument with a fretted fingerboard.

[16]Shaoxing is a city south of the Yangtze River. The opera style that originated in this area and uses its dialect is one of the major regional music drama forms in China. Its music is light and flowing, and the instrumental accompaniment is sparse or entirely absent.

"Men are made of mud, and women of water."[17]
Slave girls suffer more than other daughters.
Women worry, but slave girls feel great pain.
The magnitude of her grief is plain:
It's as large as a looming, distant peak
And constant as a winding, flowing creek.

(*On the other platform,* LÜ SHASHA *reappears.*)

LÜ SHASHA: Hey, this handsome young man seems really familiar. What movie did I see you in?

YOUTH: I am Baoyü, from the Joyful Red Courtyard.[18]

LÜ SHASHA: (*Cannot help laughing*) You've come in through the wrong door. You've confused *The Water Margin* with *Dream of the Red Chamber*. Second Master Baoyü, your appearance on the stage makes people think of Mr. Cao Xueqin, who always took the side of the beautiful, unfortunate female souls.

JIA BAOYÜ: Speaking of Mr. Cao; as compared to Mr. Shi in his treatment of women, these literary giants differed widely in their appraisals.

LÜ SHASHA: The play finished on this stage just now is a rough draft I wrote. What do you think of it?

JIA BAOYÜ: The plot material is from *The Water Margin,* but the narrative follows *Dream of the Red Chamber*.
(*Sings*)

> In the bitter sea, Yuan Yang[19] drowns.
> Jin Chuan's[20] ghost once more returns.

---

[17]A famous line spoken by Jia Baoyü, the central male character in *Dream of the Red Chamber*. According to Chinese thought, because women are more sensitive, they suffer more from the effects of pure and gentle emotions.

Dream of the Red Chamber is the outstanding classic novel of the early Qing dynasty (1644–1911). The author, Cao Xueqin, belonged to a Manchu family that had fallen on hard times. He was the first Chinese writer to use autobiographical material in a novel. At his death in 1763, he left eighty chapters; relying partially on his notes, his friend Gao E added forty more chapters to constitute the work as it is known today. Throughout its depiction of the collapse of a noble family, one of the book's main themes is the general superiority of women to men in matters of morality.

[18]In *Dream of the Red Chamber,* the living quarters of Jia Baoyü, where most of the novel's action takes place.

[19]In *Dream of the Red Chamber,* a servant girl to Baoyü's grandmother. Desired as a concubine by Baoyü's uncle, she refuses and instead commits suicide.

[20]In *Dream of the Red Chamber,* a lower-level servant girl. When Baoyü's mother

If Pan Jinlian entered *Dream of the Red Chamber,*
Twelve tragic beauties as kin would claim her.

LÜ SHASHA: (*Sings*)

Ba Jin's book *The Family*[21] has inspired me
To note recurrent pairs across the dynasties.
Does Feng Yueshan resemble Zhang Dahu?
Can Pan Jinlian be taken as Ming Feng,[22] too?

JIA BAOYÜ: (*Sings*)

Where is the Third Young Master Jue Hui?[23]

LÜ SHASHA: (*Suddenly struck by an inspiration*) No need to look any
further—you yourself are Jue Hui!

JIA BAOYÜ: Me?

LÜ SHASHA: (*Approaches him and sings*)

The Second and the Third Master[24] are twins!

JIA BAOYÜ: (*Sings*)

I will dash into *The Water Margin* to rescue the
vulnerable woman—

LÜ SHASHA: Too late. (*Sings*)

The vulnerable woman is fluttering down Purple Stone Street.

(*The two people each climb up to their respective platforms and look
around.*)

---

glimpses her flirting with Baoyü, she condemns her and orders her cast out of the
mansion. Forced to choose among humiliation or poverty, she drowns herself.

[21]The first book in a trilogy of novels, written in the 1930s by Ba Jin. Set in the earlier
decades of the twentieth century, it vociferously protests the injustices intrinsic to the
traditional Chinese family system.

[22]The maid in *The Family* who kills herself rather than endure an arranged marriage to
a wealthy old man named Feng Yueshan.

[23]One of the leading male characters in *The Family*. He views the servant class with
compassion and rebels against the patriarchal structure of the family.

[24]In *Dream of the Red Chamber*, Baoyü is called "Second Master" (i.e., the second son),
while in *The Family*, Jue Hui, the third son, is called "Third Master." Both are distinguished
by their sympathy for oppressed women, although in different time periods.

FEELING WRONGED

PAN JINLIAN: (*Sings from offstage*)

> The years have ebbed away.
> My clothes and face have changed.

(*A small gong sounds.* PAN JINLIAN *enters, dressed in the clothes of a common woman. In pantomime, she acts out the steps of making rolls.*)

JIA BAOYÜ: (*Not understanding her actions*) Please tell me, what is Elder Sister Jinlian[25] doing?

LÜ SHASHA: She's kneading dough.

JIA BAOYÜ: Ah! Kneading dough and making rolls.

(*While* BAOYU *is speaking, he imitates* JINLIAN's *movements.* SHASHA *cannot restrain herself from beginning to dance with him.* SHASHA's *movements gradually transform into a disco dance.* JINLIAN *is lost in thought as she continues to work the dough. The three people gradually approach each other, and they bump by accident.*)

PAN JINLIAN: Who's that?

(*The three people separate.* JINLIAN *covers her face with her sleeve, but she sneaks a peek and directly meets* BAOYU's *gaze. She pauses, and is struck by a mistaken idea.*)

PAN JINLIAN: Ah, I see. A perfectly matched young couple!

JIA BAOYÜ: (*Behind his sleeve, to* SHASHA) Ha ha, she thinks the two of us are lovers!

LÜ SHASHA: It's a misunderstanding. By mistake, you've blundered into the middle of my "play." In order to escape from it, just go!

JIA BAOYÜ: I most certainly will not leave!

---

[25]In *Dream of the Red Chamber,* Baoyü is surrounded by women who are older than he is. By addressing Pan Jinlian as one of them, he shows his courteous nature.

LÜ SHASHA: (*Anxiously crying out his nickname*) Prince of the Devils,[26] go quickly!

(SHASHA *pulls* BAOYÜ *offstage out of sight, and* JINLIAN *opens the door. She looks around; seeing no one, she concludes that it was only a vision.*)

PAN JINLIAN: My eyes are playing tricks on me. There's no one here. (*Sings*)

> While I was baking, my heart went rushing from
>   the room.
> In my vision, pairs of lovers walked down the street.

(JINLIAN *fantasizes about walking down the Street of Flowers. She ends her happy daydream and sinks into sadness, heaving a deep sigh.*)

PAN JINLIAN: (*Sings*)

> My hands on the kneading board shape the dough,
> But I am like dough being shaped by fate's hands.
> I share Dalang's bed, but I don't share his dreams.
> Marriages that are forced produce only woe.
> Our souls do not connect, no love is there;
> No amorous feelings, and consequently no heir.
> I must improve my mood as best I may.
> Embroidering, drawing lots, I pass my day.
> I hope Dalang will stand up like a man!
> I hope Dalang's mind shows enlightenment!
> He ought to have a husband's lofty pride,
> He ought to come back quickly to his bride,
> I'll go upstairs and have a look outside . . .
> The window opens on a vanity fair,
> Variety of every sort is there;
> Many types of people wander around,
> Onstage, drums and bamboo flutes resound;
> Kites fly high in colorful clouds and touch the sky
>   so blue,
> Educated women saunter by, a youthful crew.
> One, oh, one,
> One, two, three,
> Three, two, one,
> One, two, three, four, five, six, seven,

---

[26]Baoyü is often so called because he does not always behave according to convention.

Seven, six, five, four, three, two, one . . .
Ah, that old hat is Dalang's—here he comes!

WU DALANG: Let's go! (*Waves his shoulder pole in a dancelike movement as he sings*)

> My pole is slow, but I have flying feet.
> I wear my hat down low to hide my face.
> I plan my route so thugs and I won't meet.
> My home is certainly the safest place.

(PAN JINLIAN *descends, opens the door, and greets him as he enters.* WU DALANG *closes the door.*)

PAN JINLIAN: Dalang, you have been working hard.

WU DALANG: Whew, this business is so difficult! In Qinghe County, I suffered from the arrogance of local bullies. It was said that if we came to Yanggu County, we would be safer. I didn't expect that this area's bad guys would be even worse. They come to get my baked goods without any payment, and their leaders just take whatever they want. It's impossible to run away from those people!

PAN JINLIAN: All crows under heaven are black; where do you think you can hide from evil? Kind people are hurt by the bullies, and good horses are ridden by men. Don't falter, but hold your head up high and walk proudly. Straighten up and be a man, Dalang; don't be such a sheep!

WU DALANG: Ai, yielding a bit always gives one some breathing room. Since I'm so short, how can people not look down upon me?

PAN JINLIAN: Short? (*Encouragingly*) It doesn't matter how high or low a mountain is; if it's inhabited by a spirit, it will be famous. It doesn't matter if a man is short or tall; if he has self-respect and fortitude, he will stand up. Don't you know that Li Tai Bai[27] was less than five feet tall, but his heart was so great that he moved millions of people? Yan Pinzhong[28] was also

---

[27]The "style name" of Li Bai (701–762), one of the greatest poets of the Tang dynasty (A.D. 618–907) and of all Chinese literature. Such a name was taken by men upon reaching the age of twenty and used on more formal occasions.

[28]Style name of Yan Ying (d. 493 B.C.), a student of Confucius. An important prime minister of the state of Qi, he was noted for exemplary frugality.

short, but he brought the state of Qi into order out of utter chaos. Pang Shiyuan[29] looked ugly, but he judged hundreds of cases.

WU DALANG: All right, all right, you can talk about literature and history all you like, but it's as useless as playing classical music for cows.[30] I get nothing out of your tales of ancient sages. Let's talk about our own situation and time.

PAN JINLIAN: Certainly. There are short people who are heroes alive right now. (*Gently*) Not far from here, there is a windswept mountain. On this mountain, there is a man who is the head of an outpost. He is a famous dwarf nicknamed "The Short-legged Tiger."[31] Do you hear his nickname? Isn't he a hero and a virtuous man?

WU DALANG: Shut up! (*Hurriedly covering* JINLIAN's *mouth*) He is in rebellion against the imperial rule! To revolt is to be a traitor. You shouldn't praise him, and I certainly can't imitate him!

PAN JINLIAN: (*Angrily*) I'm not telling you to go out and become a rebel, I'm only telling you to increase your ambitions a little!

WU DALANG: Once a horse is ill fed, its fur becomes bedraggled; once you are poor, your ambitions become low. We'll just close up shop if business continues to be so difficult. From that point on, you follow me to my home village to be a farmer. I want only a little piece of land, one cow, and a warm bed for my wife and child.

PAN JINLIAN: A child. (*The subject strikes a chord in her.*) We are such a mismatch, how do you think we can possibly ever have a child? (*Depressed, she sits silently off to one side.*)

WU DALANG: That . . . (*A careful and apologetic smile*) My love, don't be angry with me. Today I've bought something I hope will make you happy. (*Fetches out something*)

---

[29]Style name of Pang Tung, who helped the ruler Liu Bei administer the land of Sichuan during the Three Kingdoms period (A.D. 222–280).

[30]*Dui niu tanqin,* a common idiom. The English equivalent is "casting pearls before swine."

[31]One of the heroes of *The Water Margin,* who fights actively against the Song government.

PAN JINLIAN: A puppet!?

WU DALANG: This wooden-headed baby is healthy and plump, smiling and giggling. Let's adopt him as our family's child. This baby will accompany his mommy and make her happy. (*Mimes playing with a baby*) "Pound the pestle hard in the pot, baby won't eat tofu that isn't hot . . ." (*Trying to amuse* JINLIAN) Mama should be smiling, mama should be smiling, she's smiling, she's smiling, ha ha . . .

PAN JINLIAN: (*Smiling wryly*) Having a wooden baby is better than having none at all. (*Mocking herself*) Today I'm married to my husband and I follow him; later, after he dies, I'll follow my son. My whole life, I'll rely on my husband and my son. This is my fate, so let's play with baby here! (*The couple plays with the puppet as they exit. The* THREE RASCALS *enter.*)

THE THREE RASCALS: (*Sing*)

> In my hand, I hold my seven-fold fan lightly;
> A birdcage on my shoulder has a thrush singing
> obediently.
> In my fish-tail slippers, I casually stroll by,
> My sleeves bearing dragons are flowing high.

(*A man's voice calls out from behind the curtain.*)

VOICE: Forefathers, wait a minute!

(*A* MODERN PUNK *rushes on, wearing Frogskin-brand sunglasses, long curly hair, a flowered print shirt, and very tight pants—the height of Hong Kong hipster style.*)

THE THREE RASCALS: (*Amazed*) Where on earth did that oddball come from?

MODERN PUNK: You of the older generation, good things always happen in pairs. If you add me to the three of you, we'll be a *pair* of pairs.

FIRST RASCAL: Who are your ancestors?

MODERN PUNK: You have a descendant in me, and I have ancestors in you. Five hundred years ago, we were together in one family. Birds of a feather flock together in any dynasty. On this kind of occasion, if you don't take me along, you'll be missing a really tasty flavor. If you do, things can only look more gorgeous. (*Does a rock and roll dance*)

FIRST RASCAL: Your clothes are all mixed up, neither male nor female. The underworld has its codes, you know. Go back, paint your face appropriately and make yourself look like a real man, and then you'll be welcome to join us.

MODERN PUNK: Right. You ancestors lead the way, and I'll change my clothes and come back.

THE THREE RASCALS: Go! (*They dismiss him with a specific underworld courtesy.*)

MODERN PUNK: Bye-bye! (*Exits, whistling*)

FIRST RASCAL: After a little walk, here we are at the corner of Purple Stone Street.

SECOND RASCAL: Hey, shorty, open the door! (*He knocks on the door. WU DALANG and PAN JINLIAN enter, startled by hearing the knock.*)

WU DALANG: Wife, the Rascals are knocking at the door. What should I do?

PAN JINLIAN: Those Rascals specialize in extorting money from people who don't fight back. If you act like a punching bag, that will only encourage them.

WU DALANG: I, I'm really afraid!

PAN JINLIAN: Dalang, go back to the bedroom and rest. I will deal with them!

WU DALANG: Wife, please be sweet and don't say anything to make them angry.

(WU DALANG *exits, and* PAN JINLIAN *opens the door. The* SECOND RASCAL *sticks his head in wishing to enter, but* JINLIAN *blocks the way. The* SECOND RASCAL *raises his head and carefully examines her.*

Stunned by her beauty, he retreats and treads on the FIRST RASCAL.)

FIRST RASCAL: Ouch! Have you run into a ghost and lost your wits?

SECOND RASCAL: When I opened the door I saw a painting, and in the painting was a flower! (*Pointing*)

FIRST RASCAL: (*Comes forward and sizes her up*) What sort of a person are you?

PAN JINLIAN: (*Neither humbly nor arrogantly*) You tell me, what kind of people are you?

FIRST RASCAL: I fly around in the sky.

SECOND RASCAL: I run around on the earth.

THIRD RASCAL: I climb around in the trees.

MODERN PUNK: (*Enters*) And there's me, too! (*He has on an ancient costume, draped askew over his shoulders.*) I am Mr. Quick-change! (*On the spot, he whitens his nose with makeup.*[32])

PAN JINLIAN: My goodness, you certainly are a colorful bunch of wild creatures! What have you come here for today?

FIRST RASCAL: We have come to find Wu Dalang and collect "head money" from him.

PAN JINLIAN: Please tell me, what is "head money"?

FIRST RASCAL: Every one of the seventy-two existing trades has a union. Even beggars have a sort of guild. Wu Dalang came to this territory to do business. All of us flew here—

SECOND RASCAL: Ran here!

THIRD RASCAL: Climbed here!

---

[32]His face thus resembles that of the "Chou" role, a clown or a villainous character in Beijing Opera and other regional music dramas.

MODERN PUNK: Transformed here!

FIRST RASCAL: Of course, we must get a percentage of his earnings—that is what we call "head money."

PAN JINLIAN: Outrageous! (*Methodically*) "Head money" is like a comb with knives for teeth. When poor people's hair is scarce, the government officials come to comb, the soldiers come to comb, the lackeys come to trim, and you rascals have come to shave. You have come too late: we have nothing for you to put in your money "clip."[33]

FIRST RASCAL: Oh! (*Rolls his eyes*) Listen to her! She's really pulling out all the stops. It seems as if she's from a real upper-crust family.

MODERN PUNK: Where do you come from? (*To the* FIRST RASCAL) If I were you, I would be careful not to get on her bad side; it could cause great pain as pointed stones would.

FIRST RASCAL: (*Turning with a toadying smile to* JINLIAN) There, Elder Sister, please allow me to introduce myself. (*Bows*)

PAN JINLIAN: Those who respect others win respect for themselves. If you respect me, I will respect you. Since you have bowed to me, I will bow to you.

SECOND RASCAL: Excuse me, ma'am, but is Wu Dalang affiliated with you?

PAN JINLIAN: We are affiliated.

FIRST RASCAL: And are connected?

PAN JINLIAN: Connected.

FIRST RASCAL: How exactly is he affiliated or connected with you?

PAN JINLIAN: He's my husband.

ALL THREE RASCALS: Aha!

---

[33]Approximating a pun on the word *fa* ("hair" or "way") in the original.

MODERN PUNK: I can't believe that you are Wu Dalang's wife.

FIRST RASCAL: Strange, how can a lovely flower like you be stuck in cowshit like this?

PAN JINLIAN: (*With an angry expression*) How dare you!

SECOND RASCAL: Wu Dalang sure has wonderful luck, just like an old bull getting to eat young, tender grass!

PAN JINLIAN: And how dare you!

MODERN PUNK: A tall beauty and an ugly dwarf—what a pair!

PAN JINLIAN: (*Extremely angry*) You, you dare say that again!?

FIRST RASCAL: Say what again? This wild flower is fragrant—I believe I'll sample her sweetness. (*Stretches out his hand and tries to caress her*)

PAN JINLIAN: You rude creep! (*Gives him a resounding box on the ear*)

FIRST RASCAL: Owwww! (*His spirit crushed, he retreats with his cohorts.*)

PAN JINLIAN: (*Angrily denouncing the* RASCALS, *sings*)

> That box on the ear should make your head spin.
> That ought to teach you to respect Pan Jinlian!
> My body is female, but a man's heart beats within.
> Though I only wear hairpins, I don't fear your weapons.
> My fist can make a person who stands on it tough.
> My arm can endure a horse's prancing hoof.
> A wilted rose lacking petals still has thorny spines;
> I dare you, you dregs, to fight me anytime!

(JINLIAN *turns and enters the room to fetch a bamboo staff.* WU DALANG *follows her back onstage, trying everything he possibly can to stop her. He roughly shoves* JINLIAN *back into the room and closes the door behind her.*)

WU DALANG: Oh no, stirring up those bad guys against us will only bring us big trouble!

PAN JINLIAN: Open the door, I'll give them hell!

(JINLIAN *beats at the closed door for a while, then turns and goes up-*
stairs. She leans looking out of the window. The RASCALS *have been*
badly shaken by JINLIAN's *outburst, but after they see* WU DALANG's
attitude of appeasement, their pretensions rise once more.)

FIRST RASCAL: That woman is really savage. Brothers, let's muster our
strength and force our way in!

WU DALANG: (*Quickly clasping his hands together in a gesture of con-*
cession) All of you, please don't be angry. The woman of the household has
a bad disposition. She's offended you, masters. I'll come and apologize for
her. Please, all of you, forgive me.

MODERN PUNK: It's not going to be as easy as that. Your wife hits
people in the face, and we won't stand for that! Brothers, let's burst into his
house and level it to the ground!

WU DALANG: Please, no, don't do that. The house is rented, and if you
destroy it, we can't possibly pay for it. Please, all of you, do a noble deed
and let me off kindly.

PAN JINLIAN: Dalang, don't beg them!

WU DALANG: Oh, please! Keep your mouth shut!

MODERN PUNK: (*Looking upstairs*) What, you still haven't given up? We
brothers are still angry at you!

FIRST RASCAL: Listen, half-pint, your wife gave me quite a slap. What a
wife owes, a husband pays. I'm going to punish you by making you crawl
on your hands and knees like a turtle.[34] (*Points between his outspread legs*)
Right between my legs.

THE THREE RASCALS: (*Jeering and hooting*) Crawl, crawl!

WU DALANG: Umm . . .

---

[34]A derogatory term for a cuckolded husband, and thus a great insult not only to Wu
Dalang but to Pan Jinlian as well.

PAN JINLIAN: (*Anxiously*) Dalang, you can't do such a thing!

FIRST RASCAL: If you don't crawl, we'll destroy your house.

THE THREE RASCALS: Destroy!

WU DALANG: Don't destroy it, don't destroy it!

FIRST RASCAL: If you don't want it destroyed, you'll have to crawl between my legs.

CROWD OF RASCALS: Crawl!

PAN JINLIAN: (*Calling out tragically*) Dalang, for my sake, behave like a man!

WU DALANG: (*Crushed*) The house is a real asset, and anger is not. What's the use of fighting?

FIRST RASCAL: You crawl to me!

WU DALANG: (*As is his habit, he resigns himself to the humiliation.*) I'm crawling, I'm crawling, I'm crawling!

(*From within, a wordless song rises:*) Ahh . . .

(WU DALANG *crawls between the* FIRST RASCAL'*s legs.* PAN JINLIAN *dejectedly hides her face. The* RASCALS *break into high-pitched peals of derisive laughter.*)

MODERN PUNK: Pan Jinlian has covered her eyes because she couldn't stand to look, so this matter isn't over yet. Your man is going to treat us to a meal at the Lion Restaurant to relieve our anger. Let's go! (*Pushes* WU DALANG *offstage*)

PAN JINLIAN: A feckless husband and a heartless world—my existence is disgraceful and pathetic!

(*From within, another wordless song rises:*) Ahhh . . .

(JINLIAN *bursts out wailing, and the lights fade. On the platform appears a* FOREIGN WOMAN.)

FOREIGN WOMAN: (*Sings to the tune of a Russian folk song*)

> Such a husband and wife,
> Such a household,
> Look at the world—
> All happy families resemble each other,
> But each unhappy family is unhappy in
>   its own way.

LÜ SHASHA: (*Appearing on the other platform*) From the few famous sentences she has said, we know who she is—Anna Karenina!

ANNA: (*Stepping down from the platform*) I am Anna, and I have floated here from my cold Moscow. Please tell me, what place is this?

LÜ SHASHA: Ancient Purple Stone Street!

ANNA: (*Looking up*) Who is that person up there?

LÜ SHASHA: An unfortunate woman just like you.

ANNA: Oh, I sympathize with her fate. Tell her to rebel like me, and rush out of her unhappy household!

LÜ SHASHA: Anna, that will not do. She cannot do what you did. Still less can she do what I did and get a divorce!

ANNA: What, you are divorced too?

LÜ SHASHA: (*Sings*)

> I also married most unhappily;
> I had a madman for a mate.
> But happiness can spring from misery;
> On Garden Street, the clouds have left
>   the sky.
> A pair that's mismatched has the right
>   to separate,
> A happy household comes after "Goodbye."

ANNA: (*Sings*)

> One China
> Two women
> On Garden Street, happy grins;
> On Purple Stone Street—painful groans!

LÜ SHASHA: Listen, what's that sound?

ANNA: It's horses' hooves!

LÜ SHASHA: It's cheering!

ANNA: It's a horse race! It's Vronski, in the horse race. The person on that horse is my lover, my betrayer . . .

LÜ SHASHA: Dear Anna with your heart on your sleeve, this is not a Moscow racetrack. This is a small county seat in ancient China. Watch Wu Song parade through the streets, and listen to the long blasts of the old-style horns!

(*As the two look inside, the lights fade.*)

THE PURSUITS

(*The old-style horns play, and a group of banner-bearers waving colored flags leads the way. Soldiers beat gongs, and hunters raise placards saying "Eliminate Evil for the People."* WU SONG, *draped in bright red, parades through the streets, urging his horse on. On the way, he waves his hand in greeting.*)

WU SONG: (*Sings*)

> Riding my wonderful horse amid firecrackers' pops,
> I ride through busy downtown toward the suburbs.
> The willow twig quite gently strokes my hat,
> The poplar bloom lightly gives my robe a pat.
> My life started poor, and poor many years I remained.
> One morning, my fate turned; banners now wave for me.
> Poor people, don't let your proud spirits wane.
> Even in triumph, your willpower must increase.
> You all have your own white-faced tigers to slay;
> Prepare for your own Jinyang Ridge fight someday![35]

(WU SONG *slowly ties up his horse's bridle. The horse neighs.* WU SONG *guides his horse with a whip in stylized, dancelike movement.*

---

[35]In Chapter 23 of *The Water Margin*, Wu Song defies the advice of others and enters an area where a tiger had previously killed many travelers. The tiger attacks him, but he kills it using only his fists. His name thus became a byword in Chinese culture for courage and skill in the martial arts.

LÜ SHASHA *holds a camera in her hand; she is like a news photographer who has come onstage to take pictures. She chooses an angle and adjusts the distance.*

(WU SONG *holds his horse and turns his head.*)

LÜ SHASHA: Don't move!

(*The flashbulb flashes and the flag-wavers arrange themselves in the camera frame, coaxing* WU SONG *into posing for a stage picture.*)

LÜ SHASHA: The expression in this stage picture is just right. (*Calling inside*) Pan Jinlian, don't cry, come quickly and see all the excitement!

(PAN JINLIAN *enters, hearing the noise from the street. She quickly looks around.* SHASHA *stealthily follows, and selects another angle from which to shoot a picture.*)

PAN JINLIAN: (*Sings*)

> Who is the bridegroom in red satin clothes?

LÜ SHASHA: (*Sings*)

> Wu Song, the coldhearted hero; watch him stand
> in his saddle and pose.

PAN JINLIAN: (*Sings*)

> All the town wants to catch a glimpse of this man.

LÜ SHASHA: (*Sings*)

> The tale of his tiger killing has long been well known.

PAN JINLIAN: (*Sings*)

> We praise him for saving the people from the tiger's might,
> He stands here before us, the hero of Jinyang Ridge fight!

(*The* FIERCE TIGER *jumps up.* WU SONG *brandishes his fist and hits the tiger, killing it.* SHASHA *snaps a picture.*

PAN JINLIAN *is dazzled by the sight. She leans on the railing and gazes at* WU SONG.)

LÜ SHASHA: Don't move. (*The flashbulb goes off. The flag-wavers once more arrange themselves, framing* JINLIAN *in another picture.*)

LÜ SHASHA: The angle for this picture is brilliant! (*Looks around*) I'm going to go fetch Wu Dalang. I'll take a picture of the whole family. (*Exits in search of him*)

(JIA BAOYÜ *enters. He sees* WU SONG *on the left and* JINLIAN *on the right. He suddenly has a strange illusion.*)

JIA BAOYÜ: (*Sings*)

> I look to the left, and I look to the right,
> My imagination begins to take flight.
> If *The Water Margin* had come from my pen,
> I would marry Wu Song to Pan Jinlian.

RED MAID: (*Hearing the sound, she enters.*) I have come to make this connection! (*Strikes a pose*)

JIA BAOYÜ: Who are you?

RED MAID: If you really want to know, I am the little Red Maid from *The Romance of the Western Chamber.*[36]

JIA BAOYÜ: Ha ha! (*Unable to contain his delight*) Sister Red Maid, it's wonderful that you've come here. Demolish this barrier of flag-wavers, and connect the hero and the beauty in marriage.

RED MAID: Right. I hope that all the star-crossed lovers in the world can find their happiness in marriage. I will destroy the barriers that separate them! Get rid of the barriers! Get rid of the frames!

(RED MAID *breaks through the "frame" of flag-bearers and pulls* PAN JINLIAN *and* WU SONG *toward each other, making them pose together.*

---

[36]In Chinese, she is called "Hong Niang." In the play mentioned, she exercises great energy and ingenuity in assisting two young lovers to get married. *The Romance of the Western Chamber*, written by Wang Shifu of the Yuan dynasty, is one of the greatest classics of Chinese dramatic literature; Hong Niang is one of the most popular characters loved by Chinese theatergoers.

WU SONG *and* JINLIAN *both feel this is improper, and they move apart in two separate directions. The flag-wavers once more come between the two people and surround each of them, as if in two separate pictures.*)

JIA BAOYÜ: Changing the position does not change the relationship.

RED MAID: It's just the same old wine in a new bottle.

FIERCE TIGER: (*Suddenly capable of human speech*) Red Maid, you cannot change the framework of this ancient text!

JIA BAOYÜ: (*Alarmed*) The tiger is speaking!

RED MAID: (*Ponders the idea*) The tiger has spoken the truth! (*Sings*)

> The hero and the beauty meet too late.
> Falling bloom and rushing stream have no
>   chance to meet.
> A large abyss will keep them separate.
> In-laws should not stand so close,
>   it's indiscreet.

JIA BAOYÜ: I am so disappointed.

RED MAID: We must bow to fate.

(JINLIAN *is still gazing in adoration at* WU SONG.)

RED MAID: Stop staring at him!

JIA BAOYÜ: I tell you, you adore him excessively.

RED MAID: You're getting a crush on him!

JIA BAOYÜ: Too much love is shining from your eyes.

RED MAID: Tragedy is bound to follow!

JIA BAOYÜ: Leave!

RED MAID: Go! (JINLIAN *does not move*) She's completely hypnotized. What can we do?

JIA BAOYÜ: I have an idea. (*Calls inside*) Any patrolling guards within hearing, come on out, and we'll wake her up with our yodeling!

RED MAID: One!

JIA BAOYÜ: Two!

(*Both, Shouting together at* JINLIAN:) Three!
(*From within, a loud shout*) Heyyyyy! (JINLIAN *and* WU SONG *both snap to awareness.*)

(*A deafening sound from the gongs and drums. The soldiers intermingle and circle the area, and the banner-bearers do likewise, moving like flowing clouds. They cover up the principals in the center of the stage.*
After the banner-bearers have passed, they reveal WU DALANG *in the center of the stage. He is holding* WU SONG *by the hand, and he takes him across to* PAN JINLIAN.)

WU DALANG: (*Sings*)

> On the street, we brothers meet once more.
> The in-laws are introduced before this very door.

(*Accompanied by the characteristic sounds of the old-style horns, they talk of the time when they were apart and tell each other the hardships that they have gone through. After the end of the horn music, the crowd of* RASCALS *appears onstage, completely drunk.*)

FIRST RASCAL: Open the door! Open the door!

MODERN PUNK: (*Calls out*) Hey, shorty, we brothers are all drunk and stuffed with food. We want your wife to accompany us and please us, so open the door and roll yourself out.

WU DALANG: My God, it's those scoundrels again! Speak of the devil, the Rascals have truly returned!

WU SONG: They've arrived at just the right time. I will come out and teach them a lesson!

WU DALANG: Sending them away will be enough. I can't bear the trouble they stir up.

PAN JINLIAN: You lily-livered coward, let your brother show you his strength. We'll watch it all from upstairs.

WU SONG: Brother and sister-in-law, do as you wish.

(PAN JINLIAN *pulls* WU DALANG *upstairs.* WU SONG *opens the door. The* MODERN PUNK *rushes in with drunken steps.* WU SONG *lightly pushes him. The* PUNK *at first staggers, and then does a series of somersaults and handsprings.*)

FIRST RASCAL: Oh no, did you run into a ghost again?

MODERN PUNK: I knocked that door down, and a godlike he-man appeared—(*Points to* WU SONG)

FIRST RASCAL: What kind of a god? I'll take a look. (*Gazes around drunkenly*) Well, well, well. It's not a spirit, it's a bridegroom. It's Pan Jinlian's lover!

WU SONG: (*Knocks over the* FIRST RASCAL *with one hand*) Do you want to die? Damn you!

MODERN PUNK: Brothers, let's get him!

WU SONG: I'm ready!

(*They fight. The* PUNK *takes off his outer clothes and uses Western-style boxing moves.* WU SONG *hits the* RASCALS, *beating them so badly that they quiver in terror. He hits the* PUNK, *who then reveals his true nature as a useless coward.*)

PAN JINLIAN: (*Clapping her hands*) Beat him up! Beat him up!

WU DALANG: Don't beat him anymore, you're going to kill him!

THE RASCALS *and the* PUNK: (*Making a kowtow together*) Great hero, spare us, spare us!

PAN JINLIAN: Brother, please avenge your sister-in-law, and make them crawl!

(LÜ SHASHA, JIA BAOYÜ, *and* RED MAID *rush out onto the platform where they chime in with their cheers.*)

JIA BAOYÜ: Evil reaps an evil harvest!

LÜ SHASHA: That's great news for everybody!

RED MAID: Crawl, crawl, crawl!

WU SONG: Crawl—

THE RASCALS *and the* PUNK: (*Jostling each other and starting to cry*) *You* crawl!

PAN JINLIAN: Splendid hero!

(JINLIAN *runs downstairs, kicks at the* RASCALS, *embraces* WU SONG, *and praises him lavishly.* WU DALANG'*s clothes split along the seams, and the dwarf suddenly grows taller.*)

THE CROWD: Oh, how can you possibly be growing?

WU DALANG: Brother, I've been squatting for quite a while, and I need to rest.

LÜ SHASHA: Fine. Everyone please take a ten-minute intermission.

(*A bell rings, and the crowd of people bows and disperses. After the intermission, they resume the scene.*
    Soft, lyrical music plays. PAN JINLIAN *is heavyhearted. She carries her serving tray out and sets the table with three wine cups. She frowns and takes one back, leaving the remaining two on the table. Her face now shows a happy expression, and she cannot restrain herself from spinning and spinning, holding the tray. She opens one side of the double door, letting in a gust of the north wind.*)

PAN JINLIAN: (*Sings*)

>Tonight, the north wind is in full cry;
>The door blows open, and snow lies piled high.
>That day, I served him welcoming wine;
>Today, this wine is to say goodbye.
>It was the misty springtime when we met;
>On this snowy evening, we now shall part.
>Why does it seem as if he entered my life
>>Just like a wild goose fluttering in?
>Why does it seem as if he now leaves
>>Flying like a yellow crane?
>Why does warmth strike me in his presence?
>Why does melancholy flood me in his absence?
>When I see him, why am I so full of words
>>I cannot say?
>When I do not see him, why do my thoughts
>>go astray?

CHORUS: (*From within*) Ahhhhhh . . .

Love did inwardly appear;
Catastrophe is very near.

PAN JINLIAN: (*Sings*)

>If only I'd been single when we met;
>I was not your sister-in-law, not yet.
>If you must go, please do not delay.
>My eyes are dazed as long as you do stay.
>I'll live in Dalang's house as I have done,
>And treat the wooden puppet as my son.
>Mornings, I'll read the words of sages great;
>Evenings, I'll pray and on texts for women
>>meditate.[37]
>Three obediences and four virtues[38] best guide
>>a wife,
>Like a penitent nun, I'll lead a moral life.

(JINLIAN *controls herself and hides her feelings. She picks up the serving tray and exits.* WU SONG *enters slowly, carrying a sack of official documents.*)

---

[37]Nü'er Jing, written by an unknown author, was a verse text that prescribed moral rules for women.

[38]According to Confucian morality, the "three obediences" a woman was expected to perform without question were to her father, her husband, and her son; the "four virtues" were fidelity, obsequious speech, proper appearance, and handicraft.

WU SONG: (*Sings*)

> I'm returning home to say good-bye.
> I'm returning home to say good-bye.
> The prefect gave a weighty task to me;
> To Kaifeng[39] now I must ride alone.
> I worry what may happen after I leave.
> In the world, there are evils;
> In the city, there are devils.
> My brother is law abiding;
> My sister-in-law is still young.
> We just met, but we'll quickly part again.
> I'll be far away, but my worries will be of here.
> My war-torn armor weighs my heart with
> great cares.
> I tread upon the snow as I return;
> It spreads under my step like broken jadeware.

(PAN JINLIAN *enters, welcomes in* WU SONG, *and bows to him in a manner appropriate to a sister-in-law. She sits opposite him.*)

PAN JINLIAN: Brother-in-law, the wine for this farewell dinner has been ready for some time now. We wait only for your brother and you to come to the table.

WU SONG: I thank you for taking such trouble, sister-in-law. My brother has not yet finished his business and returned?

PAN JINLIAN: Your brother! I reminded him to come back a little early, but he has always been slow and dull.

WU SONG: I shall go out into the street and look for him . . .

PAN JINLIAN: Wait. Have a drink; you are about to take a long trip. Today, you should be especially careful not to catch a chill. Sit down, drink some wine, and warm up. Wait for your brother to come home.

WU SONG: All right. I will relax for a while and drink a little wine. Sister-in-law, please, after you.

---

[39]The national capital during the Northern Song dynasty (960–1126), then called Bianjing.

PAN JINLIAN: No, after you, brother-in-law.

(*The two sip their wine, facing each other, and subside into silence.*)

PAN JINLIAN: The year is coming to an end, and this winter is particularly cold. That will make your journey to the capital even more difficult than usual.

WU SONG: I merely follow my orders and perform my official duties. I am not in full control of this matter.

PAN JINLIAN: Brother-in-law, do you also know how difficult not being "in full control" can make you feel?

WU SONG: Hmm . . . I do not fear being sent on a difficult task. I am only concerned that after I go, that group of Rascals will return; if so, they will certainly cause some more trouble!

PAN JINLIAN: I am not afraid of the Rascals. I only fear that if you go, you might not ever return.

WU SONG: To speak the truth, sister-in-law, men cannot be afraid when performing their duties. This trip to the capital is my way of serving my country. As to the day of my returning . . .

PAN JINLIAN: When will you return?

WU SONG: That is truly difficult to predict.

(*Sadness fills* PAN JINLIAN's *heart. The music swells.*)

PAN JINLIAN: (*Sings, to herself*)

> His return date is concealed by the snowy sky;
> Most difficult in life is to say goodbye.
> When he leaves, his footprints yet remain,
> When we part, his legacy is my pain.
> After he leaves—
> The mountains loom in rows, the waving rivers flow.
> They'll witness as he travels down the road.
> Men of heroic character I've always admired;

I know how to achieve they must always aspire.
His lucky horse neighs; together they soon will leave.
He looks powerful! The bandits he meets will all flee.
Inns with dirt floors and chickens will shelter his sleep.
In my small city, my lonely vigil I'll keep.
After he leaves—
His trip will be like the phoenix's glorious flight;
His world will glow with wondrous, magical light.
In the capital, he'll see the "Zhongtai willow,"
And in the south, he will see "a broken bridge
    under snow."
He'll taste "lichi in the deep autumn."
He'll witness "a ten-mile stretch of lotus blossoms."[40]
I hope he will find the one who knows his heart.
I hope he will become a rich man's son-in-law.
Next springtime, when the grass and flowers sprout,
I'll open the door and greet with smiling eyes
A flying, fluttering pair of butterflies!

(*At the sound of her own singing, a pure teardrop wells up and flows from* JINLIAN's *eye. She hurriedly conceals her mood and forces herself to smile.*)

CHORUS: (*From within*)

Stolid Wu Song, are you blind to her love?
Can't you sense her hidden meaning at all?

WU SONG: (*Sings*)

The flame heats the wine in the red clay stove.
At my farewell meal, I have three songs to give:
The first sinks my heart low, leaving makes me grieve,
As the chilly, ghostly wind stirs the yellow leaves.
The second makes me bold as I anticipate my trip.
I'm like a fearless stallion rearing proudly up.
The third will bring the day of reunion.
Cheer and warmth fill my heart like an autumn moon.
I may seem stern, but my spirit feels, truly.
Those lacking warmth cannot be heroes, surely.
Affection is like snow; snow is clean and pure.

---

[40]All these rare occurrences are allusions to famous and beautiful scenes. From the Tang dynasty onward, they were standard tropes presented in many well-known classical poems. Jinlian's point is to contrast Wu Song's adventurous trip with her own dull life in the small town.

>I shall emulate—
>Bao Gong's deep respect for his brother and
>   sister-in-law.[41]

(At the beginning of this song, PAN JINLIAN *finds his words comforting, but as she hears him out, she gradually loses hope.)*

CHORUS: *(From within)*

>Master Bao and Master Wu
>Lack the empathy for women of Jia Baoyü!

WU SONG: *(Proposing a toast with his winecup, sings)*

>The first cup is to wish my brother long life;
>The second is to honor his virtuous wife.
>The third cup . . . is hoping a treasured son comes soon,
>To continue forever the family name of Wu.

PAN JINLIAN: *(This hits her sore spot, and she is moved.)* The treasured son? *(A bitter smile)* Ha ha, I thank you, my brother-in-law, for your care. Your sister-in-law has a baby already.

WU SONG: You do? *(Happily)* The luck of the Wu family is just marvelous. Thanks to the powers that be!

PAN JINLIAN: *(Fetching the puppet)* Here, have a look! *(Lightly tossing it to him)*

WU SONG: A puppet?!

PAN JINLIAN: That's exactly it. *(Sings)*

>I accompany the lifeless puppet in the day;
>All by myself, I play.
>My companion is a live puppet in the night.
>How tragic and wretched is my plight!
>What good luck? What happiness?
>My hatred for my fate is limitless!

---

[41]Bao Gong, a historical figure from the Song dynasty, was an orphan who became a famous magistrate. He convicted his own cousin of hoarding grain during a famine and had him executed. When his sister-in-law, who had raised him, later complained that no one would look after her in her old age, Bao Gong replied that since she had treated him as a son, he would treat her as his mother.

WU SONG: Who does my sister-in-law hate?

PAN JINLIAN: (*Sings*)

> I first hate the rich and powerful family,
> Those who created this tragedy.
> They forced us into marriage.
> I then hate the coward without the stomach for a brawl.
> Between the Rascal's legs, he is willing to crawl.
> Look at him . . .

(JINLIAN *shows some signs of being drunk. She imitates her dwarf husband's resigned posture and weak manner of speaking.*)

PAN JINLIAN: "My spirit is broken. What use is struggle? I'll crawl, crawl, crawl!"

WU SONG: (*Displeased*) Sister-in-law, are you drunk?

PAN JINLIAN: Wine! (*Without hesitation, she drinks another half cup. She offers the bottle to* WU SONG, *making her affection for him quite plain. She drinks again.*)

PAN JINLIAN: (*Sings*)

> One can spit out the truth only after drinking wine.
> My feelings break the dike like an onrushing tide.
> I wish you and I could drink with arms entwined.
> I hate not having known you before I was wed!

WU SONG: (*Immediately disgusted*) Hold your tongue!

(WU SONG *rapidly flies into a rage. With a single touch, he flips over the wine cups.* JINLIAN *suddenly pauses and becomes aware of her faux pas. She becomes almost sober, and she is seized by panic.*)

WU SONG: (*Sings*) I'm angry as a bull who stamps with rage.

> I'm angry as a bull who stamps with rage.
> Your wine and words, though sweet, both seem
>   like poison.
> I have never been corrupted by a woman.
> Face my gaze, you moral weakling, learn a lesson!

I, who killed a tiger, without question
Live my life by sages' moral guidelines.
Whoever respects my brother is a friend of mine,
But those who shame him, I will help to die!
Before your birth, fate tied you to my brother.
Till death, you must be true to one another.
And when he's dead, true widow's tears you'll shed.
If you are chaste, I'll carve your deeds in stone.
If not, I'll force you to atone.
Make sure you fear the power that lies in this—

(*Shakes his fist and closes in on her*)

My mighty, tiger-killing iron fist!

(WU SONG *fetches his sack of official documents and prepares to go.* PAN JINLIAN *pulls at him, and tries to explain.*)

PAN JINLIAN: Brother-in-law, I'm sorry, the wine made me say something improper. But can't you understand the ache I must hide in my heart, even a little?

WU SONG: (*Still more furiously*) Do not touch me! Your behavior is simply outrageous! Go away! (*He shoves* JINLIAN *to the ground, and strides off.*)

PAN JINLIAN: (*Wailing*) Brother-in-law . . . (*Giving up all hope, she faints.*)

(*The lighting fluctuates and flickers here and there. Imperial music plays. The* PALACE GUARD *enters in single file, marching in a solemn and reverent fashion. From inside comes a cry, "The Jinlun Empress is arriving!" Empress* WU ZETIAN[42] *is revealed. Following her is* SHANGUAN WAN'ER.[43])

WU ZETIAN: You, common woman, should not feel timid or afraid. We, the Empress Wu Zetian, support your position in this matter. Straighten your body, and raise your face—

---

[42]Like all Chinese rulers, upon assuming office, the Empress Wu Zetian of the Tang dynasty adopted a reign name different from her personal name. The only formally recognized empress in Chinese history, she ruled from 690 to 704.

[43]In the Tang dynasty, an author famous for her wisdom and literary and administrative skill, much prized by the Empress Wu.

(JINLIAN *raises her face. The* PALACE GUARD *echoes the words of the empress.* JINLIAN *seems to have entered an unreal space. She slowly retreats, then screams, hides her face, and runs offstage.*)

SHANGUAN WAN'ER: Jinlian, come back, this way . . .

WU ZETIAN: Wan'er, don't startle the common woman. You have observed this situation; how do you evaluate it?

SHANGUAN WAN'ER: In my humble opinion, although Wu Song's manner may be rough, he is very clear in his moral judgments. He follows the ethical principles on every point. Inside and out, he is a paragon of Chinese moral excellence. (*Blurting out*) His heroic character truly demands our respect and love!

WU ZETIAN: (*Laughing in spite of herself*) Ha ha, you also mention that word "love." In Our opinion, Pan Jinlian has been depressed for a long time. Once she met a hero and her respect turned to love, her reaction was understandable. Just as the common woman herself said, "If only I'd been single when we met." (*Sings*)

> Even We feel the common woman's pain;
> We, who resisted orthodoxy's constraint.
> Since the first king's long-forgotten reign,
> Women long for loving in their hearts.

THE PALACE GUARD: (*Singing in chorus*)

> Yes, women long for loving in their hearts.

SMALL-TOWN MAYOR: (*Enters*) Your Majesty has come down across the dynasties to see us. I, the mayor of this small town, come to welcome you from across the ages. Please allow me to bow to Your Majesty.

WU ZETIAN: And who is the official who bows to Us so graciously?

SMALL-TOWN MAYOR: I am the seventh-rank mandarin Tang Cheng.

WU ZETIAN: Yes, you are the very Small-town Mayor who has always decided in favor of the people.

SMALL-TOWN MAYOR: That is merely the reputation the common people have generously awarded me. Your Majesty honors me too much.

WU ZETIAN: You have come at just the right time. Please make a judgment in support of the common woman Pan Jinlian.

SMALL-TOWN MAYOR: Right away, Your Majesty. (*He fetches the historical records and sings in the Henan-opera style.*[44])

> If any official serves the people ill
> He should quit and put out yams to sell.
> If you research past dynasties' statute books,
> What is written can be seen with just one look.
> In the home, the father's word is law;
> After marriage, the husband is her lord.
> If he dies, she must live as a widow,
>   and the son then is held in awe.
> When you marry a rooster, a hen you become;
> When you marry a boar, a sow you become.

WU ZETIAN: (*Not pleased*) Hmph! What are you saying?

SMALL-TOWN MAYOR: This is what I have to say, Your Majesty. I have carefully gone over the legal writings from every single ancient dynasty. There is not even one clause in support of Pan Jinlian. This woman dared to reveal her affection to her own brother-in-law! That really is a most horrible offense!

WU ZETIAN: (*A cold laugh*) Hm . . . In the royal courts of past dynasties, a man could have three wives and four concubines. An emperor could house three thousand beauties and concubines. The Taizong Emperor chose Us first, and then the Gaozong Emperor also picked Us as his fourth wife. Father and son both had the same concubine. Isn't that truly opposed to what is known as "ethical principles"?

SMALL-TOWN MAYOR: Well . . . In the royal family, these things are permitted by heaven and earth. I dare not reproach these traditions!

WU ZETIAN: So you say that royalty is allowed to be completely dissipated, but that a common woman who conceives a small affection is guilty? Pan Jinlian only revealed a bit of her depression to her brother-in-law, and also some of her adoration for him. However, you see this as "a most horrible offense." Hmmmm . . . the nobility are above, and the masses are

---

[44]Another major form of Chinese regional music dramas. Its music is prominently characterized by strong rhythms accentuated by wooden clappers.

below, and the men are above and the women below; this is completely unjust. Mr. Mayor, you had better quickly think of a way to save this common woman.

SMALL-TOWN MAYOR: I have no way, even if I could ask Bao Gong, Hai Rui, and Xü Jiujing[45] to help me. Their heads are the same as mine. (*Takes off his cotton hat and reveals a small braid hanging from his head*) I could not take much of a "cue" from them.[46]

WU ZETIAN: Gracious, and all of you were known as "the righteous officials," weren't you?

SMALL-TOWN MAYOR: The righteous officials in every dynasty can only cure a little cough or a cold. We cannot cure serious illnesses, and still less can we cure "woman's disease."

WU ZETIAN: (*Angrily*) You useless mediocrity, get out of here! (*The* SMALL-TOWN MAYOR *withdraws.*)

SHANGUAN WAN'ER: It's no wonder that the righteous official cannot fix this. Even if Your Majesty did something to shake the nation's moral standards and ethical roots, they would react with heavy pressure and all sorts of abuse. (*In a stage whisper*) "A hen takes a rooster's job of reporting the dawn," "Sexual anarchy rules the great palace."[47]

WU ZETIAN: Say whatever they want, somewhere in Our great country there must be some statute book that upholds women! (*She slowly raises her arms, imploring heaven, as the ancient lute begins to play.*)

SHANGUAN WAN'ER: It's hard, this case is as hard as climbing to heaven.

---

[45]The first two were actual historical figures with reputations as judges of exceptional integrity. For Bao Gong, see note 41. In 1565, Hai Rui (1513–1587) criticized the emperor for his land policy which hurt the peasantry, and his toleration for corruption. The monarch exiled him to Hainan Island, where he died. Xü Jiujing is the fictional protagonist of another play by the same author of this version of Pan Jinlian; he is a small-town official also known for his integrity.

[46]An approximate rendition of another pun on *fa* ("hair" or "way"), as in note 33, above.

[47]Stock phrasing of accusations by orthodox moralists against Wu Zetian.

WU ZETIAN: (*Dejectedly*) We, Wu Zetian, confess that it is beyond Our power to solve it. We think about the vastness of the world, and We feel so sad. We do not know which dynasty, which emperor, which sage can give free choice of marriage to women in order to help them climb out of their abyss.

SHANGUAN WAN'ER: Only in the far-distant future. The common woman is right in front of us. What way out is possible for her?

WU ZETIAN: People are filled with all sorts of desires; her future will be very treacherous.

SHANGUAN WAN'ER: Please look, Your Majesty: that handsome devil Ximen Qing is coming!

(*The* PALACE GUARD *changes formation and suddenly becomes a whirling riot of colors.*[48])

SINKING INTO DEPRAVITY

XIMEN QING: (*Enters, singing*)

> I dream of a thousand floral women,
> I think of hundreds of enchanting ladies,
> My life is that of a libertine.

(XIMEN QING *pursues the group of beautiful women.* WU ZETIAN *and* SHANGUAN WAN'ER *climb onto the platform together and stand there looking on.*)

XIMEN QING: (*Sings*)

> Waving fan in hand, I stroll at leisure
> I devote my life to chasing pleasure.
> My hands can gather delicate bouquets.

---

[48]The Chinese phrase *cha zi yan hong* literally refers to a beautiful flower garden in bloom, but it is often figuratively applied to a crowd of women in colorful clothes.

> I hide this knowledge from the light of day.
> I appear soft, but inwardly I'm tough,
> Like an iron fist beneath a velvet glove.

SHANGUAN WAN'ER: (*Points critically at him, and sings*)

> Oh, Ximen Qing—
> Seeming gentle and charming, but actually ruthless
> and cruel!

XIMEN QING: (*Bragging, sings*)

> In my gentleness is my beauty.
> I amble along the streets of the city . . .

(*The multicolored group shifts, covering up* WU ZETIAN. XIMEN QING, *who has been trying to find her, loses track. He gives up his intention of finding her, and ambles off.*)

PAN JINLIAN: (*Holding a forked pole, she dances onstage upstairs and begins to sing.*)

> In the middle of great bitterness,
> To reduce my heartache, I seek small delights . . .

(JINLIAN *raises the curtain. A bee buzzes about her face, and she waves her pole in an attempt to drive it away.*)

XIMEN QING: (*Enters*) Oh! (*Sings*)

> What family's jewel is as splendid as
> who I see?
> Around her face buzzes a yellow bee.
> I look from the left to the right,
> And I see beauty on the right.
> I look from the right to the left,
> And I also see beauty on the left.
> As if dreaming, I approach her, step
> by step . . .

(JINLIAN, *afraid of being stung by the bee, waves her pole about and drops it. It accidentally strikes* XIMEN QING *on the head.* MATCH-MAKER WANG *quietly enters, just in time to catch a glimpse of this event.*)

XIMEN QING: Ouch!

PAN JINLIAN: Oh, I'm sorry!

MATCHMAKER WANG: (*Aside, sings*)

> This is the working of fate,
> This is just like a play;
> This will be interesting to watch.

(*She conceals herself and peers out from her hiding place.*)

PAN JINLIAN: (*Making a traditional gesture of apology*) The bee stung my hand and I dropped my staff, which hit you by mistake. I apologize from the bottom of my heart; please don't be offended.

XIMEN QING: (*Courteously*) People sometimes do drop things; it's quite all right. I don't blame you. I return your courtesy from down here.

PAN JINLIAN: I'm grateful to you for being so understanding and kind.

XIMEN QING: (*Lifting the pole*) How can I return this to you? Please come downstairs and get it.

PAN JINLIAN: Me, come downstairs?

MATCHMAKER WANG: (*Aside*) She's coming downstairs, she's coming downstairs, but she's going to wind up on his hook!

PAN JINLIAN: (*Coming to a halt*) Coming downstairs is not convenient. Would you please toss it up to me?

XIMEN QING: Well . . .

MATCHMAKER WANG: (*Aside*) Don't hurry, take it slowly.

XIMEN QING: I will do as you wish. Would you please take your pole?

(XIMEN QING *deliberately wiggles the pole here and there.* PAN JINLIAN *retrieves it only with great difficulty.*)

PAN JINLIAN: (*Showing some feigned anger*) That really isn't a fishing pole; why are you shaking it back and forth? (*Flashes him a smile, and exits*)

(XIMEN QING *is deflated.* MATCHMAKER WANG *comes into view.*)

XIMEN QING *and* MATCHMAKER WANG: (*Together*) Aha!

XIMEN QING: (*Looking back, embarrassed*) I didn't know who it was—it's Mrs. Wang.

MATCHMAKER WANG: And I didn't know who it was, either—it's you, sir, Master Ximen Qing! (*They exchange courtesies.*)

XIMEN QING: Auntie Wang, you have come at just the right moment. You saw what happened just now. I can't hide my intention from your old, wise eyes. I want to ask you, Auntie Wang, to help me in this affair. (*Giving her silver*)

MATCHMAKER WANG: (*Looking wide-eyed at it*) Ha ha, you're my old customer, and she's my new neighbor. It's only right for me to do the matchmaking between the two of you.

XIMEN QING: I ask you, Auntie Wang, what are your new neighbor's financial circumstances? What does she love and what does she hate?

MATCHMAKER WANG: It's a long story. Let me tell it to you . . .

(*The old-style horns play some music while she tells the story.*)

XIMEN QING: According to what you say, the beauty upstairs cannot be bought with money?

MATCHMAKER WANG: If she desired money from the beginning, she would've married Zhang Dahu. Instead, the pretty woman made an unlucky marriage with Shorty Dalang. This was just like being a widow with a living husband! Then, dear me, she quietly fell in love with her heroic, handsome brother-in-law!

XIMEN QING: (*Suddenly struck by an idea*) I just thought of the best way to catch her—let's put on a show!

MATCHMAKER WANG: I understand. You'll play the lead role. I'll take a supporting part, and I'll also arrange several other minor roles. Let's craft a perfect plot. I'm sure she won't get off the hook.

XIMEN QING: This isn't the proper place for a long-drawn-out conversation. Please come to my house to talk.

MATCHMAKER WANG: Lead on, please. (*They exit together.*)

PAN JINLIAN: (*Enters, holding some needlework in her hands, sings*)

> I raise the curtain smiling, I lower it disappointed;
> I descend the stairs, holding my needlepoint.
> I open the door, but no young man can be seen.
> The small, empty alley remains calm and serene.

CHORUS: (*From within*) Deliver the finished shirt to the Wang house!

(PAN JINLIAN *circles the stage. The* RASCALS *and the* PUNK *appear and block her path. They surround and besiege her.*)

PAN JINLIAN: (*Sings*)

> Alone on a deserted street,
> I encounter my enemies . . .

MODERN PUNK: Wu Song is away on an official trip, so there's no one who can protect you now. Today, we brothers are going to settle our accounts with you!

PAN JINLIAN: In this street in broad daylight, you would dare to commit homicide?

MODERN PUNK: Not homicide, not homicide. In the first place, we won't degrade you by forcing you to come to drink with us. Second, we don't want to take your life, you old bat! But we do want you—

THE RASCALS: On your knees and crawl!

PAN JINLIAN: Ptah! Although I may be a woman, I have my pride. I would rather die than crawl like a slave!

MODERN PUNK: You do have some grit, after all. Since that's the case, don't blame us for being heartless. Raise your arms! (*The* RASCALS *grab and hold* JINLIAN *as the* PUNK *pulls out his dagger.*)

PAN JINLIAN: I was just thinking about dying anyhow. Lend me your knife, it'll be quick and clean!

MODERN PUNK: It won't be that easy. We brothers are going to slash your face, so you will be a perfect match for that ugly husband of yours.

(JINLIAN *closes her eyes. The* PUNK *sharpens his knife. He smiles coldly and pushes closer to her, getting ready to cut her face.*)

XIMEN QING: Hold it right there!

(XIMEN QING *bounds onstage, seizes the knife, and sends it flying to the ground. He speaks with righteous indignation.*)

XIMEN QING: In our clean and peaceful world, who dares commit such a crime?

MODERN PUNK: Buddy, where do you come from?

MATCHMAKER WANG: (*Quickly entering*) You may have eyes, but you are truly blind! This is the famous Sir Ximen Qing!

MODERN PUNK: Ximen, Schmimen, all men should be brothers. Bonjour[49]—have a smoke, pal. (*Presenting a Harmony Grass–brand cigarette*)

XIMEN QING: (*Knocking the cigarette away*) Could a noble-minded man such as I associate with riffraff like you? Here comes my fist!

(XIMEN QING *uses his outer garment as a weapon, and he attacks the* RASCALS *with flying fists and feet, scattering them.* MATCHMAKER WANG *helps* PAN JINLIAN *off to the side.* XIMEN QING *hauls the escaping* PUNK *back.*)

XIMEN QING: Kneel down quickly, and acknowledge that you have wronged this woman!

MODERN PUNK: (*Making a kowtow*) Lady, this man is even stronger than Wu Song. I will never, never, ever dare to touch a hair on your head. Spare my life, spare my life!

MATCHMAKER WANG: He's as pathetic and clumsy as a crab trying to pick up a rolling pea!

---

[49]In French in the original.

(*The* MODERN PUNK *turns and talks with* XIMEN QING *on one side of the stage. On the other side,* MATCHMAKER WANG *and* PAN JINLIAN *likewise converse.*)

MATCHMAKER WANG: You've had the good fortune to meet with a righteous and courageous hero.

MODERN PUNK: This act of the play is going quite well, isn't it?

XIMEN QING: You have good skill in performance; get ready to prepare the next act.

MODERN PUNK: And my bonus?

XIMEN QING: Go see my accountant and pick it up.

MODERN PUNK: (*Speaking Japanese*) Hai! ("OK!")

(*The* MODERN PUNK *calls the* RASCALS *to decorate the bedroom.* JINLIAN *fixes her hair.* MATCHMAKER WANG *leads her into the bedroom and introduces her to* XIMEN QING.)

MATCHMAKER WANG: Master Ximen, this is my neighbor Pan Jinlian. Jinlian, come quickly to thank your benefactor.

PAN JINLIAN: (*Making an obeisance*) Many thanks to Master Ximen, who saw the right thing to do and had the courage to do it.

XIMEN QING: It has been my lifelong wish to have the opportunity for such a deed. Lady, do take care of yourself, please. (*He begins to exit.*)

MATCHMAKER WANG: No, no. Just now, there's been a fight, and you've torn the front of your jacket. Why don't you come to our humble house? Sit awhile and have a cup of tea, and I'll ask Jinlian to sew it up for you. She really has a deft hand at sewing.

XIMEN QING: It isn't worth the bother, really, it's just a flimsy old jacket. How could I dare to impose on the lady to sew it up, ma'am?

MATCHMAKER WANG: No, if you had not come to her rescue just now, Jinlian would already have her looks damaged. It's only right for her to do what she can to repay you. Jinlian, what do you have to say?

PAN JINLIAN: (*Sincerely*) What you say is correct. I must repay Mr. Ximen.

MATCHMAKER WANG: (*Aside, to* XIMEN QING) It's looking good. (*To* JINLIAN) You have known kindness, and (*to* XIMEN QING) you have accepted her repayment. There is a reason for you to come together and travel down the same road. Mr. Ximen, please; Jinlian, please . . .

(*Delicate woodwind music begins to play. The three people take a few steps and enter the Wang house. MATCHMAKER WANG arranges their seating and hands the jacket to JINLIAN. She then offers tea all around, and the music stops.*)

MATCHMAKER WANG: Distinguished guest, you honor our humble home. Please have some tea, please. (*Sings*)

> The bluebird of happiness flying inside
> Sees the hero save and guard the beauty.
> Mr. Ximen, doing good is your whole life.
> You have ambition, and also you have youth.
> Every day, you practice martial arts,
> And you write with elegance and style.
> Your drugstore's very famous in these parts.
> But you've been all alone for quite a while.
> I ask you, you young man-about-town,
> When will we see you wed and settle down?

XIMEN QING: Oh, Auntie Wang, please don't mention that topic. My wife died three years ago. At first, I did think of remarrying, but it's such a huge world, and it's so hard to find a soulmate.

MATCHMAKER WANG: Mr. Ximen, don't let your outlook get too lofty. (*Testing* JINLIAN) A true mate could be at the ends of the earth, or she could be right under your nose . . .

(XIMEN QING *looks up and steals a glance at* JINLIAN. *They make direct eye contact. Her heart trembles, causing her to stop sewing and to stare off into space.*)

MATCHMAKER WANG: Jinlian, have you finished sewing? (*Louder*) Jinlian!

PAN JINLIAN: (*Coming back to reality*) I've finished the sewing, but I don't know if Master will like it or not. Is it "suit"-able?

MATCHMAKER WANG: (*With a double meaning*) It's suitable—it will surely suit his taste and heart.

XIMEN QING: Ohhhh . . .

MATCHMAKER WANG: What is it?

XIMEN QING: OHHHHhhhhh . . .

PAN JINLIAN: What is it?

MATCHMAKER WANG: Mr. Ximen, what's the matter?

XIMEN QING: (*Pointing to his stomach*) Just now when I was in the fight, I got hit here by a Rascal, and I think he may have broken something inside. It's caused a recurrence of an old pain. Ohhh . . .

MATCHMAKER WANG: Good heavens, this is a bad reward for a good man. What can we do? I'll help you to a bed and you can lie down for a while.

(MATCHMAKER WANG *supports* XIMEN QING, *secretly making a gesture to him to indicate that his plan is already 80 percent successful.* XIMEN QING *slowly lies down on the curtained bed.*)

MATCHMAKER WANG: Jinlian, I'm going to fetch a doctor. You stay here and help him a little.

PAN JINLIAN: Mother Wang, I . . .

MATCHMAKER WANG: Really, now! This worthy man got hurt while trying to save you. Can you just watch him die without even trying to help him? (*She leaves and latches the door, secretly smiling.*) It worked! (*She glides off.*)

PAN JINLIAN: (*Restlessly*) Auntie Wang, Auntie Wang . . .

XIMEN QING: (*Calling from inside the curtain*) Oh, help me!

PAN JINLIAN: (*Hesitates, and sings*)

> It's evening and we two are all alone.
> This makes my heart flutter and my face blush.
> I hear my benefactor cry and moan.
> How can I restrain my feelings' gush?

XIMEN QING: (*From inside the curtain*) Water, water . . .

(*At the sound,* PAN JINLIAN *answers, "Coming, coming," and brings him some tea. She raises up the side curtain—and leaning at the head of the bed is* WU SONG!)

PAN JINLIAN: Wu Song!

(*A loud noise from the gongs, and then the big drums suddenly join in.* JINLIAN *drops her tray and flies from the bed to the center of the stage.*)

XIMEN QING: Water, water . . .

(JINLIAN *collects herself and tiptoes back to the raised side curtain.* XIMEN QING *lies unconscious at the head of the bed. As if relieved of a heavy load,* JINLIAN *lets out a long breath and lowers the side curtain.*)

PAN JINLIAN: (*Sings*)

> My heart swims in illusion, my eyes are dim.
> I erred in thinking Ximen was Wu Song.
> In courage, the two men appear to be the same.
> They are both distinct, yet similar.
> Compared to him, though, Wu Song is far colder.
> He is more broad-minded than Wu Song.
> I see Ximen, but then recall Wu Song.
> These two men's images combine and blur.
> I love Wu Song, but I also hate Wu Song.
> I can't forget the snowy night Wu Song cruelly
>   went away.
> The bitter past replays itself before my eyes today!

(XIMEN QING *comes out from behind the curtain. He holds out both his hands seductively to* JINLIAN.)

XIMEN QING: (*Speaking gently*) Jinlian . . .

(JINLIAN *can no longer restrain herself from showing her repressed affection. She yields to his entreaty, and hides her face in* XIMEN QING's *chest. The lights dim.*)

CHORUS: (*Singing from within the curtain*)

Ah, one misstep leads to eternal regret!

LÜ SHASHA: (*Enters anxiously, sings*)

One misstep leads to eternal regret.
I ponder the cause that leads to this consequence.
Does Jinlian have a hope of getting out?
This ancient case needs trial in modern court.

(*The* HEAD JUDGE *of the people's tribunal, a woman, enters, carrying a briefcase.*)

LÜ SHASHA: Comrade Judge, welcome.

JUDGE: Comrade reporter, greetings.

LÜ SHASHA: We have an urgent matter on hand, and we'd like to consult with you about it.

JUDGE: What is the problem, and how urgent is it?

LÜ SHASHA: A divorce!

JUDGE: (*A pause*) Shasha, how many times do you want to get divorced?

LÜ SHASHA: It's not me, it's Pan Jinlian!

JUDGE: Pan Jinlian. (*A strange smile*) Ha ha, you have a rich imagination. She was a woman from a feudal society. To think that she could apply to the People's Tribunal for a divorce is a fairy tale, a sheer fairy tale!

LÜ SHASHA: Please think about this "fairy tale." Let me bring up a couple of interesting questions.

JUDGE: What questions?

LÜ SHASHA: Suppose I were Pan Jinlian?

JUDGE: You! If you were in that society, you would fall just as surely as Pan Jinlian did!

LÜ SHASHA: I would? (*Shaken up a little*) In that case, suppose Pan Jinlian were me?

JUDGE: That would be most fortunate!

LÜ SHASHA: Very well; suppose Pan Jinlian were a resident of Garden Street, and suppose she applied to the People's Tribunal for a divorce. What judgment would you render?

JUDGE: Following legal procedure, mediation would be in progress.

LÜ SHASHA: How about if mediation didn't work?

JUDGE: According to the Marriage Code, Section Twenty-five, the judgment should be as follows—(*Sings*)

> Arranged marriages have evil consequences.
> An injured woman hopes for recompense.
> Wife and husband treat each other irately,
> And each one makes the other suffer greatly.
> I'd grant her a divorce; it's only right
> That neither should be scarred in future fights.

LÜ SHASHA: The fight has not yet subsided. The present age still has its Pan Jinlian!

(PAN JINLIAN *stands on the platform with her back to the audience.*)

JUDGE: (*Calls*) Pan Jinlian!

(PAN JINLIAN *"strikes a pose." In* SHASHA's *eyes, she appears to take the form of a modern woman in a light windbreaker.*)

LÜ SHASHA: She's a modern woman, but she does resemble Pan Jinlian. She's also in an arranged marriage that has led to an unfortunate result. She has no way to free herself. She is in agony, she is changing, she is sinking . . .

JUDGE: (*Lost in thought*) How difficult it is to cure "a woman's agony"!

The Small-town Mayor didn't cure it, but we have eased it a great deal. Even so, such "difficult and complicated cases" are on the increase. The root of the problem is that we haven't gotten to the root of the problem.

LÜ SHASHA: In that case, it would be better to think about the old trage- dies. Keep looking.

(*There is a sound of muffled thunder. The two people look backward in fright.*)

JUDGE: The tragedy reaches its climax . . .

LÜ SHASHA: Ximen Qing will force her to use poison!

(XIMEN QING *anxiously enters.* LÜ SHASHA *and the* JUDGE *withdraw.*)

XIMEN QING: (*Coldly pulling* JINLIAN *down from the platform*) The bad news about us has become public knowledge, and Wu Dalang has fallen sick from anger. Matters have come to this point, and now you must tell me: were we just a one-night stand, or are we a permanent couple?

PAN JINLIAN: (*Showing no expression*) What do you mean?

XIMEN QING: A one-night stand means that we will separate here and now; but if we're a permanent couple, we will do as we had planned. (*Fetches some arsenic*)

PAN JINLIAN: (*Still showing no expression*) What is this?

XIMEN QING: (*Speaking in a staccato fashion*) It is arsenic, a deadly poison. Take advantage of serving the tea with your own hands, and send Wu Dalang straight up to heaven!

PAN JINLIAN: (*Startled*) Oh no! (*Trembling, in a low voice*) Get out. (*Bursting forth*) Get out! (*As if trying to ward off a deadly disease*) Take that and throw it away, don't let it tarnish my hands!

XIMEN QING: What, you think you still have a pure and clean body? (*A hideous grin*) You have already violated every one of the seven rules that make a good wife.[50] There is no question whatsoever concerning your crime and your guilt. You're just like a half-burned piece of firewood in the kitchen stove—even if you pull it out now, it's already become hopelessly blackened!

PAN JINLIAN: My God! (*Crumples in dejection*)

XIMEN QING: (*Speaking gently*) Jinlian, whether you kill him or not is six of one and half a dozen of the other. Since you have changed into a loach, why are you afraid of the muck?[51] Come with me, and listen to my proposal. (*Enticingly*) You and I can be together for the rest of our lives. We'll fly wing to wing, like two mandarin ducks.[52] My undying love for you lies directly before you; please, Jinlian, take it.

(XIMEN QING *goes to his knees and offers up the arsenic.* PAN JINLIAN's *hands shake crazily. After some time of being unable to reach a decision, she indicates her refusal by retracting her hands.*)

PAN JINLIAN: You, you don't really want to force me to . . .

XIMEN QING: (*In great distress, crying*) A thousand times no, ten thousand times no. I shouldn't have fallen in love with you. I'm just spellbound by you, and I can't let you go . . . If I have to live in lifelong regret, it would be better if I killed myself with the poison! (*Pretending to swallow the arsenic*)

PAN JINLIAN: (*Hurriedly stopping him*) Sir! (*Deeply moved*) You cannot die! How can I continue without you?

XIMEN QING: Either my death or Wu Dalang's! Here is the arsenic, Jinlian, for you to use as you please. (*He throws the arsenic near the hem of her skirt, and strides out.*)

---

[50]In classical China, men had seven reasons for which they could divorce their wives unilaterally: failure to bear a son, adultery, failure to serve parents-in-law satisfactorily, talking back, stealing, jealousy, or incurable disease.

[51]A type of small fish that burrows in the ooze at the bottom of ponds. The sense is that since Pan Jinlian has already wronged Wu Dalang by committing adultery, she should not hesitate to kill him, since doing so would increase her turpitude only slightly.

[52]A traditional Chinese symbol of marital fidelity and love; when one dies, the other does not mate again but dies also.

(*The lightning flashes and the thunder booms. The music plays wildly.*)

PAN JINLIAN: (*Sings*)

> The thunder crashes and roars,
> The guilt and debts of my affairs
> Weigh like a mountain on my head.
> I pull my hair, I beat my breast.
> I never had ambition to be a rich man's wife.
> I only wanted to marry a man that I liked.
> I seek good fortune, but encounter only bad:
> First, a shabby old aristocrat!
> Second, a wretched, cowardly flunky!
> Third, an icy man without empathy!
> Fourth, I fell in love with cunning,
> Soft, sugary, but ruthless Ximen Qing!

CHORUS: (*From within*)

> In a long night, you meet this Ximen,
> Or you meet that Ximen.

(*The lightning flashes and the thunder rolls once more.* ANNA KARENINA *flutters into view and bumps into the back of the half-dazed* JINLIAN.)

PAN JINLIAN: Who's that?

ANNA: (*Sings as an operatic aria*)

> My place on earth is different from yours;
> In time, my era also far away.
> I often have absurd and vivid dreams.
> Only we fellow sufferers show pity, it seems.
> Let those who follow look on us and compare
> Our tragic fates, and judge which one was fair!

(*A siren sounds, approaching from the distance.* JINLIAN *looks back.* ANNA *forcibly drags* JINLIAN *to the front of the stage. The roaring sound of a train pierces the stage as it rushes past, and its headlight flashes briefly on the faces of the two women.* ANNA *vigorously throws herself on the track and commits suicide.* JINLIAN, *unable to watch, hides her face in her sleeves. The sound of the train gradually fades, gradually fades.*)

ANNA: (*Slowly rises and sings*)

> I'm dead, and free from earthly woe.
> Pan Jinlian, do not fear to go.
> Swallow the deadly poison pill;
> Death is luring you with his call.
> Amen!
> Farewell!
> See you in hell . . .

(ANNA *crosses herself and disappears.* PAN JINLIAN *raises the arsenic and dances alone, fluttering her long sleeves and flowing skirt. As she prepares to take the poison to kill herself,* WU ZETIAN *appears.*)

WU ZETIAN: Stop!

PAN JINLIAN: Your Majesty! (*Bows down*)

WU ZETIAN: You women cannot treat life so lightly. You cannot die!

PAN JINLIAN: How can I possibly continue? Will Your Majesty please tell me what to do?

WU ZETIAN: (*Sings*)

> Worldwide, no monument fulfills my wish.[53]
> In old China, women still cry for justice.
> My sword cannot, my sword cannot
> Cut tradition's strangling net.

PAN JINLIAN. Your Majesty, please give me justice!

(PAN JINLIAN *dips her head vigorously, makes a kowtow, and begs for help.* WU ZETIAN *waves the point of her sword about uncertainly, not knowing what to do.*)

WU ZETIAN: (*Sings*)

> We cannot help the common woman escape
> the abyss.

---

[53] At the tomb of Wu Zetian there is a stone monument that, in a departure from custom, remains uninscribed.

Better to beg help from Wu Dalang than Us.
A note from him will grant you a divorce!

PAN JINLIAN: Dalang . . . (*Shakes her head*) He will never let me go.

WU ZETIAN: (*Angrily*) If he does not end the marriage, you must retaliate—kill him!

PAN JINLIAN: (*Terrified*) I dare not, I dare not!

WU ZETIAN: Oh! (*Sings*)

> Unfortunately, you are of the commoner class.
> You do not have Our power of an empress.
> We, Wu Zetian, have killed thousands of men.
> An unrequited lover—We killed!
> Political enemies—their blood We spilled!
> A twin sibling—
> In the side palace, We bestowed death upon her.
> Our own offspring
> We strangled in the crib . . . [54]
> This imperial hand is soaked in gore.
> Who reproaches Us?
> Who censures Us?
> The ages have praised imperial Wu Zetian,
> While wrongfully condemning common Pan Jinlian!

(*Three laughs and a sigh*) Ha ha, ha ha, ha ha . . . Oh! (*Disappears*)

(JINLIAN *stands up. Her state of mind is topsy-turvy. She has a vision of* WU DALANG *supported by his cane, carrying the puppet next to his chest. The puppet has sprouted five black tufts of a beard.*)

PAN JINLIAN: Dalang! (*Kneeling and imploring him*) I truly do not have the heart to hurt you or kill you. I ask you to show me some sympathy and divorce me.

WU DALANG: Divorce you?

PAN JINLIAN: While we've been married, I've broken all of the seven rules for good behavior. Please divorce me, and save my life.

---

[54]All actions actually taken by the historical Wu Zetian.

WU DALANG: (*Softly but with determination*) I, Wu Dalang, am without power and without influence, but in my hand, I do hold certain "husbandly rights." Zhang Dahu has granted you to me as a wife. You must remember, "When you marry a rooster, you become a hen; when you marry a dog, you become his mate."[55] Even chickens and dogs should grow old together. I am getting on—(*the black tufts of his hair suddenly turn white*) but even though I'm old, I won't divorce you! Even though I'm dead, I won't divorce you! (*Exits*)

PAN JINLIAN: (*Desperately looking around*) Old and no divorce! Dead and no divorce! (*Her mental state becomes unbalanced. She smiles, at first bitterly, then coldly, then idiotically.*) Ha ha, ha ha . . .

MATCHMAKER WANG: (*Anxiously entering*) Mr. Ximen urges you to start to kill Wu Dalang. You're still just staring blankly. Start, start, right away—

(PAN JINLIAN *suddenly catches sight of a whole* CROWD OF MASKED XIMEN QINGs.)

THE CROWD OF XIMEN QINGs: (*In unison*) Start!

(PAN JINLIAN *covers her ears. The* CROWD OF XIMEN QINGs *encircles her in a dance.* PAN JINLIAN *hardens her heart, makes up her mind, she dances in an intensifying whirl, and suddenly changes her expression. A lopsided red dot appears imprinted between her eyebrows.*[56] *Her sleeves shake like an agitated, pouring waterfall. She is rushed offstage by the* CROWD OF XIMEN QINGs.)

LÜ SHASHA: (*Hurrying onstage, and exclaiming in a loud voice*) You must not start to kill him!

WU DALANG: (*From inside the curtain, with his dying breath*) Ahhh . . .

LÜ SHASHA: (*Sings*)

> My cry to stop can't cross history's iron divide.
> I'm staring with my eyes in horror opened wide,

---

[55]A thought first expressed by Confucius. The Western equivalent would be the line from the Roman marriage ceremony, "Whither thou goest, Gaius, thither go I, Gaia."

[56]Hidden by the intense and dazzling movement, the actress herself places the dot on her face; it marks her as a cruel murderer.

As she makes her monstrous, fatal error.
The woman now becomes a moral leper forever.

(SHI NAI'AN *enters, holding a huge brush pen.*)

SHI NAI'AN: A stroke of the pen ends this chapter. The story is divided into two parts. Wu Song is returning!

LÜ SHASHA: Why is he coming back so soon?

SHI NAI'AN: When there is not much to tell, we may jump ahead in our narrative. Now, we are in the twenty-sixth chapter of "Wu Song Kills His Sister-in-Law."

LÜ SHASHA: One moment, please. Where did that mastermind Ximen Qing go?

SHI NAI'AN: Ximen Qing had lots of other, newly favored women. He went to the Lion brothel and embraced "Zhang Jinlian," "Li Jinlian," "Wang Jinlian," and so forth, seeking pleasure as usual.

LÜ SHASHA: (*A big sigh*) Pan Jinlian, do you regret what you have done, or not?

SHI NAI'AN: It's too late for regret now. Her chest will be sliced open, and her heart will be cut out! (*Blackout*)

KILL!

CHORUS: This is the story of a woman's fall—
            Ages of feudalism caused it all.
            The killer herself now in agony must die.
            A shocking sight to both the heart and eye.

(*The lights gradually come up, revealing the same tableau as in the beginning of the play. PAN JINLIAN runs on, her face numb. WU SONG, wearing a murderous expression, pursues her onstage. In the following section, WU SONG kills his sister-in-law. In the gloom, only the light reflected from his knife and her hair can be clearly seen.*
    PAN JINLIAN *rips open the neckband of her blouse without hesitation,*

and walks toward WU SONG. *He is not prepared for this, and he retreats in alarm.)*

PAN JINLIAN: Kill me, come on, put that knife right here—(*She pounds her breast, and she changes dementedly. In comparison with her appearance at the beginning of the play, when she was a naive and innocent young girl, she is now completely transformed.*) Ha ha, ha ha, today I can die under your hand. It's the good fortune in my bad fortune. Come on, open my chest, and rip my heart out!

(PAN JINLIAN *fiercely tears her blouse and stands revealed in a bright red brassiere. Appropriately, it seems like a cascade of fresh red blood.* WU SONG's *hand trembles. Both hold a pose.*)

WU ZETIAN: (*From within*) Spare the woman from your knife!

(WU ZETIAN, JIA BAOYÜ, the SMALL-TOWN MAYOR, SHANGUAN WAN'ER, ANNA, *and others surge onto the left platform.* ZHANG DAHU, *the* RASCALS, *the* MODERN PUNK, *and others surge onto the right platform. The two sides express their respective views in a heated debate.*)

WU ZETIAN: She's guilty, but not enough to be killed!

ZHANG DAHU: She's guilty enough to die a thousand deaths!

JIA BAOYÜ: The root of her guilt lies in social conditions!

ZHANG DAHU: The guilt is in the woman herself!

SMALL-TOWN MAYOR: Even the best judge cannot make a fair determination in this case . . .

RASCALS: Open her chest and rip out her heart!

MODERN PUNK: (*Jeering*) Cut off her limbs, let her blood flow!

JUDGE: (*From within*) This illegal punishment is forbidden!

(*The* JUDGE *and* SHI NAI'AN *rush onstage separately.*)

THE CROWD: (*Attentively*) Chief Justice?

JUDGE: (*In the middle of the stage, sings in a powerful and resonant voice*)

> This is the story of a woman's fall—
> Ages of feudalism caused it all.
> I wished to save her, but she'll soon be dead.
> My heart cannot overrule my head.
> We should not follow ways we know are evil;
> The moral of this story's deep and doleful!

SHI NAI'AN: (*In a loud voice*) My book does not deal with matters from later generations! Wu Song, steady your hand and kill her!

(WU SONG *slashes once and opens her chest. Blackout. The crowds of people disappear. A single follow-spot illuminates* PAN JINLIAN *directly. She holds her heaving bosom with the blood pouring out, until she is lying in a pool of blood.* LÜ SHASHA, *holding an electric guitar, slowly approaches the audience.*)

LÜ SHASHA: (*Sings*)

> On my new guitar, some ancient songs I play.
> To know of ethics, listen to what all authors say.

The End

March 25, 1986
Revised draft written in the village of Kong Long[57]

---

[57]Not the name of an actual place, but literally, "the home of the dinosaurs." This line is therefore the author's final comment on Chinese traditional morality.

Sangshuping Chronicles

by Chen Zidu, Yang Jian, and Zhu Xiaoping*
Translated by Cai Rong

Cast of Characters

LI JINDOU, about forty-six, a production team leader

XÜ CAIFANG, about eighteen, his widowed daughter-in-law

YÜ WA, about twenty, a seasonal farmhand from Gansu

LI FULIN, about twenty-eight, a sexually unbalanced and mentally malad-
 justed man

YUE WA, about twelve, Li Fulin's sister

CHEN QINGNÜ, about seventeen, Li Fulin's bride

WANG ZHIKE, about thirty, a "murder suspect"

MIAN WA, about eight, Wang's son

ZHU XIAOPING, about seventeen, an educated youth from the city

LI JINMING, about sixty, a stockman of the production team

DIRECTOR LIU, about thirty, a commune cadre

REPRESENTATIVE, about forty, representative of the seasonal farmhands

BAO WA, about twenty-nine, head of the militiamen

BAO WA'S WIFE, about twenty-five

LI JINCAI, about fifty, father of Li Fulin and Yue Wa; Li Fulin is his eldest
 son

AUNT JINCAI, about forty-five, mother of Li Fulin and Yue Wa

THE SIXTH AUNT, about fifty, a matchmaker

LI FULONG, about sixteen, Li Fulin's brother

---

*This play was based on a series of stories by Zhu Xiaoping. Published in *Jüben* (Drama) in 1988, it was staged by the Central Drama Academy in the same year under the direction of Xu Xiaozhong, the president of the Academy. Chen Zidu is currently pursuing his M.F.A. at California State University in Long Beach. He taught at the Central Drama Academy and was a professional director and actor in China. Yang Jian is an editor of *Xijü* (Theater), published by the Central Drama Academy. Zhu Xiaoping is a noted writer in China and has been publishing novels and novellas since the early 1980s. He is currently a screenwriter at the Beijing Film Studio. This translation is based on the text published in *Jüben*, April 1988, pp. 4–28.

LI JINSHENG, about fifty, group leader of the Poor Peasant Association, husband of the Sixth Aunt

LI JINGUI, about fifty, Party group leader

LI FUQUAN, about twenty-five, an accountant

LI JINFA, about fifty, a commune member

SISTER CUIPING, about twenty-three, a peasant

LI FUGUI, about twenty-eight, her husband

LIU CHANGGUI, about fifty, secretary of the Party branch of the production brigade

QINGNÜ'S MOTHER, about fifty, a character who appears in a scene of illusion

LI FUMIAN, about twenty-four, late wife of Wang Zhike, a character who appears in a scene of illusion

Some local cadres who come to estimate the yield of the production team, seasonal farmhands, villagers of Sangshuping, onlookers, militiamen, policemen, the ox "huozi" (played by the actors), neighboring villagers, manager of the seasonal farmhands' market—all played by CHORUS MEMBERS.

Time: Around 1968–1969

Setting: Loess plateau in Shanxi

Scene: A huge revolving stage able to turn 360 degrees is needed. In front, there is a vast stretch of sloping yellow earth, which would extend all the way to the horizon if not for the ⌒⌒ shaped cut in its middle left by the vicissitudes of life and the ancient weathered rocks by the side of the cliff on its left. The yellow earth coils silently like a drawing of the enigmatic Eight Diagrams.[1] This is echoed at a distance on the right by an unfathomable old well left behind from the Tang dynasty.

At the back of the stage on the right side is a dark cave dwelling set against the face of the rocks and the cliff. On the left is another cave for keeping oxen or storing fodder. Twisted roots and gnarled branches of aged pines hug the lintel of the door to the cave.

Before the play starts, the yellow earth slope is facing the audience. Set off by the black velvet backdrop and the side curtains, the land appears awe inspiring, dignified, ancient, barren, and desolate. Some cold light from the right dimly reveals the contour of the rocks.

With one toll of the bell, solemn, slow, and ancient, the stage gradually darkens.

---

[1]The Eight Diagrams consist of an arrangement of single and divided lines in eight groups of three lines each. According to *Book of Changes,* these diagrams symbolize heaven, earth, thunder, wind, water, fire, mountain, and lake.

PRELUDE

(*A rumble of distant thunder can be heard.* LI JINDOU *comes running from a distance, shouting and beating a gong. Light increases.*)

LI JINDOU: It's gonna rain! The wheat is gonna be ruined! Be quick, everyone. Let's shout!

(VILLAGERS *of Sangshuping hurry to join him, clanging gongs, drums, and various utensils. Raising their faces toward the sky, they bellow at the top of their lungs.*)

VILLAGERS: (*Shouting*)

> Black Dragon, Black Dragon, move on,
> In the south you can drop down.

(*Someone sets a beat; the clamor becomes more rhythmical.*)

VILLAGERS: (*Bellowing*)

> Black Dragon, Black Dragon, (*rap*) move on, (*rap-tat-tat*)
> In the south, (*rap*) you can drop down. (*rap-tat-tat*)

(VILLAGERS *from the neighboring village of Chenjiayuan rush onto the stage from the other side, beating gongs and drums and whatever they can find. Cursing those from Sangshuping, they begin to yell.*)

NEIGHBORING VILLAGERS: (*Shouting back to their neighbors*)

> Black Dragon, Black Dragon, stay
> In the north you can play.

(*Finding a cadence, their shouting also becomes more orderly.*)

> Black Dragon, Black Dragon, (*rap*) stay, (*rap-tat-tat*)
> In the north, (*rap*) you can play. (*rap-tat-tat*)

(*Exasperated, people from Sangshuping begin to curse those from Chenjiayuan.*)

VILLAGERS FROM SANGSHUPING: Damn you, you motherfuckers, how dare you ask the rain to stay!

NEIGHBORING VILLAGERS: You fuckers. You wanta drive the rain to us?

LAD FROM SANGSHUPING: See if you dare to cross the ditch. I'll rack the shit out of you.

LAD FROM CHENJIAYUAN: See if you dare to step over the ditch. I'll skin you alive.

WOMAN FROM FROM SANGSHUPING: You sluts!

WOMAN FROM CHENJIAYUAN: You bitches!

(*There is a hubbub of cursing from both sides. Suddenly somebody sets the rhythm. As a result, the uproar becomes more methodical.*)

VILLAGERS FROM SANGSHUPING: Chenjiayuan, (*bong, bong, bong*) fuck your mothers! (*bang, bang, bang*)

VILLAGERS FROM CHENJIAYUAN: Sangshuping, (*bang, bang, bang*) fuck your mothers! (*bong, bong, bong*)

(*An explosive thunderbolt. The rain pours down. People who were busy cursing a moment ago flee in all directions. Light changes with music.*)
(*Singing off stage by the* CHORUS:)

> The bright sunny May,
> The wheat in the fields turns amber,
> After harvest, bread we'll make,
> The bride enters the wedding chamber.

(*The* CHORUS, *dressed in modern costume, enters singing from deep stage.*)

CHORUS: (*Singing*)

> China was born on this yellow earth,
> The descendants of the Dragon in the East it nursed,
> Great Yu's[2] footprints were once all over the land,
> Where dashed King Wu's[3] chariot grand.
>
> Traversing the dense, impenetrable mountain peaks,
> Walking out of the dream of five thousand years,
> History raises the same queries:
> "When will you wake up, Dragon in the East?"
>
> Even if ahead there's a difficult path,
> Even if there are mountains to climb ever higher,

---

[2]A legendary tribe leader in ancient China famous for taming the waters.
[3]King Wu was the founder of the Zhou dynasty in the ninth century B.C.

Even if there are mountains to climb ever higher,
To themselves, the question they'll always ask,
They'll seek and search, never retire.

(*As the singing subsides, the* CHORUS *disperses.*)

(*Light changes*)

Act One
Scene One

(*At the side of the sloping fields of Sangshuping. Local cadres who come to estimate the yield are drawing near, picking their teeth after a hearty meal.*)

DIRECTOR LIU: Jindou, Jindou!

OTHER CADRES: J-i-n . . . d-o-u!

(*Braying of a donkey can be heard.*)

LI JINDOU: Coming.

(*Pulling ZHU XIAOPING with him,* LI JINDOU *comes running from a distance.*)

LI JINDOU: Director Liu, here's a little something from our team.

(LI *and* ZHU *serving tea and cigarettes to* DIRECTOR LIU *and his group.*)

DIRECTOR LIU: (*politely*) You shouldn't have.

CADRES: Li Jindou, you shouldn't have.

LI JINDOU: We're much obliged that you traveled this far. Director Liu, I hope the food was at least enough?

DIRECTOR LIU: Fine. All right, now, let's go look at the crops in the fields.

(DIRECTOR LIU *and the cadres walk to the fields and inspect the crops.*)

ZHU: (*To* LI) Team leader, if you don't need me, I'm taking off.

LI JINDOU: Oh, son, you can't go.

ZHU: Anything else you want me to do?

LI JINDOU: Estimation of the yield is a big thing for our village. (*Whispering*) A low estimation and we'll be able to get something out of the crops, otherwise we get nuthin' for our labor. You city kids are smart and have seen more of the world. You've got to help me deal with them.

ZHU: How in the world could I help?

LI JINDOU: Of course you can. Watch what I do. There're lots of tricks in this business.

DIRECTOR LIU: (*From the fields*) Jindou, Comrade Jindou . . .

LI JINDOU: Coming, coming.

(LI *walks to meet* DIRECTOR LIU *and the other cadres who are coming out of the fields.*)

DIRECTOR LIU: Congratulations, Comrade Jindou. You've got good crops.

LI JINDOU: Oh, they're OK.

CADRE B: They're just OK? Look at the grain, round and full. You can hardly walk in the fields. Out of every *mu*[4] you can get at least . . .

DIRECTOR LIU: Two hundred and ten *jin*.[5]

LI JINDOU: My!

DIRECTOR LIU: What d'you mean?

LI: (*Smiling*) If every *mu* could yield two hundred and ten, I'll eat my hat.

CADRE C: Then, how much would you say?

LI JINDOU: If you ask me, at most a hundred and forty, or fifty . . .

---

[4]One *mu* equals about one-sixth of an acre.
[5]One *jin* equals about a pound.

DIRECTOR LIU: A hundred and forty or fifty?! Pah! If it's only a hundred forty or so, I'll eat it for you.

(*Suddenly, a donkey brays.*)

LI JINDOU: (*Toward the braying sound*) That damned ass, bellowing after a bellyful. Somebody take it home. (*Turning to* DIRECTOR LIU) My dear director, when have you ever seen a yield of two ten around here? You've worked in the fields, you know what's it like. How can it yield two ten, what with getting scattered in the fields and wasted on the threshing ground? Besides, there's no guarantee about the freaking weather.

DIRECTOR LIU: No more arguments. Two ten. Let's go.

LI JINDOU: Please, dear director. Why in such a hurry? Let's talk about it. How about another go?

DIRECTOR LIU: (*Getting impatient*) Look at you! Li Jindou, do we have to go through this every year? You fight like crazy over a couple of pounds. We're all making contributions to the country. This is not a marketplace—what makes you think you can haggle like this?

LI JINDOU: Director Liu, please hear me out.

CADRE B: Li Jindou, look here. I've been working in this county for more than ten years and I've seen you get into trouble quite a few times over this kind of wrangling. You've been a cadre a good twenty years—you should know better. But you still have that small-farmer mentality.

LI JINDOU: (*Grumbling*) What small-farmer mentality? Every year the quota is so high. What am I going to tell the commune members?

DIRECTOR LIU: Li Jindou, watch your mouth. Don't you know what situation we're in?

LI JINDOU: I know, I know! The whole country is flourishing!

DIRECTOR LIU: The situation's not just great. It's fantastic. Therefore, we poor and lower-middle peasants should make greater contributions.

LI JINDOU: Yeah, yeah. We should make contributions. We should offer our souls . . .

DIRECTOR LIU: So, what's there to talk about? Let's go.

LI JINDOU: My dear leaders, please. Every year at this time, you overestimate. Two hundred or three hundred, it's easy for you to say. But after the harvest, there is "loyalty grain" and there is "devotion grain" to be delivered to the state. What's there left for us peasants? (*Getting more and more agitated*) The little ones must be fed and the grown-ups have to eat to work the fields. All these years we've heard that the situation is getting better. (*He seems to be losing his self-control.*) Well, it's getting better all right. But after working our butts off for a year, we peasants don't even have a slice of white bread on our table. How do you expect us to live?

(*Everyone is shocked.*)

DIRECTOR LIU: (*Loudly*) Li Jindou!

(LIU *throws the hot tea in his cup at* LI JINDOU.)

CADRES: Jindou, how dare you!

(LI *is shaken.*)

DIRECTOR LIU: (*Less sternly*) Our country is big and we've got lots of people. You're hard-pressed, but who isn't? Anyway, your grain won't be filling my mouth, so cut out this nonsense.

LI JINDOU: How dare I talk nonsense! We peasants don't have the guts. Let's be reasonable.

(LI *takes the teacup from* DIRECTOR LIU *and walks toward* ZHU XIAOPING *to fill it up.*)

DIRECTOR LIU: Be reasonable? Bah! Fuck reason. Do you know how much surplus grain the higher-ups have set for a small commune with a couple of thousand people like ours?

ZHU: What? The crops aren't in yet and they've already figured out our surplus grain?

DIRECTOR LIU: What do you know, young puppy! Let's go.

(*Frantic,* LI JINDOU *grabs* DIRECTOR LIU*'s sleeves, begging desperately.*)

LI JINDOU: Director, please. When d'you ever see us getting two ten out of a *mu* in Sangshuping? Please reestimate for us. We're all old neighbors. You'll make yourself very popular here if . . .

DIRECTOR LIU: Why are you grabbing me? Want a fight?

(DIRECTOR LIU *moves to push away* LI JINDOU. LI *raises his arm to fend* LIU *off and accidentally elbows him.* LIU *slaps* LI *across the face. The* VILLAGERS *swarm over.* LI JINDOU *starts to sob while the local* CADRES *pull him this way and that, trying to joke it off.*)

CADRES: Jindou, why are you acting like this?

DIRECTOR LIU: Sangshuping is the hardest to deal with every year at this time. Let's go.

(*Still sobbing,* LI JINDOU *stands up from the ground to stop* DIRECTOR LIU.)

LI JINDOU: Director, please don't go. Have some dinner first. (*To* ZHU XIAOPING) Sonny, the director wants to go. Run and tell your Second Aunt to prepare food for the cadres. Good food.

ZHU: (*Angrily*) I'd rather feed the dogs. (*To the cadres*) You can't go. First tell us why you can just hit people. Why?
(DIRECTOR LIU *and the rest are surprised.*)

LI JINDOU: (*To* ZHU) Let it pass. We peasants don't count for nuthin'. Can't make a big fuss of it.

ZHU: We can't let him hit you for nothing. (*To* DIRECTOR LIU) You must apologize to our team leader.

DIRECTOR LIU: Who the hell is this kid?

CADRE A: A kid from the city.

DIRECTOR LIU: I see, a rebel, are you? You wanta practice armed rebellion here? Huh?

ZHU: Don't know what you're talking about. See if you dare to hit him again.

DIRECTOR LIU: What if I do? What are you going to do about it?

ZHU: You don't expect to get away with it, do you?

DIRECTOR LIU: Take him to the commune for me! I was just thinking that I need to make an example of someone who sabotages the summer harvest.

(ZHU XIAOPING *grabs a shoulder pole from a* VILLAGER *and charges at* DIRECTOR LIU. *Several* CADRES *attempt to stop* ZHU *but are driven back by him.*)

LI JINDOU: Stop it, kid! A dozen *jin* of wheat aren't worth your life. I can't deal with it. You have your backup, but what shall we do?

ZHU: You bully poor peasants and take advantage of them. But you just wait until you hear who my old man is . . .

(XÜ CAIFANG, *disheveled and sloppily dressed, steps out of the crowd.*)

XÜ: The kid's old man is a high-ranking official in the provincial revolutionary committee.

(*The local* CADRES *are stunned.*)

DIRECTOR LIU: Who's the kid's father?

(LI JINDOU *shoves* XÜ CAIFANG *aside.*)

LI JINDOU: I told you not to touch him. The kid's old man is quite a big shot. Even the head of revolutionary committee of the prefecture has to humor him.

DIRECTOR LIU: (*Blaming* LI) Jindou, you S.O.B. Why didn't you tell me? (*To* ZHU XIAOPING) Look here, kid . . . (*Intending to talk to* ZHU.)

ZHU: (*Grabbing* LIU's *collar*) Unless you apologize to our team leader, you're not seeing the end of me yet.

DIRECTOR LIU: Damn you, Li Jindou, tell him to let go.

(LI *hurries over to them, trying halfheartedly to break them up.*)

LI JINDOU: Enough. It's all right. Let go. The director hasn't decided on the estimate yet.

DIRECTOR LIU: Exactly. We can talk about the estimate according to policy.

LI JINDOU: (*Enthusiastically*) Let go, kid. Let go.

ZHU: (*Stubbornly*) No!

LI JINDOU: Sonny, please do this for our village. Let go.

(ZHU *releases his hand, cursing and complaining.*)

DIRECTOR LIU: This is outrageous.

LI JINDOU: Director Liu, what about the estimate?

DIRECTOR LIU: Jindou, you'd better give him a piece of your mind. You let this happen again, and I won't set the estimate at a hundred and seventy, ever. (*To the* CADRES) Let's go.

CADRES: (*To* LI JINDOU) Fuck! (*Getting offstage with* DIRECTOR LIU)

(*The* VILLAGERS *gather around* LI JINDOU, *not believing what they have heard.*)

VILLAGERS: How much did he say? How much?

LI JINDOU: (*Excitedly*) A hundred and seventy, a hundred and seventy. That'll do, by god!

(*The* VILLAGERS *are excited as well; then they look at* LI JINDOU, *gradually fall silent, hanging their heads.*)

AUNT JINCAI: It worked out fine. After meeting the quota, we should still have about a dozen *jin* of wheat per *mu*. We don't have to go hungry next spring.

(*Someone begins to weep in the crowd.* WANG ZHIKE *slowly walks onto the stage from afar, carrying a stake.*)

LI JINDOU: What the fuck are you crying about? Don't you know how to be happy? (*He is also wiping tears away from his own eyes.*) Folks, I told you last night that come what may, losing face or flesh, I'll plead for us and get us some grain to feed ourselves. It's done. This is better than anything. This year our food ration can be raised to . . .

(BAO WA *Sees* WANG ZHIKE, *who stands silently to one side of the crowd.*)

BAO WA: Wang Zhike, what the fuck are you doing here? Why aren't you working?

(WANG *stares at* BAO WA *indignantly and puts down the stake with a thump.*)

BAO WA: Hey, you murderer! You want to resist supervised reform?

VILLAGERS: Get out of here. Get out of here.

LI JINDOU: (*Reproachfully*) Bao Wa! (*To* WANG) Zhike, you can knock off today also. What d'you say?

(*Shouldering the stake,* WANG *exits in anger.*)

VILLAGERS: What's the grain ration? How much?

LI JINDOU: This year our basic grain ration can be raised to three hundred ninety-five. Two hundred for kids sixteen and under.

(*The crowd breaks into happiness. The madman* LI FULIN *runs wild in the crowd, shouting, "Fulin get a bride."* YUE WA *chases after him.*)

LI JINDOU: Folks, listen to me. We should thank the student kid for this. Fuquan!

LI FUQUAN: I'm here, Uncle.

LI JINDOU: Enter two days' worth of workpoints for the lad.

WOMEN: What about yourself?

LI JINDOU: None for me.

VILLAGERS: But why?

LI JINDOU: (*Self-mockingly*) I almost screwed up. (*Everyone laughs.*)

LI JINDOU: Hey, you. (*To* XÜ CAIFANG) What are you wasting time for? Go and boil some eggs for the kid. Go on.

XÜ: All right. Xiaoping, come and get them. It won't be a moment. (*Exits*)

LI JINDOU: Everybody get ready. After we hire the seasonal farmhands tomorrow, we'll start the harvest.

(*The crowd scatters in a merry mood.* ZHU XIAOPING *turns to go and sees* LI JINMING, *who has been squatting there smoking all this while by the side.*)

ZHU: Uncle Jinming, why aren't you going home? Isn't it feeding time for the ox?

LI JINMING: Good kid. You did us a great service. (*Standing up to go*) Li Jindou certainly is a shrewd one. Pushed you to the front. Inexperienced as you are, you did it. But what if you didn't have a big shot for a dad?

(ZHU *keeps silent.*)

LI JINMING: (*Singing*)

> Big brother, listen to your sister,
> The road of the world is hard to travel . . .

(*Exits humming*)

(*Amid the music, the stage turns slowly to the left.* ZHU XIAOPING, *lost in thought, gradually disappears from view with the revolving of the stage.*)

Scene Two

(*Music. The chorus members, dressed as* FARMHANDS, *enter with the music. They walk toward the four corners of the stage.*)

FARMHANDS: (*Singing*)

> The slopes are overflowing with the
> golden wheat of Qinchuan,[6]
> To help with harvest, the farmhands
> left Shaan'gan,[7]
> In the steps of our ancestors,
> We follow our great-grandfathers.
>
> We walk and walk,
> Far, far away from home,
> Drop by drop, tears are flowing,
> Oh, my heart is drowning.

(*The* FARMHANDS *sing and move in dancing steps counter to the revolving of the stage.* YÜ WA, *with a* banhu[8] *on his shoulder, walks in the line, teasing the birds in the trees mischievously. The stage stops revolving as the singing ends.*

At the farmhands' hiring area, early morning, a number of MANAGERS *enter calling out to the* FARMHANDS. *The* REPRESENTATIVE *of the group steps forward from the chorus.*)

REPRESENTATIVE: This is it. No more haggling. We won't accept anything under three twenty.

(*The* MANAGERS *walk aside and discuss the price among themselves indignantly in low voices.* LI JINDOU *and* ZHU XIAOPING *hurry on.*)

LI JINDOU: Already noon and you're not doing business yet? What's going on?

MANAGERS: Here comes Jindou.

(*They group around* LI JINDOU, *talking with him under their breath.*)

MANAGER B: Fine, we'll do what you said.

(LI JINDOU *slowly walks toward the center of the stage.*)

LI JINDOU: Let's get going.

(*The* FARMHANDS *quickly gather around him.*)

---

[6]Qinchuan is in Shaan'xi Province.

[7]Shaan'gan refers to the northern part of Shaan'xi Province and the eastern part of Gansu Province, which are less fertile than the Qinchuan area.

[8]A *banhu* is a Chinese fiddle.

LI JINDOU: Sangshuping is the first bidder. We need twenty wheat cutters. The pay for level fields is a dollar fifty per *mu*, the slopes a dollar sixty.

(*Disappointed, the* FARMHANDS *return to their place and squat down.*)

FARMHAND A: Thought we had a Monkey King.[9] He's just a stray monkey after all.

FARMHAND B: Much ado for a quiet fart.

(*The* FARMHANDS *burst out laughing.*)

LI JINDOU: No time for chatting. Easy to be sarcastic. I might be a greenhorn but I know what's what. This is what we can offer this year. You want to take it, you come with me. Otherwise, . . .
(*The* REPRESENTATIVE *of the farmhands slowly approaches* LI JINDOU.)

REPRESENTATIVE: Older brother, you must be somebody to bid first.

LI JINDOU: Of course.

REPRESENTATIVE: Aren't you going a little too far? The crops are great this year. The wheat is thick in the level fields and the slopes are hard to work on. Three fifty wouldn't be asking too much.

LI JINDOU: Three fifty? Good heavens. You might as well put a noose on my neck. You want us to starve?

REPRESENTATIVE: Older brother, three fifty isn't asking too much at all. That's what they are offering over to the east.

LI JINDOU: I don't give a damn what they offered. This is the best we can do. Why don't you go where you can get your three fifty? (*He moves aside and squats down, puffing away at his pipe.*)

REPRESENTATIVE: (*To the* MANAGERS) Hey, folks, I say, we had the first bidder. What about the rest of you?

---

[9]The Monkey King is a character in the classic novel *Journey to the West*. It is noted for its fighting ability and resourcefulness.

MANAGER A: If he can't afford you, forget about us.

MANAGERS: That's right. That's right.

REPRESENTATIVE: What the fuck is going on? People always give and take in this market. Why the hell is he doing all the bidding today?

LI JINDOU: (*Complacently*) I'm not bragging about it, but others may not even be able to offer this much.

REPRESENTATIVE: Fine. I'll make it snappy. I'll make the first move. Three twenty.

LI JINDOU: At most one sixty, that's what I say.
(*The* FARMHANDS *gather to discuss the offer among themselves.*)

FARMHAND A: Odd. Why are there no other offers?

FARMHAND C: They're in it together. Nobody raises the pay so we have to give in.

FARMHAND B: (*Quietly to the* REPRESENTATIVE) The guy's playing dirty, if you ask me.

REPRESENTATIVE: All right. I'll take my chances. Three.

(LI JINDOU *remains silent.*)

REPRESENTATIVE: Motherfucker. This is the last time I'll give in. Two eighty. If you agree, let's get going. Otherwise, we go somewhere else.

FARMHANDS: (*Eagerly*) What do you say?

(LI *keeps smoking without saying a word. The* REPRESENTATIVE *is at his wit's end. The cicadas are clamoring under a blazing sun. The* FARM-HANDS *begin to be flustered.*)

FARMHAND A: (*To* LI) Well, say something. It's getting late.

(*Several* FARMHANDS *get together to talk with each other. After a while, they suddenly turn to* LI *and hold him up to make him talk.*)

REPRESENTATIVE: (*Irritated*) I say, yes or no, you've got to say something. You know the tricks of the market. You can't expect us to cut down the price ourselves.

LI JINDOU: There's no rush. I'm not worried. There're enough farmhands. If you don't want to do it, others sure will.
(*The* FARMHANDS *throw* LI *down in anger.*)

LI JINDOU: My dear brother, it won't do for a traveler to be rude and unreasonable. To tell you the truth, what do we have to eat if we don't harvest the wheat? Every year we depend on you guys to get it in. If you don't work, what do you have to eat? Don't you let the money you got from over there go to your head. I know your area. You don't want my money? Fine. But I'm afraid you won't even have soup to drink back home. You of all people want to be unreasonable? Who do you think you're fooling?

REPRESENTATIVE: (*Angrily*) You son of a bitch. Think you can trash people like this? Let's step outside.

LI JINDOU: (*With a tremble in his voice*) Fine, count me in. Who's afraid of you? (*He feigns taking off his shirt, challenging the* REPRESENTATIVE *for a fight. Suddenly, he stops and turns to him.*) Wait a minute. (*Unexpectedly*) Hey, I say, kid, how many brothers do you have?

REPRESENTATIVE: (*Surprised*) I'm the only one. What has that got to do with it?

LI JINDOU: Fuck. I'll never fight an only child.

REPRESENTATIVE: How's that?

LI JINDOU: I'd never want to cut off your family line. Come on, get me someone who has a brother.

REPRESENTATIVE: You!

(*An old farmhand walks over.*)

OLD FARMHAND: Let it go. Over there to the east may be a different story.

LI JINDOU: (*Getting more energetic at this*) That's more like it. All right, I'll give in a little. I'll sacrifice. Level fields a dollar seventy, slopes one eighty. If you want to accept, let's get moving. You'd have made five bucks already but for all the wrangling.

(*The* FARMHANDS *look at each other in dismay.*)

YÜ WA: (*Grumbling*) The crops are so good this year and that's all you're offering? It wasn't anything like this last year, and you offered two bucks.

LI JINDOU: (*Slapping his thigh*) You are on! On this market there's no taking it back. This young man said two bucks. I accept. Two bucks.

YÜ WA: Now, wait a minute. I didn't mean two bucks.

(*Complaining, the* FARMHANDS *pull* YÜ WA *aside.*)

OLD FARMHAND: Sonny, be careful what you say on the market. Once offered, you can't take it back.

LI JINDOU: All right, all right. I'm not going to be so hard on you. You've already wasted so much time. I'll add ten cents to it. Two ten, what do you say?

(*The* FARMHANDS *are silent.*)

OLD FARMHAND: In my opinion, the offer's OK. Let's accept it. If we work harder and cut a couple of *mu* more, we can make up the difference.

REPRESENTATIVE: (*Seeing no alternative*) All right, we'll accept.

LI JINDOU: Fine. Deal.

(*The crowd breaks up.* LI *and* ZHU *begin to choose among the* FARM-HANDS. *Those picked out stand to one side.* YÜ WA *wants to elbow his way into the group.* LI JINDOU *stops him.*)

LI JINDOU: Look here, sonny. I'd love to give you a job, but you're still young. It's tough over there at my place. If you ruin your health, what will you do the rest of your life?

(YÜ WA *walks aside dejectedly. The* REPRESENTATIVE *jumps up.*)

REPRESENTATIVE: You're going too far. A moment ago you controlled the market. Now you're being so picky. Let me tell you, if you leave out this kid, you can forget about us all.

(*The* FARMHANDS *echo him in one voice.* ZHU XIAOPING *pulls* LI *to one side.*)

ZHU: Team leader. Let's take him.

LI JINDOU: No way. I'm looking for farmhands, not a dumb lad who's only good for show.

OLD FARMHAND: Hey, compadre. You're going too far today. Who ever saw someone who hires like you? I've seen many things in my times and been a farmhand all this while. I've never seen anyone like you. Everyone has to work and live. We all have this trouble or that. Just don't overdo it. Even a rabbit will bite when he's cornered.

LI JINDOU: Fine, fine. I'll shut up. After what you've said, I'll take even a couple of the blind and crippled. (*He turns to go.*)

OLD FARMHAND: Wait a minute. (*Pointing to the* REPRESENTATIVE) What about him?

LI JINDOU: (*Glancing at him*) For him, level fields are one fifty and slopes one sixty. This is it, take it or leave it.

(*The* REPRESENTATIVE *squats down to one side furiously.*)

OLD FARMHAND: Brother, join us. Or what are you going to eat today?

REPRESENTATIVE: (*Swallowing the insult*) All right.

FARMHAND C: Let's go!

FARMHANDS: Let's go!

(*Lively and cheerful music breaks forth. The* FARMHANDS *quickly run toward the four corners of the stage as it begins to slowly turn to the right. The* FARMHANDS *dance to the music and move in the opposite direction.*)

Scene Three

(*At the entrance of the village.* ZHU XIAOPING *runs to the side of the cliff and calls into the village.*)

ZHU: The farmhands are here!

(*As the stage revolves, a group of jubilant girls and women chatting and jabbering dash out of their cave dwellings to the entrance of the village accompanied by the music.* XÜ CAIFANG, *disheveled and slovenly, runs along with the crowd.*

The stage stops. In the fields, the arrival of the farmhands has brought much life to remote Sangshuping. The isolated village suddenly is seething with excitement. The FARMHANDS *and* VILLAGERS *dance happily together.* XÜ CAIFANG *and a couple of women snatch the white kerchief dropped by* YÜ WA *and tease him with it, dancing around.*)

LI JINDOU: Start—cut—ting!

(*The* FARMHANDS *and* VILLAGERS *change to a wheat-cutting dance of bold and dynamic movement in time with the music. One row after another they bend down and straighten up. The handsome, delicate-looking* YÜ WA *works deftly with his sickle, leaving the other* FARMHANDS *behind. A moment later, he starts to sing a folk song.*)

YÜ WA: (*Singing*)

> The woods across from me
> Hides in my heart
> She is the living soul
> In my life . . .

(*The stage turns to the right with the singing.* YÜ WA *and the others gradually disappear from view.*

Hiding under the cliff, XÜ CAIFANG *is listening to the intoxicating song. Suddenly* LI JINDOU *walks up, in a dark mood, and drags* XÜ *off without a word.*

Light changes as the music fades.)

Scene Four

(*On the road at the entrance of the village, in front of* BAO WA's *cave dwelling.* LI JINDOU, *cursing, forces* XÜ CAIFANG *to go to* BAO WA's *home.*)

LI JINDOU: Move on, move on! You damn girl. You stirred up the trouble. You couldn't possibly expect me to send you there in a grand sedan chair, could you?
(XÜ *squats down and refuses to move.*)

LI JINDOU: You bitch. Your man had been dead not even a couple of days and you were already fooling around, first the truck driver of the commune, and you were even flirting with the heads of the commune. You let people spit at our door and call us names. How can your dad show his face in the village?

XÜ: (*Defiantly*) Don't blame me. That's all backbiting. Nothing else.

LI JINDOU: (*Getting more furious*) Shut your trap. Last year you tried to run off with the cloth seller. Was that also backbiting?
(XÜ *is silent.*)

LI JINDOU: Move along. Don't even try to be stubborn. If you don't apologize to Bao Wa, there won't be any peace for you.

XÜ: Why should I? He spit on me and swore at me first. I only talked back once and you want me to apologize to him?

LI JINDOU: (*Angrily*) If you hadn't egged his woman on to fight with him, how in the world would he have come to our door and cursed us up and down the street? (*Taking off his shoes to beat her*) Are you going or not? You could save yourself another beating.

(XÜ *weeps, feeling wronged.*)

LI JINDOU: What's there to cry about! Go this minute, or else . . . (LI *raises his shoes.* XÜ *jumps up and runs toward* BAO WA*'s home.*)

LI JINDOU: That's right. I see you were born an ox that won't move unless whipped. (*Turning to call into* BAO WA*'s cave*) Bao Wa, Bao Wa.

(BAO WA *answers from inside.*)

LI JINDOU: (*To* XÜ) Be polite to him. (*Exits slowly*)

(BAO WA *comes out of his cave dwelling, wiping his hands.*)

BAO WA: (*Looking around*) Who is it?

XÜ: (*Jumping up*) Me.

BAO WA: (*Taken aback*) You? Sounded like your dad.

XÜ: (*Sarcastically*) Guess he's been feeding you so long his call is more pleasant to your ears.

BAO WA: (*Turning to go*) What the hell do you mean by that?

XÜ: Nothing. Just answering you.

BAO WA: Just answering me? You compared me to an animal. You foul-mouthed bitch.

XÜ: (*Bitingly*) How dare I? You're a decent, clean man, the village's militia team leader. You won't even talk with other women. I know you don't sleep with your wife at night.

BAO WA: (*Enraged*) You fucking bitch. What do you want from me?

XÜ: I came to offer myself for a flogging, to spare you the trouble of coming to my home to help hold the club. Well, you don't have to wear your shoes down for me.

BAO WA: (*Snatching off his shoes*) You fucking bitch! See if I don't slap you upside your face.

(BAO WA'S WIFE *'s voice can be heard in the distance.*)

BAO'S WIFE: Bao . . . Wa, come . . . and . . . help.

BAO WA: Coming . . .

(BAO WA'S WIFE *comes downhill with a bundle of firewood on her back, humming a tune of the local opera.*
Putting his shoes back on, BAO WA *goes to meet his wife.* XÜ CAIFANG *tears off her jacket hastily to show her upper body dressed in a sleeveless undergarment. Coming out of her hiding place, she rushes to* BAO WA *and covers his mouth with her hand. Stupefied,* BAO WA *lets himself be dragged by* XÜ *toward his cave.*)

BAO'S WIFE: (*In a singing tone, not knowing what is going on*) Bao Wa, what are you doing?

(*Seeing* BAO WA'S WIFE, XÜ CAIFANG *pushes away* BAO WA.)

XÜ: (*Picks up her jacket from the floor, pretending to be cross*) Look at you, so impatient! This is no place for a kiss . . .

(BAO'S WIFE *is speechless.*)

BAO WA: (*Too confused to explain*) Just now it wasn't she who was hugging me, I hugged her. No, no, no, I hugged her, not she hugged me . . . My god, what am I saying!

(BAO WA'S WIFE *stares at* BAO WA *and* XÜ *fiercely. She throws the bundle of firewood at* BAO WA.)

BAO'S WIFE: I'll kill myself. I don't want to live anymore. You're shameless, Bao Wa. Doing this in broad daylight. You told me there's nothing between you two. I saw you with my own eyes today. I'll kill myself!

(BAO WA *pushes away the bundle and picks himself up only to be shoved into the cave dwelling by his wife. Flaring up,* BAO WA *grabs a huge rolling pin and charges out.*)

BAO WA: You bitch. I'll beat the living daylights out of you.

BAO'S WIFE: You're fooling around with that slut. I don't want to live . . .

(BAO WA *thrusts his wife into the cave. Noise of fighting can be heard.*)

XÜ: (*Gloating*) That's right. Beat her to death. If she dies, you can have me.

(BAO WA *darts out brandishing the rolling pin.*)

BAO WA: Throw mud at me, would you, you bitch. See if I don't smash your damned head.

XÜ: (*Unflinching*) See if you dare. You lay hands on me and I'll take you to the county courthouse and sue you for rape.

BAO WA: (*Speechless*) You! . . .

XÜ: Your wife saw us just now. Consider yourself lucky if they let you go after three years in prison. What did I ever do to you that you must help my dad and Cang Wa beat me up?! Now you've had a taste of your own medicine! See if you dare to bully me again!

(BAO WA *is dumbfounded. After a while, he turns to return to the cave.*)

(*On the cliff, cursing from women and children can be heard.*)

> "Shameless bitch,
> Every man she wants to catch.
> A soul snatcher and a husband killer,
> She is Concubine Yang,[10] the disaster."

(*Defiantly,* XÜ *swears back at them. Assuming the posture of a victor, she nonetheless bursts into tears.*

The stage turns to the right. XÜ *walks toward the small path on the slope, sobbing.*)

Scene Five

(*By the side of the old well from the Tang dynasty.* YÜ WA *is playing the* banhu. XÜ CAIFANG *draws near, attracted by the music. The madman* LI FULIN *comes over woodenly from the other side, shouldering a pitchfork. He moves close to* YÜ WA, *fixing his eyes on the* banhu *in* YÜ WA's *hand.*)

YÜ WA: (*Smiles and nods at him*) Enjoying your soup?

LI FULIN: (*Dully*) Yeah, yeah.

(*All of a sudden,* LI *bawls at the top of his voice.*)

LI FULIN: (*Singing*)

> The lad of eighteen goes to Ganzhou
> And brings back a bride called Xiuxiu.

---

[10]"Concubine Yang" refers to Yang Yühuan (719–756), the favorite concubine of Emperor Xuanzong of the Tang dynasty. She was accused of bringing about the moral corruption of the court and was strangled to death during the An Lushan rebellion in 756.

> Xiuxiu is sixteen,
> The prettiest thing you've ever seen . . .

(XÜ *comes up to* LI, *friendly.*)

XÜ: (*Coaxing*) Fulin. Enough of that. Go back home.

LI FULIN: (*Imitating her foolishly*) Go back home. Yeah, yeah.

(*Suddenly,* LI *throws himself at* XÜ *and cries out crazily.*)

LI FULIN: Have fun with my woman, have fun with my woman.

XÜ: (*Trying to stop him*) Fulin! Stop being silly . . .

LI FULIN: (*Imitating her*) Fulin. Stop being silly.

(*Mumbling to himself,* LI *jumps at* XÜ *and begins to tear at her clothes.* XÜ *tries to dodge him and cries out in alarm.*)

XÜ: Yue Wa, Yue Wa.

(YÜ WA *comes over, trying to intercede, but is jostled aside.* YUE WA *hurries up at the hullabaloo.*)

YUE WA: (*Trying to check him*) Fulin, brother, Caifang's not your woman . . .

LI FULIN: She my woman. Brother have fun with his woman! (*He pushes* YUE WA *away.*)

YUE WA: (*Crying out in distress*) Brother! . . .

(LI *freezes.* YUE WA *turns away and begins to sob in distress.*)

LI FULIN: (*Perplexed*) Sis, sis. Brother don't have fun with woman no more. Sis not cry.

(LI *takes a toy made from nutshells from his neck and tries to tease* YUE WA *with it.* YUE WA *continues to sob.* LI *is desperate.*)

LI FULIN: Sis not cry. Brother beat himself. Beat himself. Brother don't want no woman all life. (*He slaps himself harshly.*)

YUE WA: Please, brother. Stop that. If you want a girl, Dad and Mum will get one for you. Their hearts are already broken over this. Mum said we'll get you a wife even if we have nothing to eat and drink.
(LI *listens with a blank expression on his face.*)

YUE WA: Brother, let's go home.

(LI *stands up and walks away, shouldering the pitchfork. He resumes singing a folk song in a loud voice.*)

YUE WA: (*Solicitously*) Sister Caifang, are you all right?

XÜ: I'm all right. You go back home.

YUE WA: OK. (*Hurries off*)

XÜ: Hey, you . . .

YÜ WA: Yes?

XÜ: Thanks. If it weren't for you here just now . . .

YÜ WA: It was nothing. What's there to thank me for? Well, elder sister, you're all right?
(XÜ *chuckles.*)

YÜ WA: What is it?

XÜ: You didn't even ask how old I am and you addressed me as elder sister.

(YÜ WA *looks down, embarrassed.*)

XÜ: Weren't you the one who led the singing this afternoon?

YÜ WA: (*Nodding shyly*) No great singer.

XÜ: (*Innocently*) It was great. Everyone said so in the village.

(YÜ WA *remains silent.*)

XÜ: Hey, you, what's your name?

YÜ WA: Yü Wa. Surname's the same character as the elm.

XÜ: Yü . . . Wa . . .

YÜ WA: That guy, what's wrong with him?

XÜ: Name's Fulin, the village loony.

YÜ WA: Loony?

XÜ: That's right. A sex maniac. He *was* an honest lad. But his family was too poor to find him a wife, so his marriage was delayed. By the time he was almost thirty he still didn't have a woman for himself. He took it too much to heart, got himself sick. When he has an attack, he chases women around. Poor man.

(YÜ WA *gazes at her.*)

XÜ: Hey, you. Why are you staring at me?

YÜ WA: (*Jerking himself out of it*) Oh, nothing.

XÜ: Hey, kid, well, YÜ WA, how old are you?

YÜ WA: Twenty.

XÜ: Oh. I say, where're you from?

YÜ WA: Pingliang.

XÜ: (*Pensively*) Ping . . . liang. (*Suddenly*) Do you have mountains there?

YÜ WA: No, it's flat as far as you can see, enough to run a horse to the ground.

XÜ: (*Yearningly*) Really? (*Goes over to the well and fiddles with the ropes*) Do you have a family?

YÜ WA: (*Without thinking*) I do.

XÜ: (*Surprised*) You do? You've a family?

YÜ WA: Yeah, there's my dad, my mum, my sisters and brothers, and . . . (*Suddenly realizes what she is talking about*) Oh, what do you mean by family?

XÜ: I mean . . . your own . . .
(YÜ WA *shakes his head without a word.*)

XÜ: Why didn't you get yourself a family?

YÜ WA: We're poor. My mum's blind and . . .
(LI JINMING *comes on from afar, humming some folk song.*)

LI JINMING: (*Singing*)

> The sun is setting,
> It's setting,
> Thinking of my sweetheart,
> In my haste I took the wrong path . . .

(*Hearing him approaching,* XÜ *turns and exits on a run.*)

YÜ WA: Great Uncle, drawing water?

LI JINMING: Yeah.
(YÜ WA *takes the bucket from* LI *and helps him.*)

LI JINMING: You're one of the farmhands?

YÜ WA: Right.

LI JINMING: Good.

YÜ WA: Uncle, who's that girl?

LI JINMING: She's Caifang. The wife of Li Jindou's eldest son. Sold to be his adopted daughter from across the mountains at twelve. Nowadays, we call this adopted daughter. Actually it's child bride. I tell you, not easy for her to suffer through it until her marriage with his son at seventeen. But who'd have expected that her husband would fall into a ravine working in the fields hardly six months later and . . .

YÜ WA: Then she's a widow?

LI JINMING: Well, Li Jindou was afraid that she might not want to stay with the family so he readopted her as his daughter.

YÜ WA: Why did he do that?

LI JINMING: Why? That Li Jindou's calculating, I tell you. All he wants is to remarry the girl to his second son, Cang Wa, to save himself a few bucks.

YÜ WA: Remarry his second son?

LI JINMING: Now you got it. That second son of his is sick with swollen joints.[11] He can eat all right but can't work. How can Caifang agree to that? As the old saying goes, you can have fair-weather friends, but a couple's stuck together for good . . .

YÜ WA: Why didn't she run away then?

LI JINMING: Run away? She gets beaten up if she does that. But the more you beat her the more she wants to run away. Well, young fellow, why are you asking all this?

YÜ WA: Nothing really. Uncle, you do have deep wells here.

LI JINMING: My dear kid, the well's not merely deep, it's seen many years. It was left by His Majesty the first emperor of the Tang. It's called "Intoxicating Spring." Last year when they were breaking up old things,[12] some guys from the province came and looked around. They said that it's a treasure and asked us to take good care of it. Looks like this Tang well—

(LI *realizes that* YÜ WA*'s mind is elsewhere and he is staring into the distance where* XÜ CAIFANG *has disappeared. He smiles and walks away with his bucket.*)

(YÜ WA *continues staring.*)

(*From afar,* LI JINMING*'s singing can be heard.*)

> The well on the hilltop,
> From our ancestors we got,

---

[11]This refers to Kaschin-Beck disease.

[12]In the beginning years of the Cultural Revolution, traditional customs and cultural objects from the past were condemned and often destroyed by the Red Guards as "relics" of feudalistic China.

How deep is the well, you want to know?
A good fifty meters you'll have to go.

(*Light dims.*)

Scene Six

(*On the village ground in front of the livestock shed. Lights grow brighter as the sounds of gongs and drums get livelier and livelier. Though it is already dark, lit by the gas lamps the ground is as bright as day. In the center of the ground there is a square table; sitting behind on two sides are the* MUSICIANS *and the* DRUMMER, *wearing the same old-fashioned spectacles. The* VILLAGERS, *male and female, young and old, encircle the table on all sides.*

After beating the drums and gongs with all their might to enliven the atmosphere, BAO WA, LI FUGUI *and several others stop to rest.* LI JINDOU, *with a pipe in his mouth, saunters in to stand behind the table in the middle of the threshing ground.*)

LI JINDOU: Folks! Our harvest is damn near done today. When we knocked off, some kids suggested that we have some fun and put on a play. Normally, with a harvest like this year's, we should have some fun. After the political movements of these last couple of years, we really shouldn't put on the old superstitious stuff. But with such a bumper crop this year, let's make an exception tonight. You guys can go back home and do some cleaning up on your own afterward. Now let's have the play "The Story of Funu." I'll be Miss Tao Funu.

(*The* DRUMMERS *start to beat the drums and gongs dexterously. Acting the female role,* LI *walks to the middle of the ground and strikes a pose.*)

LI JINDOU: Ai ya. (*Singing*)

On the slopes, the grass is green,
And the flowers fragrant and intoxicating,
They stir up feelings of love in a young girl
like me.

VILLAGERS: (*Shouting and yelling*) Jindou has a hoarse voice. He doesn't suit the role. Get your ass off. Let's have someone else.

LI JINDOU: Fuck. I haven't shown you my stuff yet. (*To the* MUSICIANS) To hell with them. Let's go on.

(*Some impatient youngsters step up and push* LI *off.*)

VILLAGERS: (*To* YÜ WA) Hey, you, kid, you act Xü Xun.

YÜ WA: Fine. I'll be Xü Xun. But who'll be Tao Funu?

XÜ CAIFANG: (*Boldly*) Let me.

(*The* VILLAGERS *are surprised, but they soon quiet down.*)

YÜ WA: (*Reciting introductory remarks*) Since time immemorial, there has always been happiness. Beautiful scenery is bountiful throughout this land. Let's not waste the wind, the flowers, the snow, and the moon; let's not idle away the spring, summer, autumn, and winter. We present morals, ethical codes and principles, we perform the loyal, the filial, the virtuous, and the wicked, the false, and the evil. Today we sing and act in the painted hall, and through our stories of these vicissitudes of life we offer you a piece of advice.

(YÜ WA *moves to the middle in a dramatic gait to the accompaniment of music.*)

YÜ WA: (*Sings*) With my jade flute I climb the eastern tower and roll up the painted curtain. (*Speaks*) Ah, what an exquisite garden! Under the red pomegranate flowers amid the green willows, a girl dressed in a floral skirt is coming out from the flowers and willows holding her *pipa*. She is no other than Miss Funu. But, oh, where is she now? (*Looking left and right*) Ah, there she is, coming out from behind the rockery. (*Singing*)

(*She is crossing the small bridge, playing her* pipa. (XÜ, *acting as Tao Funu, pretends to go across the bridge.*)

XÜ: (*Singing*)

> To dissipate my spring sorrow, I'm playing a *pipa*
> to pass the time,
> My unhappiness I hid from my dear parents.
> Strolling over the bridge, I am suddenly flooded
>   with feelings;
> Slowly plucking the strings, I tell the flowing water
>   —my worries.

YÜ WA: (*Singing*)

> Her song of "Hubo shi"[13] carries hidden bitterness,

---

[13]The name of a music tune used in traditional music dramas.

I cannot help but play the flute to join in.

XÜ: Who is it that plays the flute to join in with my *pipa*? Oh!

(*"Funu lifts her head excitedly and meets the eyes of "Xü Xun." YÜ WA and* XÜ CAIFANG *gaze at each other with a peculiar light in their eyes.*)

(*Light changes amid music*)

(*Lost in their thoughts,* XÜ CAIFANG *and* YÜ WA *walk from the left of the stage, which is revolving to the right.*)

XÜ: Yü Wa, take me with you. Let's go to a far, far away place.

YÜ WA: (*Emotionally*) Caifang, . . . no, I can't, I can't afford to marry you. I . . .

XÜ: You don't have to marry me. No, it doesn't have to be a marriage. I'll go with you.

YÜ WA: But, I'm too poor to keep a wife.

XÜ: Yü Wa, take a good look at me. I was born in utter misery. Never had a good day in my life. I don't mind hardships, I don't mind being poor. As long as you treat me right, I'll even go begging with you. Even that would be sweet.

YÜ WA: Caifang! Wait until the harvest is over. Let's go back to Pingliang.

XÜ: Yü Wa!

(*A pair of actors symbolizing love dance in the spotlight behind* XÜ CAIFANG *and* YÜ WA. *The singing of the* CHORUS *emerges off stage.*)

> Grab the arm and lift the hand,
> Turn him around and give him a kiss,
> Like feeding firewood into the stove
> Burning hot, it's hard to part.

(*The dancers gradually fade from view as the song stops. A ring of shimmering lights suddenly appears around* XÜ CAIFANG *and* YÜ WA. *Light changes. The shimmering lights abruptly turn into torches in the hands of angry* VILLAGERS *surrounding the couple.*)

Scene Seven

(*At the entrance of the village.*)

VILLAGERS: Beat him! Beat him!

LI JINDOU: Beat him! Beat him to death! See if the fucking son of a bitch ever dares to steal another person's wife!

(*Frightening whizzing sound of clubs violently landing on* YÜ WWA, *off-stage.* YÜ WA's *pitiful cries are heard and then they gradually die down.*)

LI JINMING: That's enough! He's passed out.

LI JINDOU: Drag him over here for me!

(BAO WA *and several young men drag* YÜ WA *onstage and throw him to the floor.*)

BAO WA: (*Muttering to himself*) He's good at pretending. (ZHU XIAO-PING *comes out of the crowd.*)

ZHU: Team leader, we can't beat people up like this.

BAO WA: A sound beating is the least we do to a wife stealer.

LI JINDOU: Cut it out. Go ahead and beat him. I'm the law in Sangshu-ping.

LI JINMING: (*Bitterly*) Jindou! Beat him again and you're going to have a life on your hands!

(*The* VILLAGERS *are stunned.*)

LI JINDOU: (*Cursing*) The bastard. All right, we'll let him off lightly. Somebody, go and get that damn woman for me.

(*Several village women push the tightly trussed* XÜ CAIFANG *onto the stage.*)

LI JINDOU: (*Giving an order*) Come back home with me. You'll see what I am going to do with you.

(LI *turns to go. Suddenly he realizes that* XÜ *is not following him but is instead walking toward* YÜ WA. LI *steps in front of* XÜ.)

LI JINDOU: (*Fiercely*) Stop. (*Finding himself ignored*) Stop right there.

XÜ: (*In a low voice but sternly*) Don't you block my way.

LI JINDOU: I'm your dad. Get the hell back home.

XÜ: You're not my father. You're a Li, my surname is Xü. Get the hell out of my way!

LI JINDOU: Go ho—

XÜ: (*Furiously*) Get out of the way! Let me pass.

(LI JINDOU *steps aside involuntarily.* XÜ *drags herself toward* YÜ WA *in spite of her pain.* LI JINDOU *suddenly understands what is going on. Throwing himself on the floor, he starts to howl with tears in his eyes.*)

LI JINDOU: My poor Man Wa! You never thought about your poor dad! How could you have died before me! Heaven be my witness. It took me twenty *jin* of corn to get you a wife. I've sweated blood all my life for you. See what I got in the end, blamed by all! How can you be so cruel to cut off our family line . . . (*Rolling around on the floor, hitting the ground with his fists and beating his head on the floor*) Good Lord, open your eyes and have mercy. How am I going to live on?

(*With tears in their eyes, the* VILLAGERS *help* LI *back to the village. The crowd breaks up with only* LI JINMING, ZHU XIAOPING, XÜ CAIFANG, *and* YÜ WA *left.* ZHU XIAOPING *unties* XÜ CAIFANG. XÜ *throws herself on* YÜ WA.)

XÜ: (*Calling out in a low voice*) Yü Wa, Yü Wa. It's all my fault, all my fault.

LI JINMING: Caifang, his legs are badly hurt. We'd better get him some medicine fast. You stay with him. Me and the student kid will get some medicine from the village.

XÜ: Yes, yes! Please, do hurry.

(LI JINMING *and* ZHU XIAOPING *exit in haste.* XÜ *continues to call out to* YÜ WA.)

XÜ: Yü Wa, Yü Wa, open your eyes. It's me, Caifang. I'm with you.

YÜ WA: (*Slowly coming to*) Caifang . . .

XÜ: (*Wiping the blood off him*) Yü Wa, do you have any regrets?

YÜ WA: No. I'll never regret it even if they beat me to death.

XÜ: Yü Wa, does it hurt?

YÜ WA: No, Caifang.

XÜ: But it hurts me here right to the heart.

YÜ WA: Don't cry, there's a good girl. I wasn't hurt too badly. With you supporting me, we can still make it back to Pingliang. When I'm all right, I'll sing for you.

XÜ: Yü Wa!

YÜ WA: Caifang!

(ZHU XIAOPING *hurries up with some medicine.*)

ZHU: (*Panting*) Caifang, something's happened. Your dad wants to send Yü Wa to the commune's "study class" in the name of the production team and accuse him of abducting women. Uncle Jinming is trying to reason with him.

(XÜ *is speechless.*)

YÜ WA: Caifang, don't be afraid of him. We can sue him.

XÜ: Who are you going to sue? I'm just afraid you'll never be able to bring up the matter.

YÜ WA: Then, I'll fight them to the death.

XÜ: (*Throwing herself into his arms*) Yü Wa, don't be silly. What if you end up half dead? How would you expect me to live on?

ZHU: You'd better make up your minds fast. When Bao Wa comes with his men, it'll be too late.

(XÜ *begins to calm down. She silently takes the medicine from* ZHU *and sets about dressing* YÜ WA's *wounds.*)

XÜ: Yü Wa, . . . you leave first.

YÜ WA: What about you?

XÜ: Didn't you tell me that you'll be here every year?

(YÜ WA *is silent.*)

(ZHU *and* XÜ *help* YÜ WA *to his feet.* XÜ *ties his bundle on his back for him.*)

XÜ: (*Steeling herself*) Go, Yü Wa. I'm yours. Wherever you go, just remember that . . .

YÜ WA: All right. Little one, I'll be back. You wait for me.

XÜ: I will, Yü Wa.

(YÜ WA *starts to leave and stops, turning back.*)

YÜ WA: Caifang, my dear, you wait for me. I'll be back.

XÜ: I will wait . . .

(*The* FARMHANDS *enter with music and line up along the edge of the stage. As it revolves to the left, they move in the opposite direction in dancing steps.* XÜ *and* ZHU *help* YÜ WA *join the line. The chorus moves forward in gallant and firm strides. A song is heard.*)

> China was born on this yellow earth,
> The descendants of the Dragon in the East it nursed,
> Great Yu's footprints were once all over the land,
> Where dashed King Wu's chariot grand . . .

(*Light dims as the music fades.*)

Act Two
Scene One

(*Close to the village ox shed. Lights reveal* SIXTH AUNT, LI JINCAI, *and his wife,* AUNT JINCAI, *looking at one another in deep distress. A moment later,* LI JINDOU *enters, eating noodles from the bowl in his hand.*)

LI JINDOU: What's up?

ALL THREE: Jindou.

LI JINDOU: (*Jokingly*) Jincai, you don't want to worry yourself sick like your son, do you?

SIXTH AUNT: Damn you, Jindou. We're worried to death and you're still in a mood for jokes.

LI JINDOU: What's eating you?

(*The LIs open their mouths to say something and then stop.*)

SIXTH AUNT: Well, it's this. In the spring Brother Jincai offered a good price of two hundred dollars and asked me to find a girl for Fulin. I found one from the Chen family in Chenjiagou east of here. The girl's name's Qingnü, and a virgin, mind you. We had agreed that besides the two hundred paid upon the engagement, the Lis need only to send them some money in compensation for bringing her up and then we can have the wedding the next first lunar month. But . . .

LI JINDOU: We still have plenty of time until then.

AUNT JINCAI: But the Chens sent us word this morning that . . .

SIXTH AUNT: They say the girl's family is short of money right now and Qingnü's mother urges Brother Jincai to pay them the last five hundred "final settlement" money and arrange a wedding earlier . . .

AUNT JINCAI: They also said that we'd better not delay this wedding for their daughter . . .

LI JINCAI: We're not at the end of the year when the production team can distribute money yet. Where do we get the money from? They're pushing us against the wall. Brother Jindou, do you think our production team can loan . . .

LI JINDOU: Well, Brother Jincai, this is a knotty problem.

(JINCAI *looks at him imploringly.*)

AUNT JINCAI: Brother Jindou, do think up something for us, please. Otherwise, how can we have a clear conscience as parents?

LI JINCAI: Fulin wasn't able to afford a wife, all because we were sick. We used up all we had then. He lost his mind and we feel so . . .

LI JINDOU: Let me think.

(*He puts down his bowl, lights his pipe, and reflects. His eyes suddenly light up.*)

LI JINDOU: Brother Jincai, I've an idea, but I don't know if you can bring yourself to do it.

LI JINCAI: As long as we can get a wife for our Fulin, we'll do anything.

AUNT JINCAI: That's right.

LI JINDOU: Fine then. Brother Jincai, Yue Wa's old enough for marriage. A girl will get married sooner or later. I was thinking, why not give her up to a family as an adopted daughter . . .

AUNT JINCAI: You mean as a child bride?

LI JINDOU: No. no. Not a child bride. An adopted daughter.

AUNT JINCAI: Right, adopted daughter.

LI JINDOU: If you give Yue Wa up, you can get five hundred. That'll solve the problem for Fulin.

(*Comprehension suddenly dawning on them, the LIs nod their heads in agreement.*)

AUNT JINCAI: All these years Fulin brought Yue Wa up. If Fulin finds out that he gets a wife in exchange for his sister, well . . .

LI JINDOU: Well, who said you have to tell him everything? I'll go visit my sister-in-law in Gansu tomorrow and ask around in her village.

(*Quick curtain*)

Scene Two

(*The stage is divided into two parts, showing both the inside and outside of* LI FULIN*'s cave dwelling.* YUE WA, *her hair done in a married woman's fashion, has dressed in a garment with flowery patterns against a red background. She huddles in a corner of the* kang,[14] *looking perplexedly at her parents and the others present.* AUNT JINCAI *is packing a bundle without looking up at anyone.*)

LI JINSHENG: Our Yue Wa isn't a little kid anymore. She looks lovely made up like this.

LI JINFA: You're right. Yue Wa, you'll have enough to eat there in Gansu. Much better than it is here.

LI JINSHENG: The kid is grown up and it's natural that she should be married. Coop her up at home and she'll end up an old maid . . .

VILLAGERS: That's right. Exactly.

(*Everybody chimes in, trying to comfort* YUE WA *with sweet talk and coaxing words. The girl looks at the* VILLAGERS *without fully understanding what is going on. From time to time, she steals some glances at her parents.*)

YUE WA: (*Abruptly*) Mum, do I have to go?
(*Everyone laughs.*)

YUE WA: Dad, do I really have to go?
(*Everyone present bursts into laughter again.*)

AUNT JINCAI: Yue Wa, be a good girl. If you don't go, what about your brother's marriage?

YUE WA: Didn't you say that the engagement would be after the harvest? And anyway, after the engagement, why can't I stay home? We'd still have the money to have a wedding for brother. Why must I go now?

---

[14]A brick bed that can be warmed by a stove connected through a tunnel underneath the bed. It is often used in Northern China.

AUNT JINCAI: There, there. Don't be silly. We've found a good family for you. Do what you're told and you'll get less scolding and beating there. Then Mum'll worry less.

YUE WA: All right. I'll remember what you said. Mum, where's brother?

AUNT JINCAI: Sweetie, be watchful. Don't do anything that'll offend your in-laws. Do what they want you to do. Keep them in good humor and they may like you . . .

YUE WA: All right. I'll remember it. Mum, where's brother?

AUNT JINCAI: (*Stopping her*) Shh, Yue Wa.

(*People whisper among themselves.*)

YUE WA: Okay, I won't say anything. Mum, I'm going.

(AUNT JINCAI *stops her and hands her a small bundle.* YUE WA *puts the nutshell toy in her mother's hand.*)

YUE WA: Mum, give this to my brother . . .

AUNT JINCAI: All right.

YUE WA: Mum, don't cry. I'll leave in smiles.

AUNT JINCAI: Child, here, kowtow to your Uncle Jindou to thank him.

(YUE WA *kneels down to* JINDOU.)

LI JINDOU: No need to thank me. As long as you have a good life over there, your uncle will be happy. Let's go. I have to be back early tomorrow morning.

(YUE WA *stands up, trying hard to hold back her tears. She makes a couple of funny dancing movements to cheer up her mother and makes for the door, where she stops, taking a final look at her parents, the* VILLAGERS, *and her small cave, and then charges out of the door, covering her face with her hands.*)

AUNT JINCAI: (*In a heartbreaking tone*) Yue . . . Wa!

(*Quick curtain.*)

(*The chorus of* VILLAGERS *walks to one side of the stage and sings.*)

> China was born on this yellow earth,
> The descendants of the Dragon in the East it nursed,
> Great Yü's footprints were once all over the land,
> Where dashed King Wu's chariot grand.
>
> Traversing the dense, impenetrable mountain peaks,
> Walking out of the dream of five thousand years,
> History raises the same queries:
> "When will you wake up, Dragon in the East?"
>
> Even if ahead there is a difficult path,
> Even if there are mountains to climb, ever higher,
> To themselves, the question they'll continue to ask,
> They'll seek and search, never retire.

(*Lights grow brighter with music. The stage slowly turns to the right.* LI JINDOU *walks uphill holding* YUE WA's *hand.* ZHU XIAOPING *is leading the way with a flashlight in his hands.* XÜ CAIFANG *runs up to them out of darkness and wraps a shawl around* YUE WA's *shoulders. She wants to say something but checks herself. She turns around and disappears into darkness.* LI JINDOU, ZHU XIAOPING, *and* YUE WA *walk off.*

Suddenly, with a loud, shrill wailing, LI FULIN *dashes out of his cave dwelling and runs after the group, holding the toy* YUE WA *left him.*)

LI FULIN: Yue Wa! Yue Wa, . . . I want my sister back. I want my sister back!

(LI FULIN *runs after them, shouting and crying. Finally, he falls down, rolling around like a child throwing a tantrum.*

The song continues.

Light dims.)

Scene Three

(*The wedding ceremony; a stylized dance. Singing of the* CHORUS *off stage*)

> After harvest, shouldering the bridal sedan chair,
> We left home with piping and drumming in the air,
> Let me ask you, miss, why are you unhappy?
> You're already one of the man's family.

You're married, yes, you're married.
Why do you go to the man's house?
Cooking, washing, and cleaning,
And bearing children for your spouse.

(LI JINDOU *enters, shouting amid the happy wedding music.*)

LI JINDOU: The wedding chair is here,
                  The bride is smiling from ear to ear.
                  The groom goes up to meet his dear.

(*Three couples from Sangshuping come up to help* CHEN QINGNÜ, *whose head is covered with a piece of red cloth, to step off the sedan chair.* LI JINCAI, *his wife, and* LI FULONG, *who is there on his brother's behalf, walk up to meet the bride.*)

LI JINDOU: The newlyweds thank their friends and relatives.

(CHEN QINGNÜ *and* LI FULONG, *standing side by side, make three bows to everyone present.*)

LI JINDOU: Present the bride with a fortune.

(*Several women tie two bundles of tree twigs they have prepared for the occasion to the ankles of* CHEN QINGNÜ.[15] *Taking advantage of the opportunity, they lift the cloth on the bride's head to take a peep.*)

BAO WA'S WIFE: I say, isn't she the girl in the commune's propaganda team who acted Li Tiemei?[16]

SISTER CUIPING: You got that right. What a pretty girl.

(*Hearing this, the* VILLAGERS *start to talk all at once among themselves.*)

LI JINDOU: Bride and groom enter the wedding chamber, they'll live happily ever after.

---

[15]A custom that symbolizes the transformation of the identity of the bride from a maiden to a married woman.

[16]Li Tiemei is a major character in the revolutionary opera *Red Lantern*, a story about a revolutionary family during the War of Resistance against Japan (1937–1945).

(*Amid piping and drumming,* LI JINDOU *and the* VILLAGERS *send the couple into the wedding chamber.*

The stage turns opposite to the direction in which the group is moving. Light changes.)

Scene Four

(*Outside* LI FULIN's *wedding chamber, at night.* LI JINDOU, *in control of the situation, sees off the* VILLAGERS *who came for the wedding.*)

LI JINDOU: Brother Jincai, brother Jincai.

LI JINCAI: (*Running up*) Coming. I'm here.

LI JINDOU: It's about time. Let Fulin go to the wedding chamber.

LI JINCAI: (*Calling toward backstage*) Mother, get Fulin out here.

(AUNT JINCAI *and* LI FULONG *come up, pulling* LI FULIN *with them.*)

LI JINDOU: Fulong, it's time you gave the sash to your brother Fulin.

(LI FULONG *reluctantly takes off the red sash that he wears to perform the wedding ceremony for his brother and puts it on* LI FULIN. LI JINCAI *and his wife lead* FULIN *to the bedroom, giving him some last-minute advice along the way.*)

LI JINCAI: Fulin, you wanted a wife, and your dad and mum found you one. Now you two have a good life together . . .
(*Soon all leave the cave and close the door behind them.* LI JINDOU *and* LI JINCAI *exit, talking to each other.*)

AUNT JINCAI: (*Calling into the room*) Qingnü, blow out the light and go to bed early. (*Exits*)

(*It is quiet both inside and outside the wedding chamber. In a little while, the light in the room is blown out. In accordance with local custom, several* YOUNGSTERS *tiptoe to the window, listening intently.*

Suddenly, a bloodcurdling shriek is heard from the chamber, followed by LI FULIN's *shouts and screams. The* YOUNGSTERS *disperse in a rush.*)

LI FULIN: You're not my sister. I want my sister. I don't want a wife!

(*Noise of things being broken inside the room is heard. The door is jerked open and a disheveled* CHEN QINGNÜ *runs out and cowers to one side, terrified.*)

QINGNÜ: (*Transfixed*) He's not my husband. He's not my husband.

(*The illusion of* QINGNÜ'S MOTHER *appears in a spotlight.*)

QINGNÜ'S MOTHER: Don't cry, my daughter. If we didn't marry you off, where'd we have gotten the money to get a wife for your brother?

QINGNÜ: I got into the bridal chair without knowing what was going on. But when I stepped off the chair, I saw him. He looked strong, healthy, and handsome. He looked fine . . .

QINGNÜ'S MOTHER: Dear, don't cry. How could we have afforded your brother's marriage if we hadn't married you off?

QINGNÜ: But in just a flash, how could he turn into, into . . . Ma, you didn't tell me the truth.

QINGNÜ'S MOTHER: Don't cry, my child. If we hadn't married you off, where'd we have gotten the money to get a wife for your brother?

QINGNÜ: Let me come back home, please.

QINGNÜ'S MOTHER: Don't cry, my girl. If we hadn't married you off, where'd we have gotten the money to get a wife for your brother?

QINGNÜ: (*Dully*) No, no. You won't let me come back home. I know it . . .

QINGNÜ'S MOTHER: Dear, your engagement money is . . .

QINGNÜ'S MOTHER *and* QINGNÜ: (*Together*) spent on your (my) brother.

(*Spotlight dims.*)

Scene Five

(*By the side of the old well.* QINGNÜ, *unkempt and bedraggled, sits in a daze.* SIXTH AUNT *enters with a laundry basin.*)

SIXTH AUNT: Qingnü, Qingnü. (*Louder*) Qingnü!

QINGNÜ: (*Startled*) Oh, it's you, Aunt.

SIXTH AUNT: What is it? Fulin beat you up again?

(QINGNÜ *hangs her head.*)

SIXTH AUNT: (*To herself*) We all thought once he's got a woman his sickness will be gone. Who expected that . . .? Qingnü, tell your aunt if you're unhappy. Don't hold it inside. If your health is ruined, you're done for.

QINGNÜ: Aunt, how am I going to make it?

(SIXTH AUNT *is lost in thought.)*

QINGNÜ: Aunt, Fulin's sickness, will it get better?

SIXTH AUNT: What sickness? If you ask us mountain people, he got sick all because he held too much inside himself when he couldn't have a wife . . .

QINGNÜ: Then, it can be cured?

SIXTH AUNT: It's not exactly hard. But you're a virgin—it won't be easy for you to do.

QINGNÜ: (*Pleading*) Please, Aunt. Let me know. It was my rotten fate to be married to a lunatic. If I can help him get better, I'll do anything.

SIXTH AUNT: Fine then. He got sick because of women. If you don't sleep together, if he doesn't have you, how's he going to get rid of his pent-up passion?

QINGNÜ: (*Shyly*) Aunt, Fulin . . . He's sick. He doesn't . . .

SIXTH AUNT: (*Straightforwardly*) He's sick, but you're not. As long as you don't get annoyed and are patient with him. Go slow to turn him on, and when you have kids . . .

QINGNÜ: (*Embarrassed*) Aunt!

SIXTH AUNT: Silly kid. It doesn't sound good, but it'll work.

(After a while, QINGNÜ nods silently.
  Quick curtain.)

Scene Six

(Inside LI FULIN's wedding chamber, at night. When the light goes on, QINGNÜ is leaning on the door, waiting for FULIN. There is wine and food on a small table set up at the center of the large brick bed. After a while, QINGNÜ sits down on the kang *and begins to make herself up, filled with happy expectation. LI FULIN enters with a farm tool on his shoulder, singing a ditty stupidly.)*

LI FULIN: *(Singing)*

> The lad of eighteen went to Ganzhou,
> Brought back a girl called Xiuxiu . . .

(Scared, QINGNÜ moves aside.)

QINGNÜ: *(Quietly, to test his reaction)* Fulin, Fulin . . .

(LI FULIN stares at QINGNÜ with a blank expression on his face. Frightened, QINGNÜ cowers to one side. Then she tries to make LI wash his face but winces back when she sees his face. Seeing QINGNÜ so terror stricken, FULIN chuckles foolishly. He puts down the towel and moves woodenly toward the kang *and discovers the food on the table. All of a sudden, he turns to leave.)*

QINGNÜ: Fulin! I, I cooked that food for you.

(LI again turns to go.)

QINGNÜ: Fulin!

FULIN: I go piss. *(Rushes out)*

(QINGNÜ sits down on the edge of the kang *uneasily. When FULIN returns, she again moves to one side in fright. FULIN sits down and begins to gobble the food.)*

QINGNÜ: Fulin, there's no rush. Here, here's wine.

(*She scrambles onto the central area of the brick bed where the small table for wine and food is set, pours a glass of wine, and holds it out to* FULIN *with trembling hands.* LI *stares at her uncomprehendingly.* QINGNÜ *tries a sip for herself to show him.* FULIN *grabs the glass and pours it into his mouth. He chokes and starts to cough.* QINGNÜ *leans over* FULIN *to pound his back with her fists.*)

QINGNÜ: Told you there's no rush . . .

(LI FULIN *grabs* QINGNÜ*'s hand and smells it. Then he holds the lamp to take a good look at her and removes the flower in her hair.*)

FULIN: (*Chuckling*) See how much you love him. So seductive . . .

QINGNÜ: (*Patiently*) Fulin, what do men get married for? What does a wife do?

(FULIN *thinks for a while.*)

FULIN: (*Rhythmically*) What does a wife do? During the day she'll do the cooking, at night on her breasts you'll be resting, and she'll bear you children. What does a wife do . . .

QINGNÜ: (*Anxiously*) Why did you send a bridal sedan chair for me?

(FULIN *reflects in a stupor.*)

QINGNÜ: Don't you want to have fun with your woman? Sleep with her?

FULIN: (*Hysterically*) Have fun, yeah, yeah, have fun.

QINGNÜ: (*Excitedly*) Fulin. (*Throws herself into his arms*)

(QINGNÜ *weeps from agitation for her fate but also for her husband.* FULIN *becomes unusually quiet, letting* QINGNÜ *snuggle in his arms and caress him. Perhaps he is thinking of a dream in his childhood, a beautiful and distant dream.*)

FULIN: (*Singing*)

> The lad of eighteen goes to Ganzhou
> Brings back a bride called Xiuxiu.

Xiuxiu is sixteen,
The prettiest thing you've ever seen . . .

QINGNÜ: (*Longingly*) Fulin, let's have children . . .

FULIN: (*Suddenly*) Fulin want children, Fulin want children. (*He tears at* QINGNÜ's *clothes.*)

QINGNÜ: (*Scared*) Fulin, take it easy . . . (*Taking off her clothes*)

FULIN: (*Running all around the room*) Fulin want children. Fulin want children . . .

(QINGNÜ *helps to undress* FULIN. *Suddenly the toy left by* YUE WA *drops from the pocket of* FULIN's *coat.* FULIN *snatches it from* QINGNÜ *and mumbles to himself dumbly.*)

FULIN: Sister . . . Where's my sister? Is this my sister? . . .

(QINGNÜ *suddenly realizes what is going on. She throws her arms around* FULIN.)

QINGNÜ: Fulin, stop that. Your sister is married. You got a wife instead. You got me.

FULIN: I don't want no wife. Get back my sister for me. Give me back my sister.

QINGNÜ: (*Persists*) Fulin. Listen to me. Qingnü will cook for you. She'll have children for you . . .

(FULIN *starts to beat* QINGNÜ *violently.*)

FULIN: I don't want no wife. I want my sister.

(*Finally,* FULIN *brutally cuts off* QINGNÜ's *braids with a sickle.* QINGNÜ *shrieks and runs out of the room.*)

FULIN: (*Sobbing*) I don't want no wife. I want my sister . . .

(*Light changes with music; the singing of the chorus emerges offstage.*)

"The Double Ninth Festival,[17] how cheerful,
The red sorghum on the slopes is plentiful,
With longing,
Sis, by the roadside your brother is waiting."

Scene Seven

(*On the hilltops by the side of the cornfields.* LI JINDOU*'s shouting in a singsong voice is heard from afar.*)

LI JINDOU: Break time, break time.

(*In twos and threes, with their farm tools in their hands, the* VILLAGERS *come out of the fields to take a break.*)

VILLAGE LAD: Sister Cuiping, who are you making the sole of the shoe for?

SISTER CUIPING: I'll tell you only if you don't tell your mum.

LAD: You're on.

SISTER CUIPING: For your old man.

(*The* VILLAGERS *burst into laughter.* QINGNÜ *approaches from a distance. She seems to be forever looking for something.*)

XÜ CAIFANG: Qingnü, (*solicitously*) are you tired?

(QINGNÜ *shakes her head with a bitter smile.* XÜ CAIFANG *pours a bowl of water for* QINGNÜ.)

XÜ: Let's move over there to cool off.

(*The* YOUNGSTERS *stop chatting and look at* QINGNÜ.)

XÜ: Any news about the divorce?

QINGNÜ: (*Shaking her head*) They didn't approve.

---

[17]So called because the festival falls on the ninth day of the ninth month in the lunar calendar.

XÜ: Why?

QINGNÜ: The higher-ups said that, that we're still living together, so we must be getting along fine and . . .

XÜ: Why didn't you tell them that he's sick?

QINGNÜ: I did. But they say he can get better.

(XÜ *sits down without a word.* QINGNÜ *is on the point of taking off her coat.*)

QINGNÜ: (*Suddenly*) Where's my sickle? (*She turns to go.*)

XÜ: Qingnü. (*Getting up to go over to* QINGNÜ) What's come over you? Look, you're holding it in your hands.

(QINGNÜ *smiles, feeling embarrassed.*)

XÜ: See, you've got yourself into such terrible shape!

QINGNÜ: (*With a wry smile*) It's the same for every woman.

XÜ: Don't talk nonsense. (*Sitting down to one side, covering her face with her hands*)

(QINGNÜ *slowly takes off her coat, with only her underblouse on.*)

LI JINFA: Such a pretty wife. That fool Li Fulin certainly has his own kind of luck.

SISTER CUIPING: He must've done something good in his previous life.

BAO WA'S WIFE: What a shame. Such a pretty girl, but she's still a virgin.

(*Hearing this, the* VILLAGE YOUNGSTERS *all gaze at* QINGNÜ.)

(LI FULIN's *singing can be heard in the distance.*)

> The lad of eighteen goes to Ganzhou
> Brings back a bride called Xiuxiu.

Xiuxiu is sixteen,
The prettiest thing you've ever seen . . .

VILLAGE LADS: Look! Fulin's coming.

(FULIN *enters without any expression on his face, shouldering a pair of water buckets. He puts them down and, getting a bowl of water for himself, goes to sit by himself to one side. After drinking his water, he sits cross-legged, staring at the sky. The* VILLAGE LADS *talk among themselves while drinking from the water bucket. At a wink from one of them, they gather around* LI FULIN.)

LAD A: Fulin, do you have a wife?
(FULIN *nods woodenly.*)

LAD B: You sure you got a wife?

FULIN: Yeah.

LAD C: But who?

FULIN: (*Searching around stupidly, points to* QINGNÜ) Her.

LAD B: Who says Qingnü's your wife?

FULIN: She is.

LADS: No, she isn't.

FULIN: She is.

LAD C: I tell you, she isn't.

FULIN: I say she is.

LAD D: Have you slept with your wife?

(FULIN *is speechless.*)

LADS: See? Snap out of it. You haven't even slept with her once. How come she's your wife?

(*The* LADS *purposely turn around to go in order to make* FULIN *angry.* FULIN *pants heavily. He wants to say something but cannot. Suddenly, he charges at* QINGNÜ *and grabs her wrists before she has time to react.*)

FULIN: She is my wife, I tell you.

(*The* VILLAGE LADS *turn to surround them.*)

LADS: No, she is not.

FULIN: (*In a loud voice*) Yes, she is!

(FULIN *unconsciously looks for something on the ground. Suddenly, he bends down and tears a piece of cloth off* QINGNÜ*'s blouse.* QINGNÜ *screams and curls up on the ground. Everyone is stunned.*)

LADS: (*Mischievously*) That doesn't count. You tore other women's clothes before. It doesn't mean anything. Qingnü's not your wife.

(FULIN*'s face whitens with anger.* QINGNÜ *realizes things are getting out of hand. She wrenches herself away from* FULIN *with a loud cry and dashes away.* XÜ CAIFANG *tries to stop* FULIN *but he shoves her back.* FULIN *charges after* QINGNÜ. *The* VILLAGE LADS *follow them, jeering and taunting* FULIN. QINGNÜ *shrieks as she is caught by* FULIN *and thrown to the ground.* FULIN *tears off* QINGNÜ*'s pants in the presence of the crowd. The* VILLAGERS *quickly gather around.*)

FULIN: She's my woman. I bought her, exchanged my sister for her.

(FULIN *takes off, holding* QINGNÜ*'s pants high, cruelly but naively. The chorus, dressed as* VILLAGERS, *scatters gradually. Unexpectedly, a broken but spotlessly white statue of an ancient maiden comes into view, representing time immemorial and all the women sacrificed over the centuries.* XÜ CAIFANG *solemnly and respectfully covers the statue with a piece of yellow silk. The chorus follows the girl and kneels down around the statue. The stage slowly turns to the left when the music starts.*)

> China was born on this yellow earth,
> The descendants of the Dragon in the East it nursed,
> Great Yü's footprints were once all over the land,
> Where dashed King Wu's chariot grand . . .

(*Music lingers as the stage slowly darkens.*)

Act Three
Scene One

(*Inside the ox shed. The* VILLAGERS *are holding a public meeting to criticize and denounce the "murder suspect"* WANG ZHIKE.)

BAO WA: (*Shouting slogans*) Leniency to those who confess their crimes and severity to those who refuse!

VILLAGERS: (*Repeating after him*) Leniency to those who confess their crimes and severity to those who refuse!

BAO WA: Fess up!

WANG: I don't know. I didn't kill anybody.

BAO WA: Bullshit! You give us the same crap at every meeting.

LI JINDOU: Let our villagers talk.

(*The* VILLAGERS *look at each other hesitantly.*)

LI JINDOU: Who'd like to be the first? (*To* BAO WA) You take the lead.

(BAO WA *takes out the speech he has prepared.*)

BAO WA: Dear team leader Li Jindou and dear group leader of the poor peasants Li Jinsheng, the east wind is blowing and the battle drum has sounded. Who's afraid of whom in this world? With tre-tre-tremen-dous rage, let me announce, I mean, denounce the murder suspect Wang Zhike's heinous crimes. Er . . . (*To* LI JINDOU) Second Uncle, what's this word?

LI JINDOU: Fuck off. You think you can earn five workpoints like this?

SISTER CUIPING: (*Interested*) What? You can earn five workpoints?

(*The* VILLAGERS *begin to whisper to one another.* BAO WA'S WIFE *pulls* BAO WA *back to his seat.*)

LI JINSHENG: Next?

(LI JINMING *snores loudly.*)

LI JINDOU: Jinming!

LI JINMING: (*Wakes up with a start*) Is the meeting over? (*Stands up to go*)

(*The* VILLAGERS *laugh.*)

LI JINDOU: What the fuck's so funny?

LI JINSHENG: We're holding this meeting to criticize and denounce. We should also expose his crimes.

SISTER CUIPING: I'll expose him.

BAO WA: (*Shouting*) Leniency to those who confess their crimes and severity to those who refuse!

VILLAGERS: (*Following suit*) Leniency to those who confess their crimes and severity to those who refuse!

VILLAGER A: (*Shouting*) Be stubborn and you'll—

LI JINDOU: (*Cutting him short*) That's enough.

SISTER CUIPING: (*Straightforwardly*) Listen to me, Wang Zhike. I'll expose you. The other day I passed your house and heard you say to your kid that . . .

LI JINDOU: (*Eagerly*) What did he say?

SISTER CUIPING: He said, "Dad has liquid food and Mian Wa, you have solid food so you can grow up quick." Let me ask you, what do you want him to grow up to be?

VILLAGERS: Yes, out with it. What do you want him to grow up to be?

SISTER CUIPING: (*Faster*) You, Wang Zhike, you're a murderer. See how you spoiled your kid? He's already seven or eight, but you still carry him round on your back and in your arms. Who else spoils his kids like you? I have more. The kid's not a baby anymore, but you're still feeding him by hand—

LI JINDOU: (*Interrupting*) That's fine. That's fine. Now you can go back to your seat.

SISTER CUIPING: I haven't finished yet.

LI JINDOU: Keep the rest for your ancestors.

SISTER CUIPING: Team leader, I didn't do anything to offend you. Why should you curse my ancestors? I'm also a poor peasant. I've never done anything wrong to offend you leaders.

LI FUGUI: Enough of that nonsense. You gossipy woman. Get the hell home now!

SISTER CUIPING: I'm not done yet. I want to speak out. The wheat we got from the team last year—

LI FUGUI: What the fuck are you talking about? Go back home!

(LI FUGUI *takes off a shoe to beat* SISTER CUIPING. *The couple gets into a fight. The room is in an uproar.*)

LI JINDOU: (*Pounding the table*) Stop that! Those who won't will have their workpoints taken away!

(*The crowd quiets down.* SISTER CUIPING *picks herself up from the floor.*)

SISTER CUIPING: All right, team leader. I won't say anything more. Okay?

LI JINSHENG: Let's get on with the meeting. Wang Zhike, stand up!

LI JINDOU: Confess how you killed the stranger, the cloth peddler.

(*The* VILLAGERS *shout slogans.*)

WANG: I have nothing to say. I didn't kill anybody.

BAO WA: You didn't? Tell me then how did the guy die? What? You want to eat me? You ingrate. How did we Lis treat you? The cave where you had your wedding was dug for you by us Lis. But as soon as your wife died, you changed your son's surname to yours.

(WANG *glares at* BAO WA *indignantly.*)

BAO WA: (*Shamed into anger*) Lower your head!

(WANG *suddenly raises his head and by chance catches* BAO WA *on the chin.* BAO WA *squats down, crying out in pain. Several* MILITIAMEN *come up to hold* WANG *down but are sent staggering by him. The angry crowd surrounds* WANG, *kicking and beating him.* WANG *has to squat down with his arms over his head to protect himself. Seeing this,* MIAN WA, *who has been looking on from the slope outside, runs into the shed.* XÜ CAIFANG *pulls him back.*)

LI JINDOU: (*Stopping the crowd*) Enough. Stop it. Wang Zhike, with your attitude, you'll only get severe punishment.

LI JINSHENG: Now Fuquan will announce the decision on murderer Wang Zhike.

LI FUQUAN: Wang's private garden plot will be taken back; he won't be allowed to raise any poultry. Your family's food ration will be lowered to one hundred and eighty-two for the year.

SISTER CUIPING: (*Involuntarily and good-hearted*) Oh, how can they live on . . .

LI FUQUAN: Shut up.

LI JINDOU: We'll stop here today. If you behave like this again next time, don't blame us for not being nice. That's it. Meeting over.

(*The* VILLAGERS *and* LI JINDOU *exit. Comforting* MIAN WA, XÜ CAIFANG *leads him to his father. The child stands in front of* WANG, *not knowing what to say. Seeing his son,* WANG *smiles at him, trying to laugh it off. Then he squats down, offering to carry* MIAN WA *on his back. Gazing at his father for a minute,* MIAN WA *turns around and walks over to one side.* WANG *straightens up slowly, glances at* MIAN WA, *and goes uphill.* MIAN WA *tags behind at a short distance.*

The stage revolves to the right. The chorus, dressed as VILLAGERS, *enters and stands in a corner.*)

VILLAGERS: (*Singing*)

> Our backs turned to the sky,
> Every day we run low and high,
> What are we busy for?
> To get something to feed us all.
>
> We live in this way from day to day,
> Whoever fights for our grain
> Will have nothing to gain.
> Yes, he'll have nothing to gain.

(WANG *and* MIAN WA *trudge on in the direction opposite to the turning stage. Lights gradually change.*)

Scene Two

(*In the burial ground of* LI JIAGOU. WANG ZHIKE *and* MIAN WA *approach.*)

WANG: Wife. We're here to see you.

(MIAN WA *runs up to the tomb and kneels down.* WANG *does the same.*)

WANG: Wife, we cannot live here anymore. I haven't killed anybody but they say I did. We must have something to eat, but they have lowered our ration. I want to leave. I really want to bring Mian Wa with me and go to a place far, far away from Sangshuping. But I, I cannot leave you here. Sixteen years, I've been here. If you and your dad hadn't kept me, an orphan like me wouldn't even have known what a home is like. But I haven't had a chance to repay you yet. How can the two of you leave the world before us?

(LI FUMIAN *steps forward from the chorus.*)

LI FUMIAN: Husband, you had no father and mother. We cannot let your family line die after you. After I'm dead, let the kid have your surname. If you miss me, you can name our son Wang Xiaomian. As long as you stay here near us, my dad and I will rest in peace in the underworld.

WANG: Wife, we won't leave here, we won't. We'll be with you even if we have to die here.

(LI JINDOU *slowly enters.*)

LI JINDOU: Zhike, you're here.

(WANG *pulls* MIAN WA *to his feet and turns to go.*)

LI JINDOU: Zhike, . . . Have a smoke with me.

(WANG *stares at him without a word.*)

LI JINDOU: I see. You're still angry about what happened today. I know how you feel. But there's nothing I can do about it. Let me make it clear right here in front of your wife's grave.

WANG: I didn't kill anyone. I'm innocent.

LI JINDOU: You didn't kill anyone? You can repeat this to me, and to the villagers. But I'm afraid the cops won't buy it.

(WANG *is silent.*)

LI JINDOU: See, you've nothing to say to that. That year you and the cloth peddler went to Gansu together, he was robbed and killed. You said that you and he had separated long before that, but who's your witness? Who saw you two part?

(WANG *is speechless.*)

LI JINDOU: You see, you've no witnesses. Now look, we're talking about a murder here. The higher-ups trusted the case to us. How dare we be slack?

(WANG *keeps silent.*)

LI JINDOU: Though you're not one of us Lis, Mian Wa's grandfather and I were of the same generation. We didn't hand you over to the police; instead we kept you under the team's supervision. We Lis took pity on you. If the higher-ups find out, you'll probably end up in prison.

WANG: I'm not afraid, I'm innocent. I didn't commit any crime.

LI JINDOU: Innocent? Tell it to the cops.

WANG: No. Why should I?

LI JINDOU: No? I know you can't go and tell them that. After all, we're in the same village, and you're brother Jinhong's live-in son-in-law. If you went, who's going to take care of your kid?

LI FUMIAN: (*Aside*) Then what do you think he should do?

LI JINDOU: If you ask me, you should take Xiaomian with you and go back to your hometown in Longdong.

LI FUMIAN: You mean he should leave here?

LI JINDOU: That's right. Though you have no relatives there, it is, after all, where you grew up. Better than here.

(WANG *remains silent.*)

LI JINDOU: What do you say? If you promise to go, the team will give you fifty or so pounds of grain plus ten bucks or so. What do you say?

WANG: (*Suddenly realizing his intention*) Li Jindou, you . . .

LI JINDOU: What do you mean?

WANG: For all that talk, you were only trying to drive us out of here! Now I understand.

LI JINDOU: Who's trying to drive you out of here? Look at you. You took my goodwill for bad intentions. (*Pause*)

LI FUMIAN: Husband, go—leave here.

WANG: (*Aside*) What? You also want me to go?

LI FUMIAN: Husband, Sangshuping won't tolerate a Wang family here. That old cave dwelling you have now originally belonged to a Li. It's a part of the Li family property.

WANG: (*Aside*) Don't say any more. I won't go, that's that. (*To* LI JINDOU) Don't drive me to the wall or I really will kill someone.

LI JINDOU: You . . . ! Wang Zhike, if that's what you say, don't blame me for whatever happens later. Fumian, my niece, you heard what he said. Don't blame me now. (*Exits*)

WANG: Wife, I won't go. I'll die and be buried here. (*He throws himself down on his knees in front of the grave.*)

(MIAN WA *snuggles up to* WANG ZHIKE. LI FUMIAN's *shadow lingers on. The* CHORUS *pulls* LI FUMIAN *back into the line, singing.*)

> Live or die, I won't desert you,
> Die or live I won't leave the valley
> Alive, we eat from the same bowl,
> Dead, we'll share one grave.

(*Light dims.*)

Scene Three

(*In a big barn near the village ox shed. Several village VIPs are listening to* LI FUQUAN *reading the written complaint to be submitted to the police.*)

LI FUQUAN: ... As listed above, we poor and lower-middle peasants in Sangshuping are very, very indignant with the murderer Wang Zhike, who threatened to kill and murder as re-re-talia-tion against the revolutionary masses. We u-u-u-unanimously request that the police arrest the counter-revolutionary Wang Zhike and protect our—

LI JINDOU: All right, all right. No need to go on. Well, as long as it makes clear how we poor and lower-middle peasants feel, it'll be enough. Does anyone have anything more to say?

(*People start to talk among themselves.*)

LI JINSHENG: The team leader asked you if you've got any other opinions.

LI JINGUI: I say, second brother, this isn't quite right. Let's just label him counterrevolutionary and keep him here in the village to reform through labor under our supervision.

LI JINDOU: Nonsense. In that case our team has to supply a grain ration for the prisoner. Don't you know that grain rations for prisoners in the county jail are provided by the state? If you've got more grain in your house than you know what to do with, how about taking care of a couple of prisoners there?

LI JINGUI: What the fuck are you talking about?

LI JINSHENG: Who else has any objections to the complaint?

VILLAGERS: No.

LI JINSHENG: In that case, put your fingerprints on the complaint.

(*People gather to leave their fingerprints.* LI JINDOU *moves aside, lost in thought.*
  The scene freezes for a moment. The chorus of VILLAGERS *enters.* LI JINMING *steps out of the chorus.*)

LI JINMING: Jindou, you realize this is filing a suit in court?

LI JINDOU: (*Aside*) A suit? No, not at all. This is a letter of accusation from us poor and lower-middle peasants.

LI JINMING: Come on, this isn't just a letter. It's a written complaint. Jindou, out with it. You did this all because you didn't want the cave dwelling to fall into the hands of a Wang. But haven't you thought about what this may do to Wang Zhike? This may cost him his life.

LI JINDOU: (*Aside*) But our team needs that cave to put our stone mill in right now.

LI JINSHENG: (*To* LI JINDOU) Second brother, we're done. Your turn to put down your fingerprint.

(LI JINDOU *walks toward the table and rolls up his sleeves, making a great show of preparing to make the print.* LI JINMING *returns to the chorus. The stage slowly moves to the right with the music. The table with the complaint on it suddenly collapses under the pressure of* LI JINDOU's *hand. Though falling down with the table,* LI *firmly puts his print on the paper.*
  Light gradually goes out.)

Scene Four

(*Outside the village, at the edge of the fields on the slope.*

The stage gradually lights up. The mixed voices of the chorus are heard: they have dressed as VILLAGERS *and are shouting out orders to the ox.* LI JINMING *walks down from the slope.*)

LI JINMING: Okay, Harelip, your dad is here.

(*With another burst of orders to the ox, two members from the chorus hold up a prop of an ox head.*)

LI JINMING: (*Loudly*) Fugui, fuck your ancestors. That's our own plow ox. How do you expect the animal to pull the plow when you've struck it so deep in the soil?

LI FUGUI: (*From the chorus*) How will the corn grow if I don't plow deep?

LI JINMING: You think it's the same as you planting in the belly of your wife, the deeper the better? (*To the audience*) Every farm job will need the animal, right? It does the heaviest work for us. If we hurt it, who'll work for us?

(*Suddenly a crack of the whip is heard from the chorus. The actors raise the ox head and low, imitating the ox.*)

LI JINMING: Fugui, how dare you whip Harelip! You fucking son of a bitch, why didn't you try this on your dad? Harelip, jab the asshole of that bastard. See if he doesn't feel the pain.
(LI FUGUI *steps out the chorus, shouting.*)

LI FUGUI: This is it. I've had enough. I can't do the job.

LI JINMING: You don't want to do it? Fine. See what the fuck you can come up with to feed yourself without the workpoints.

LI FUGUI: Uncle Jinming, you scold me this way and that all day long. If you don't beat the animal, how will it work for you? I quit.

LI JINMING: What do you have to complain about? The animal isn't human so you can beat it all you want?

LI FUGUI: (*Indignantly*) Fine, fine. The animal is human and I'm not.

LI JINMING: That's more like it. The animal is our treasure, the lifeline of our village. You think you could plow our hundred or so *mu* of land?

(LI JINMING *walks aside to mix fodder for the ox.* ZHU XIAOPING *steps out of the chorus.*)

ZHU: Brother Fugui, where's Uncle Jinming?

LI FUGUI: (*Angrily*) Making love to Harelip over there.

ZHU: What's wrong? You look so upset.

LI FUGUI: Go and find out from your Uncle Jinming if Harelip is human or just an ox.

(LI FUGUI *returns to the chorus.*)

ZHU: Uncle Jinming. Uncle Jinming.

LI JINMING: Hey, I'm here. What do you want me for, kid?

ZHU: The team leader wants Harelip to send firewood to the commune.

LI JINMING: He's not available. (*Complaining*) Jindou, the bastard!

ZHU: He has to run errands for the commune. What do you mean he's not available?

LI JINMING: (*Muttering*) Fuck his ancestors. The ox has hardly had a break, now you want it to work again. The animal is going to die from this.

ZHU: Uncle Jinming . . .

LI JINMING: (*Seeing no alternative*) All right. Here, take the ox with you.

(ZHU *takes a whip from the chorus.*)

LI JINMING: Kid, don't whip the ox. Remember to give .it some water when you get there.

ZHU: I know.

LI JINMING: What do you know? You're a city kid. You don't know how precious an animal is. Promise me you won't whip him on the road.

ZHU: Uncle Jinming, don't worry. I won't beat him.

LI JINMING: What if you did?

(ZHU *does not know what to say.*)

LI JINMING: If you want to do it, you might as well beat me first.

ZHU: How can I beat you like an ox?

LI JINMING: That's right. Shouldn't beat anyone.

ZHU: All right then, I'm leaving.

LI JINMING: Now go, go.

(*The ringing of the bell on the ox's neck is heard. The chorus exits as the stage revolves to the right.*)

LI JINMING: Hey, kid. Take it easy. When it's uphill, give the ox a hand. Don't just let him do it on his own. (*Hitting himself a couple of times*) Now, Harelip, your dad just took a beating for you. If the kid beats you on the road, let me know and I'll . . .

(*The lowing imitated by the chorus is heard from time to time. The light gradually goes out.*)

Scene Five

(*Outside the cave of* WANG ZHIKE. *A path leading to the cave is seen.* BAO WA *hurries up opposite the direction the stage is turning. When he walks up to the cave, the voices of* WANG ZHIKE *and his son can be heard.*)

WANG: Hurry up and have your meal. Dad has a job to do.

MIAN WA: Dad, let's eat together.

(BAO WA *hesitates and stops. Then he reluctantly goes up to the door and calls into the cave.*)

BAO WA: Zhike, Zhike.

(WANG *comes out of the cave.*)

BAO WA: Zhike, you're wanted for a meeting.

(*Hanging his head,* WANG *walks toward the slope silently.* BAO WA *follows at a distance. The stage slowly turns to the left and stops when* WANG *gets to the cliff. Suddenly,* WANG *sees something, stops short, and draws back in fear. Two* POLICEMEN *appear in the distance.* WANG *jerks himself free from* BAO WA *and runs back as fast as he can.*)

WANG: Mian Wa, Mian Wa!

(BAO WA *catches up with* WANG *and holds him down with the help of several strong men who have been attracted by the noise. The two* POLICEMEN *draw up and put handcuffs on* WANG. MIAN WA *runs up from a distance, crying wildly.*)

MIAN WA: Dad, Dad! Where're you going?

(*Struggling with all his might,* WANG *turns to look at* MIAN WA.)

WANG: Mian Wa, Dad's leaving. There's food in the pot . . .

(*At last,* WANG *is pushed and dragged off. The stage slowly turns to the left. The sound of the jeep driving off is heard from a distance. The cliff is crowded with onlookers. Some are silent, some look on indifferently. Freeing himself from those who are trying to stop him,* MIAN WA *runs up the cliff, shouting in tears.*)

MIAN WA: Dad, Dad! Don't leave me behind!

(MIAN WA *and the* VILLAGERS *move to the left with the stage and disappear from sight. Light gradually goes out.*)

Scene Six

(*On the ground outside the village's ox shed. The brigade secretary* LIU CHANGGUI *and* LI JINDOU *come up, talking to each other.*)

LIU: Jindou, the commune revolutionary committee is going to be formally set up tomorrow. Have you heard about it?

LI JINDOU: The kid told me about it yesterday. He went to the commune to deliver firewood.

LIU: Good. So you knew about it. The commune is going to hold a meeting to celebrate it and will treat the leaders from the county and district to a dinner.

LI JINDOU: (*Echoing* LIU) Of course. Of course.

LIU: The preparatory group has assigned every team some job to get ready for the meeting.

LI JINDOU: (*Alert*) Secretary Liu, we've already delivered the firewood as we were supposed to.

LIU: You understand that's only a small part of it. Considering the fact that your team is not exactly well off, . . .

LI JINDOU: Well, do you want us to send some people to help?

LIU: As to people to help, we have enough of that.

LI JINDOU: Then, what does the commune want us to . . .

LIU: Those teams in better shape have all contributed something, for example, pigs, lambs, poultry, eggs, dried fruit, and whatnot. The thing the commune is looking for is an ox for beef.

(*The chorus, dressed as* VILLAGERS, *enters.*)

VILLAGERS: An ox? An ox?

LI JINDOU: To kill a farm animal is illegal.

LIU: That's a revisionist law passed before 1966.

LI JINDOU: Right, right. That's a revi . . . eh, revist law.

LIU: The commune's heard that you've an old good-for-nothing ox. Is that correct?

LI JINDOU: I'm afraid you're wrong.

LIU: Jindou, don't try to piss me off. It won't work. Those in the commune saw it delivering firewood yesterday. That's why I was sent here to see you.

(LI JINDOU *is dumbfounded. In the chorus the old ox Harelip suddenly lows deeply.*)

LIU: That's the ox, isn't it?

LI JINDOU: No, no! This won't do!

LIU: Why not? They'll pay you for it.

LI JINDOU: (*Still loudly*) But why? Why kill the ox?

(LI JINMING *steps out of the chorus.*)

LI JINMING: What's going on?

LI JINDOU: The commune wants to buy Harelip and kill it.

(LI JINMING *blinks his eyes in disbelief.*)

LI JINDOU: (*To* LIU) My dear Secretary Changgui, please tell them for us that we won't sell the ox. It can still work.

LIU: (*Also getting desperate*) Jindou, how do you expect me to tell them that? They're not negotiating with us. They want us to send the ox to them. Even the forty dollars payment is out of the account of the brigade. Who knows if they're going to pay us back.

(LI JINMING *moves aside silently.*)

LI JINDOU: Whatever they say, this won't do. To get some beef? We might as well kill it for ourselves. Forty dollars for a big ox, this is robbing us.

VILLAGERS: Right. This is robbing us.

LIU: Fine, fine. I did what I was supposed to do. If you have the nerve and the backing, go tell this to the commune yourself! (*Exits in a rage*)

LI JINDOU: Wait, Secretary! Secretary Liu!

LI JINMING: (*Muttering to himself*) We won't even let people touch it, but they want to kill it for its meat. We won't lay our hands on it, but they want to kill it.

LI JINDOU: (*Furious*) Fine, they won't get him alive! (*Exits indignantly*)

(*The chorus breaks up to reveal HARELIP, played by two actors. It looks at the VILLAGERS, alarmed and bewildered. A distraught LI JINMING crawls on the ground, seeming to be looking for something. Suddenly, he snatches a wooden plow from a VILLAGER and charges at HARELIP with a loud cry.*)

LI JINMING: (*Beside himself with grief*) Let's kill him here! Kill him here! Don't let them have him alive. (*He swings the plow at HARELIP with all his might.*)

(HARELIP *gives a pitiful cry, rolls on the ground, and struggles to his feet. The light gradually changes into a bloody red along with the music.*
Simultaneously, the scene turns into a terrifying dance in slow motion, in which the VILLAGERS chase after the old ox HARELIP madly, beating him as he tries frantically to find his way out. HARELIP dodges, rolls on the ground, and wails piteously. All of a sudden, it stands up on its hindlegs, with a loud howling, looking around in pain and confusion. In the midst of this madness, BAO WA pulls the trigger of his rifle. HARELIP is shot and falls down in his own blood. With his last breath, HARELIP pulls up his wounded body and crawls toward LI JINMING, wailing plaintively.
The old ox HARELIP is dead. LI JINMING is heartbroken, and the VILLAGERS of Sangshuping are indignant. To the accompaniment of music the CHORUS kneels down with faces raised questioningly toward the sky in deep, bitter grief, singing.)

> China was born on this yellow earth,
> The descendants of the Dragon in the East it nursed,
> Great Yü's footprints were once all over the land,
> Where dashed King Wu's chariot grand . . .

(*As the scene concludes, the deafening tolling of ancient bells resounds in the music.*)

(*Light dies out.*)

Epilogue

(*In the vicinity of the small storage cave. The rumble of thunder and pouring rain is heard. BAO WA runs toward the cliff, shouting and panting.*)

BAO WA: Team leader, team leader—something's wrong. The storage cave collapsed!

LI JINDOU: What about Jinming?

BAO WA: He's getting the fodder out of the cave.

LI JINDOU: That won't do. It's pitch-dark in the cave. He can't handle it by himself. (*Turns to run down the slope*)

(LI JINMING *exits before* LI JINDOU *with a bundle of fodder on his shoulder.* LI JINDOU *turns to get into the cave. At* BAO WA*'s summoning, the* VILLAGERS *hurry to the cave in the rain. Suddenly, there is a loud crash in the cave. The* VILLAGERS *are stunned.*)

BAO WA: (*Calling out madly*) Team leader, team leader!

(*Quick curtain.*)

(*Singing of the chorus emerges off stage*)

> The first month is early spring,
> It's white all over the hilltops,
> After winter comes the spring,
> Year after year, we work and no one stops.

(*The stage lights come up.* XÜ CAIFANG *is making shoe soles in front of her cave dwelling.* ZHU XIAOPING *approaches from the slope.*)

ZHU: Caifang.

XÜ: (*Getting up to meet him*) Why, it's you, Xiaoping. Come on in.

ZHU: Well, I'm here to say good-bye to you.

XÜ: (*Surprised*) Why?

ZHU: I'm going to join the army. All procedures have been taken care of in the county.

XÜ: Oh. When are you leaving?

ZHU: Early tomorrow morning.

XÜ: (*After a while*) Good. You can forget all about this desolate land when you're over the mountains.

ZHU: How can I? I won't ever forget Sangshuping and all of you. Though I haven't been here long, I've learned so much. I'll come back and see you. (*Turning round to go, and stops*) I heard that your dad's busy arranging the wedding for you and Cang Wa. I can't be of any help, but you should make up your mind.

(XÜ *looks at him silently.*)

(*A deranged* CHEN QINGNÜ *approaches from a distance, cradling a doll in her arms, humming a tune.*

CHEN QINGNÜ: (*Singing*)

>Looking for my sweetheart I go over the
>   mountains,
>Oh, the white peony,
>We can only see each other in the dreams,
>Oh, the white peony . . .

ZHU *and* XÜ: Qingnü, you . . .

CHEN QINGNÜ: (*Fixing* ZHU *with a blank stare*) Do city girls get married?

(ZHU is *not sure how to respond.*)

CHEN QINGNÜ: Why aren't you saying anything?

ZHU: Yes, they do.

CHEN QINGNÜ: How?

ZHU: Well, the same as we do here.

CHEN QINGNÜ: (*Smiling sadly*) The same! Women are the same all over the world. (*Walks off laughing insanely*)

ZHU: Qingnü, Qingnü. (*Runs after her*)

(XÜ CAIFANG *sits vacantly, lost in thought. After a while,* LI JINDOU, *now with one leg broken, limps from a distance with a small bundle on his arm.*)

LI JINDOU: Caifang.

(XÜ *remains silent.*)

LI JINDOU: It's getting cold. Your mum and I made some coats for you. Try this one on and let me see.

(XÜ *makes no move.*)

LI JINDOU: Caifang. Have you made up your mind? Whatever is on your mind, at least let us know.

XÜ: No, I can't do it.

LI JINDOU: But why? A widow remarrying to her brother-in-law is a common thing in our area. You know that.

(XÜ *acts as if not hearing him.*)

LI JINDOU: My good girl. Please leave a way out for your dad . . . Man Wa left us early and you were so young when you lost your man. Dad knows it hasn't been easy for you . . . But we've got to move on with our lives.

(XÜ *still keeps silent.*)

LI JINDOU: Since you came to us at twelve, it's been a good ten years. How can you really have the heart to leave your dad and your mum uncared for?

(XÜ *refuses to say anything.*)

LI JINDOU: Man Wa, my son! Why did you have to go before your dad?

XÜ: Dad, Dad, please don't cry, please . . .

LI JINDOU: I know my Caifang is a good girl and loves her dad. You grew up with your brother Cang Wa. Though he has swollen joints, he can still have a family. If you agree to this, you and Cang Wa can start a family and continue our family line when you have a couple of kids. If you still want to leave us, you can after that. Caifang, my dear girl, please do this for us! Your dad is begging you! Please! (*Suddenly kneels down before* XÜ CAIFANG)

XÜ: Dad, I can't agree to that. I just can't.

LI JINDOU: (*Disappointed*) Fine, then. (*He has no choice but to stand up. He turns round to leave. After a few steps*) Dad took pity on you, but you don't care for your dad. All right, you can't have everything your way. Willing or not, tonight, you and Cang Wa will have your wedding! (*Exits*)

XÜ: Dad, Dad! (*Stands and looks into the distance woodenly; to herself*) Tonight . . . Yü Wa, why aren't you here by now? I . . . I'll have to be going.

(*With the music,* XÜ CAIFANG *walks toward the Tang well distractedly. The stage slowly turns to the left. The chorus, dressed as* VILLAGERS, *sings:.*)

> The well on the hilltop,
> From our ancestors we got,
> How deep is the well, you want to know?
> Way down you'll have to go.

(*As the song subsides, lights dim. By the side of the well, the fire from* LI JINDOU's *pipe glimmers as the stage gradually lights up, showing* LI *squatting by the well with his head hanging down. A moment later, he wipes away his tears, gets on his feet leaning on a stick, and walks off. He turns to look at the well now and then. Light changes with the music. The* CHORUS *enters from the depth of the stage, singing.*)

> China was born on this yellow earth,
> The descendants of the Dragon in the East it nursed,

Great Yü's footprints were once all over the land,
Where dashed King Wu's chariot grand.

Traversing the dense, impenetrable mountain peaks,
Walking out of the dream of five thousand years,
History raises the same queries:
"When will you wake up, Dragon in the East?"

Even if ahead there is a difficult path,
Even if there are mountains to climb, ever higher,
To themselves, the question they'll continue to ask,
They'll seek and search, never retire.

The End

Old Well

(A film script)

Script by Zheng Yi, Directed by Wu Tianming*
Translated by Yu Shiaoling

Synopsis

Old Well is a village deep in the Taihang Mountains. There are mountains upon mountains, rocks upon rocks, but there is no water. Over many generations, the people of this village have dug 270 dry wells, the deepest one being more than fifty meters deep. The most cherished wish of the villagers is to find water on their land.

Sun Wangquan, an educated youth returned from the city, is determined to use what he has learned at school to drill a well and find water. Wangquan comes from a poor family—all five men in his family are bachelors, too poor to marry. For the sake of finding water and finding a wife for his younger brother, Wangquan agrees to marry the young widow Duan Xifeng, sacrificing his love for Zhao Qiaoying.[1]

Under the leadership of Sun Wangquan, the villagers succeed in drilling a well and finally finding water.

As the world continues to turn, life goes on.

---

*Wu Tianming is currently living in Los Angeles but frequently goes to China to direct films and television dramas. Before he came to the United States in 1989, he was the head of the Xian Film Studio, bringing it to national prominence and becoming one of the most important figures who permanently altered the Chinese cinematic landscape in the 1980s. He has been one of the best-known film directors in China since 1982. Among his films, *A River without Navigation Mark* (1982) and *Life* (1984) won him national recognition. *Old Well* (1986), which won four grand prizes, including the best film prize at the Tokyo Film Festival in 1987 and the best film award at the Golden Rooster Awards in China in 1986, established his status as an internationally acclaimed film director. His most recent film, *Changed Face* (1996), won the best film prize at the Tokyo Film Festival in 1996.

This translation is based on the film script published in *Old Well: Chinese Masterpieces—Film*, edited by Jiao Xiongping (Taipei: Wanxiang Publishing, 1990), pp.13–88.

[1]In rural China, it is customary for the bridegroom's family to pay a "bride price" to the bride's family. The Sun family is too poor to afford such expenses. By agreeing to marry the young widow Duan Xifeng, Sun Wangquan not only does not have to pay a "bride price" but also receives a thousand-dollar payment from Xifeng. His family can use this money to "buy" a bride for his younger brother.

Title sequence:
   The logo of Xian Film Studio appears on the screen against the backdrop of the stone horses of the Tang Tombs.
   Two muscular arms holding a hammer and pounding at a steel drill. A picture of arms swinging a hammer forms the backdrop of the entire sequence.
   A view of a well from the bottom up: the mouth of the well looks like a small silver plate, then it becomes bigger and bigger until blue sky fills the entire screen.

Cast of Characters

SUN WANGQUAN: Zhang Yimou
ZHAO QIAOYING: Liang Yujin
GRANDPA WANSHUI: Niu Xingli
XIFENG: Lu Liping
SUN WANGCAI: Xie Yan
SUN FUCHANG: Ping Lanting
MAD GRANDUNCLE (Sun Wanshan): Zhao Shiji
SUN FUGUI: Hao Jiaoyong
XIFENG'S MOTHER: Mu Mu
XIZHU'ER: Tan Xihe
CHUNMEI: Li Jingjing
SAN ZE: Zhang Yuan
ZHI'ER: Hou Xiaolin
WANGQUAN'S YOUNGER BROTHER WANGLAI: Qian Huande
THIRD AUNT: Ting Weimin
WANGCAI'S MOTHER: Zhang Muqin
CHIEF ENGINEER SUN: Li Jinbang
PARTY BRANCH SECRETARY OF SHIMEN COUNTY: Lu Hui
AN EXPERT WELL DRILLER: Cheng Shenglin
Director: Wu Tianming

At a lively open-air theater, Party branch secretary SUN FUCHANG is passing out cigarettes to several old peasants. GRANDPA WANSHUI asks: "How much did this show cost us?"

CHUNMEI and ZHI'ER are buying melon seeds from a vendor.

Two old peasants sit at the foot of a wall, looking around. Theatergoers pass in front of them. A group of people crowd around the foot of the wall looking at something.

A dozen or so school badges are pinned on a piece of black cloth.

SUN WANGCAI (*offscreen*): "It's too expensive. Can you make it cheaper?"

SUN WANGCAI (squatting in the midst of the crowd): "OK. I'll buy one!"

VENDOR: "Pick any one you want."

SUN WANGCAI: "I'll just take this one."

SUN WANGCAI proudly pins the badge of the Taiyuan Institute of Technology on his lapel.

XIFENG stands under a tree, holding her daughter Xiuxiu and waiting for the show to begin.

Colorfully dressed women and children mill around.

Backstage, actresses are busily putting on makeup.

SANZE comes to the village driving a tractor. QIAOYING stands on the tractor, holding a television set in a box.

WANGQUAN, who is sitting on the roof, sees QIAOYING.

The tractor stops. QIAOYING busily greets the people around her.

WANGQUAN looks at QIAOYING.

CHUNMEI and ZHI'ER squeeze themselves onto the tractor.

CHUNMEI touches the television: "Is it colored?"

QIAOYING: "No, it's black and white."

QIAOYING busies herself with something.

XIZHU'ER (*offscreen*): "Qiaoying!"

QIAOYING quickly answers.

XIZHU and WANGCAI, who are sitting on a tree, smile broadly at QIAOYING.

WANGQUAN (*offscreen*): "Qiaoying!"

QIAOYING turns around.

WANGQUAN calls her cheerfully: "Qiaoying!"

QIAOYING tells CHUNMEI: "Watch this thing for me." She then hurriedly jumps down from the tractor.

WANGQUAN beams happily. He pulls QIAOYING onto the roof and the two of them sit side by side. WANGQUAN'S YOUNGER BROTHER sensibly walks away.

XIFENG notices them . . .

WANGQUAN and QIAOYING sit on the roof, chatting. They are a little embarrassed by the teasing from XIZHU, WANGCAI, and other young people.

With a long face, XIFENG walks offscreen holding the crying little XIUXIU.

In front of the stage, villagers dressed in their festive clothing excitedly wait for the show to start.

Dots and streaks appear on the screen of a 14–inch black-and-white TV; WANGQUAN adjusts the buttons.

WANGCAI stands on a big rock atop the mountain, holding a long pole and turning the aluminum antenna attached to the pole.

WANGCAI asks: "Hey, get any picture?"

WANGQUAN gives orders: "To this side."

WANGQUAN, QIAOYING, XIZHU, SANZE, and several other young people crowd around the television and try to adjust it, but they fail to get any picture. QIAOYING sits dejectedly on a rock.

QIAOYING looks at the mountain below: "Our ancestors must have been blind to put the village here."

CHUNMEI and ZHI'ER look in the same direction as QIAOYING.

The Old Well village lies quietly in the embrace of the mountains, shrouded by cooking smoke curling upward and evening mist.

The young people walk down the mountain slope, carrying the antenna and the TV set, chatting and laughing. QIAOYING and WANGQUAN walk in the rear.

QIAOYING: "Hey, what about a song?"

WANGQUAN rubs the back of his head: "My voice is no good. You sing."

QIAOYING stands still, looks at the mountain below, and starts to sing in her youtful and loud voice:

"My darling goes down to the river to wash clothes,
Her knees kneeling on a stone.
Oh, my little darling!"

People from down the mountain roar with approval.
Several women sitting in the courtyard are laughing.
Children eating supper are laughing.

WANGQUAN and QIAOYING smile at each other. From the mountain below comes the voice of their friends teasing them: "Wangquan, you sing a song!"

WANGQUAN and QIAOYING walk down the mountain slope. WANGQUAN sings in his hoarse voice:

"Her hands are pink, her hands are white.
She takes off her clothes and swings her pigtails.
Oh, my little darling!"

The village street is flooded with silver moonlight. Several young people carry water buckets and lanterns, chatting and laughing as they walk from the village.

WANGQUAN and QIAOYING are climbing a mountain path while carrying water buckets on their shoulder poles. WANGQUAN puts down his buckets in the middle of the road. The minute QIAOYING puts down her buckets, her legs feel like jelly and she falls down. WANGQUAN helps her up. Laughing and panting, they sit by the roadside wiping the sweat away from their faces.

QIAOYING: "What a terrible place! You have to walk more than ten miles just to get a drink of water!"

WANGQUAN looks at QIAOYING. She looks radiant in the morning light. He gazes at her, entranced. QIAOYING looks at WANGQUAN with her bright shining eyes.

WANGQUAN lowers his head to hide his emotions. He removes his sweat-soaked T-shirt: "Aren't they drilling a well in Xijing now?"

QIAOYING turns the question on him: "It's been ages. They've drilled more than a hundred dry holes. Where is the water?"

WANGQUAN has no reply. From the valley below comes young people's shouting. The two stand up and walk to the edge of the slope, yelling at the people below: "Hey—" From the mountain above also comes young people's loud cry. WANGQUAN and QIAOYING turn around and call to the people above: "Hey—"

The young people's calling echoes through the endless mountains and cliffs.

At the well site in Xijing, an EXPERT WELL DRILLER pulls WANGQUAN's father, SUN FUGUI, up with a rope. His whole body covered with mud, FUGUI lies near the well in a state of utter exhaustion. The well driller gives him a lighted cigarette and goes offscreen.

WANGQUAN and QIAOYING come along on the mountain path, carrying water buckets.

WANGQUAN: "Let's go to the well and have a look."

QIAOYING: "Ai."

They put down their load, say hello to several members of the drilling team huddled around a fire, and walk toward the well.

WANGQUAN and QIAOYING walk to the well.

QIAOYING: "Uncle Fugui."

FUGUI nods. WANGQUAN squats near the mouth of the well and takes out a cigarette from the pocket of his pants. He lights it from his father's cigarette.

FUGUI: "We dug another three inches today." He is seized by a fit of violent coughing.

WANGQUAN looks at his father coughing with a pained expression. He gets up and walks away.

WANGQUAN and QIAOYING walk away carrying water buckets.

At SUN WANGQUAN's house. In the light of a dim oil lamp, SUN FUGUI is stitching the sole of a cloth shoe; GRANDPA WANSHUI sits on the brick bed, smoking a pipe.

WANSHUI: "Eight hundred dollars is too little. But one gets a husband, and the other gets a wife. It's better than having both brothers remain bachelors."

FUGUI answers woodenly: "It's good, but . . . it's unfair to Wangquan."

WANSHUI: "Why is it unfair? Is it fair to have a whole household of bachelors? I'll make the decision on this matter."

WANGLAI is asleep on the brick bed. WANGQUAN's mad GRAND-UNCLE WANSHAN sits at a corner of the bed, humming a folk song. His face is dirty and his hair is disheveled.

WANSHUI (*offscreen*): "That girl from the Zhao family is like a foreign cigarette—looks pretty but doesn't taste good. She won't be satisfied staying in Old Well village."

The door opens with a squeak and WANGQUAN comes in. FUGUI puts down the shoe sole, takes out a big bowl of steaming hot gruel from the stove, and puts it on the table. WANGQUAN takes a few pieces of salted vegetables with his chopsticks and starts eating by the brick bed. The sound of a dog barking can be heard from time to time.

WANSHUI looks at WANSHAN: "Second Brother, go to bed."

FUGUI helps his mad uncle lie down. WANSHUI also gets into bed. After a while he says, "Wangquan, go to Xifeng's house tomorrow to do some masonry work."

In the kitchen of XIFENG's house, eggs are being poached in a pot, giving off waves of steam. XIFENG carefully turns them with a ladle. The sound of chiseling stone comes from the courtyard.

XIFENG'S MOTHER (*offscreen*): "Has that Zhao-family girl come back?"

THIRD AUNT (*offscreen*): "That's right. I heard she didn't pass the college entrance exam. That hussy, whenever WANGQUAN sees her, he loses all self-control."

XIFENG'S MOTHER holds little XIUXIU while sitting in front of the stove and adding firewood to it. THIRD AUNT sits next to her, gossiping.

XIFENG: "Mother, don't add any more wood." She goes offscreen.

XIFENG'S MOTHER and THIRD AUNT look toward the courtyard.

WANGQUAN is chiseling a trough for feeding pigs. THIRD AUNT moves closer to XIFENG'S MOTHER.

XIFENG is drying dishes while listening intently to what they are saying.

THIRD AUNT (*offscreen*): "Those two got to know each other when they were in school together . . ."

THIRD AUNT whispers in the ear of XIFENG'S MOTHER: "I heard . . ."

XIFENG comes onscreen. She walks to the stove and scoops the poached eggs into a bowl: "Mother, let's give them the thousand dollars they asked for." She walks to THIRD AUNT while holding the bowl: "Third Aunt, it's settled. You give them our reply." She goes offscreen.

XIFENG walks to WANGQUAN: "Uncle Wangquan, take a rest."[2]

WANGQUAN puts down his tools, takes a towel from XIFENG to dust himself. He follows her into another room.

XIFENG sits on the edge of a brick bed embroidering a shoe-pad and stealing a glance at WANGQUAN from time to time. WANGQUAN sits at a table eating his eggs with gusto.

XIFENG: "Uncle Wangquan, the way you eat really reminds of my Xiuxiu's dad. The way you smoke and work also looks familiar."

WANGQUAN, eating, asks: "How did Brother Laifu have the accident? I was at school in the city at the time."

XIFENG: "All because he was drilling that well at Song Gou . . ."

WANGQUAN: "Song Gou?"

XIFENG nods: "They were going to use explosives. When that dead devil of mine[3] lit the charge, they should have pulled him out of the well. But I don't know what happened, the rope got all tangled up in the winch . . . People were running around in circles . . . By the time they straightened out the rope, the dynamite exploded . . ."

WANGQUAN finishes his last drop of egg soup. XIFENG comes over quickly to take the empty bowl and puts it on the table. She hands him a cigarette and lights it.

---

[2]Xifeng calls Wangquan "uncle," referring to him in relation to her daughter, to show her politeness by avoiding directly calling his name.
[3]Referring to her dead husband.

XIFENG: "Now that we finally got you to come over to our house, I really shouldn't talk about these unhappy things . . ."

WANGQUAN inhales deeply, picks up the shoe sole on the brick bed and looks at it. XIFENG takes out several ten-dollar bills from her pocket and timidly puts them on the table.

XIFENG: "Uncle Wangquan, please take this money and buy yourself some new outfits. Don't always dress so shabbily. Although our family is not rich, we can still spare some cash."

WANGQUAN is dumbfounded: "What's this for?"

XIFENG blushes. She takes the empty bowl and walks out.

XIFENG's MOTHER sits by the kitchen door shelling corn. Little XIUXIU stands on the side throwing corn kernels on the ground. A flock of birds pecks at them near her feet.

XIFENG comes over, holding the empty bowl.

XIFENG'S MOTHER asks happily: "Did he take the money?"

XIFENG nods and walks into the kitchen.

XIFENG'S MOTHER stands up. She goes offscreen.

WANGQUAN thumbs the stack of bills on the table.

XIFENG'S MOTHER (*offscreen*): "Want to have some more?"

WANGQUAN quickly withdraws his hand and bows slightly: "No more, thank you."

XIFENG'S MOTHER comes onscreen: "Have a little snack first. Xifeng is going to cook dinner soon. Come, have another cigarette . . ." She notices that WANGQUAN did not take the money on the table. She is a little disappointed but tries to hide her feelings with a smile: "Xifeng really has good judgment . . ." She sits on the edge of the brick bed and says to WANGQUAN: "When we set the date for you to come over, we will finally have someone to depend on."

WANGQUAN: "What date?"

XIFENG'S MOTHER stands up: "What date? The wedding date . . ."

XIFENG'S MOTHER: ". . . Didn't your grandpa and dad tell you?"

It finally dawns on the bewildered WANGQUAN. Annoyed, he gets up and goes offscreen.

WANGQUAN quickly walks out of the room and picks up his tools.

THIRD AUNT, who has been eavesdropping by the door, is alarmed: "Hey, Wangquan, what happened? You're leaving? Wangquan!"

WANGQUAN walks away angrily. THIRD AUNT tries to catch up with him.

WANGQUAN keeps walking. THIRD AUNT chases after him, trying to calm him down: "They don't mind your family being poor because they really like you. All they ask you is to move in with your wife's family. What's wrong with that? You know something? Young widows really know how to please and take care of their men . . ."

WANGQUAN walks away with big strides.

THIRD AUNT yells at the receding figure of WANGQUAN: "Wait till you eat from the same pot with her, you'll know what a fine woman she is!"

On a moonlit night near the foundations of a fallen-down and deserted house, a grim looking QIAOYING sits on a broken stone wall surrounding a small courtyard. Footsteps approach; she raises her head.

WANGCAI and WANGQUAN enter from outside.

QIAOYING stands up; WANGCAI and WANGQUAN come toward her. WANGCAI takes out a piece of paper from his pocket and hands it to QIAOYING: "This is a letter of introduction. I secretly put the official seal on it."[4] He walks away satisfied with what he has done.

WANGCAI suddenly remembers something when he is outside the wall. He leans over the wall and says to them: "Tell you something, why don't you go on to Taiyuan for several days after you get your marriage certificate tomorrow? . . ."

QIAOYING gazes at WANGQUAN.

---

[4]In China, an official certification issued by would-be couples' working units or places of residence is required for them to get a marriage certificate from the civil bureaus of the government.

WANGCAI (*offscreen*): ". . . take a honeymoon trip . . ."

WANGQUAN looks at QIAOYING.

WANGCAI (*offscreen*): ". . . When the rice is cooked, there's nothing they can do!"

QIAOYING looks at WANGQUAN expectantly.

QIAOYING sits down, looking at the stones around her.

WANGQUAN walks over to her and sits beside her. WANGCAI walks away humming a popular song:

> "You ask me how much I love you,
>   how deeply I love you.
> Why don't you think about it?
> The moon knows my heart's secret . . ."

On a main road outside the village, a raging WANSHUI is in hot pursuit.

On the road beneath the mountain cliff, QIAOYING and WANGQUAN hurriedly walk away, carrying bundles of their belongings. WANSHUI stops them with a furious shout: "Stop!"

Startled, they turn around. WANSHUI runs up to them and stands like the statue of a demon.

At WANGQUAN's house, the MAD GRANDUNCLE is picking up broken pieces of bowls, pots, and pans. Gruel is spilled all over the place.

WANSHUI sits immobile on the brick bed. WANGQUAN squats on the ground, his body curled up.

QIAOYING stares at WANSHUI defiantly.

WANSHUI turns around to stare at QIAOYING, but does not flinch.

WANSHUI (*offscreen*): "You may leave, you're not my grandson . . ."

QIAOYING turns to look at WANGQUAN.

WANGQUAN squats on the ground, listening.

WANSHUI (*offscreen*): ". . . you've had enough? Get out! Break your younger brother's engagement, finish off your granduncle and me. Get out! Out!"

WANGQUAN lifts his head.

QIAOYING looks at WANGQUAN, holds her breath with expectation.

WANSHUI looks at WANQUAN with hatred.

WANGQUAN lowers his head.

QIAOYING begins to lose all hope, turns around and leaves.

WANGQUAN looks deeply dejected.

The MAD GRANDUNCLE throws the broken bowls on the floor, breaking them into smithereens.

In the kitchen of QIAOYING's house, QIAOYING is chopping vegetables on a cutting board without any expression on her face.

WANGCAI: (*offscreen*) "Listen to me, swallow your disappointment . . ." WANGCAI is sitting in front of the stove, helping QIAOYING tend the fire.

WANGCAI: "Forget about it. Wangquan's puny arms are no match for big fists. His grandpa is a real devil-god."

QIAOYING throws down her knife. She comes to the stove and lifts the lid of a pot.

WANGCAI continues: ". . . there's no need to get so angry. You know what his grandpa is like. He even beat up the Dragon King forty years ago. Who dares to cross him? Besides, there are plenty of good men around. What cock doesn't want a hen?"

QIAOYING adds a ladleful of water to the pot. She takes another ladle of water and walks to the front of the stove. As soon as WANGCAI finishes talking, she throws the water on the fire in disgust. Smoke and dust rush out from the stove and fill the whole kitchen.

WANGCAI is stunned.

At Xijing construction site, FUGUI, the WELL DRILLER and others hide in a stone cave. XIZHU suddenly turns off the electric switch. The whole area around the well falls silent.

FUGUI, as he is being lowered into the well, argues with the WELL DRILLER.

FUGUI: "I told you it won't work, but you insisted on setting it up that way. Let it go!" WELL DRILLER: "There are so many fucking strange things in your village. It's so windy at the bottom of the well that you can't light the explosive."

FUGUI's voice sounds fainter and fainter: "That has never happened in our village!"

WELL DRILLER: "Slowly, slowly."

FUGUI yells after he gets to the bottom of the well: "OK, OK."

A rope hangs loose around the mouth of the well.

From the well comes the colliding sound of steel drills. Suddenly there is a huge explosion. Fire spews out from the well, followed by a thick, black smoke. (*Fade out.*)

(*Fade in.*) A bloodstained mat covers SUN FUGUI's body. WANGLAI bends over the mat, weeping bitterly. WANGQUAN kneels on the ground, stupefied. QIAOYING helps WANGQUAN to his feet. Several people carry the body on a stretcher and walk back to the village.

MAD GRANDUNCLE quickly comes over and looks in the direction of the wailing people.

People carrying the corpse disappear into the distance.

MAD GRANDUNCLE opens wide his buffalolike eyes, lowers his head, and stares at the bloodstains on the well.

In an outburst of crazy rage, he throws rocks, carrying poles, iron buckets, steel drills, and everything else into the well.

From inside the blood-splattered well come dull echoes.

A blood-colored coffin is placed in front of the memorial tablet of SUN FUGUI. On the table there are fruits, steamed buns, and other foodstuffs. Coiling incense smoke envelops the memorial tablet. (*Fade out.*)

(*Fade in.*) WANGQUAN and WANGLAI, in heavy mourning clothes, kneel in front of the coffin. WANSHUI sits on the brick bed, smoking his pipe in silence. MAD GRANDUNCLE intermittently hums a folk song.

WANSHUI: "Quanzi, your marriage with Xifeng, your dad . . ."

WANSHUI (*offscreen*): ". . . he did agree."

WANGQUAN looks at the coffin in front of him, then lowers his eyes. (*Fade out.*)

(*Fade in.*) A bloodred sun hangs in the sky.

Flocks of sheep graze on the mountain slope. Shepherds are singing folk songs.

Several people stand or sit around the well, all keeping perfectly still.

WANGQUAN leans against the well platform in silence.

WANSHUI squats near the well with his back to the stone wall. ZHANG SANHUO, the head of the country's drilling team, sits on a pile of rocks, listlessly playing with a measuring tape.

SUN FUCHANG sits with his body hunched, smoking and not saying anything.

ZHANG SANHUO takes out a cigarette and comes over to light it from FUCHANG.

FUCHANG stays still.

WANGQUAN: "Team leader, according to what you said, our village is being given a death sentence."

ZHANG SANHUO lights his cigarette: "It's not exactly a death sentence. We say it's a 'water-deprived area,' based on the technology we now have. The main problem is that we can't decide accurately where the site of the well should be. Our technology is not up to the task."

WANSHUI stands up and leaves.

Under a setting sun, WANSHUI walks away with heavy steps.

The raucous music of a band of *suona*.[5] The street of the village is crowded with people. QIAOYING comes pushing her bicycle. A wedding procession passes. Beside a table, several young people lift a newlywed couple in the air.

QIAOYING watches from the crowd.

---

[5]A double-reeded wind instrument.

The newlyweds are placed on top of each other on the table.

Pushing her bicycle through the crowd, QIAOYING walks away in disgust.

Against the background of a picture-filled wall, XIFENG sits on a bench, beaming with happiness. WANGQUAN is decked out in a new outfit from head to toe. THIRD AUNT adjusts his collar button and pushes him to sit on the bench. WANGQUAN suddenly notices—

QIAOYING stands in the middle of the street, leaning against her bicycle and staring at WANGQUAN and XIFENG.

WANGQUAN awkwardly stands up.

QIAOYING scrutinizes the cowardly WANGQUAN with a cold gaze.

A big red character reading "Happiness" hangs on the wall.

Cold moonlight comes through the window and shines on the brick bed in the bridal chamber. WANGQUAN and XIFENG lie on the bed, separated by a distance.

XIFENG turns around to look at WANGQUAN. WANGQUAN lies in bed with his clothes on and his back to XIFENG.

WANGQUAN is wide awake, staring vacantly into space. From outside comes the sound of footsteps treading and breaking tiles. XIFENG turns around: "Who's there?" The shadows of several persons disappear from the window; hurried footsteps fade into the distance.

In an alley in the moonlight, WANGCAI, XIZHU, and SANZE are running breathlessly. They stop at a corner of a wall to have a smoke.

XIZHU: "That fucking Wangquan really has some self-control. We have been listening for several nights now but he hasn't done it."

SANZE is bent over from the cold: "My feet are frozen stiff."

WANGCAI: "Such a delicious young widow, how can Wangquan resist the temptation?"

They burst out laughing, singing a ditty as they walk away:

> "The first hour has struck,
> Brother and sister-in-law are embracing,
> Lights are turned out in their building . . ."

A crisp autumn day. On a mountain path strewn with red leaves, WANGQUAN has just turned a corner around a ditch, carrying a stone slab on his back. Dying from thirst and sweating profusely, he looks in the direction of the village and yells, "Hey, who's there? What about a drink of water?" In the distance, a young woman carrying water buckets stops.

WANGQUAN's face appears by the roadside.

QIAOYING, sitting on her shoulder pole, turns around to look at him with a cold stare.

WANGQUAN, holding his breath, tries to get away.

QIAOYING (*offscreen*): "Hey, where are you going? . . ."

QIAOYING: ". . . You must feel guilty for what you've done, so you don't even dare to have a drink of water?"

WANGQUAN hesitates for little while, then comes closer and stands stiffly in front of her. QIAOYING scoops a dipper of water from her bucket: "What's the matter? Are you waiting for me to serve you?" WANGQUAN takes the dipper from her, squats down, and is about to drink the water. QIAOYING removes the kerchief from her head and starts to shake it.

QIAOYING shakes her kerchief vigorously.

Scraps of straw keep falling into the dipper. WANGQUAN is taken aback, then starts to blow the straw away.

He sips the piercingly cold spring water as he continues to blow at the scraps of straw. He finishes drinking and gives back the dipper to QIAO-YING. She takes it and throws it into her bucket. Carrying her water buckets on a shoulder pole, she walks offscreen. WANGQUAN stands there numbly, gazing after her.

QIAOYING's graceful figure gradually disappears in the distance.

On a mountain road, WANGQUAN walks toward the camera, carrying a stone slab on his back.

WANGQUAN staggers along on the mountain road with the stone slab on his back.

Nighttime in XIFENG's bedroom. She pulls up the quilt to cover her face and starts sobbing.

WANGQUAN turns around.

XIFENG continues to sob under her quilt.

WANGQUAN hesitates for a while, then moves closer to her and pats her lightly on her trembling quilt. XIFENG bursts out crying; WANGQUAN is compelled to cover up her mouth with his hand, which she instantly grabs and starts kissing passionately. Moved by her emotion, WANGQUAN reluctantly opens her quilt. XIFENG seizes this opportunity to hug him.

XIFENG holds WANGQUAN tightly in her embrace.

WANGQUAN cuddles XIFENG, kissing her sympathetically. Her bitter sobs finally turn into tears of joy. (*Fade out.*)

(*Fade in.*) The big red character, "Happiness," hangs on the wall. (*Fade out.*)

(*Fade in.*) XIFENG lies contently in WANGQUAN's arms.

Early morning. The door of their bridal chamber opens; WANGQUAN pops his head out to look around. Carrying a chamber pot, he walks to the latrine.

Old Well village after a snowfall.

On a small path outside the village, a woman holding a child is scraping snow with a ladle.

XIFENG'S MOTHER is scooping up snow with a bamboo dustpan.

WANGCAI'S MOTHER and FUCHANG are also packing snow into a bucket.

WANSHUI and a dozen or so villagers are busily loading and carrying snow back to the village.

WANGQUAN (*offscreen*): "Grandpa!"

WANSHUI raises his head to look.

WANGQUAN, SANZE, and WANGCAI run toward him, huffing and puffing.

SANZE: "We went down into the Eastern Spring Well to copy the inscription, but those sons of bitches from Shimen village . . ."

WANGQUAN: "What the old people said is right! Our village and Shimen village jointly drilled the Double Spring Well. The Western Spring Well belongs to them . . ."

WANGQUAN: ". . . the Eastern Spring Well belongs to us."

WANGQUAN shows FUCHANG an opened cigarette box: "Look, this is the inscription. There is an inscription at the bottom of the Eastern Spring Well. We just went down and copied it."

WANGCAI says angrily: "Those motherfuckers in Shimen village had the well all to themselves for more than ten years. Now they want to continue to monopolize it and wouldn't let us go down!"

WANGQUAN: "More than a dozen of their men stood guard over the well."

With a long face FUCHANG walks offscreen.

WANSHUI waves his hand: "Let's go!"

WANGQUAN: "Let's go!"

On the mountain road, led by WANSHUI, WANGQUAN, and FUCHANG, the villagers of Old Well march forward, carrying clubs and hoes.

At the Double Spring Well, about a dozen people from Shimen village hurriedly move rocks and sand to fill the well.

The PARTY BRANCH SECRETARY of Shimen urges them on: "Faster, faster!"

The villagers of Old Well angrily march on the mountain road.

The people of Shimen village hurry to fill the well.

The villagers of Old Well run toward the well.

WANGQUAN (*offscreen*): "What are you people doing?"

WANSHUI (*offscreen*): "Stop!"

The people of Shimen are caught by surprise.

The villagers of Old Well come to the well.

WANSHUI: "Stop!"

The Shimen people all stand around the well, staring at each other in astonishment.

The villagers of Old Well continue to arrive in large numbers. WANSHUI and WANGQUAN stand at the front of their contingent and look at their adversaries with hatred in their eyes.

The people of Shimen stare back blankly. The PARTY BRANCH SECRETARY of Shimen whispers to a young man near him: "Blacky, go back to the village to get help!" The young fellow runs away quickly.

Villagers of Old Well stand their sticks, clubs, and hoes on the ground, creating an awesome noise.

The PARTY BRANCH SECRETARY of Shimen smiles grimly at WANGQUAN: "Sun Wangquan, I was just about to look for you. Where did you get that inscription? Young man, you should base what you say on facts and not make up a story."

WANGQUAN: "What do you mean by making up a story?"

The PARTY BRANCH SECRETARY of Shimen: "We just went down the well to take a look . . ."

The SECRETARY continues: "There is a tablet down there all right, but it doesn't have the words you copied on it. Look at the trouble you've created with your tall tale!"

WANGQUAN is too angry to say anything. He steps forward and grabs the PARTY BRANCH SECRETARY of Shimen.

WANGQUAN: "You go down with me!"

PARTY SECRETARY: "Go down where?"

WANGQUAN is getting impatient: "Go down with me!"

The PARTY SECRETARY pushes WANGQUAN away: "You go down by yourself! You go down by yourself!"

WANGQUAN runs forward: "Wangcai, let's go down!" He hurriedly grabs the rope attached to the well and slides down.

The PARTY SECRETARY of Shimen glances at his counterpart.

FUCHANG remains calm.

On the mountain road, the villagers of Shimen swarm forward, carrying all kinds of weapons in their hands and on their shoulders.

The Shimen PARTY SECRETARY turns to look.

The Shimen people keep coming.

Pleased with himself, the Shimen PARTY SECRETARY looks at his counterpart again.

FUCHANG looks on coldly.

The Shimen villagers one after another take up their positions around the well, looking fierce and threatening.

The Shimen PARTY SECRETARY lights up a cigarette.

FUCHANG smokes in silence.

Several hundred villagers with their forest of weapons have the well tightly surrounded.

WANGQUAN climbs out of the well, then grabs the Shimen PARTY SECRETARY in exasperation: "You've chopped it!" FUCHANG rushes forward to separate them: "Wangquan, what's the matter?"

FUCHANG: "What's the matter? Wangquan, tell us slowly!"

WANGQUAN: "They . . ."

WANGQUAN: ". . . they've chopped off the inscription on the tablet!"

FUCHANG turns to the Shimen PARTY SECRETARY: "My friend . . ."

FUCHANG: ". . . you and I are like the blind man playing trumpet, we both know the scores in our head. We the people of Old Well have survived without drinking the water from this well, but you're chopping off the inscription . . ."

FUCHANG: ". . . how can you commit such a despicable act?"

The Shimen PARTY SECRETARY: "Despicable act? We only go by the tablet, not by the people. If you can't produce the tablet, forgive us for being rude." He turns around to address his own people, "This is the well of our Shimen village—fill it!"

Several young men of Shimen are about to move.

WANGQUAN yells at them: "You don't dare!"

The PARTY SECRETARY of Shimen straightens up his neck: "Fill it!"

At this time, someone from Old Well village calls: "Party secretary, I have the tablet!" FUCHANG turns to look.

THIRD AUNT hurriedly pushes through the crowd.

THIRD AUNT: "Secretary, let me tell you something. We used to have a tablet in my house. My old man told me there's an inscription on it. When that Emperor Daoguang had this well drilled for us, both our villages paid for it. It's this well. How can this well belong to Shimen village alone?"

FUCHANG asks her anxiously: "Where's the tablet?"

THIRD AUNT: "The tablet? I heard it used to be in the Guanyin temple . . ."

FUCHANG: "Make your story short. Tell us where it is now."

THIRD AUNT: "Now . . ."

THIRD AUNT answers in embarrassment: ". . . it's in our latrine. We use it as a stepping stone in our latrine."

From the Shimen camp comes laughter mixed with ridicule.

WANGQUAN waves his hand: "Wangcai, Goudan, let's go get it!"

WANGQUAN and several other young people squeeze their way out from the crowd.

The dark mouth of the well.

The PARTY SECRETARY of Shimen looks nervously at FUCHANG.

FUCHANG looks back calmly.

Shimen villagers: the face of an old man.

Old Well villagers: the scornful look of an old man.

Shimen villagers: a middle-aged man staring coldly at the opposite side.

Old Well villagers: a young man's look of hatred.

The mouth of the Double Spring Well.

Two villages face each other: tension and animosity run deep.

The dark mouth of the well.

WANGQUAN and several young men come back carrying a tablet. They push through the crowd and drop the tablet on the ground.

WANGQUAN: "Take a look!" The villagers of Shimen respond with jeering laughter: "We don't want to look! It's got dog shit on it! It stinks!"

FUCHANG says to the PARTY SECRETARY of Shimen: "My friend, you're more educated than I. You decide what to do." After he finishes speaking, he leaves.

The PARTY SECRETARY of Shimen is stunned by FUCHANG's action.

FUCHANG pushes his way through the crowd and walks away.

The PARTY SECRETARY of Shimen gives a snort: "Let's see if he can eat us up or shit on us! Fill the well!"

The Shimen people begin to fill the well while yelling and shouting.

WANSHUI (*offscreen*): "So be it . . ."

WANSHUI yells at the top of his lungs: ". . . We haven't fought with weapons for several decades now. We're not afraid to die or become ghosts! Fight!"

The villagers of Old Well charge into the ranks of their Shimen opponents with fury. Suddenly, several hundred people from the two villages are thrown into a melee.

Two villages continue to battle each other in the midst of loud cries.

Several young people are tangled together, fighting.

One young man's throat is being choked.

One young man is being dragged on the ground.

WANGCAI wrestles another young man to the ground.

WANGQUAN pushes the PARTY SECRETARY of Shimen to the ground and punches him repeatedly.

A Shimen young man hits WANGQUAN on the head with a club.

Blood immediately gushes out from WANGQUAN's head.

WANGQUAN lies on the ground unconscious; XIFENG throws herself on him.

XIFENG holds WANGQUAN, one hand covering his injured head.

The PARTY SECRETARY of Shimen pushes forward and kicks WANGQUAN ferociously.

XIFENG tries to shield WANGQUAN.

XIFENG's bloody hands scratch the PARTY SECRETARY's face.

XIFENG holds the PARTY SECRETARY's legs in a tight grip.

XIFENG'S MOTHER lunges forward, knocking the SECRETARY down. Mother and daughter firmly hold him down to the ground.

XIFENG pinches and hits him.

XIFENG'S MOTHER beats him mercilessly. The SECRETARY cries out aloud.

XIFENG tears and pulls him with all her strength.

WANGQUAN regains consciousness and looks at the well.

Rocks and sand are being dumped continuously into the well.

People are locked in a tangled battle near the winch.

Rocks are thrown into the well.

WANGQUAN crawls with difficulty toward the well.

GOUDAN knocks a young man's head on the ground.

ZHI'ER cries out in pain.

Shouting wildly, CHUNMEI tears open a Shimen young man's mouth.

Spadeful after spadeful of earth are shoveled into the well.

WANGQUAN crawls to the mouth of the well, blocking several spades from filling the well. A basketful of earth is dumped on him.

Another basketful of earth is dumped on WANGQUAN's head.

WANGQUAN makes up his mind to risk all and jumps into the well. All around him his friends cry out in alarm: "WANGQUAN!"

The mouth of the well looks like a full moon or a big millstone.

In XIFENG's house. WANGQUAN lies unconscious on the brick bed, his head wrapped in bandages. XIFENG and her mother, WANSHUI, and FUCHANG sit quietly. The door opens with a squeak, and they all turn around to look.

QIAOYING appears at the door. She closes the door lightly, walks to the brick bed, and puts down a roll of gauze, one box of absorbent cotton, and two bottles of liquid medicine on the edge of the bed. She looks at WANGQUAN in silence.

WANGQUAN remains unconscious.

XIFENG looks at QIAOYING with gratitude, then looks at the medicine she has brought.

The medicine stays on the edge of the brick bed. Casting a sidelong glance at XIFENG, QIAOYING turns around and leaves.

QIAOYING walks out of the house. XIFENG's mother gets up from her seat and watches her leave.

A view of the tablet of the Eastern Spring Well.

ZHANG SANHUO (*offscreen*): "The day the fight broke out, the county Party committee sent us to investigate the case . . ."

ZHANG SANHUO says to CHIEF ENGINEER sun from the provincial capital: ". . . The Party branch secretary of Shimen instigated the fight, resulting in two persons being severely injured and a dozen or so people slightly injured. The secretary has been expelled from the Party . . ."

WANGQUAN and FUCHANG are looking at ENGINEER SUN's business card with curiosity. It reads:

> Sun Jinbang
> Chief Engineer
> Hydrogeology Research Institute
> Shanxi Province

ZHANG SANHUO points at FUCHANG: ". . . This one here is a shrewd one. He quickly left the scene of fighting without trying to stop it. He was given a warning by the Party. This well is now awarded to Old Well village."

ZHANG SANHUO then points at WANGQUAN: "This is our hero who jumped into the well."

WANGQUAN smiles good-naturedly, and they all walk toward the Eastern Spring Well.

CHIEF ENGINEER SUN walks to the well and squats down, feeling the grooves around the mouth of the well.

FUCHANG, holding a thermos bottle, tells SUN: "This well was drilled during the reign of Daoguang, emperor of the Qing dynasty. It doesn't have any water now. It won't do us any good even if we get it."

CHIEF ENGINEER SUN: "You don't use a winch to draw water?"

FUCHANG: "When people are in a hurry, they just use rope. It's been several hundred years. All these marks were made by the rope."

FUCHANG is about to return ENGINEER SUN's business card to him.

ZHANG SANHUO: "Engineer Sun gives it to you."

FUCHANG says: "Oh," respectfully holding the business card in his hand. WANSHUI steps forward to take a closer look.

MAD GRANDUNCLE (*offscreen*): "Who's that person?"

WANSHUI, FUCHANG, and the others turn around to look.

MAD GRANDUNCLE comes herding a flock of sheep. He waves to WANGQUAN. WANGQUAN goes over to explain to him: "That person is a chief engineer from the provincial capital. He comes here to inspect our work. Granduncle, why don't you go with your sheep?"

MAD GRANDUNCLE stares at him and shows a toothless grin: "Don't try to fool me. You think you can steal earth from the Earth God? I know who he is. He is a geomancer to look for water for us."[6]

MAD GRANDUNCLE comes over, points his finger at CHIEF ENGINEER SUN, and says mysteriously: "The Mountain God has told me that you people wouldn't dare to drill a well anymore."

---

[6]A geomancer is a fortune-teller who specializes in finding auspicious sites for building houses, tombs, and so forth.

WANSHUI: "Second Brother, don't talk nonsense! Go tend your sheep."

WANGQUAN and WANGLAI push MAD GRANDUNCLE up the mountain slope. MAD GRANDUNCLE yells all the way: "The geomancer is useless, the well driller is useless, even the Dragon King and Well King are also useless . . ."

MAD GRANDUNCLE (*offscreen*): ". . . It's no use! No one dares to drill a well! No use! No one dares to drill a well!"

FUCHANG tells CHIEF ENGINEER SUN: "He's Wangquan's granduncle. When he was young he was buried for one day and one night at the bottom of the well during a well-drilling operation. When they finally rescued him, he became like this."

They all gaze at the departing MAD GRANDUNCLE with heavy hearts.

At Hougou. WANGQUAN walks to a dry well. (*Handheld shot.*) Several broken-down stone houses stand near the well. ENGINEER SUN and his party come over.

SANHUO goes over to WANGQUAN.

SANHUO: "When did this well run dry?"

SANHUO goes over to WANGQUAN.

SANHUO: "When did this well run dry?"

WANGQUAN: "It's been dry for a long time."

FUCHANG, WANSHUI, and ENGINEER SUN walk to the dry well. FUCHANG busily pours water from the thermos; WANSHUI takes out two cans of fruit from his bosom and tries to open them. ENGINEER SUN leans against a rock, catching his breath.

SANHUO: "Where are the people who used to live here?"

WANGQUAN: "Originally four or five families lived here. When the water dried up, they moved away."

ENGINEER SUN: "The well is dry?"

WANGQUAN: "Yes, it's been dry for a long time."

FUCHANG takes two cups of water to ENGINEER SUN and SANHUO:

"This well was drilled shortly after the Liberation in 1949. When the well ran dry, the five families that lived here moved away."

ENGINEER SUN throws a stone into the well: "How deep is this well?"

FUCHANG: "About twenty to thirty meters."

WANGQUAN and WANSHUI try to open the cans with a kitchen knife on a nearby rock.

ENGINEER SUN asks SANHUO: "Sanhuo, do you still have any places left in your study class?"

SANHUO: "We still have three slots open."

ENGINEER SUN: "Can you give me a slot?"

SANHUO: "What do you want it for?"

ENGINEER SUN: "I can use it."

SANHUO looks at WANGQUAN and nods understandingly: "All right."

ENGINEER SUN: "Little Sun!"

ENGINEER SUN: "Little Sun, your county's Bureau of Water Conservancy is going to organize a hydrogeology study class. I'll give lectures there. Do you want to come?"

WANGQUAN grins happily. WANSHUI holds two cans of fruit and solicitously hands them to his two guests. SANHUO notices WANSHUI's finger, cut by the can, "You cut your finger."

WANSHUI puts his bleeding finger in his mouth and sucks it, beaming: "It's nothing!"

In WANGQUAN's house, WANSHUI, MAD GRANDUNCLE, WANGQUAN, and WANGLAI sit around a small table, drinking.

In a merry mood from drinking, WANSHUI begins to spin old tales: "During the great drought of 1935, my grandpa, your great-grandpa, died from praying for rain. He was somebody. He hanged the Dragon King on a walnut tree and beat him. People from miles around all knew Sun the Second! He was really somebody . . ."

MAD GRANDUNCLE, with a dull look on his face, empties a cup of wine.

WANSHUI: "Your granduncle became this way from digging a well . . . Wanglai, go get the potatoes."

WANGLAI stands up.

WANSHUI puts a package of cigarettes on the table.

WANGLAI walks to the stove and takes out the potatoes from the pot. WANSHUI looks at WANGQUAN: "Quanzi . . ."

WANSHUI: ". . . it takes three generations to produce a talented person, and ten generations to produce a genius. As I see it, people of your generation are educated and have a broad vision. Maybe . . ."

WANSHUI: "Your generation will produce a genius."

WANGQUAN smiles good-naturedly.

WANSHUI: "Your younger brother doesn't have a strong character . . ."

WANGLAI is eating noisily.

WANSHUI says to WANGQUAN: "My grandson, we all depend on you! Go to the county town and learn all you can, then find water for Old Well village. So . . ."

WANSHUI: "The Suns, the Duans, the Lis, and the Zhaos of our village may plant their roots here securely. So our ancestors who died for the well and water may rest in peace." WANGQUAN listens to his grandpa's fervent words as he eats.

WANSHUI downs a cup of wine.

MAD GRANDUNCLE chews his food absentmindedly.

WANSHUI says to WANGLAI: "Pour some wine for grandpa."

WANGQUAN looks at WANGLAI: "Pour the wine."

WANGLAI pours.

WANSHUI raises his cup with both hands, looks at his eldest grandson, and says excitedly: "Quanzi, Grandpa proposes a toast to you—drink!"

WANGQUAN takes the cup and empties it in one gulp. He then pours another cup and holds it respectfully in his hands: "Grandpa . . ."

WANGQUAN: ". . . you drink."

WANSHUI takes the cup and also finishes it in one mouthful. He gazes at his grandson and wants to say something, but he doesn't know how to say it.

WANSHUI finally says: "Quanzi, your relationship with Qiaoying, I really shouldn't have interfered. But for the sake of this well, for the sake of your younger brother, I had no other choice . . . That girl has big ambitions—our Old Well village is not good enough for her. I was right. She is leaving now. I've said long ago that she would leave sooner or later."

WANGQUAN pours for himself and drinks. He does not say anything, but a thousand thoughts weigh on his mind.

SANZE drives a tractor, speeding on the asphalt road toward the county town. WANGCAI sits on the tractor. The engine makes a deafening noise.

The tractor stops in front of the county Bureau of Water Conservancy. WANGQUAN pops out his head from the reception room. WANGCAI calls excitedly: "Wangquan!" ZHANG SANHUO helps WANGQUAN take his luggage to the tractor.

ZHANG SANHUO asks WANGCAI: "You came to pick up Wangquan?"

SANZE: "Yes."

WANGCAI picks up the tool bag: "How come it's so heavy?"

WANGQUAN: "There are several surveying instruments in it, and also the books Chief Engineer Sun gave me."

WANGCAI: "You've finally graduated."

WANGQUAN: "I still have a lot to learn."

SANZE: "Get on the tractor."

WANGQUAN shakes hands with ZHANG SANHUO.

ZHANG SANHUO: "If you need anything, come see me."

The tractor speeds on a street in the county town.

WANGCAI: "Your grandpa came to see you several days ago but he couldn't find the place. He is fine, but misses you very much."

WANGQUAN: "Is Wanglai still tending sheep?"

WANGCAI: "Yeah."

WANGQUAN: "Sanze, where are you going?"

SANZE (*offscreen*): "To pick up Qiaoying."

WANGCAI: "We go to the First High School to pick up Qiaoying. She's just come back from the provincial capital and is staying at Teacher Wang's place."

In front of the county's First High School, WANGCAI helps QIAOYING carry her bags from the school. The doorkeeper OLD ZHAO says to them: "Zhao Qiaoying, Sun Wangcai, time to go?" They bid him good-bye as they get ready to leave. QIAOYING sees WANGQUAN standing by the tractor.

WANGQUAN appears a little uneasy.

OLD ZHAO: "Hey, isn't that Wangquan? You've been graduated for two or three years, but you've never come back for a visit."

OLD ZHAO comes over to shake hands with WANGQUAN.

WANGQUAN says apologetically: "I've been busy, just couldn't find the time."

SANZE: "Wangquan, shall we go?"

They fill the tractor's water tank with water, then take off. The tractor bumps along on the winding mountain road. WANGQUAN and QIAOYING sit on either side of the driver's seat. WANGCAI hangs on the water tank, swinging back and forth.

At the entrance to Old Well village. Several dozen villagers, carrying empty buckets and basins, follow the tractor to the village. More people on both sides of the road impatiently run toward the tractor with their pails and pots.

The tractor stops.

Villagers swarm up, tightly encircling the tractor.

People are shouting and yelling, creating a great commotion. SANZE unties the water hose, preparing to dispense water to the waiting crowd.

WANGQUAN takes down his luggage and walks toward the village.

WANGCAI helps QIAOYING carry her luggage and they also head toward the village.

A street in the village. SUN FUCHANG comes out of an alley carrying an empty bucket. He sees WANGQUAN.

FUCHANG is pleasantly surprised: "Wangquan! You're back."

FUCHANG puts down his bucket, says enthusiastically to WANGQUAN: "Several days ago . . . come, come, come . . ." FUCHANG gives WANGQUAN a cigarette and continues: "Several days ago, I went to the county town to look for people to find water for us. Can you guess what they said?"

WANGQUAN is busy saying hello to his friends.

XIFENG comes out of an alley with a bucket on her arm. She is seized with happiness as she sees her husband.

FUCHANG (*offscreen*): "They told me that I'm begging for alms holding a golden bowl. They said you're our homegrown expert for locating sites for wells. You looked for water for Xixiang . . ."

WANGQUAN sees XIFENG and says to her, "Leave that there . . ."

WANGQUAN: "I'll get it later."

FUCHANG says to XIFENG: "I'd like to have a talk with Wangquan."

XIFENG nods, walking to the other end of the village in high spirits.

FUCHANG tells WANGQUAN earnestly: ". . . during your internship, you located wells for several villages in Xixiang. Is that true? Won't you locate a well for our village?"

QIAOYING passes under an archway carrying her bags and bumps into XIFENG. QIAOYING looks calm and composed.

XIFENG lowers her eyes and brushes past QIAOYING.

QIAOYING and WANGCAI walk by carrying their luggage.

FUCHANG calls them: "Wangcai, come over here. I have something to say to you. Put down your luggage."

QIAOYING and WANGCAI reluctantly walk toward FUCHANG and WANGQUAN, and put down their luggage.

WANGQUAN says in embarrassment: "Uncle Fuchang, our village is in a limestone area. It's hard to find water here!"

FUCHANG's expression becomes grave: "It's hard to find water? Does that mean our village will never find water?"

From the other end of the village comes the sound of people shouting. FUCHANG and the others turn around to look.

A herd of sheep is frantically scrambling for water.

Several sheep push their way to a bucket of water.

A girl forcibly pushes the sheep away.

everal sheep knock over a bucket of water.

The whole herd swarms forward.

WANGQUAN and WANGCAI quickly rush toward the sheep.

Several sheep closely follow GOUDAN, who is carrying a bucket of water.

A hand takes the bucket away. The sheep bleat.

Two sheep put their heads in a bucket to drink water.

Several women struggle to take the bucket away from the sheep.

Several girls chase away the sheep.

A girl pulls a sheep away from a basin with all her strength.

People and sheep are locked in a fierce battle over water.

WANGCAI and WANGQUAN pull and kick the sheep to drive them away.

A girl picks up a can of water and pushes her way out of the herd of sheep.

Several sheep reach over to drink from a bucket.

WANGQUAN takes a bucket from XIFENG while trying to chase the sheep away.

Several sheep follow a girl with a water bucket and chase after her.

Several sheep tightly surround a water bucket.

Two frenzied sheep surround a water bucket.

MAD GRANDUNCLE blocks those people who are chasing the sheep.

GOUDAN pushes MAD GRANDUNCLE to the ground: "What are you doing? Grandpa!"

A herd of sheep pushes this way and that way.

Several sheep are fighting for water.

QIAOYING is driving the sheep away.

CHUNMEI carries a pail of water and steps over the sheep.

People and sheep press close together. FUCHANG yells: "Drive these sheep away! Drive these sheep away!"

The sheep are running wild.

A sheep butts a water bucket, tilting it.

People fight sheep. MAD GRANDUNCLE uses his body to block people from chasing the sheep.

MAD GRANDUNCLE is pushed to the ground.

A stampede of sheep keeps coming.

A frightened little girl cries loudly.

QIAOYING chases away several sheep, and raises her head to look.

MAD GRANDUNCLE holds a lamb in his arms, laughing at this spectacle of people fighting with sheep over water.

On a village street. FUCHANG and WANGQUAN walk back home, their clothes covered with water stains.

FUCHANG sighs: "Oh, this is really terrible. Those sheep have gone mad from thirst."

They sit down.

FUCHANG says to WANGQUAN as he takes out a cigarette: "Is the Responsibility System good? Of course it is good! How can the government's policy not be good? Right now the land has been divided. From now on I don't have to worry about the affairs of this village."

WANGCAI and QIAOYING come over and sit down, exhausted. WANGQUAN gives a cigarette to WANGCAI; he also lights one himself.

FUCHANG: "Now I'm not concerned about anything, but I have one unful-filled wish ... Quanzi, won't you give me a hand? I've been a Party branch secretary for twenty years. I have built the Dazhai-style terraced fields,[7] filled ditches, dug dry reservoirs ..."

FUCHANG: "... drilled a dozen dry wells ... In short, I didn't accomplish anything real for the village. Now they're promoting young people to be cadres. Before I step down, I would like ..."

WANGQUAN listens.

FUCHANG says excitedly: "... to dig a well while I am still in office ..."

QIAOYING listens.

FUCHANG (*offscreen*): "... to leave something to our children and grand-children in this village ..."

FUCHANG: "... to earn some good karma for myself. Then my heart will be at peace, and people won't curse me after I die."

FUCHANG: "Now I am still in charge. I'll listen to you, Quanzi, also the two of you ..."

WANGCAI and QIAOYING listen.

FUCHANG (*offscreen*): "... you people are the only high school graduates in our village. I put my bet on you. Let's give it everything we've got, let's work together ..."

FUCHANG: "Even if all the people of this village have to tighten their belts for two years, it's still worth it. It's the same Taihang mountain, I just don't believe ..."

---

[7]Dazhai, a production brigade in Shanxi Province, was famous for its terraced fields built and cultivated on formerly barren mountains by the villagers to demonstrate their spirit of conquering nature and self-reliance. The slogan that guided Chinese agriculture during the 1960s was, "In agriculture, learn from Dazhai." But Dazhai's terraced-field method, which requires tremendous human resources, did not work well in many other rural areas.

WANGQUAN is visibly moved.

FUCHANG: ". . . the piece of earth under our Old Well village doesn't have water! If you people find water . . ."

QIAOYING listens.

FUCHANG: "I'll have a monument built to you!"

QIAOYING asks: "What if we don't find water?

FUCHANG: "If you don't find water, I'll still have a monument built!"

FUCHANG: "I want to tell the descendants of our village to give up hope of water, and never to drill any more wells."

WANGQUAN stands up with a heavy heart, picks up his luggage, and leaves.

FUCHANG gazes at the departing WANGQUAN: "Quanzi, please say something."

WANGQUAN stops, turns around, and says with determination: "Uncle Fuchang, you've said it. We'll drill this well, even if we have to drill to the eighteenth level of hell, even if I have to give up my life."

WANGQUAN throws his bag on his shoulder and walks away.

FUCHANG looks at the receding figure of WANGQUAN with gratitude; he then turns to look at QIAOYING and WANGCAI.

QIAOYING and WANGCAI watch WANGQUAN disappear into the distance. They then turn to look at the Party branch secretary who has so much faith in them.

In a small alley in the morning. WANGCAI carries a backpack, comes to a breach in the wall of QIAOYING's house.

WANGCAI calls her: "Qiaoying! Qiaoying!"

A door opens, and QIAOYING'S MOTHER pops out her head: "She's left. Weren't you supposed to go to the mountains?"

WANGCAI is about to leave, but suddenly he turns to look in the direction of the courtyard.

In the courtyard, QIAOYING's underwear and bras are hanging on a clothesline.

WANGCAI's mouth twitches a little. He turns and walks away.

On a winding mountain road. WANGQUAN stretches out his hand to help QIOAYING, but she ignores him and climbs up by herself. WANGCAI stands on a big rock, waiting for QIAOYING. QIAOYING stretches out her hand, and WANGCAI pulls her up.

WANGQUAN looks helplessly at QIAOYING, then follows her up.

WANGCAI and QIAOYING walk back and forth on the mountain top. WANGQUAN comes down on a very steep trail. He comes to a big rock and looks at the mountains around him.

WANGCAI calls out: "Wangquan, are you mad . . ."

WANGCAI calls from the mountain top: ". . . one minute you want us to climb to the top, next minute you want us go down in a ditch. Are you playing tricks with us?"

WANGCAI and QIAOYING come down, panting all the way.

WANGQUAN bends over a rock, testing the run of the mountains with a surveying instrument.

WANGQUAN puts away his instrument and looks into the distance.

The mountain ranges rise and fall, peaks rising one higher than the other and sometimes overlapping each other. WANGQUAN sits on the grass, opens his folder to take notes. WANGCAI and QIAOYING sit under a big tree, eating lunch. WANGCAI takes QIAOYING's canteen from her.

QIAOYING glances at WANGQUAN.

WANGQUAN is busy drawing something on the paper.

QIAOYING comes over, puts a piece of dry pancake on WANGQUAN's paper folder. She then returns to her original place. WANGQUAN looks at her and takes a bite.

QIAOYING sits down.

WANGCAI sucks at QIAOYING's canteen and takes a few drinks. He says jokingly: "Ai, I'm not even as lucky as the mouth of this canteen. It has kissed you so many times."

QIOAYING seems angry: "You devil!"

WANGCAI looks at QIAOYING, smiling rascally.

WANGQUAN (offscreen): "Let's go!" The two of them turn around.

WANGQUAN gathers up his paper folder and stands up: "Let's go over to the other side of the mountain to take a look." He walks offscreen.

WANGCAI: "Do you want to kill us? We've been walking for more than two weeks. My legs have just about given up. Aren't we going down today?" He turns to look at QIAOYING after he finishes speaking.

QIAOYING doesn't say anything.

WANGCAI is reassured and lies down on the ground: "We two can't walk anymore. If you want to go, go by yourself."

QIAOYING picks up her canteen and backpack and walks offscreen.

WANGCAI hurriedly gets up.

QIAOYING follows WANGQUAN to the far side of the mountain.

WANGCAI resentfully spits on the ground.

Early morning in XIFENG's house.

XIFENG'S MOTHER is sweeping the brick bed.

QIAOYING (offscreen): "Sun Wangquan!"

XIFENG'S MOTHER pops out her head to look.

WANGQUAN answers, carries his tool bag on his back, comes out from the eastern room, and leaves with QIAOYING.

XIFENG'S MOTHER looks displeased.

Tall cliffs.

WANGQUAN and QIAOYING climb up by following the narrow mountain trails.

More tall mountain peaks. Rocks fall into the deep ravines, creating hollow echoes.

WANGQUAN and QIAOYING sit by the roadside to rest.

Bored, QIAOYING throws rocks into the ravines.

They sit quietly, listening to the echoes of falling rocks in the ravines.

They both remain silent.

WANGQUAN glances at QIAOYING, asks her with reserve: "You hate me, don't you? The last time we met in the mountains . . ."

WANGQUAN: ". . . you didn't even want to give me a drink of water."

QIAOYING is annoyed: "So was it a dog that drank that half dipper of water?" She picks up her bag and walks away.

WANGQUAN: "So I only deserve half a dipper of water . . ." He stands up.

QIAOYING walks in front, WANGQUAN follows her.

WANGQUAN: ". . . not only that, you shook all that straw and dirt into my water."

QIAOYING turns around to look at WANGQUAN: "How ungrateful you are! You could have died."

WANGQUAN listens in embarrassment.

QIAOYING (*offscreen*): "That day was so hot and you had been walking for a long time. If I didn't make you drink slowly, your lungs would explode."

WANGQUAN's heart beats faster. He finally understands the reason for her behavior several months ago. Ashamed and happy, he walks behind her on the mountain path.

The mountain peak in the glow of the setting sun. WANGQUAN and QIAOYING come out from a clump of shrubs.

They climb up a mountain slope.

WANGQUAN watches happily as QIAOYING walks ahead of him; he hastens to catch up with her. They feel intoxicated with happiness in the warm rays of the setting sun and surrounded by endless mountain scenery.

In the kitchen of XIFENG's house, XIFENG fills two bottles with water and puts them in WANGQUAN's tool bag.

WANGQUAN is eating breakfast. XIUXIU sits on a small stool, having a temper tantrum.

WANGQUAN looks at XIUXIU: "Eat! You don't want to eat?"

XIFENG comes over and sits down. She wraps up a stack of steaming cornmeal pancakes in a towel for WANGQUAN to take with him.

XIFENG'S MOTHER (*offscreen*): "What a pampered lord. He used to empty the chamber pot everyday, but today he thinks it will sprain his back if he does it."

Seeing that WANGQUAN does not move, XIFENG yells to the outside: "Mother, he's eating. Can't he do it later?"

XIFENG'S MOTHER (*offscreen*): "Humph! You always have an excuse for him."

XIFENG'S MOTHER walks out the kitchen door with a basket of corn in her hands, complaining as she winnows the corn: "Ah, still sitting on his butt without stirring. What makes you think you're so important today?"

XIFENG says softly to WANGQUAN: "What are you waiting for? Go . . ."

WANGQUAN shovels several mouthfuls of food into his mouth: "If you want to go, you go! Who ever heard of the men of Old Well village emptying chamber pots? I'm not a hired hand in your family. Even a hired hand . . . doesn't empty chamber pots!"

XIFENG'S MOTHER rushes to the door holding the basket: "Sun Wangquan! You think you're a big shot now. We gave you a home and a wife, but you've become so conceited you forget who you are."

XIFENG tries to quiet her down: "Mother!"

XIFENG'S MOTHER: "What do you mean by working as a hired hand? Are my daughter and I landlords? Just think, you're a secretary of the Communist Youth League . . . Let me tell you, if you can't explain everything to my satisfaction today, don't come back to this house tomorrow!"

WANGQUAN slams down his bowl on the table, picks up his tool bag, and walks to the door. He says angrily: "You think I care!" He turns around and goes offscreen.

XIFENG'S MOTHER yells after him: "Get out, get out!"

XIFENG chases after him.

In XIFENG's room, WANGQUAN pulls the wardrobe open to take out his clothes. XIFENG rushes over to grab him.

XIFENG: "Wangquan, what are you doing? Just yield to her a little and this whole thing will soon pass."

WANGQUAN takes several of his clothes and is about to leave. XIFENG holds him back with all her strength.

XIFENG begs him: "Wangquan, haven't you noticed that I missed my period? I think I'm having . . . In the future, I'll empty the chamber pot, OK?"

WANGQUAN is struck dumb.

In XIFENG's room at night, WANGQUAN is reading in bed. XIFENG sits against the wall mending her cotton jacket, WANGQUAN's black cotton jacket draped over her shoulders.

XIFENG speaks as she sews: "Are you still angry at Mother? For the sake of arranging our marriage, Mother has used every ounce of energy in her body. My dad died early. All these years, Mother and I, a widow and an orphan, were bullied by others . . ." XIFENG pins her needle on a picture hanging on the wall behind her, "Mother has a sharp tongue, but her heart is good." XIFENG tenderly and playfully takes the book from WANGQUAN's hand and throws it on the table.

XIFENG: "All right, all right. A great person should be largehearted. Won't you forgive Mother just this once?"

WANGQUAN sits up, takes off his sweater, and gets under his quilt.

XIFENG affectionately snuggles up to him: "Hey, feel my tummy."

WANGQUAN doesn't move: "Oh, it's still too early."

XIFENG: "I've calculated the date. After we're finished with the harvest, the baby will be due. I hope it's a boy, so he can go digging wells with you when he grows up."

WANGQUAN grins.

XIFENG: "Why do you laugh?"

WANGQUAN: "All you can think of is digging wells."

XIFENG looks at WANGQUAN; after a short silence, says to him: "You want to think of a name for our child?"

WANGQUAN doesn't say anything.

XIFENG: "I've thought about it. The first word will be decided by my mother—it will be my father's surname, Duan. I choose the second word—it will be your name, Sun, and you get to choose the third word. Find a good word from all the books you have read. What do you say?"

WANGQUAN: "I can't think of anything right now . . . or, we can call him 'Jing,' meaning 'well.' "

XIFENG: "Well? Duan Sunjing? It's a real tongue twister."

WANGQUAN: "You'll get used to it after you say it a couple of times."

XIFENG says softly: "Well . . . ?" Both of them burst out laughing.

The door of XIFENG's room squeaks open. WANGQUAN lazily walks to the latrine and empties the chamber pot into the manure pit.

WANGQUAN comes out from the livestock shed leading a donkey.

WANGQUAN collects manure from a pigsty.

WANGQUAN is chopping up hay with a fodder chopper. XIFENG adds hay to the chopper. WANGQUAN's knife rises and falls steadily in rhythm with her movements.

XIFENG'S MOTHER and XIUXIU are shelling corn.

WANGQUAN and XIFENG are chopping up hay.

XIFENG'S MOTHER takes the dried corn down from a tree.

In the small courtyard, XIFENG's family is busy doing different chores.

XIFENG's room is full of people and cigarette smoke. WANGQUAN is studying charts on the brick bed.

QIAOYING comes over with a stack of calculations, saying to WANGQUAN: "297, 379."

WANGQUAN: "What is the number for Guai'er Gou?"

QIAOYING: "379."

WANGQUAN spreads out a topographic map and looks at it.

The topographic map is spread out on the brick bed. (*Fade out.*)

(*Fade in.*) The winch makes a squeaking sound as WANGQUAN is lowered into a well. (*Fade out.*)

(*Fade in.*) At the mouth of the well, an exhausted WANGQUAN is pulled up on a rope.

(*Fade in.*) CHUNMEI is lowered into the well. (*Fade out.*)

(*Fade in.*) FUCHANG is being pulled up from the well. (*Fade out.*)

(*Fade in.*) XIZHU is lowered into the well. (*Fade out.*)

(*Fade in.*) A mud-covered CHUNMEI is pulled out from the well. (*Fade out.*)

(*Fade in.*) SANZE is swallowed by the dark mouth of the well. (*Fade out.*)

(*Fade in.*) Broken rocks pile up on the construction site. XIZHU, CHUNMEI, and GOUDAN keep turning the winch, exhausted from their work. WANGQUAN is gathering up the electric wires. SANZE and several girls are keeping warm by a fire.

QIAOYING and ZHI'ER are dozing, leaning against a shack.

SANZE and the others are sleeping by the fire.

XIZHU and GOUDAN laboriously turn the winch, and WANGCAI is being pulled up from the well. He lies on the ground, bone-tired.

WANGCAI: "Oh my legs! I'm about to fall apart. I call it quits!" He struggles to get up: "Let's all go back to the village tonight and attend a blind singers' concert that I've arranged."

XIZHU: "You arranged? Didn't we all pay for it?"

WANGCAI: "Never mind who paid for it, let's go!"

SANZE: "I'm dead tired; let's quit!"

XIZHU doesn't dare to leave. He looks at WANGQUAN.

WANGQUAN looks at everybody: "All right, all right, I let you all off tonight."

XIZHU, GOUDAN and the others leave in high spirits.

Nighttime on a village street. Wooden clappers are tied to a pole and beaten by a stick controlled by strings. Under a table, a pair of feet are busily treading a footboard connected to the strings. An old blind man is blowing at a *suona* through his nostrils. He holds two cigarettes between his teeth; puffs of smoke come out from his mouth to the rhythm of the music.

A middle-aged peasant is obviously delighted by the performance.

A group of middle-aged women watch with interest.

CHUNMEI and a group of girls crowd around at the foot of a wall. WANGCAI, XIZHU, and SANZE stand in front of the stage.

WANSHUI and FUCHANG watch from a corner.

A campfire is burning brightly. Women and children stand against a wall.

The street is full of people. Several big lightbulbs make the street as bright as daylight. On the stage, several blind musicians are playing musical instruments.

The old blind man takes out the cigarettes and puts a paper flower in his mouth. He starts to play the *suona* with his nostrils, causing the flower petals to turn magically.

CHUNMEI and the group of girls laugh with delight.

WANGQUAN holds XIUXIU and sits together with XIFENG. XIFENG is cracking melon seeds, her belly protruding. QIAOYING stands on the outside of the crowd, unsmiling and coldly watching WANGQUAN and XIFENG. She lowers her eyes and then turns to look at the stage.

XIZHU, WANGCAI, SANZE, and others push to the front of the stage, watching the performance excitedly.

After the old blind man finishes playing, he beats a gong several times.

WANGQUAN turns to say something to XIFENG. WANGCAI and his gang yell: "Sing something sexy and interesting."

QIAOYING looks at WANGQUAN and XIFENG chatting and laughing together. Her expression changes and she pushes her way through the crowd.

The blind musicians adjust their instruments.

QIAOYING squeezes herself in between WANGCAI and XIZHU. XIZHU leans his shoulder and then his body on QIAOYING and elbows WANGCAI. WANGCAI pushes XIZHU away and guards QIAOYING.

WANGQUAN looks at them.

QIAOYING intentionally laughs and jokes with WANGCAI.

WANGQUAN looks at them with displeasure. XIFENG notices her husband's expression, and looks in the same direction.

QIAOYING, WANGCAI, and the others keep up their lively chatting and laughing.

WANGQUAN feels very uneasy, all kinds of emotions crowding into his heart. WANGCAI's yelling can be heard: "Sing a song quickly! A sexy one . . ."

The blind musicians start to play an interlude.

A pretty blind woman plays a fiddle and sings: "During the first month of my pregnancy, I came down with an illness. My head ached and I felt bored. I felt bored and didn't want to move. I ended up craving for food." Before she finishes her song, she is interrupted by WANGCAI and others, jeering, "It's too tame, too tame. Sing something sexier."

The blind musicians on the stage don't know what to do. WANGCAI and the others keep booing and hooting.

WANGQUAN: "I'm tired; let's go home."

XIFENG knows what's on WANGQUAN's mind; she seconds his suggestion: "It's past Xiuxiu's bedtime. Why don't we go home." They walk toward the back of the stage.

QIAOYING leaves WANGCAI's group and pushes her way forward, looking in the direction of where WANGQUAN was sitting.

WANGQUAN and XIFENG are not to be seen in their original place. WANGQUAN, holding XIUXIU, is leaving from the back. XIFENG closely follows him.

QIAOYING lowers her head and joins the other girls.

The leader of the blind singers (*offscreen*): "My dear elders, fellow villagers, and comrades . . ."

The leader of the blind singers: ". . . please forgive us. Don't make it hard for us poor blind people . . ."

All the villagers look at the stage. The leader of the blind singers continues: ". . . We don't dare sing anything pornographic. Not that we don't want to, we don't dare . . ."

FUCHANG listens. The leader of the blind singers (*offscreen*): ". . . Chairman Mao and the Communist Party have educated us for many years. How can we not . . ." Seeing the situation is getting out of control, FUCHANG gets up and leaves.

The leader of the blind singers: ". . . have any political awareness?"

WANGCAI is getting impatient: "Oh, cut it out. What 'awareness'? We tell you to sing, you just sing! Go ahead and sing! Sing!"

The leader of the blind singers: "We live under the leadership of the Communist Party no matter where we are. If the Party branch secretary gives us permission . . ."

WANGCAI (*offscreen*): ". . . The Party branch secretary? He's slipped away."

The blind woman: "Who are you?"

XIZHU puts his arm around WANGCAI and says teasingly: "Him? He's the son of the Party branch secretary—probably be secretary himself soon!"

The leader of the blind singers hesitates for a while, then says: "That will do." He turns to the blind singers: "All right, we'll sing."

The blind old man: "We'll sing 'Picking Beans.' " The audience cheers.

A middle-aged man grins from ear to ear.

Several young people are laughing.

A group of children listens with curiosity.

A young man is smiling. The interlude is playing.

WANGCAI waits excitedly.

The blind woman begins to sing: "In July, in August . . ."

Two middle-aged men listen. The blind woman continues to sing: ". . . a girl about seventeen or eighteen is picking beans . . ." WANGCAI and a group of young men join her in singing the last line: ". . . Oh my sweetheart."

The blind woman smiles stealthily with closed lips.

The blind old man energetically plays the *suona*.

Two old men laughingly look on.

A group of girls and young women listen.

The blind woman: "A man comes from the east side, a scoundrel . . ."

Several middle-aged men listen. The blind woman sings: "He takes me . . ."

QIAOYING, CHUNMEI, ZHI'ER, and other young girls shyly huddle together. The blind woman sings: ". . . into the sorghum field . . ."

WANGCAI and his friends sing in unison: "Oh my sweetheart!"

The blind woman smiles with closed lips.

WANGCAI asks: "To do what?" His question makes everybody rock with laughter. XIZHU and his friends become breathless from laughing.

In the morning, to the music of Beijing Opera played on an electronic organ, QIAOYING and several girls are warming themselves by a campfire.

A tape recorder sits on a rock.

WANGCAI, XIZHU, SANZE, and others are dancing a funny-looking disco.

QIAOYING laughingly pokes at the fire.

Two girls beam with smiles.

The campfire burns brightly.

SANZE is sweating from dancing. WANGCAI practices his dance steps in high spirits.

ZHI'ER leans against a shack eating a flat cake and watching her friends dance.

Two girls are smiling broadly.

CHUNMEI dances clumsily as if doing a *yangge* dance.[8]

QIAOYING stays by the fire, feeling happy and smiling.

WANGQUAN silently gathers up tools and safety helmets.

A girl smilingly looks at WANGCAI.

XIZHU dances with joy.

WANGCAI is exhausted from dancing.

A young man is bent over with laughter.

WANGCAI, XIZHU, and SANZE keep on dancing.

On the platform of the well, QIAOYING and several girls are warming themselves by a fire. WANGCAI and his friends are absorbed in dancing.

XIZHU nudges WANGCAI: "Hey, Prince Liang, tell me the truth, did you expend all your energy on that blind woman last night? Don't be embarrassed to tell your good friend!"

WANGCAI: "Shut up! You yourself are a shriveled bedbug. Just look at you, besides your arms and legs, nothing in your body is firm!" Everybody bursts out laughing.

A girl comes over and whips WANGCAI with a tree branch: "You devil!"

WANGCAI jumps up in front of the girl: "Devil? With your looks, even if you pay me two thousand dollars I wouldn't want to touch you."

CHUNMEI walks past WANGCAI and scolds him: "You're really shameless!"

XIZHU: "You don't want to touch her? You're like an old crow dead for more than two years. All you have left is a hard beak. You don't want to touch her? Don't you steal young women's underwear and bras to satisfy your craving?"

QIAOYING raises her head to look.

WANGCAI becomes angry. He grabs XIZHU: "You, you're lying!"

XIZHU: "Whoever lies will get scabs on his head! Do you dare to take off your clothes to show us now? You may be wearing someone's bra!"

---

[8]A rural folk dance popular in North China.

Young men and young women all rush forward: "Take off his clothes!" They push WANGCAI down on the ground.

ZHI'ER looks on uneasily.

WANGQUAN watches intently.

After a moment of scuffle, XIZHU pulls out a white bra from WANGCAI's clothes. "See, what did I say? What did I say?" He waves the bra triumphantly.

QIAOYING looks cross.

ZHI'ER lowers her head.

QIAOYING suddenly stands up and goes offscreen.

WANGQUAN looks at QIAOYING.

QIAOYING leaves in anger. Bypassing the shack and the graveyard, she walks back toward the village.

WANGQUAN turns around.

XIZHU is still holding the bra and shouting. WANGCAI springs at XIZHU and grabs the bra, "I do what I like—it's none of your business. Someone has a woman in the open . . ."

WANGQUAN looks glum. WANGCAI (*offscreen*): ". . . and another one on the sly. Why don't you dare do something about that?" The others all try to quiet them down: "That's enough, that's enough . . ."

WANGQUAN shouts at them: "Stop this nonsense! Go down the well!"

At the mouth of the well. WANGQUAN, holding on to the rope, is being lowered down.

WANGCAI is already in the well. He stretches out his hand to help WANGQUAN come down, yelling, "Down . . . all right!" As soon as WANGQUAN reaches the bottom of the well, he slaps WANGCAI.

WANGCAI is stunned. Covering his face with his hands, he asks: "What's the matter? What's the matter?"

WANGQUAN: "What's the matter? Whose bra did you steal?"

WANGCAI: "It's none of your fucking business. Is it against the law to think about women? What kind of secretary of the Communist Youth League are you? You just hit me!"

WANGQUAN: "Hit you?" He punches WANGCAI again in the chest.

WANGCAI is struck down to the ground.

WANGQUAN kicks him.

WANGCAI bursts out crying, feeling wronged: "Wangquan, you have a woman at home and another outside. You can sleep with either one as you please. But I . . . I've lived all these years without ever . . . touching a woman. How can I be considered a man? Go ahead and beat me! I don't want to live this fucking life anymore!"

WANGQUAN looks at WANGCAI, saddened, and turns his face.

WANGCAI lies on the ground, wailing loudly.

The winch axle turns slowly, pushed by four rods. (*Fade out.*)

(*Fade in.*) The young people strenuously push the rods. (*Fade out.*)

(*Fade in.*) The rods keep turning. WANGQUAN, QIAOYING, SANZE, XIZHU, WANGCAI, CHUNMEI, and two other young people push the turning rods, their bodies covered with mud.

The young people turn round and round in the mud, pushing the rods.

The wheels of a handcart are covered with mud. CHUNMEI pushes the cart to a side pit. She slips and falls into a mud hole together with the cart. She cries out in alarm: "Ah, Qiaoying!"

WANGQUAN, WANGCAI, and QIAOYING rush over to help.

WANGQUAN and others drag CHUNMEI out. CHUNMEI's face and body are covered with mud. She cries as she spits out the sand in her mouth. WANGQUAN tells CHUNMEI: "Go up to change your clothes." He then pulls up the cart from the mud hole.

WANGCAI and QIAOYING help CHUNMEI get into the well-bucket.

WANGCAI: "People up there, pull someone up! Up!"

QIAOYING walks to the side pit.

The rope goes up. Sand and mud fall down, falling into WANGCAI's eyes. He curses: "Hey, you people up there, what are you fucking doing?"

CHUNMEI also yells from the well-bucket: "What are you doing?"

ZHI'ER and others turn the winch. From the bottom of the well comes WANGCAI's shouting: "People up there, you motherfuckers, what are you doing?" XIZHU (*offscreen*): "What's he shouting about? Go take a look." ZHI'ER walks to the mouth of the well and looks down.

The bamboo matting that reinforces the wall of the well is being pushed out of shape. Sand and mud keep falling down. A disaster is imminent.

ZHI'ER quickly runs to the winch, crying out in alarm: "Hurry! Turn quickly!"

XIZHU, GOUDAN turn the winch with all their strength.

ZHI'ER joins the others to turn the winch.

A screaming CHUNMEI is being pulled up.

A booming sound is heard. The well platform caves in.

The platform collapses; dust and smoke fill the air. Members of the drilling team fall into the caved-in pit, crying out in alarm.

At the bottom of the well, rocks, mud, and sand fall down like flood water. WANGCAI only has time to cry out once before he is buried in a pile of sand and rocks.

At the collapsed well, in a cloud of dust, members of the drilling team shout and struggle to free themselves. XIZHU and others rush to the mouth of the well and yell desperately: "Wangquan! Wangquan!"

In the well, QIAOYING cries: "Wangquan! Wangquan! Wangquan!"

WANGQUAN calls anxiously: "Wangcai! Qiaoying! Where are you?"

QIAOYING: "I'm here!"

WANGQUAN: "Don't cry, don't cry, I'll light the lamp. I'll light the lamp."

After some fumbling, WANGQUAN strikes a match, which shines on their frightened faces. WANGQUAN raises the match to locate the lamp.

WANGQUAN walks along the wall to where the lamp is. His match burns out; he quickly strikes another one and lights the lamp.

QIAOYING draws closer to WANGQUAN, still badly shaken: "Where is Wangcai?"

WANGQUAN's lips are trembling: "Wang . . . Wangcai?"

Holding the lamp high, they begin to look for him. Rocks and mud pile high in the passageway leading to the pit shaft.

The two of them look in the direction of the mud pit; there is no one there either.

They again look at the sand-and-rock-filled pit shaft, and it finally dawns on them: "Wangcai!" They throw themselves on the rock pile and start digging furiously, calling their friend's name as they dig.

Rescue work is progressing urgently on the collapsed well platform. Rock after rock is being moved away.

The well-bucket is filled with rocks and pulled up.

XIZHU and SANZE pull the rope with all their strength.

The well-bucket goes up quickly.

FUCHANG, while steadying the well-bucket with his hands, urges on his co-workers: "Faster! Faster!" Everyone works with maddening speed in the midst of confusion and chaos.

There is dead silence inside the side pit of the well. After a long while, WANGQUAN struggles to get up and drags an unconscious QIAOYING to a flat place. He sits down against a stone wall.

Shortly after, QIAOYING comes to and murmurs to herself: "Wangcai is dead! Wangcai is dead!" She suddenly throws herself into WANGQUAN's arms: "Quan! We're going to die too. Quan, I did all this for you. For you! I was planning to help you drill this well and then leave this place together, you and I . . . It's too late now!" She cries bitterly. Deeply pained, WANGQUAN holds her tightly in his arms. (*Fade out.*)

(*Fade in.*) The lamp wick is burning down. Dark shadows are everywhere. QIAOYING (*offscreen*): "Quan . . ."

QIAOYING: "This is . . . our fate. I'm glad that I can die with you. It's worth it." QIAOYING lowers her head to kiss WANGQUAN's chest. She then raises her head and gazes at him affectionately. WANGQUAN embraces her tightly and kisses her madly. (*Fade out.*)

(*Fade in.*) WANGQUAN and QIAOYING are locked in a passionate kiss.

(*A series of lap dissolves.*)

Endless mountain ranges.

Towering peaks.

Mountains roll on endlessly like waves.

A siren is heard. An ambulance speeds by and disappears at the end of a highway.

After a heavy snowfall, a Beijing jeep is seen driving along a mountain road; it then stops at the village. PARTY SECRETARY WU, his secretary Mr. Zhou, and several others get out of the car.

Villagers crowd in front of SUN FUCHANG's house. Several musicians are playing funeral music. GRANDPA WANSHUI and SANZE come to the door to lead Secretary Wu's party inside.

WANGCAI's coffin is placed in the courtyard. SECRETARY WU and his entourage come forward through the gathered crowd. SECRETARY WU silently shakes hands with SUN FUCHANG. The cover of the coffin is lifted to let relatives and the leadership say farewell to the deceased.

In the coffin, WANGCAI's head is wrapped in white bandages with only his nose showing. He wears a brand-new army cap and student uniform.

SECRETARY WU solemnly raises his head to look at the dead man's mother.

WANGCAI'S MOTHER, silently weeping, puts her son's belongings one by one into the coffin.

A package of Phoenix-brand cigarettes is placed beside WANGCAI's pillow.

SECRETARY WU is deeply grieved and looks on in silence.

A book, *Love Poetry,* is placed beside WANGCAI's pillow; a stack of old magazines with movie stars on their covers rests on the other side of the pillow.

WANGCAI'S MOTHER sobs.

She places two fountain pens and the school badge of the Taiyuan Institute of Technology on WANGCAI's chest. Then, she covers her son's body with a red brocade coverlet.

MR. ZHOU walks to SECRETARY WU and tells him: "Secretary Wu, two comrades from the county Bureau of Cultural Affairs wish to see you."

SECRETARY WU turns to the two cadres.

The man cadre says: "Secretary Wu, it has been reported by the masses that a young man by the name of Sun Wangcai in this village invited a band of blind singers to sing pornographic songs. We've come to investigate this case."

The woman cadre is about to take out the documentation. SECRETARY WU waves his hand in disgust and sends them away.

The sounds of firecrackers and the nailing of the coffin are heard. SECRE-TARY WU turns around to look.

A hammer is pounding heavily on the nails on the coffin.

The sound of wailing fills the courtyard.

The nails on the coffin are bent from the pounding.

WANGCAI'S MOTHER falls to the ground, weeping. CHUNMEI and ZHI'ER, who are supporting WANGCAI'S MOTHER, are also choked with tears.

On the deserted well platform, a tiny figure is moving rocks.

MAD GRANDUNCLE throws a rock into the well. From deep in the well comes the echo of rocks striking against each other.

MAD GRANDUNCLE carries another rock to the well and throws it down.

The rock falls into the pitch-dark mouth of the well, sending forth a pro-longed echo.

In the hospital room, QIAOYING is receiving intravenous feeding. WANGQUAN sits quietly on a stool beside her bed.

A patient walks by on crutches.

WANGQUAN: "Sanze is going to town to haul some goods. I'll go back with him later."

QIAOYING: "He's just been here."

WANGQUAN stretches out his hand to touch the adhesive strip on QIAOYING's arm and makes it secure.

QIAOYING slowly lifts her fingers to stroke WANGQUAN's hand.

WANGQUAN raises his eyes, gazing at her lovingly.

QIAOYING looks at him quietly.

WANGQUAN's loving face.

QIAOYING: "That well, are you still going to drill it?" WANGQUAN nods.

Under a cliff, FUCHANG, WANGQUAN, CHUNMEI, XIZHU, and others carry tools in their hands and walk up from a back slope. They look in the direction of the well.

On the desolate well platform, a small kneeling figure is doing something.

FUCHANG and others walk toward the well. They stop.

WANGCAI'S MOTHER slowly raises her head.

WANGQUAN, FUCHANG, and others silently stand in front of her.

WANGCAI'S MOTHER finishes tying the last strip of red cloth on the rope. She stands up and leaves. The coil of rope on the ground is tied with a strip of red cloth every two or three feet. The numerous strips of red cloth tied to the long rope reach all the way to the top of the platform.[9]

WANGQUAN, FUCHANG, and others look up at the platform, a pang of sadness swelling in their hearts. They all turn to look at the old woman who tied these red strips.

WANGCAI'S MOTHER walks along the small path in the graveyard and gradually disappears from view.

In the courtyard of XIFENG's house, the door opens with a squeak. WANGQUAN comes out holding a chamber pot and empties it into the manure pit.

---

[9]In Chinese culture, the color red symbolizes good luck and happiness.

Chickens come out from their coop. Little XIUXIU feeds them with corn.

WANGQUAN is smoking while looking at his family at work.

XIFENG pours pig feed into the pig trough.

XIFENG'S MOTHER is sweeping the courtyard.

Little XIUXIU also plays with a broom to imitate her grandma's action.

XIFENG is sifting flour. Her mother follows a donkey around a millstone, turning round and round and continuously stirring the kernels of corn on the surface of the millstone. WANGQUAN frowns and takes a deep puff on his cigarette.

At the site of the well. Snow covers the graves, the footpaths, and the distant mountains. QIAOYING wears a red down jacket and walks toward the well. WANSHUI squats in front of the shack, his hair and beard covered by snow. He sits there still like a statue, gazing at the well platform.

On hearing footsteps, WANSHUI raises his eyes and sees QIAOYING standing before him.

QIAOYING: "Grandpa Wanshui."

WANSHUI stands up and says to her kindly: "Qiaoying, you're out of the hospital now? Have you recovered?"

QIAOYING nods.

WANGQUAN (*offscreen*): "When did you come back?"

WANGQUAN stands on the well platform.

QIAOYING (*offscreen*): "A while ago."

QIAOYING walks toward the platform. WANSHUI looks at the young couple affectionately.

WANGQUAN and QIAOYING stand facing each other, not knowing what to say. Hearing WANSHUI's footsteps, they turn around.

His back hunched, his hands in his sleeves, WANSHUI shuffles away slowly, circling the snow-covered graveyard.

QIAOYING turns to look at WANGQUAN.

WANGQUAN laughs a hollow laugh, then begins to pick up the tools scattered on the platform.

QIOAYING (*offscreen*): "Where's Wangcai buried?"

WANGQUAN points with his chin—the snow-covered grave.

QIAOYING gazes at the grave for a long time, her eyes turning moist. She turns around slowly to look at WANGQUAN.

WANGQUAN looks at WANGCAI's grave with a heavy heart, then at QIOAYING. He quickly avoids her gaze and walks toward the mouth of the well.

WANGQUAN walks to the mouth of the well and squats down. QIAO-YING follows him. Touching the red cloth tied to the rope, she wants to say something but checks herself. WANGQUAN lights a cigarette.

WANGQUAN smokes in silence.

QIAOYING looks at him, not saying a word.

WANGQUAN numbly squats on the ground, puffing away at his cigarette.

QIAOYING's expression seems to calm down; she turns her eyes to the vast expanse of snowy field.

FUCHANG (*offscreen*): "The county government . . ."

In the street of Old Well village, villagers are having a meeting.

FUCHANG stands on the rostrum and addresses the gathered crowd: ". . . has decided to provide a machine to help us drill this well. The county will also give us twenty thousand dollars. This is the first time in the history of our village that such a good thing has happened! . . ."

FUCHANG: ". . . But to drill to the depth Wangquan's design calls for, we still need another twenty thousand dollars . . ."

The villagers in front of the rostrum, mothers and daughters, old and young, sit here and there in the street. Some of them are doing needlework; some are smoking; some are coaxing their children. They seem unconcerned about what the Party branch secretary is telling them.

FUCHANG (*offscreen*): ". . . the draught animals, the farm tools have already been divided. The tractors have also been contracted out. Other than the poplar trees by the ditch, there's nothing that we can sell or pawn. Even if we convert all the property our team owns, the most we can pool together is ten thousand dollars . . ."

FUCHANG: ". . . tell me, what should we do?" After he finishes speaking, he goes to sit by WANGQUAN.

WANSHUI anxiously looks at the unresponsive audience.

ZHANG SANHUO, WANSHUI, FUCHANG, and WANGQUAN sit on the rostrum, looking very lonely.

None of the people in the street says anything.

FUCHANG, WANSHUI, and WANGQUAN gaze at each other in despair.

WANSHUI finally stands up, moving a few steps toward the front of the rostrum: "Haven't you heard the saying 'people work to death, buffaloes die from thirst, don't marry your daughter to Old Well village'? Generation after generation of our young men can't find wives. Brothers share one woman. It's a shame! Shame! We make our ancestors lose face! . . ."

Two women listen.

A middle-aged man knits his brows.

WANSHUI (*offscreen*): ". . . The big families of our village, the Suns, the Duans, the Lis, the Zhaos . . ."

An old man listens.

WANSHUI (*offscreen*): ". . . so many have died from drilling wells . . ."

WANSHUI: ". . . give our lives but don't want to give money? I have one foot in the grave and my days are numbered. I don't have any money, but I've asked my grandsons . . ."

There is a black coffin on a bench.

WANSHUI (*offscreen*): ". . . to carry this coffin here. Maybe we can get a few . . ."

An old man looks at the coffin.

Another old man silently smokes his pipe.

WANSHUI (*offscreen*): ". . . When I die, as long as we can see water, . . ."

WANSHUI: ". . . just wrap me in a mat and let wolves and dogs drag me and chew me up!"

A villager (*offscreen*): "Let wolves and dogs drag and chew, if we find water . . ."

A middle-aged man twists his nose and looks in the direction of the voice.

Villager (*offscreen*): ". . . If we don't find water, then we'll be throwing our money into a bottomless pit!"

FUCHANG replies with a retort: "Speaking of bottomless pits, our ancestors have filled many of them. We don't need to go to other places . . ."

FUCHANG continues: ". . . just take a look around Blue Dragon Ridge, you can find several dozen dry holes! For many generations, this is the first time we've tried to locate our well by scientific methods. Like a bride riding the bridal sedan chair—this is Wangquan's first try. He has traveled from Shanxi to Hebei, then from Hebei to Shanxi, covering a distance of several thousand *li* at least. The geomancers we had before, they were all wined and dined by us, but they either fooled us or made wild guesses with their compasses. The most they did was to put a washbasin over a proposed site to see whether water drops collected in it. The well that Wangquan has located . . ."

Same scene as before. XIZHU sits in the middle of a crowd, warming himself by a fire: "It looks like we have to shed our blood. Even just for the sake of finding a wife, we must drill this well immediately! Last month I went to Qinchuan to see my prospective wife. Do you know what she said to me? Let me imitate what she said: You're good in every way, but I definitely would not go to your Old Well village and drink your water that tastes like horse urine."

SANZE, WANGLAI, and others laugh.

SANZE: "How much will you give?"

XIZHU: "You name a figure. You've contracted the team's tractor and made bundles and bundles of money with it. How much will you give?"

SANZE: "I'm saving my money in order to buy a high-priced bride. Right now I only have enough to buy two legs; I still lack the upper body."

The young men sitting around the fire all laugh.

FUCHANG calls to them: "Why are you people making so much noise?"

FUCHANG: "I believe in Wangquan's well!" He takes out a roll of money and walks to ZHI'ER, who is keeping record: "I'll give one hundred dollars. Put it under Wangcai's name." ZHI'ER is stunned; she lowers her eyes to write down WANGCAI's name on the paper.

WANGCAI'S MOTHER looks at the rostrum.

Two or three girls look perplexed.

A woman holding a child forgets to look after her child.

An old man numbly chews his finger nails.

An old man stops smoking, gazing at the rostrum.

XIFENG looks at WANGQUAN.

A man (*offscreen*): "Wangquan knows what he's doing—let him speak."

WANGQUAN: "What can I say? I do feel we can find water where I've located the well. But we haven't reached the depth the design of the well calls for. Our problem now is money."

WANSHUI continues: "That's right. He is our own son. Would he lead his fellow villagers to ruin? . . ."

XIFENG looks at WANGQUAN on the rostrum.

WANSHUI (*offscreen*): ". . . Let's talk about how we can raise money."

WANGQUAN does not look at XIFENG.

WANSHUI: "This is an old tablet. I asked Wangquan to polish it last night."

XIFENG awkwardly turns her already heavy body and walks away.

WANSHUI (*offscreen*): ". . . We'll carve on this tablet the donors' names and the amount they contributed, and the phrase 'Leave a good name for a thousand generations.' "

WANSHUI: ". . . We'll also carve an inscription detailing the hardships of our well drilling!"

He finishes talking. Seeing that there is no response, he returns to his seat.

The street is full of people, but no one says anything.

The black tablet stands on the rostrum, it does not have any words carved on it yet.

SANZE (*offscreen*): "If we find water we can write history . . ."

SANZE: ". . . What can we write if we don't find water?"

GOUDAN, who is standing not far from the foot of a wall, says cheekily: "We can say how much we have sacrificed, how much money we raised, and how hard we worked, only to add another mechanized black hole for our village!"

Everybody laughs.

WANGQUAN: "We can write that too!"

WANGQUAN stands up angrily: "We can say we are a bunch of good-for-nothings, and tell our descendants never to drill another well! Or else we can flee to greener pasture by following the Blue Dragon River . . ."

WANGQUAN (*offscreen*): ". . . Abandon our old village, never to come back!"

SANZE, XIZHU, and others curl their lips, turn silent.

Shouting is heard from outside the gathered crowd. People turn around to look. Two young men carrying a sewing machine make their way through the crowd, followed by XIFENG and her mother.

WANGQUAN raises his head when he hears the shouting.

Two young men carry a sewing machine to the rostrum; XIFENG walks up with her big belly sticking out in front of her. She glances at WANGQUAN, then says shyly to the villagers in front of her: "My Wangquan was responsible for locating this well. If he doesn't find water, we won't be able to pay for the village's loss even if we give up everything we own. Now please show favor to him and pool money to drill this well . . . We're rather hard up and we don't have any cash . . ." She touches the sewing machine that she is donating and continues: "If we really can't find water, please don't say we're leaving the village in a moment of anger. We've been here for several hundred years. Who has ever left? If our generation can't find water, there'll be another generation. We'll find water sooner or later. Heaven has eyes."

As soon as she finishes speaking, people begin to applaud.

A woman carrying a child smiles.

WANGCAI'S MOTHER smiles proudly, gratified.

WANGQUAN looks at his wife with gratitude.

XIFENG looks at WANGQUAN.

WANGQUAN lowers his head, not knowing whether he is happy or ashamed.

XIFENG comes down from the rostrum and sits beside her mother. Her mother is very pleased and draws her daughter closer to her. Suddenly the audience bursts into warm applause. People turn around to look.

CHUNMEI pushes herself through the crowd carrying a television set. Several young men behind her carry two or three cabinets, embroidered pillows, and brocade quilts. The atmosphere at the meeting becomes lively. People heatedly discuss who the generous donor might be.

WANGQUAN and FUCHANG put everything on the rostrum. CHUNMEI counts the items, then stands on the stage.

CHUNMEI holds back her emotions and tells the villagers: "These are Zhao Qiaoying's contributions. She's left. She said she will never come back . . ." Her voice trembles. After a slight pause, she continues: "These things are her dowry. This television is new, it's still good . . . Qiaoying said that because of the high mountains, we can't use it here but we can sell it . . ." CHUNMEI is too emotionally stirred to say anymore. She comes down from the stage with her head lowered.

The noisy meeting suddenly becomes quiet.

WANGQUAN remains on the rostrum, dumbfounded.

Several girls keep quiet.

A group of children calms down.

XIFENG and her mother look on in silence.

Three girls look on.

SANZE and XIZHU look on.
An old man looks on with raised head.

An old woman looks on with her hand covering her mouth.

An old man remains silent.

FUCHANG lowers his head in silence.

An old man looks on without any expression on his face.

WANSHUI knits his eyebrows.

The rostrum is filled with the villagers' contributions: bolts of cloth, dress materials, quilt covers, sheets, silver coins, antiques, jewelry, eggs, walnuts, doors, bicycles, wardrobes . . . (*Fade out.*)

(*Fade in.*) On the black tablet are carved four big characters that mean "Leave a good name for a thousand generations." Beneath these four characters is "A Record of Drilling Wells in Old Well Village," carved in intaglio design. A sequence of white characters appears against the black background of the stone tablet.

A Record of Drilling Wells in Old Well Village

During the period before the third year of the Yongzheng Emperor of the Qing dynasty, fourteen wells were drilled, no water was found, and more than ten people died.

During the reign of the Daoguang Emperor of the Qing dynasty, eighteen wells were drilled, no water was found, five people died.

In the second year of the Xuantong Emperor of the Qing dynasty, three wells were drilled, no water was found, two people died.

In 1912 one well was drilled, no water was found, Sun Jinchang died in his work. In 1914 two wells were drilled, no water was found, Sun Jinfu and Duan Yanzhang died when they fell into the well.

In 1918 three wells were drilled, no water was found, Sun Wangman and Zhao Renhou were killed when the well collapsed.

In 1922 two wells were drilled, no water was found, Duan Junlai was buried by a mudslide.

In 1926 two wells were drilled, no water was found, Sun Tingmao, Li Menglong, and Zhang Falai were killed when the well collapsed.

In 1928 one well was drilled, no water was found, Li Genggeng fell to his death. In 1931 two wells were drilled, no water was found, Sun Jinyang died from smoke inhalation.

In 1936 one well was drilled, no water was found, Sun Zeliang was killed when the well collapsed.

In 1939 three wells were drilled, no water was found, Sun Jiming, Duan Shian, Zhao Tianshou, Li Chenglin died in their work.

In 1942 Sun Zuwen, Sun Kaocheng, Sun Huairen, Duan Shiqing, Zhao He were killed by Japanese soldiers while trying to protect the well.

In 1943 two wells were drilled, no water was found, Sun Wenchang died when he fell into the well.

In 1948 one well was drilled, no water was found, Sun Wuduan, Sun Shengyong died from smoke inhalation.

In 1950 three wells were drilled in Xipo, no water was found, Li Dashan died when he fell into the well.

In 1961 armed fighting broke out over the well in Xipo, Sun Yingyuan and Duan Zhenqing died.

In 1964 one well was drilled in Nanshi Gou, no water was found.

In 1966 three wells were drilled in Woyang Ping, no water was found, Sun Heyuan was killed when the well collapsed.

In 1968 one well was drilled in Qinglong Ling, no water was found, Sun Weibin, Duan Chengyuan died in their work.

In 1973 three wells were drilled in Guai'er Gou, no water was found.

In 1979 one well was drilled in Xipo, no water was found, Duan Laifu was killed by an explosion.

In 1982 a well was drilled in Xifen Po, Sun Wangcai was killed when the well collapsed.

On January 9, 1983, the first mechanically drilled deep well was completed in Xifen Po, with a water flow of fifty tons per hour.

(*Dissolve to:*) The four big characters—"Leave a good name for a thousand generations"—appear at the top of the stone tablet. (*Dissolve to:*)

The logo of Xian Film Studio

Produced in 1987

Notes on Translators

KIMBERLY BESIO is an assistant professor in the Colby College Department of East Asian Studies. She received her Ph.D. from the University of California at Berkeley. Her research concentration is in traditional Chinese fiction and drama, and she has published on a variety of topics, including history and theatricality and women's voices in traditional drama.

RONG CAI received her Ph.D. in Chinese and comparative literature from Washington University in St. Louis. Her research interests are in contemporary Chinese fiction and drama. She has taught at Colby College and joined the faculty of Illinois State University in 1997.

THOMAS MORAN is an assistant professor of Chinese at Middlebury College. He received his Ph.D. in East Asian literature from Cornell University, and his research focuses on contemporary Chinese literature and reportage. He has published translations of short stories by Shi Tiesheng and Han Shaogong. He was in the audience at the February Seventh Theater on the evening of November 8, 1985, for what turned out to be the last Beijing performance of *WM*.

DAVID WILLIAMS received his Ph.D. in theater arts from Cornell University and is currently associate professor of English at Providence University in Taichung, Taiwan, where he also acts and directs. His anthology of English-language plays containing images of the Chinese was published in 1997.

XIAOXIA WILLIAMS taught English at Liaoning University before she came to the United States. She received her M.A. in city and regional planning from Cornell University.

YAN HAIPING is an assistant professor of theater and comparative literature at the University of Colorado at Boulder. She received her B.A. in Chinese literature from Fudan University and her Ph.D. in theater and critical theory from Cornell University. Her teaching, research, and extensive publications focus on twentieth-century drama and critical theory. She is the author of several creative works, including the prize winning historical drama *Li Shimin, Prince of Qin,* and a collection of prose narratives on gender, culture, and global politics.

YU SHIAOLING is an associate professor of Chinese at Oregon State University at Corvallis. She received her Ph.D. in Chinese literature from the University of Wisconsin, Madison. She has published extensively in the areas of contemporary Chinese literature and traditional Chinese drama, including an anthology titled *Chinese Drama since the Cultural Revolution.*

DATE DUE
